Housing and Financial Stability

This book brings together politics, law, financial services regulation, economics and housing policy in the analysis of mortgage lending and macroprudential policy in the UK and US.

The book addresses the relationship between housing policy, credit and financial instability in light of the recent global financial crisis, and proposes both short and long-term solutions. Although it is not known where the next crisis will come from, history suggests that it will have credit and property at its source. Thus, it is important that the UK and other countries look more broadly at what should be done in terms of policies, institutions and tools to make the housing market and mortgage lenders more resilient against a future crisis. This book sets out a number of workable proposals. Central to this work are questions relating to the quantitative macroprudential measures, such as loan-to-value (LTV) and debt-to-income (DTI) restrictions, and whether these can be used to any significant extent in western democracies and, if employed, whether they are likely to be effective. In particular, the book questions the political legitimacy of their use and the potential consequences for the institutions, such as central banks, promulgating such policies. Preserving financial stability in very uncertain market conditions is of key importance to central bankers and other regulators, and macroprudential policy is a rapidly growing subject for both legal and economics study.

This book will therefore be of interest to financial professionals, policy-makers and academics.

Alan Brener is Deputy Director of the Centre for Ethics and Law at University College London and a Teaching Fellow at University College London's Law Faculty. He has a PhD from Queen Mary University of London and LLM from UCL. He has worked for many years in financial services and its regulation.

Routledge Research in Finance and Banking Law

Available:

Law and Regulation of Mobile Payment Systems
Issues arising 'post' financial inclusion in Kenya
Joy Malala

Management and Regulation of Pension Scheme
Australia: A Cautionary Tale
Nicholas Morris

The Regulation and Supervision of Banks
The post crisis Regulatory Responses of the EU
Chen Chen Hu

Regulation and Supervision of the OTC Derivatives Market
Ligia Catherine Arias-Barrera

Value Added Tax Fraud
Marius-Cristian Frunza

Trust and Distrust in Digital Economies
Philippa Ryan

Credit and Creed
A Critical Legal Theory of Money
Andreas Rahmatian

Housing and Financial Stability
Mortgage Lending and Macroprudential Policy in the UK and US
Alan Brener

For more information about this series, please visit: www.routledge.com/Routledge-Research-in-Finance-and-Banking-Law/book-series/FINANCIALLAW

Housing and Financial Stability

Mortgage Lending and Macroprudential Policy in the UK and US

Alan Brener

Routledge
Taylor & Francis Group
LONDON AND NEW YORK

First published 2020
by Routledge
2 Park Square, Milton Park, Abingdon, Oxon OX14 4RN

and by Routledge
52 Vanderbilt Avenue, New York, NY 10017

Routledge is an imprint of the Taylor & Francis Group, an informa business

British Library Cataloguing-in-Publication Data
A catalogue record for this book is available from the British Library

Library of Congress Cataloging-in-Publication Data
A catalog record has been requested for this book

ISBN: 978-0-367-35553-1 (hbk)
ISBN: 978-0-429-34151-9 (ebk)

Typeset in Galliard
by codeMantra

For Fiona and David and my father, Leon

Contents

Figures

Acknowledgements

This book draws on both my own experience and research over several decades in financial regulation and policy formation and implementation. Additionally, it develops the thoughts and views of a number of senior officials in government, regulation, politics and the financial services industry. I am grateful for their cooperation and the frankness with which they expressed their opinions which were all provided on the understanding that they were speaking in a personal capacity and that what was said would not be attributed.

I am also indebted to the intellectual support of my two PhD supervisors: Professor Rosa Lastra, Sir John Lubbock Chair in Banking Law, and Dr Costanza Russo both at Queen Mary University of London, whose knowledge, judgement and guidance have been invaluable. I am also grateful for the advice and support of Professor Patricia McCoy, Liberty Mutual Insurance Professor of Law at Boston College.

Finally, but not least, writing this book would not have been possible without the support and good humour of my wife, Fiona, and son, David, and my father, Leon, who have made themselves experts on the book's contents and, as always, provided superb guidance over the years. Nevertheless, all the faults and errors remain mine – a perfect rule for domestic bliss.

1 Introduction – housing, mortgages and society

The financial crisis precipitated by the events of 2007/8 could be described as a world "undone by mortgages".[1] It was based on an obsession with housing and the means to finance their purchase. In 1896, the architect Hermann Muthesius joined the German embassy in London as a special attaché with a brief to report on British housing. He wrote to the Grand Duke Carl Alexander of Saxe-Weimar stating, "no nation has identified itself more with the house".[2] The UK, more recently, has been described as a

> nation bewitched by property…home-ownership still stands its ground along with weather…as Britain's public conversation of choice. House price surveys…command the front page; while the TV schedules are dominated by the generic pap of Location, Location, Location, Property Ladder, Trading Up or, for the more aspirational, Grand Designs.[3]

Ioannis Kapodistrias, the great European statesman and first president of Greece, considered that "only by owning land will they respect the property of others".[4] In his view, having a home of one's own was desirable to help ensure political stability. Home ownership has been described as "a source of personal identity and status", providing "a sense of place and belonging".[5] It can establish both memory and hope. Over the last hundred years, this has become central to a socio-political understanding of how a popular demand for owning a home reflects a desire for security and optimism for the future.

1 Richard Brome, 'The English moor' (published 1640, University of Missouri Press, Columbia, 1984), Rashley, Act 1, Scene 1.

2 Quoted by Tristram Hunt MP during the debate on the Housing and Planning Bill, 2 November 2015, Hansard, column 777.

3 Tristram Hunt, 'How the English became obsessed with property' (New Statesman, 2 February 2004).

4 Ioannis Kapodistrias, Letter to A. M. le Chevalier Eynard, February 1830, 'Correspondence de Comte Capodistrias', (1839), 3, Geneva, 472–473, Bibliothèque Université De Genève.

5 Shelley Mallett, 'Understanding home: a critical review of the literature', (2004) *The Sociological Review*, Vol. 52, No. 1, 63–89, 66.

Residential housing mortgages have provided the fuel to satisfy this desire. This has been mirrored by the involvement of banks in housing finance in, for example, the US since the 1920s and in the UK from the 1970s. This has changed the composition of bank lending and balance sheets. The rapid growth in this lending was at the heart of the recent financial crisis in the UK and in a number of other countries. The consequential financial instability threatened not just the global financial system but has spread to the "real" economy and is likely to have had a significant influence on the political system.[6]

As a consequence, international cooperation and national initiatives have developed macroprudential policymaking to improve financial stability. These steps have both measured and highlighted risks to financial stability and implemented actions to help reduce these risks. The latter policies broadly fall into two groups of instruments or "tools": those that seek to reduce bank lending by increasing the cost to banks of rapidly increasing credit, and those that placed quantitative restrictions on such lending particularly for house purchases.

Many of these actions mirror those employed by microprudential supervisors. In addition, both macroeconomic and fiscal policies may also have macroprudential effects. This work considers these aspects in relation to residential mortgages and their respective relationships and merits. It does not cover areas such as "buy-to-let" or "equity release", since these types of transactions have their own dynamics and operate in ways which are more akin to investment products.

Central to this work are questions relating to the quantitative measures, such as loan-to-value (LTV) and debt-to-income (DTI) restrictions, and whether these can be used to any significant extent in Western democracies and, if employed, whether they are likely to be effective. At its centre is their political legitimacy and the potential consequences for the institutions promulgating such policies.

The answer, at least in part, may exist in a different area of regulation: that regulating conduct of business. The recent financial crisis revealed serious deficiencies in the conduct of mortgages sales both in the US and UK. Superficially, both responded with similar sets of new regulations. However, the underlying regulatory concepts were different. The US focus is on standardising the structure of mortgages to make it easier for customers to understand and to compare mortgage offers. The UK's approach is much more paternalistic evidencing a lack of trust in the consumer's judgement with new regulations designed to protect customers from themselves.

Accepting that conduct of business regulation in the UK has its limitations and has suffered many substantial failures, this book proposes that it may still provide a more effective alternative to reliance on LTV and DTI measures to curb a mortgage lending bubble.

6 Guillermo Cordero and Pablo Simón, 'Economic crisis and support for democracy in Europe', (2016) *West European Politics*, Vol. 39, No. 2, 305–325, 317. See also Matthew Goodwin, 'The Great Recession and the rise of populist Euroscepticism in the United Kingdom', in Hanspeter Kriesi and Takkis Pappas (eds), *European populism in the shadow of the great recession* (ECPR Press, Colchester, 2015), 273–286, 281–284.

However, UK regulation in this area could benefit from incorporating some aspects of the US's approach. The regulation of mortgage selling in the UK has followed a path set in the 1980s, largely designed to protect wealthy customers from abuse by their trusted investment advisers. There are limitations to this approach, and US financial services' policymaking could provide innovative examples for use in the UK. This work highlights three particular aspects.

First, the US "qualified mortgage" is a largely unknown concept in the UK. This provides a mechanism for policymakers, including politicians, to set limits to the public "risk appetite", balancing consumer protection, ensuring financial stability and meeting societal expectations and aspirations. Second, there does not appear to have been any assessment of the role of sound conduct of business policies employed by, for example, the Veterans Administration (VA), a significant Government Sponsored Enterprise (GSE), during the financial crisis. While other GSEs, such as Fannie Mae and Freddie Mac, failed and were rescued by the Federal government, the VA was unaffected and prospered, as did those borrowers it served. It is possible that the VA's support for mortgages was successful for reasons other than good conduct of business policies, but this is an aspect which merits further research. Additionally, there is scope for much greater, and possibly more effective, innovative regulatory policy in this area by making use of the extensive data available on potential borrowers rather than the current reliance on long customer interviews examining sources of income and the customers' assessment of their expenditure and future intentions.

Conduct of business policy in this area may be hampered by the structure of regulation in the UK. Macroprudential policymaking is undertaken within the Bank of England while conduct of business policy is the responsibility of the Financial Conduct Authority. Moreover, it is not entirely clear that the macroprudential policymakers fully understand the difference between credit and affordability risk and the importance of this distinction for both conduct of business and macroprudential policy. This issue and the results of interviewing senior current and former regulators indicate a possible disjunct between the two sets of policymakers and how conduct of business policy, in relation to mortgages, may provide important support for macroprudential policies.

As mentioned, the rapid expansion of credit to support house purchases has been central to almost all financial crises particularly in the latter part of the 20th and early years of 21st centuries. This may be due to a variety of reasons including increasing household formation, ready access to credit and cultural norms.[7] For example, Germany has one of the lowest homeownership rates in

7 Germany provides an interesting comparison. Germans continue to save rather than consume. However, equity investments are seen as too volatile and bank and savings deposits, the traditional place for German savings, continue to have very poor rates of return. However, based on anecdotal information, Germans continue to rent since rent increases are controlled and tenancies are long term and heavily protected. However, moving to a new tenancy can be very expensive so most Germans simply do not move. Instead, many are using their savings to buy

Europe.[8] This appears largely due to a well-developed private rental sector and high levels of tenant protection with modest rent rises, many of which are subject to statutory controls. In the UK, however, since the financial crisis the option of owning a home of ones' own has faded for those who currently do not have sufficient funds to put down a large deposit and cannot prove that they can afford a mortgage.[9]

Macroprudential policy may have the unequal task of attempting to suppress house price booms as it seeks to maintain a lid on the pressure cooker of an asset bubble. Moreover, macroprudential policy is predicated on its ability to identify sufficiently early potential risks to financial instability and root causes and to deploy the necessary macroprudential tools in time and to effect. The evidence that this would happen is not robust. Further, in the UK a major reason for such a high demand for housing, house price inflation and rapid credit creation is the significant deficit in the supply of housing. Government policy in this area has, at the very least, failed to support macroprudential policy and may be running counter to its objectives. This highlights the constraints on macroprudential policy since there are significant limits on its ability to influence fiscal and socio-economic policy.

In summary, although discussions on macroprudential policy go back to at least the early 2000s, the difficulties inherent in this form of regulation, coupled with a reluctance to interfere when asset prices rose rapidly, meant that it took the recent financial crisis for its importance to be fully recognised. Macroprudential policy is at a very early stage. Nevertheless, there is a danger that it may become too narrowly focused. To avoid this happening it needs to address, both conceptually and operationally, a range of issues. These include the following: the political and institutional legitimacy of macroprudential policy; how it relates to microprudential and conduct of business regulation; the need to manage excessive expectations; and recognition that any belief that macroprudential policy can be "fine-tuned" is a chimera. At the same time, macroprudential policy has a tendency to expand its scope as risks are perceived to migrate from one area to the next.

Further, macroprudential authorities need to consider the wider economic and societal issues and the effectiveness of some of the macroprudential tools and their potential for unintended consequences. Finally, it is possible that LTV and DTI limits may simply not work in the face of market forces, political interference and the lack of any willing constituency reinforcing such measures. It is possible that too many expectations are balanced on the columns of

---

new properties which they let out in turn, which provides a much higher and stable rate of return. German households own 75% of all housing but only 43% live in their own homes. The balance is rented out by one household to another, European Central Bank, 'Housing finance in the Euro area', (March 2009) Occasional Paper Series, No. 101, 34.

8 Eurostat, Housing statistics, Eurostat (June 2019).

9 *Daily Telegraph*, 'Is the British dream of home ownership dead?' (3 January 2015).

macroprudential policy while the countervailing forces of monetary policy and political expediency may help to create instability in the structure.

Consequently, macroprudential policy needs to be subject to realistic expectations with limited "role responsibility creep", and policymakers need to reinforce the public and political legitimacy of their role. Moreover, macroprudential policy needs to be coordinated with monetary and fiscal policy. Finally, it should not neglect the importance of conduct of business affordability assessment regulations in helping to contain the growth of credit in the economy.

Chapter 2 examines the importance of financial stability and the geopolitical concept of the "turbulent frontier" applied to macroprudential policy. It is likely that the latter will be extended to encompass one aspect of the economy after another, and complicate its relationship with macroeconomic, microprudential and fiscal policies.

Chapter 3 is focused on the quantitative macroprudential tools restricting mortgages for housing, their use in Asia in the 1990s and more recently in other jurisdictions and the reasons militating against success as the markets find ways of circumventing its effect.

Chapter 4 assesses US mortgage conduct of business regulatory policy since the recent financial crisis and its vulnerability both to reliance on the provision of information to borrowers and the weakness in regulatory policy governing mortgage intermediaries, and contrasts this with the approach taken in the UK. Further, the US "qualified mortgage" is an approach unknown in the UK, and this chapter considers whether the UK could adopt the concept as a means of limiting the risk of over-selling mortgage credit.

Chapter 5 considers UK conduct of business and mortgage regulation including its path dependency and also the effect of work on behavioural economics and increased regulatory paternalism in the development of regulatory policy. The chapter also examines some of the societal effects of mortgage affordability assessment regulation.

Chapter 6 considers the very real problems of expanding macroprudential policy, in particular those with quantitative effects, since these policies start to encroach on the role of the elected government and may challenge the political legitimacy of macroprudential policymakers. The latter are very conscious of this issue and in the UK have tried to shy away from employing effective macroprudential tools in this area.

Chapter 7 examines US Federal intervention in the housing market and considers the success of the VA and its employment of conduct of business policies which may have been responsible for protecting borrowers, the VA and significant elements of the economy from failures in this area during the financial crisis. This may support the use of such measures both for consumer protection and as instruments of macroprudential policy.

Chapter 8 returns to the central issue that the propensity to over-borrow to buy a home is implicit in a number of economies both for cultural reasons and due to the significant lack of house building over recent decades. Unless this issue is addressed with significant home building programmes, a number of countries will continue to face the risk of a financial crisis every few years and macroprudential policies will have to be developed to continue to suppress increasing demand for mortgages to finance the purchase of the scarce resource of housing.

In conclusion, it is evident that macroprudential policy operates at the point where law, economics and politics intersect. The consequences are that quantitative macroprudential policy tools may be ineffective in the face of market forces and if employed to any significance extent may undermine the legitimacy of the macroprudential policymakers. Nevertheless, it may be possible to learn from other jurisdictions and to consider the employment of measures such as "qualified mortgages" and more innovative methods for assessing mortgage affordability and to operate conduct of business policy in coordination with macroprudential objectives. In addition, politicians need to understand the implications of a lack of significant house building not just in societal terms but also the threat it poses for financial stability.

2 Macroprudential policies

Rationale, scope and issues

There is a close relationship between the growth of credit, the demand for, and supply of housing and the risks these pose to financial stability. In recent years these, and other risks, have led to the development of macroprudential policy. The latter's role has been keenly debated. Macroprudential policy is still at a very early stage of development and too much may be expected of it. There is a concern that too narrowly focused a view, which excludes its socio-economic consequences, may result in challenges to the legitimacy of macroprudential policymaking. This is a particular issue if macroprudential policymakers attempt to restrict access to mortgages limiting the ability of individuals to acquire a home of their own. While macroprudential policy needs to be connected to its jurisdictional social and political context, there is merit in looking at what other countries are doing and learning from them.

There are additional concerns that macroprudential policy may over-reach and continually seek to control the next 'valley' mirroring the expansion of colonial powers always fighting on a 'turbulent geo-political frontier'. Additionally, macroprudential and microprudential policies may pull in opposite directions as each strives to meet opposing objectives. There is considerable scope for unintended consequences in this new area of policymaking, and it may be an illusion to believe that it can be 'fine-tuned'. There may be too great a focus on controlling credit expansion using diktats limiting mortgage loan-to-value (LTV) and debt-to-income (DTI) ratios and too little consideration of how conduct of business regulation may assist. The latter is an aspect often neglected when considering financial stability.

The innovative use of the mortgage affordability assessment as part of conduct of business regulations could protect both borrowers and the stability of the financial system.

2.1 Introduction

Larry Summers is recorded as saying that he "would submit that the financial history of the last 40 years demonstrates that often when real estate operators are thrilled about credit availability, financial crisis is only a few years away".[1] This supports the general view that the failure to have a broad regulatory and economic perspective across the economy and the consequential build-up of economic distortions, particularly in the areas of property and mortgages, were at the root of the recent financial crisis.[2] Macroprudential policy aims to address this issue by taking an over-arching view of potential threats to financial stability and implementing actions to prevent these coming to fruition.[3] Nevertheless, macroprudential policy is in its infancy. Andrew Haldane has stated that

> the state of knowledge about macroprudential regimes today is roughly where monetary policy was in the [1940s].[4]

Macroprudential policy comes in two main forms: narrow policies which seek to buttress the "resilience of the financial system" by building, for example, increased capital buffers, and more widely drawn policies which seek to damp down a rapid expansion of credit.[5] Nevertheless, some consider that macroprudential policy, beyond a certain point, is a chimera since markets are too complex to map and comprehend and that action in response to macroprudential "signals" will be too slow.[6] These are valid concerns, but the consequences of inaction are worse, and there are effective mechanisms which can be employed to enhance and protect financial stability and which avoid some of the issues with macroprudential policy. These are discussed later.

This chapter considers three broad themes: the relationship between credit growth, the housing market and the risk of financial instability; the purpose and role of macroprudential policy in curbing the growth of credit and protecting financial stability, and the main issues with macroprudential policy. There are other possible perspectives. For example, Noyer concentrates on the important but more limited aspects of macroprudential policy governance and the identification of "market failures".[7] These are important aspects. However, this approach may be too narrow. This chapter highlights a significant element, encapsulated in the themes mentioned earlier, that it is important to broaden the view taken

1 *Financial Times*, 'There are big risks in a hasty rollback of financial regulation', (8 January 2017).

2 Charles Goodhart, 'The macroprudential authority: powers, scope and accountabilities', (2011) *OECD Journal: Financial Market Trends*, No. 2, 5. www.oecd.org/finance/financial-markets/48979021.pdf.

3 Christian Noyer, 'Macroprudential policy: from theory to implementation', (April 2014) Banque de France, Financial Stability Review, No. 18, 7–11, 7.

4 Andrew Haldane, 'Macroprudential policies – when and how to use them', (April 2013), IMF seminar 'Rethinking Macro Policy II: First Steps and Early Lessons', Washington, DC.

5 Emilios Avgouleas, *Governance of global financial markets* (Cambridge University Press, Cambridge, 2012), 268–269.

6 Daniel Awrey, 'Macroprudential financial regulation: panacea or placebo', (2009) *Amsterdam Law Forum*, Vol. 1, No. 3, 17.

7 Noyer, supra note 3, 7.

of macroprudential policy. Too narrow a focus may undermine the "legitimacy" of macroprudential policy, set unachievable expectations, produce unintended consequences and divorce it from its socio-economic context.

Initially, it is important to understand the objectives of macroprudential policy. Broadly, it can be said that the aim of macroprudential policy is to reduce serious systemic financial risk.[8] The EU's European Systemic Risk Board has defined macroprudential policy as: "contribut[ing] to the safeguard[ing] of the financial system as a whole, including by strengthening the resilience of the financial system and decreasing the build-up of systemic risks".[9] This chapter looks at aspects of these interpretations. It also considers what is encompassed by the phrase "systemic financial risk". This analysis includes consideration of what is meant by the term "financial instability" and the development and objectives of macroprudential policy since "at the same time banking regulation needs to be cognizant of the effect of regulation on the wider economy".[10]

This is particularly important since the nature of banking has changed substantially in the last fifty or so years. For example, in the UK, it reflects both social and cultural changes as well as a transformation in financial markets regulation. These are often said to have started in the 1980s but the roots of these changes developed much earlier with banks starting to fund new asset classes coupled with a decline in class delineation in the structure of the banking industry.

The initial changes, in the UK, can be seen in the late 1960s and early 1970s with lending focused on commercial property. This resulted in a major financial crisis in the early 1970s. This was followed by the growth in bank lending to finance the acquisition of residential property as the banks took over an area of business previously dominated by the building society sector. Housing markets and credit have a special role in magnifying risk in financial system.[11] It is

8 Steven Schwarcz, 'Systemic risk', (2008) *Georgetown Law Journal*, Vol. 97, 193–249, 202, emphasises the importance of defining what needs to be controlled. There are a wide range of definitions. For example, the Basel Committee for Banking Supervision, 'Core principles for effective banking supervision', (2012), 2, defines macroprudential policy as, "applying a macro perspective to the microprudential supervision of banks…to address systemic risk; and [measures to reduce]…both the probability and impact of a bank failure".

9 European Systemic Risk Board, 'Recommendations on intermediate objectives and instruments of macro-prudential policy', (4 April 2013), ESRB/2013/1, 2013/C 170/01, Section 1. The Bank of England sees it as the: "remove[al] or reduc[tion] of systemic risks with a view to protecting and enhancing the resilience of the UK financial system", 'Instruments of macroprudential policy: a discussion paper', (December 2011), 7. However, the IMF's definition focuses more on the use of prudential tools, "Macroprudential policy [is] the use of primarily prudential tools to limit systemic risk", 'Key aspects of macroprudential policy', (10 June 2013), 6.

10 Frederic Mishkin, 'Prudential supervision, why is it important and what are the issues?', in Frederic Mishkin (ed), *Prudential supervision* (University of Chicago Press, Chicago, 2000), 27–26.

11 Markus Brunnermeier and Isabel Schnabel, 'Bubbles and central banks: historical perspectives', (2014) Gutenberg School of Management and Economics & Research Unit 'Interdisciplinary Public Policy' Discussion Paper 1411, 21–22, property bubbles are a constant feature throughout the period studied (page 8).

the growth in credit, particularly used to acquire residential property, coupled, in some instances, with the development of securitised assets that changed the banking landscape in recent decades in the UK. In the UK, this has been a relatively recent issue. Historically, banks did not lend against the security of property.

In part, this derives from the social perception of the purpose of banking. Unlike many other jurisdictions, banking has been culturally acceptable as a "gentlemanly profession" in the UK for at least the last two hundred years.[12] The elevated status of banks was based on their role in facilitating markets in the prestigious areas of bill-broking and the financing of governments and international trade and development. Banks avoided lending against the security of residential property. This latter area of business was left to the more déclassé small regional building societies. However, since legislative changes in the early 1970s, developments in prudential regulatory policy and the ending of the building society mortgage interest rate cartel in the early 1980s, bank lending has concentrated on residential mortgages with, currently, two-thirds of bank balance sheets devoted to this type of lending.[13] This has increased risk. In the event of default, the security may be illusionary for a variety of reasons, including the social obloquy that attaches to evicting borrowers. As a banker told me, they are not in the business of casting families out into the street.

Moreover, mortgage lending produces very illiquid balance sheet assets. Concern over the value of these assets and their illiquidity has frequently resulted in those who provide finance to banks withdrawing their funds, resulting in a liquidity crisis and a subsequent solvency debacle. Thus, it can be said that "mortgage credit growth has become a…dominant driver of financial crisis risk, and mortgage credit overhang now weighs more on economic performance in recessions".[14] There is a strong argument that, in the UK, the deregulation of mortgage lending and the development of bank lending in this area in the 1980s was the foundation of macroeconomic instability.[15] At its heart is a combination of factors including the growth in bank mortgage lending, the difficulties in pricing the assets and its inherent risks, the threat to trust that this engenders and the centrality of housing in producing both a wealth-multiplier effect and as a popular means of helping to provide for the future.

There is something analogous, in macroprudential policy, to the idea of the "turbulent frontier" in geopolitics.[16] Essentially, empires over-extend themselves

12 William Rubinstein, *Capitalism culture and decline in Britain* (Routledge, London, 1993), 39.

13 Òscar Jordá, Moritz Schularick and Alan Taylor, 'The great mortgaging: housing finance, crises and business cycle', (2014) Federal Reserve Bank of San Francisco, Working Paper Series 2014–23, 4.

14 Ibid., (Jordá, Schularick and Taylor), 31–32.

15 Peter Malpass, *Housing & the welfare state: the development of housing policy in Britain* (Palgrave Macmillan, Basingstoke, 2005), 122.

16 John S. Galbraith, 'The "turbulent frontier" as a factor in British expansion', (1960) *Comparative Studies in Society and History*, Vol. 2, No. 2, 150.

by allowing their attention to focus on their frontiers – where there is always trouble. The next valley is occupied to suppress the disturbance which in turn becomes manifest in a second valley and so on. Similarly, regulation, in general, and macroprudential policy, in particular, is drawn towards new frontiers as risk is perceived to spread. This may well be the correct approach, but it requires a disciplined approach to policymaking which appreciates what is happening and determines priorities. Otherwise, there is a risk that macroprudential policy may attempt to engage with too many areas and lose focus. Faced with a never-ending turbulent frontier, the Emperor Diocletian created the Roman "Tetrachy" in order to increase imperial focus on what was important. By analogy, it may be necessary for the UK's Financial Policy Committee (FPC), for example, to divide itself into two or more committees. Each would focus on different aspects of risks including those related to technology and infrastructure. This might appear cumbersome but this approach would ensure that sufficient attention was devoted to all the potentially important areas.

In addition, there are a number of structural issues with macroprudential policy including the relationship with microprudential regulation. It is possible that macroprudential and microprudential policies may work in opposite directions with potential conflicts between their respective objectives. Macroprudential policy may also fail to consider wider economic and societal issues. These factors may include limits on the ability of people to aspire to own their own home.

Further, too much may be expected of macroprudential policy since it may be too difficult to identify issues sufficiently early and both the capacity and will to intervene in time may be lacking. This is coupled with a belief that macroprudential policy can be "fine-tuned".

Moreover, macroprudential tools appear to be jurisdiction-specific since their effectiveness may depend on market and organisational structures. In addition, macroprudential policies may be linked to political structures and fiscal measures. Nevertheless, there is merit in looking at other jurisdictions including the approach adopted in the US.

In view of the limited previous use of macroprudential policy, there is little knowledge and experience as to how they would work in practice. Consequently, there exists the potential for unintended consequences. For example, a limit on loan-to-income (LTI) multiples may come to be seen as an acceptable target both by borrowers and lenders, rather than an upper boundary.

Finally, macroprudential policy may lack both political and institutional legitimacy. This concern is coupled with issues over accountability and may deter the use of macroprudential policies either at all, or at the right time. Consequently, during a property boom the Bank of England's FPC may not consider that it has sufficient "legitimacy" to impose significant LTV and LTI or DTI restrictions. This perception may also be shared by others in the political and media world.

Economic research on mortgage regulation has focused on LTV and DTI macroprudential tools. There has been little on the role of the conduct of business aspects of mortgage lending beyond the limits of consumer protection. This aspect, including assessing the ability of borrowers to afford the mortgage, is, apparently, rarely mentioned or considered by the FPC. This book suggests that innovative use of the mortgage affordability assessment should form a major element of the quantitative measures available for macroprudential policy. If developed and applied appropriately, this approach could protect both borrowers and the stability of the financial system. My central theme is to rebalance the perception of macroprudential policy with what conduct of business regulation can achieve to support it.

In summary, macroprudential policy needs to be subject to realistic expectations with limited "role responsibility creep", and the policymakers need to establish the public and political legitimacy of their role. Macroprudential policy must be coordinated with monetary and fiscal policy and with those undertaking similar responsibilities in other jurisdictions. Finally, it should not neglect the importance of conduct of business regulation in restricting the growth of credit in the economy.

2.2 The structure of financial systems

There are a number of ways of looking at financial systems. Understanding these different perspectives, as mentioned earlier, is important as the need to understand the various structures may determine macroprudential policy. Under any form of analysis, financial systems are complex and subject to unpredictable shocks which transmit their effect with "non-linearity" (i.e. the effects and causes are difficult to model and predict).[17] Haldane described the financial system as being on a constant "knife-edge" where, for reasons that are difficult to model and hence forecast, "even a modest piece of news might be sufficient to take the system beyond its tipping point".[18]

A financial system is connected via a myriad of agents, each with only a limited perspective on the whole system, and subject to "bounded rationality".[19] Many of the linkages in the system arise from a number of common factors such as shared depositor bases and mutual interactions in the interbank market.[20]

This complexity has been identified by recent analysis which instead has concentrated on a small number of individual financial institutions and their direct effect on systemic risk.[21] This highlights both the role of these firms in their

17 Bank for International Settlements, Committee on the Global Financial System, 'Macroprudential instruments and frameworks: a stocktaking of issues and experiences', (2010) CGFS Papers No. 38 (CGFS), 19.

18 Andrew Haldane, 'Rethinking the financial network', speech at the Financial Student Association, Amsterdam, 28 April 2009.

19 See Chapter 5 for a brief analysis of the concept of "bounded rationality".

20 Committee on Economic and Monetary Affairs hearing, 15 February 2016, 3.

21 Nikola Tarashev, Claudio Borio and Kostas Tsatsaronis, 'Attributing systemic risk to individual institutions', (2010) BIS Working Papers No 308, 21. The collapse of the Crown Agents is an example of the importance one organisation may have in the development of a bubble and subsequent financial collapse. It would have been be difficult to predict its significant influence in advance of the crisis in the early 1970s. The Crown Agents was a government agency which

exposure to systemic risk and in the transmission of instability. This latter aspect is considered later in this chapter. However, the complexity of the financial system means that any attempt to gain a view of the whole to prevent financial instability is likely to fail. However, it may be possible to concentrate regulatory efforts on a few more precise areas. To be successful what is meant by "financial instability" needs to be understood.

2.3 What is understood by the term "financial instability"

The phrase "financial stability" is not an abstract term, since it relates to the individual actions of, and the consequences on, firms operating in the financial sector. It also has a deep resonance within the wider economy and affecting both political actors and internationally, with countries connected by trade and investment. Importantly, it is closely tied to the general population who rely on the financial system and who are contributors to its existence. Consequently, systemic risk has been defined as "the risk or probability of breakdowns in an entire system, as opposed to breakdowns in individual parts or components".[22]

There are a number of ways of looking at financial stability. However, all assume a large element of economy equilibrium and consider what could distort this balance. This approach is important since how these distortions are perceived can determine how and when the macroprudential policy should be imposed and which "tools" are best in the circumstances. This form of analysis is also central to how distortions to the equilibrium are measured, since if the disturbance cannot be detected, any macroprudential regulatory action may be too late.

There are three broad types of threat to financial stability.[23] The first category of threat could arise from an irrational fear, based on a rational analysis ("all customers want to be at the head of the queue to get their money out at the same time"), or a concern founded on some change in an institution's "fundamental" financial strength (e.g. a significant fall in the value of assets held by a bank and thus a consequent threat to the bank's solvency). The risk of contagion then spreads to such an extent that it threatens the financial system as a whole.[24]

The second type of threat could arise from "either a shock from within the financial system or from one which is exogenous" which affects something which

---

made significant loans to "secondary banks" in the prelude to the UK's financial crisis in the early 1970s, *Report by the committee of inquiry into the circumstances which led to the Crown Agents requesting financial assistance from the Government in 1974* (HMSO, London, December 1977), 32 and 69.

22 Rosa Lastra, 'Systemic risk, SIFIs and financial stability', (2011) *Capital Markets Law Journal*, Vol. 6, No. 2, 197–213, 199.

23 Claudio Borio and Mathias Drehmann, 'Towards an operational framework for financial stability: "fuzzy" measurement and its consequences', (June 2009) BIS Working Papers No. 284, 5–8.

24 Douglas Diamond and Philip Dybvig, 'Bank runs, deposit insurance, and liquidity', (1983) *The Journal of Political Economy*, Vol. 91, No. 3, 401, 402.

is common across some or all the financial system. It could relate to a tangible problem such as a breakdown in the payments system or, more conceptually, by a failure in trust across the financial system. The crisis, in the latter situation is brought about by "the inability to distinguish solvent from insolvent institutions".[25] Rather than financial "contagion" spreading as a series of collapsing dominos my experience is that of markets seizing at more or less the same time as banks and other financial institutions seek to ascertain their own financial positions and to conserve liquidity and reduce external liabilities coupled with a simultaneous lack of trust in the financial position of other institutions.[26]

There is a third type of thread analysed by Minsky and, subsequently, developed by Kindleberger, describing the "endogenous cycle view of financial instability". Here the financial system is seen as inherently unstable with a "propensity [for] disaster".[27] There is some "displacement" event which starts the process of accelerated credit provision and increased money supply coupled with a rapid growth in asset prices leading to a "bubble" and eventual collapse.[28] It is very difficult, ex-ante, to identify the "displacement event". It could be an element of financial deregulation, some form of innovation, or significant new trading patterns (e.g. the emergence of China as part of the international economic system or the collapse of the Soviet Union).

It is clear from the recent financial crisis that institutional and market systemic risks are inter-related and that a failure of even a small bank can have severe market implications.[29] Instability can develop rapidly, transmitted via interconnected financial markets, and can spread beyond the banking sector.[30]

2.4 The transmission of financial instability

In any financial system, there exist a number of flaws and highly interconnected systems appear to magnify these and facilitate their transmission.[31] This magnification is increased by the propensity of financial firms to "herd" and to move in the same direction together.[32] The recent financial crisis highlighted how instability may be transmitted across global economic systems. The mechanisms

25 Franklin Allen and Douglas Gale, 'Financial contagion', (2000) *The Journal of Political Economy*, Vol. 108, No. 1, 1, 3.

26 Markus Brunnermeier and others, 'The fundamental principles of financial regulation', Geneva Reports on the World Economy (International Center for Monetary and Banking Studies and Centre for Economic Policy Research, 2009), 13.

27 Charles Kindleberger, *Manias, panics and crashes* (Macmillan, London, 1978), 15.

28 Ibid., (Kindleberger), 16–19.

29 Supra note 8, (Schwarcz), 202.

30 Ibid., 243–245.

31 It mirrors microcosm communities in nature. For example, see Robert May, 'Will a large complex system be stable?', (1972) *Nature*, Vol. 238, 413–414.

32 Emilios Avgouleas, 'The global financial crisis, behavioural finance and financial regulation: in search of a new orthodoxy', April 2009) *Journal of Corporate Law Studies* Vol. 9(1), 23–59, 28.

include common exposure to the same categories of distressed assets, direct exposure to failing institutions, over-reliance on financial infrastructure provided by firms in difficulties and the effect on markets of forced asset sales amplified by "marked-to-market" accounting.[33] The failure of trust is at the root of all this; both between institutions and across markets. It is the equivalent of a depositors' bank run where distrust in the institution is infectious and immediate. Once trust is lost it is very difficult for it to be regained. Frequently, it requires outside intervention whether by the government or by, for example, J. P. Morgan in halting the panic of 1907.

There have been attempts to distinguish the transmission mechanisms between those that relate to bank balance sheet assets and those that relate to bank capital.[34] In practice, the instability mechanism sweeps backwards and forwards across both sides of bank balance sheets. It may, for example, start with market concerns about bank balance sheet asset values resulting in withdrawals of deposits and short-term funding followed by a write-down of other balance sheet asset values, which may trigger bond issue clauses and so on.

There are three key elements relevant to the transmission of financial instability through the financial system: the build-up of financial imbalances in the economy, the transmission systems which causes the build-up of these imbalances and how their effects are transmitted to the wider economy.[35] These imbalances will normally be expressed in rapid asset, invariably, property price growth. However, it is the form of financing which is critical to macroprudential policy since an analysis of twenty-three "bubbles" found that debt financing causes the greatest concern.[36] For example, canals and railways financed in the 18th and 19th centuries in the US and UK by equity had little effect on the wider economy when the issuing companies failed. However, the system is much more likely to fracture if the bubble is financed by debt.[37]

The risks to financial stability can be analysed into those which occur over a period of time and those which spread across financial sectors. Those with a "time-series dimensional" develop with the build-up, over time, of financial imbalances. Those with a "cross-sectional dimension" indicate imbalances crossing

33 Luis Jácome and Erlend Nier, 'Macroprudential policy: protecting the whole', (March 2012) *IMF Finance and Development*, 1–6.

34 Sami Alpanda, Gino Cateau and Cesaire Meh, 'A model to analyse macroprudential regulation and monetary policy', (2014) BIS Working Paper No. 461, 4–6.

35 David Aikman, Andrew Haldane and Benjamin Nelson, 'Curbing the credit cycle', (November 2010), Columbia University Center on Capitalism and Society Annual Conference, 'Microfoundations for modern macroeconomics', New York, 17.

36 Supra, note 11, (Brunnermeier and Schnabel), 22.

37 In the build-up to the secondary banking collapse in the early 1970s UK bank borrowing rose by 148% between 1971 and 1973 and bank lending to the property sector rose by over 800% from 1971 to 1974. This was reflected in a rise in the capital valuations of property of some 25% in each of the years 1972 and 1973, Margaret Reid, *The secondary banking crisis, 1973–1975* (Macmillan Press, London, 1982), 62–63.

over into other sectors at a "single point in time due to the interconnections (direct or indirect) of the financial system".[38] The two aspects of financial instability are clearly linked as "the unwinding of financial imbalances poses more concerns to policymakers if shocks cause strong spill-over effects within a highly connected financial system".[39] This form of analysis would mean that the roles of both the macroprudential and the microprudential authorities are twofold: to have sufficient capital and liquidity buffers to support individual financial institutions through the lesser trials and to provide the management of individual firms and the regulators with time to mitigate the more powerful threats. This is important, since in order to be successful, macroprudential policy needs to have a clear understanding of what is meant so that the right macroprudential structures can be designed and the correct "tools" employed. However, macroprudential policy, unlike monetary policy, lacks clear, measurable objectives.

Consequently, financial instability appears to be the norm. The whole financial structure is inherently fragile and subject to frequent stresses which, depending on a range of factors, have the potential to cause the system's collapse at any time. This gives the macroprudential policymaker an important but limited role: to keep a look-out for the bigger squalls and to ensure that microprudential regulators take the necessary collective actions. This analysis underpins the subsequent consideration of macroprudential policy. The inherent fragility of the system provides the macroprudential regulator with a constant dilemma of when to exercise its powers and to intervene.

2.5 When to intervene in the market and discretion in applying macroprudential policy

Since, as mentioned earlier, macroprudential policy is anticipatory and much of its effectiveness comes from the ability of the regulator to "signal" its concerns to the market, it is important to intervene as early as possible. However, the indicators of financial imbalance are likely to be confused. For example, the US economy started to turn at the end of 2006 with major problems in the financial markets starting at the end of 2006 and into the spring of 2007, but economic growth continued into 2008.[40] It is possible that certain lead-indicator ratios such as the increase in credit as a percentage of GDP or rapid asset price inflation should provide the macroprudential regulator with the data to act very early in the financial cycle. However, as discussed later in this chapter this places the

38 Claudio Borio and William White, 'Whither monetary and financial stability? The implications of evolving policy regimes', (February 2004) BIS Working Paper No. 147, 17.

39 Gabriele Galati and Richhild Moessner, 'Macroprudential policy – a literature review', (2011), BIS Working Papers No. 337, 1.

40 Claudio Borio, 'The financial cycle and macroeconomics: what have we learnt?', (2012) BIS Working Papers No. 395, 3–5 argues that the "financial cycle" is much less frequent than the "business cycle".

regulator in a difficult position in relation to politicians, the financial services industry and borrowers since the start of the financial cycle may not appear to be an issue viewed from the perspective of those looking at the business cycle. In 2005, the then Chairman of the Federal Reserve stated that any central bank intervention to correct "cyclical imbalances" would be too late and "misguided".[41] This was supported by Bernanke and Gertler.[42]

There are also questions whether the decision, and the extent to which action is taken, are best determined by inflexible "rules" or, at the other extreme, left wholly to the judgement of the policymaker. If a rules-based approach is taken, the indicators used and the rules applied need to be transparent and easily understood by the market.[43] The FPC does not see itself as constrained by, for example, automatic macroprudential "triggers". Instead the committee exercises its judgement in determining policy.[44] However, there is a risk that a system based on simplicity misses key factors. "There may also be 'softer' factors to take into account using information from the microprudential supervisors (e.g. increasingly lax underwriting, more frauds, mis-priced risk, etc.)".[45] Moreover, in carrying out any analysis the macroprudential policymaker needs to act with "simplicity and humility" since macroprudential policy "cannot be expected to eliminate the credit cycle"...and macroprudential policy needs to operate with "simple rules augmented by regulatory judgement".[46]

The tendency, with macroprudential tools, has been to limit non-discretionary rules to the sphere of capital, liquidity and leverage regulation.[47] This approach

41 Alan Greenspan, 'Reflections on central banking', remarks at a symposium sponsored by the Federal Reserve Bank of Kansas City, Jackson Hole, Wyoming, 26 August 2005.

42 Ben Bernanke and Mark Gertler, 'Should central banks respond to movements in asset prices?', (2001) *The American Economic Review*, Vol. 91, No. 2, 253, who saw the main role of the central bank as remediation action following a collapse in asset prices.

43 The Bank for International Settlements', Committee on the Global Financial System is in favour of a strict rules-based macroprudential regime:

> Experience with monetary policy suggests that policymaking works best when it is fairly predictable and transparent. The same is likely to hold true for macroprudential policy. When leaning against the financial cycle, where timely policy action is particularly important, explicit guidelines or well-articulated principles for macroprudential policy actions should help to counter political and institutional resistance.
>
> Supra, note 17, (CGFS), 6

44 Paul Tucker, Simon Hall and Aashish Pattani, 'Macroprudential policy at the Bank of England', (2013) *Quarterly Bulletin*, Vol. Q3, 192.

45 Bank for International Settlements, Committee on the Global Financial System, 'Operationalising the selection and application of macroprudential instruments', (2012) CGFS Papers No. 48, 16.

46 Supra, note 35, (Aikman, Haldane and Nelson), 25.

47 Rules have the advantage that once in place they require no further justification and act automatically, Claudio Borio, 'Implementing a macroprudential framework: blending boldness and realism', (2010), BIS Paper, 10.

dovetails with the microprudential rules. In addition, capital requirements fulfil a range of roles (e.g. to act as a buffer if losses are sustained by the bank, to encourage shareholders to oversee bank management since their investment is effectively held hostage against the undertaking of excessive risk and to act as a price signal to the market as the strategy of the bank develops in the context of economic and market conditions). For example, rules-based dynamic capital provisioning may fulfil this market-signalling function as well as act as a brake on bank asset growth. Much of the success of this approach will depend on how markets read the signals against a background of rapidly rising asset prices, possibly inflated by other sources of credit and finance. It is possible that the signals, in these circumstances, are too muted and the provisioning required too little.[48] Much will depend on how macroprudential regulatory actions are transmitted through the market and into the broader economy. Aspects of this issue are considered later in this chapter. However, it may be the case that capital requirements which attempt to establish a high level of uniformity across all banks, for example, in terms of the allocation of risk-weights, may in turn encourage a "uniformity of behaviour which is itself a source of instability".[49]

Moreover, the longer credit controls are in place the greater the risk for avoidance. For example, in Spain while dynamic provisioning was useful in mitigating the credit cycles, credit growth continued as borrowers moved to smaller lenders which were less constrained by provision limits.[50] This issue of avoidance, or "leakage", may undermine many aspects of macroprudential policy and is considered in more detail later in this chapter. It is worth noting that leverage ratios are much more difficult to avoid and may have an important market "signalling" effect but may still be ineffective in the face of large amounts of non-banking mortgage lending.[51] Consequently, it is against this background of uncertainty and serious policy disagreements that a subsequent section of this chapter considers the issues involved in the design and application of macroprudential policy. However, before turning to this it is important to reflect upon an important aspect of what may be described as both macroprudential policy "hubris" and

48 Financial Stability Board, 'Peer review of Spain', (January 2011), 5, "[T]he Spanish dynamic pre-provisioning scheme...was a well-designed counter-cyclical measure, but of insufficient scale and extent to provide much of a mitigant to the Spanish housing cycle." Charles Goodhart, 'Lessons for monetary policy from the Euro-area crisis', (2013), 4, Bank of Greece conference on 'The crisis in the Euro-area', in Athens, on 23–24 May 2013, 383, 386.

49 Jean-Pierre Landau (Deputy Governor of the Banque de France), 'Bubbles and macro prudential supervision', speech, at the conference on 'The future of financial regulation', Banque de France and Toulouse School of Economics, Paris, 28 January 2009, 5.

50 Gabriel Jiménez and others, 'Macroprudential policy, countercyclical bank capital buffers and credit supply: evidence from the Spanish dynamic provisioning experiments', (2015) Working Paper, Universitat Pompeu Fabra.

51 Emilios Avgouleas, 'Bank leverage ratios and financial stability: a micro and macroprudential perspective', (October 2015) Levy Economics Institute, Bard College, Working Paper No. 849, 24–25.

its perceived vulnerabilities. Macroprudential policy seeks to establish control using a variety of powerful "tools" but at the same time sees, as in the example of Spanish dynamic provisioning mentioned earlier, the effect of these mechanisms become less potent.

2.6 Housing markets and credit and their link to systemic risk

It was the failure to note, and address, the build-up of systemic risk in the recent financial crisis that threatened not just individual financial institutions but the financial system as a whole.

The analysis of the causes is important since the effectiveness of macroprudential policies depend on the weight given to each of the suggested reasons.[52] Some blame the recent financial crisis on the development of a classic housing price "bubble" with rising house prices fuelling the demand for credit.[53] There are a range of explanations given for the rapid rise in house prices leading up to 2007. Goodhart considers that the way housing finance was undertaken "was at the centre of the crisis" in a range of countries including the US.[54] Some have suggested that the large global trade imbalances were the underlying cause for this excess credit.[55] These resulted in both an increase in the supply of credit and low interest rates which, in turn, encouraged increased demand for both credit and housing. Others strongly believe that the increased prevalence of securitisation and financial innovation allowed lenders to increase their provision of home loans.[56] Aspects of financial innovation in the US and the role of government-sponsored enterprises are explored in Chapter 7. Finally, there is a view that government and its agencies interfered in the housing market and

52 Less explored are the organisational structural of both banks and regulators and cultural reasons for the crisis. They can be grouped into three broad but over-lapping areas: the desire of individuals and organisational departments to self-restrict their areas of responsibility to those aspects with which they feel comfortable; a short organisational "attention span" due to changes in personnel, re-assessed priorities, new initiatives, etc.; a reluctance to use all the powers available hoping that the problem will resolve itself, Timothy Malloy, 'Regulation, compliance and the firm', (2003) *Temple Law Review*, No. 76, 451.

53 Ryan Bubb and Pasad Krishnamurthy, 'Regulating against bubbles', (2014) *University of Pennsylvania Law Review*, Vol. 163, 1553; Edward Glaeser, Joshua Gottlieb and Joseph Gyourko, 'Can cheap credit explain the housing boom?', (2010), National Bureau of Economic Research, Working Paper 16230.

54 Charles Goodhart, 'Property finance has been the main common factor', (Written evidence to the Parliamentary Commission on Banking Standards, House of Commons, 24 October 2012).

55 Ouarda Merrouche and Erlend Nier, 'What caused the global financial crisis?—evidence on the drivers of financial imbalances 1999–2007', (2010) IMF Working Paper, WP/10/265, 29.

56 Adam Levitin, Andrey Pavlov and Susan Wachter, 'Securitization: cause or remedy of the financial crisis', (2009) Georgetown University Law Centre, Research Paper No. 1462895 and University of Pennsylvania Law School, Institute for Law and Economics, Research Paper No. 09-31.

through legislation and financial operations created an unsustainable boom in credit availability and home buying.[57]

In addition, economic modelling has failed to recognise the central role of banks, the growth of bank balance sheets, coupled with asset prices increases, and the role of banks in the increasing level of debt in the economy.[58] This combined with periodic bursts of "euphoric expectations", together with increased financial inter-connectedness, has been at the heart of most financial crises.[59] All these explanations contain the common threads of a demand for housing coupled with the provision of excess credit. Broadly, macroprudential policy aims to control the level of credit available.

While there are a number of definitions of macroprudential policy, it is clear that the broad objective is to protect the financial system as a whole from "systemic risk". There are a number of views on what constitutes "systemic risk".[60] These range from an unexpected change in prices in credit and asset markets as result of disturbances in financial markets "which lead to a danger of failure of financial firms which in turn threatens to spread so as to disrupt" other financial systems.[61] This can arise from correlation of returns on the asset-side of bank balance sheets since "banks prefer an inefficiently high correlation of asset returns ('herd [effect]'), giving rise to systemic or aggregate risk".[62] This can produce a period of high financial instability where risk can no longer be priced. Financial instability can also be seen as the result, or cause, of a break down in trust. In the recent crisis, lenders would not lend to other financial institutions who in turn would not lend – in a version of the prisoners' dilemma where co-operation was not possible.[63]

As mentioned, the origins of the recent financial crises lay in the rapid build-up of credit and its relationship to property prices in the period preceding the collapse.[64] This form of systemic risk is not a recent phenomenon. It was a major factor in the three most recent property crises in the UK (i.e. the secondary banking crisis in the early 1970s, the small banks crisis 1990–1994 and the

57 Atif Mian, Amir Sufi and Francisco Trebbi, 'The political economy of the US mortgage default crisis', (November 2008) National Bureau of Economic Research, Working Paper No. 14468.

58 Atif Mian, Kamalesh Rao and Amir Sufi, 'Household balance sheets, consumption and the economic slump', (2013) *Quarterly Journal of Economics*, 128, 4, 1687–1726,1693, 1724.

59 Hyman Minsky, *Can 'it' happen again? Essays on instability and finance* (Routledge, London, 1982) 150–151.

60 Supra, note 8, (Schwarcz, 'Systemic risk'), 202. See also Jean-Claude Trichet, 'Systemic risk', The Clare Distinguished Lecture in Economics and Public Policy at the University of Cambridge, 10 December 2009, describing systemic risk as a "seizing-up of the financial system".

61 Philip Davis, *Debt, financial fragility and systemic risk* (Clarendon Press, Oxford, 1992), 118.

62 Viral Acharya, 'A theory of systemic risk and design of prudential bank regulation', (2009) *Journal of Financial Stability*, Vol. 5, 224, 225.

63 Lucian Bebchuk and Itay Goldstein, 'Self-fulfilling market freezes', (2011) *Review of Financial Studies*, Vol. 24, No. 11, 3519, 3521.

64 Mathias Drehmann, Claudio Borio and Kostas Tsatsaronis, 'Anchoring countercyclical capital buffers: the role of credit aggregates', (2011) Bank of International Settlement Working Paper 355, 1.

most recent financial crisis). In all these cases, "it is clear that a rapid build-up of private credit was a lead indicator of the crisis to follow".[65]

An analysis of financial crises in five countries in the latter part of the 19th century and early 20th century found close links between the growth of credit and a rapid expansion in both equity and property markets.[66] In all cases this resulted in a rise in bad debts, destroying many banks and threatened the financial infrastructure.[67] There is an argument that the depression in the US in the 1930s had its roots in the residential property boom of the 1920s.[68] One review found that of twenty-three countries that had booms in both property prices and credit before the recent crisis, twenty-one experienced either a financial collapse or a significant drop in GDP growth.[69] However, of the seven countries that experienced a boom solely in property prices only two had a systemic financial crisis.

Nevertheless, there is a distinction to be drawn between the consequences of major falls in equity prices compared with the periodic collapses of the housing market seen during the second half of the 20th century. Crises involving major equity falls are more evenly spread while housing price crises are much more clustered and, in addition, approximately 40% of house price escalations were followed by property value collapses.[70] Housing price falls are not as deep (no more than 30% on average) but have a more widespread and longer lasting effect on the economy (due to a broader wealth effect) and much stronger and faster consequences for the banking system due to the additional provisioning costs, enhanced capital ratios and a reduced willingness to lend.[71] The "wealth

65 Julia Giese and others, 'The credit-to-GDP gap and complementary indicators for macroprudential policy: evidence from the UK', (2014) *International Journal of Finance and Economics*, Vol. 19, No. 1, 25, 26.

66 Giovanni Favara and Jean Imbs, 'Credit supply and the price of housing', (2015) *American Economic Review*, Vol. 105, No. 3, 958–992, 984.

67 Charles Goodhart and P. Delargy, 'Financial crises: plus ca change, plus c'est la meme chose', (1999), Special Paper No. 108, London School of Economics Financial Markets Group, 261, 263. Post-1990s crises parallels those in the late 19th and early 20th centuries with an over-investment in property coupled with weakly regulated banking systems, Barry Eichengreen and Michael Bordo, 'Crises now and then: what lessons from the last era of financial globalization?', (2002), National Bureau of Economic Research, Working Paper 8716.

68 Alexander Field, 'The interwar housing cycle in the light of 2001–2012: a comparative historical perspective', in Eugene White, Kenneth Snowden and Price Fishback (eds), *Housing and mortgage markets in historical perspective* (National Bureau of Economic Research, University of Chicago Press, Chicago, 2014), 39–80.

69 Christopher Crowe and others, 'Policies for macrofinancial stability: options to deal with real estate booms', (2011a) IMF Staff Discussion Papers, SDN/11/02.

70 IMF study of asset price cycles, 'When bubbles burst', (2003), IMF World Economic and Financial Survey, Chapter II, 61, 63.

71 Ibid., IMF, 63 on the "wealth effect" which describes the relationship between asset prices and consumer spending. There appears to be a psychological link between an increase in the value of an individual's shareholding or house price and their propensity to spend, Filippo Altissimo and others, 'Wealth and asset price effects on economic activity', (2005) European Central Bank Occasional Paper Series 29, 34.

effect" is stronger for house price growth compared with that for share price increases.[72] As a consequence housing crises are more difficult to unwind.[73] In the US, the house price decline following the recent financial crisis lasted at least six years.[74]

The evidence suggests that the loan security provides the 'currency' to support the growth in lending. Leveraging the value of this collateral has a multiplier effect on credit since increased credit availability increases demand for property and this in turn raises house prices.[75] The higher property values in turn provide great security for more loans and so on. If asset prices fall the multiplier effect is reversed. The result amplifies and spreads through the economy.[76]

There is also something special about economic recessions which follow a rapid expansion in credit coupled with a house price boom. It appears that these types of economic troughs are longer and deeper and affect many other parts of the economy and have a deleterious effect on the whole economy.[77] Consequently, it is fair to say that housing markets are exceptional and are not like other markets in their economic effect. This is probably due to residential property forming the major part of personal wealth with the resulting large "amplification effect" mentioned earlier.[78] Moreover, there is a close inverse relationship between house price increases and the decline in savings correlated with increased consumer spending.[79]

In addition, the value of a household's equity in their home (the rising value of the property, less the outstanding mortgage) represents future aspirations since it provides an opportunity to buy a bigger home, possibly to accommodate a growing family or a move to somewhere new to find work or a better job.[80] In other words, the equity in a current home represents not only the deposit for the next but also hope for the future. This is an important but neglected

72 Karl Case, John Quigley and Robert Shiller, 'Comparing wealth effects: the stock market vs. the housing market', (2005) *Advances in Macroeconomics*, Vol. 5, No. 1, Article 1, 26.

73 Supra, note 70, (IMF), 72–73, house prices declines lasted on average four years.

74 Carmen Reinhart and Kenneth Rogoff, *This time is different* (Princeton University Press, New Jersey, 2009), 226.

75 Òscar Jordà, Moritz Schularick and Alan Taylor, 'Betting the house', (December 2014) National Bureau of Economic Research, Working Paper 20771, 37.

76 Nobuhiro Kiyotaki and John Moore, 'Credit cycles', (1997) *Journal of Political Economy*, Vol. 105, No. 2, 211, 212. "The system's reaction to shocks is highly nonlinear. Once in a crisis regime, even small shocks are subject to amplification, leading to significant...risk", Markus Brunnermeier and Yuliy Sannikov, 'A macroeconomic model with a financial sector', (2014) *American Economic Review* 104, 379, 381–382.

77 Stijn Claessens, Ayhan Kose and Marco Terrones, 'What happens during recessions, crunches and busts', (2008b) IMF Working Paper, WP/08/274, 34.

78 Jeremy Stein, 'Prices and trading volume in the housing market: a model with down-payment effects', (May 1995), *The Quarterly Journal of Economics*, Vol. 110, No. 2, 379, 380–383.

79 Dan Andrew, Aida Caldera Sánchez and Asa Johansson, 'Housing markets and structural policies in OECD countries', (2011) OECD Working Paper No. 836, 56.

80 Supra, note 78, (Stein), 383.

perspective in many economic assessments. However, it is a major reason why access to homeownership is high on the political agenda in both the UK and US and in many other jurisdictions – and why this issue cannot be left solely to technocratic judgements.[81] The involvement of politics in macroprudential policy and the latter's role in house price growth and access to credit is considered later in this and subsequent chapters.

2.7 The role of credit

As mentioned earlier, systemic financial instability is frequently caused by a combination of a rapid increase in credit and residential property price inflation. The empirical evidence indicates that the credit system itself acts a "potential source of financial instability and not merely as an amplifier of shocks".[82] The quality of bank credit assessment processes commonly appear to deteriorate during a property asset price boom in part due to the agency effect of mortgage intermediaries and the difficulty in establishing "true" asset prices in a booming market.[83] These issues were explored before the start of the recent financial crisis and the conclusion was that "excessive credit created 'imbalances' and a risk of financial instability".[84]

The view that "financial crises are credit booms gone wrong" has been known since at least the 1970s and proponents of this perspective have recently been "rediscovered" following the 2007/2008 financial crisis.[85] In Minsky's analysis, money acts as a "veil of finance" between a real asset (e.g. a building), the borrower and the lender with banks acting as the intermediary with the creation of debt obligations. The result is uncertainty and potential instability.[86] Subsequent work indicates a strong correlation between monetary policy, rising household debt and house prices coupled with lax underwriting and mis-priced

81 Stijn Ferrari, Mara Pirovano and Wanda Cornacchia, 'Identifying early warning indicators for real estate-related banking crises', (2015) ESRB Occasional Paper No. 8, 5 for an example of the wholly technocratic approach.

82 Moritz Schularick and Alan Taylor, 'Credit booms gone bust: monetary policy, leverage cycles and financial crises, 1870–2008', (2012), *American Economic Review*, Vol. 102, No. 2, 1029–1061, 1042.

83 Franklin Allen and Elena Carletti, 'Systemic risk from real estate and macroprudential regulation', (2013), *International Journal of Banking, Accounting and Finance*, Vol. 5, Nos. 1–2, 28.

84 Claudio Borio and Philip Lowe, 'Asset prices, financial and monetary stability: exploring the nexus', (2002) BIS Working Papers, No 114, 27.

85 Henry Kaufman, 'Debt: the threat to economic and financial stability', (1986) *Economic Review, Federal Reserve Bank of Kansas*, Vol. 71, No. 10, 3, 6, ("The build-up of debt in the economy is due to a variety of factors including financial deregulation and innovation, the development of securitisation and financial internationalisation and tax structures and a lack of 'debt prudence'").

86 Hyman Minsky, 'The financial instability hypothesis: an interpretation of Keynes and an alternative to "standard theory"', (1977), Hyman P. Minsky Archive, Paper 38, 4–6.

risk.[87] There is also a correlation between an increase in household debt and a subsequent fall in GDP growth.[88]

It is the interaction between asset prices, particularly in the housing sector, and credit that makes macroprudential policy necessary to control credit growth.

2.8 The definition of macroprudential policy

Macroprudential policy is a new and inchoate area.[89] This section seeks to explain what it includes and its relationship with the more traditional microprudential form of regulation.

EU Regulation has defined macroprudential policy as the

> oversight of the financial system…in order to contribute to the prevention or mitigation of systemic risks to financial stability…that arise from developments within the financial system and taking into account macroeconomic developments, so as to avoid periods of widespread financial distress.[90]

In this context, the financial system includes "all financial institutions, markets, products and market infrastructures".[91]

However, UK legislation has avoided defining macroprudential policy. It instead provides the Bank of England with broad objectives, organisational and governance mechanisms and specific macroprudential tools (e.g. The Bank of England Act 1998 (Macroprudential Measures) Order 2013).[92]

Macroprudential policy can be analysed into four main aspects: the monitoring and identification of risks to financial stability; the prevention of these risks; the containment and control of these risks in order to reduce their occurrence and to limit their effect and, finally, if severe financial instability occurs to prevent, or reduce, its transmission to areas of the economy beyond the financial services system (i.e. the so-called "real economy").[93] Macroprudential policy includes financial markets as well as institutions. Additionally, it encompasses

87 Matt Waldron and Fabrizio Zampolli, 'Household debt, house prices and consumption in the United Kingdom: a quantitative theoretical analysis', (2010) Bank of England Working Paper No. 379, 3–4.

88 Atif Mian, Amir Sufi and Emil Verner, 'Household debt and global growth', (2015) National Bureau of Economic Research Working Paper No. 21581, 22.

89 Bank of England, 'The role of macroprudential policy: a discussion paper', (November 2009), setting the ground work for the establishment of the Financial Policy Committee.

90 EU Regulation No. 1092/2010 of 24 November 2010 on European Union macroprudential oversight of the financial system and establishing a European Systemic Risk Board, Article 3.

91 Ibid., (EU 1092/2010), Article 2.

92 House of Lords' European Union Committee, 'The future of EU financial regulation and supervision', (2009).

93 There are a number of views on how systemic risk is transmitted. Augustin Landier, David Sraer and David Thesmar, 'Banks' exposure to interest rate risk and the transmission of monetary policy', (2013) NBER Working Paper 18857 (75), 459–512.

the financial systems' infrastructure including the payments systems and the arrangements which ensure trust and the integrity of, and across, global markets. These include, for example, credit rating agencies and external auditors. Moreover, macroprudential policy needs to look across borders, and over the longer term, in order to ascertain what risks to financial stability may be building up with implications for financial stability.

Macroprudential policymakers also need to be aware of any severe operational issues including those not directly related to financial services. For example, a significant breakdown in the farm payments and support system may have widespread effects on the ability of farmers to meet their debts. Finally, macroprudential policy must not shy away from areas with a political dimension. For example, in the context of this book, the failure to build anything approaching the necessary number of new homes each year in the UK increases both house prices and the demand for more credit. The result may be greater risks to financial stability from an expanded growth in credit and inflated asset prices. Part of the concern expressed in this work is that those that operate macroprudential policy may not comprehend its full scope and the need for the Bank of England's macroprudential mandate to extend to a range of areas which traditionally have been outside the Bank's scope. This is likely to be seen as encroaching on public policy, such as house building, with implications for the political legitimacy of the Bank of England. These aspects are developed in Chapters 6.

Moreover, transnational macroprudential policy may be even more complex since, for example, the European Central Bank has no responsibility for financial services outside banking.[94] Similarly, the membership of the European Systemic Risk Board's governing board consists primarily of central bankers since it is perceived that

> if you put together central banks in such a body you are going to have the right people in the right place because it is going to force these central banks to be more active on the essential thing, which is detecting systemic risks....[95]

Bringing central bankers together may assist in identifying risks to financial stability, many of which may have cross-border implications, at the same time it may limit the necessary broader perspective. Although the governing board includes representation from the European authorities responsible for other financial areas, such as insurance and asset management, its focus on central banks is likely to be a significant weakness. Part of the reason for this apparent narrow focus may lie in the history of macroprudential policy.

94 See the oral evidence given by Jacques De Larosière to the House of Lords European Union Committee for its 14th Report of Session 2008–09, 'The future of EU financial regulation and supervision', 149.

95 Ibid., 150.

2.9 The development of macroprudential policy

The risks of bank maturity transformation to financial stability have long been known. It is claimed that it was while considering this subject that the term "macroprudential" was first used when it was recorded "in the minutes of a meeting 1979 of the Basel Committee on Banking Regulation and Supervisory Practices discussing the potential collection of data on maturity transformation in international bank lending".[96] This was developed further by Andrew Crockett, the General Manager of the Bank of International Settlements, in a speech in October 2000, considering both microprudential and macroprudential policy and the need to develop the latter system of financial supervision of banks.[97] This highlighted the risk to the whole economy as a result of individual, rational actions by financial institutions, which collectively threaten the system as a whole. This narrow approach is mirrored by microprudential regulation and supervision which seek to limit the risk of failure of individual financial institutions. The latter "approach was seen as treating aggregate risk as independent of the collective behaviour of institutions.... Crucially, this excluded the possibility that actions could appear individually rational but, in the aggregate, result in undesirable outcomes, owing to the externalities involved".[98]

Crockett explained that the only difference between these two forms of regulation is in their objectives and "the conception of the mechanisms influencing economic outcomes. It has less to do with the instruments used in the pursuit of those objectives".[99] The differences between microprudential and macroprudential policy can be best illustrated by considering the perspective of the microprudential supervisor instructing a bank to improve its capital position. "The regulator does not care whether the bank adjusts [its capital ratio] via the numerator or via the denominator—that is, by raising new capital or by shrinking assets."[100] This is an example of the "fallacy of composition" where what is a rational action for individuals in a group has an adverse consequences for the group, and hence individuals, as a whole.[101] The similarities between microprudential and macroprudential supervisory tools are considered later in this chapter.

Additionally, there is a view that financial stability can be enhanced by improving the ability of financial firms to enter and exit the market with the least

96 Piet Clement, 'The term 'macroprudential': origins and evolution', (2010) *BIS Quarterly Review*, March, 59.

97 Ibid., (Clement), 63.

98 Ibid., (Clement), 64.

99 Andrew Crockett, 'Marrying the micro- and macroprudential dimensions of financial stability', (BIS speech on 21 September 2000), 2.

100 Samuel Hanson, Anil Kashyap and Jeremy Stein, 'A macroprudential approach to financial regulation', (2011) *Journal of Economic Perspectives*, Vol. 25, No. 1, 5.

101 Ricardo Caballero considered this issue in his paper, 'A fallacy of composition', (1991), National Bureau of Economic Research Working Paper 3735.

disruption via workable recovery and resolution plans. This will require less focus on the traditional methods of microprudential regulation.[102] The development of macroprudential policy may also complicate the role of the Bank of England which has to operate both a monetary policy regime alongside macroprudential and microprudential policies.[103] The clear interaction between macroeconomic policy and macroprudential policy is considered in the next chapter.

As mentioned, macroprudential policy objectives include "strengthening the resilience of the financial system" to economic downturns and other shocks and by "leaning against the financial cycle reducing the probability or magnitude of a financial crisis".[104] It is anticipatory: it seeks to prevent a serious systemic problem developing.[105] Its effects are as much psychological as operational since it acts on the expectations of financial institutions.[106]

Moreover, the macroprudential policymaker may seek both to control the rapid growth of credit and to limit the increase in the price of the asset being financed. This may be at odds with the aims of both investors in the bank and the microprudential supervisor. The latter two groups have an aligned interest in increasing the profits of the bank. The microprudential supervisor is keen to increase retained earnings which strengthen the bank's capital and, at the same time, make it easier to attract new investors to supply new capital. Additionally, constraining the growth of credit has its disadvantages since setting "limits to credit expansion" may have "a consequential effect on the economy" and have political implications.[107] This approach, discussed in more detail later, is itself controversial since the central banking view, prior to the financial crisis, was not to target asset price rises, since it was impossible to determine whether these were due to systemic imbalances or changes in economic fundamentals.[108] However, the evidence from the recent crisis is that a policy of passivity in the face of an asset price bubble is expensive in view of the cost of "cleaning up the mess".[109] However, it is difficult to identify a bubble and to act with the necessary speed. This is "coupled with the difficulty of gently deflating these bubbles" providing "serious impediments to such proactive approaches".[110] These issues raise questions over whether macroprudential policy can provide

102 Geoffrey Wood and Ali Kabiri, 'Firm stability and system stability: the regulatory delusion', in John Raymond LaBrosse, Rodrigo Olivares-Caminal and Dalvinder Singh (eds), *Managing risk in the financial system* (Edward Elgar, Cheltenham, 2011), 181–193.

103 Charles Goodhart and Rosa Lastra, 'Interaction between monetary policy and bank regulation', (Report to the European Parliament, 21 September 2015), 7–11.

104 Supra, note 17, (CGFS), 2.

105 Supra, note 49, (Landau), 1.

106 Supra, note 35, (Aikman, Haldane and Nelson), 24.

107 Supra, note 49, (Landau), 3.

108 Ben Bernanke and Mark Gertler, 'Monetary policy and asset price volatility', (2000) National Bureau of Economic Research Working Paper 7559, 6–9.

109 Supra, note 11, (Brunnermeier and Schnabel), 21–22.

110 Ibid., 22.

a "backstop for systemic risk containment".[111] This approach is developed further in the next chapter.

Nevertheless, again as mentioned earlier, there may be something special about rapid growth in property prices and the interaction with an accelerated growth in bank credit which necessitates a highly proactive approach.[112] Options for macroprudential policy limiting house price growth are considered in the next section. It is a central theme of this book that since the more traditional macroprudential tools for limiting credit growth may not be effective other options need to be considered.

2.10 The role of banks in asset price growth and the employment of macroprudential policy to control this

Macroprudential policy is needed both for financial markets and businesses since they demonstrate an aspect of the economic concept known as the "tragedy of the commons".[113] There is no single "owner" of the financial system and consequently, in the lead-up to the financial crisis, banks and other financial institutions developed products and operated in such a way as to threaten the stability of the system as a whole. Financial stability meets the definition of a "public good" in that there is no rivalry and no exclusivity in that financial stability is indivisible, in that its benefits are available to all "its enjoyment by one jurisdiction does not reduce the amount available to another country".[114] In economic terms the benefits accrued to the financial institutions but the risks were not internalised and, in many instances, fall on the state and taxpayers.

This risk to the stability of the system is magnified by the ability of banks to create money.[115] Left to their own devices banks will create money using

111 Rosa Lastra, 'Systemic risk and macroprudential supervision', in Niamh Moloney, Eilís Ferran and Jennifer Payne (eds), *The Oxford handbook of financial regulation* (Oxford University Press, Oxford, 2015), 317.

112 Stefan Gerlach, 'Housing markets and financial stability', speech at the National University of Ireland, Galway, 20 April 2012), 1–6 and Michael Bordo and Jeanne Olivier, 'Monetary policy and asset prices: does 'benign neglect' make sense', (2002) IMF Working Paper, WP/02/225, 24–25, 11, found that financial crises are triggered when house prices have peaked. In an analysis of fifteen advanced economies during the period 1970–2002 they identified twenty distinct housing booms, of these eleven were followed by an economic collapse and of these eleven, six involved banking crises. There is some correlation between the size of the property market in relation to the whole economy and the effect of the housing boom on the economy. highlighting this relationship between high property prices and the growth of credit.

113 First articulated in 1833 by William Foster Lloyd, 'Checks to population', (reprinted in 1980) *Population and Development Review*, Vol. 6, No. 3, 473, 483, using the example of overgrazed common land where while there is a collective, as opposed to an individual, interest in its conservation nothing is done.

114 Supra, note 111, (Lastra, 'Systemic risk'), 313.

115 For example, the development of the discounted bill of exchange as a form of money created by banks turned business and commercial promissory notes into negotiable instruments.

short-term debt instruments. Consequently, it is important that "central banks should not be reluctant to deploy [their various] tools...in an effort to contain excessive private money creation".[116] It is the special function of banks to create money as they carry out the process of "maturity transformation".[117] The transformation of maturity can be reversed as long-term assets held by banks are then, in turn, changed, via securitisation, into shorter-term commercial paper liabilities which can be sold to another financial institution and then used as part of another maturity transformation process and so on. In parallel, banks will transform risk; both by increasing and decreasing risk. The extent and the speed of this process are at the heart of concerns with the stability of the financial system.

As mentioned earlier, part of the rationale for macroprudential policy is the need to limit rapid asset price growth. However, the view of central banks prior to the financial crisis was not to target asset price rises since it was impossible to determine whether these were due to systemic imbalances or changes in economic fundamentals.[118] More recently, this view was reiterated by the Governor of the Banque de France who said that asset prices should not be targeted by central banks. The latter should be limited to two broad objectives: "price and financial stability".[119] The governor was critical of some who have "suggested including asset prices in the index targeted by the central bank". He saw this "as a distinctly sub-optimal solution, as it would essentially amount, in practice, to moving to a situation with one instrument, monetary policy, aiming at a combination of two objectives, price and financial stability".[120] This can be contrasted with the views of Padoa-Schioppa who considered that monetary policy, working in tandem with microprudential supervision and backed by the availability of emergency liquidity, would be sufficient to ensure financial stability.[121] He saw "banking as a system" in which the "pursuit of financial stability occupies a 'land in between' monetary policy and prudential supervision".[122] As mentioned

116 Jeremy Stein, 'Monetary policy as financial stability regulation', (2012) *The Quarterly Journal of Economics*, Vol. 127, 57, 91.

117 "At the heart of banking is...maturity transformation, or more simply, banks borrow at a shorter term and lend at a longer term in respect of the duration of their deposits and loans. This is the essence of banking...This is a benefit to the economy and society because it allows longer-term borrowing by companies and by all of us to buy houses. But it makes banks inherently illiquid". 'Financial Stability – objective and resolution', speech by Andrew Bailey at the Pro Manchester Business and Professional Services Conference, Manchester, 17 March 2011.

118 Supra, note 108, (Bernanke and Gertler), and Bernanke and Gertler, 'Should central banks respond to movements in asset prices?', (2001) *The American Economic Review*, Vol. 91, No. 2, 253.

119 Christian Noyer, 'Monetary policy and macroprudential policy' speech at a conference on 'The future of monetary policy', Banca d'Italia, Rome, 30 September 2010.

120 Ibid., (Noyer).

121 Tommaso Padoa-Schioppa, 'Central banks and financial stability', speech in Jakarta, 7 July 2003. See also Tommaso Padoa-Schioppa, 'Central banks and financial stability: exploring the land in between', in V. Gaspar, P. Hartmann and O. Sleijpen (eds), *The transmission of the European financial system* (European Central Bank, Frankfurt, 2003).

122 Tommaso Padoa-Schioppa, *Regulating finance: balancing freedom and risk* (Oxford University Press, Oxford, 2004), 94 and 97.

earlier, the relationship between monetary policy and macroprudential policy is considered in the next chapter.

As mentioned, it is clear that macroprudential policy is, at best, a set of broad objectives. It is the variety and use of a range of macroprudential "tools" which defines this form of regulation. In contrast, microprudential regulation is based on promulgating rules, both substantive and procedural, for regulated firms coupled with effective supervision of how firms comply with these requirements. The next chapter considers a subset of the full macroprudential "tool-kit", their effectiveness and the limitations on their use. The use of conduct of business rules is often neglected as a macroprudential tool. This work advocates using these regulations as well as limiting asset price growth by substantially increasing the supply of housing to help reduce pent-up demand for homes and credit.

The next sections consider the macroprudential policy framework and the issues and limitations of the current approach to macroprudential policy.

2.11 The macroprudential policy framework

As mentioned, macroprudential policy differs from microprudential regulation in that the former is, in practice, a set of broad objectives and has a number of methods which may be employed most of which are derived from, or match, those used by other forms of regulation. An analysis of the macroprudential "tools" and the effectiveness of those focused on LTV and DTI is set out in the next chapter.

The starting point came in November 2010, when the G20 Leaders "called on the FSB, IMF and BIS to do further work on macroprudential policy frameworks…".[123] Subsequently, the Bank for International Settlements' Committee on the Global Financial System suggested seven principles for the design and operation of macroprudential policy.[124] These include ensuring that there is a strong macroprudential regulator with "strong accountability" and clear objectives. This organisation needed to collect and analyse data from the markets and microprudential supervisors and "[understand] the interconnectivity of markets and financial institutions, both domestically and cross-border" and co-operate with other cross-border agencies. The authoritative macroprudential regulator needed to develop "both traditional and less familiar macroprudential tools" and have a strong "communication strategy" setting out policies linked to ensuring financial stability and to "manage public expectations about what can be achieved with macroprudential policy".[125]

The macroprudential regulator will usually rely on the microprudential supervisors to implement and enforce the designated tools. Systemic risk changes over

123 FSB, IMF and BIS, '*Macroprudential policy tools and frameworks progress report to G20*', October 2011, 3.

124 Supra, note 45, (CGFS Papers No. 48), 40–42.

125 Supra, note 45, (CGFS Papers No. 48), 40–42.

time.[126] Consequently, it will need to adapt the use of these tools to counteract growing vulnerabilities in the financial system by assessing the two key dimensions of risk mentioned earlier: cross-sectional and time series.[127]

The issues and limitations of the current approach are considered next.

2.12 Macroprudential policy and the concept of the "turbulent frontier"

As mentioned earlier, the concept of the "turbulent frontier" used in the context of geopolitics lends itself to an analysis of financial services regulation, in general, and macroprudential policy, in particular. In its original form the analysis of the "turbulent frontier" puts forward the proposition that provincial "governors, charged with the maintenance of order, could not ignore disorder beyond their borders" and consequently, they took action "to eliminate the disorderly frontier" which "in turn produced new frontier problems and further expansion".[128] In developing this idea in regulatory policy, as well as geopolitical terms, there probably need to be other dynamics in operation including sufficient "turbulence" and factors which "push and pull" towards intervention and action.[129] The "turbulent frontier" concept is particularly appropriate when the governor's power is increasing. This growth of power leads to a concern "with everything that happens anywhere" and the need to protect the ever-expanding frontier is "a process with few natural limits".[130] It is compounded by the perception that regulators are very ready to perceive instances of "market failure" based on their tendency to have a "latent distrust of market system" solutions and hence to favour regulation and direct intervention in the market.[131]

First, there needs to be "turbulence". In terms of financial services this may take the form of some threat to financial equilibrium. For example, it could involve a rapid expansion of credit in a new and growing area such as "buy-to-let" properties. Macroprudential policy would indicate the need for data, the acquisition of regulatory powers over this area and possibly macroprudential action in the form of a recommendation to microprudential supervisors. Second, there would need to be some "push" for macroprudential intervention. This could come from individual members of the FPC or from the Treasury Select

126 Xavier Freixas, Luc Laevan and José-Luis Peydró, *Systemic risk, crises and macroprudential regulation* (MIT, Massachusetts, 2015), 259.

127 Douglas Elliott, 'Choosing among macroprudential tools', (2011) The Brookings Institution, 4.

128 Supra, note 16, (Galbraith), 168.

129 Susan Woodward, 'The long intervention: continuity in the Balkan theatre', (December 2013) *Review of International Studies*, Vol. 39, No. 5, 1169, 1172–1173.

130 Robert Jervis, 'Unipolarity: a structural perspective', in John Ikenberry, Michael Mastanduno and William Wohlforth (eds), *International relations theory and the consequences of unipolarity* (Cambridge University Press, Cambridge, 2011), 265–266.

131 Thomas Barthold, 'Issues in the design of environmental excise taxes', (1994) *Journal of Economic Perspectives* Vol 8, No. 1, 133, 143.

Committee or wider government and media interest. A Deputy Governor of the Bank of England would want to avoid being described, in public by, for example, the Treasury Select Committee as "being asleep at the wheel".[132]

The "turbulent frontier" concept also applies to microprudential and conduct of business policy where there is always one more area to be regulated. This can be seen in the UK, as over the years conduct of business regulation has spread from investment business to general insurance to first charge residential mortgages to retail banking business to unsecured credit to "crowd funding" to second charge and buy-to-let mortgages and so on. However, in most instances, the drive to regulate these areas has not been "pushed" by the regulator. Instead, the initiatives have largely come from politicians, machinery of government restructures (i.e. the demise of the Office of Fair Trading and the transfer of responsibility for most aspects of unsecured lending to the FSA) and EU legislation. In some cases, the regulator has expressed reluctance to take on these new responsibilities. This is particularly true when the FSA was assigned responsibility for aspects of competition regulation.[133]

Similarly, macroprudential policy has no boundaries and its frontier is ever expanding. As described above, there is sufficient evidence of both policy push and pull, incrementally, to extend the purview of macroprudential policy frontier by frontier. This approach contains the risk of over-reach as "policymakers may soon find themselves extending the range of measures and inadvertently drift into credit allocation. And the temptation to resort to capital controls to underpin macroprudential instruments could at some point become quite strong…".[134]

A wide-ranging perspective is undoubtedly correct but an overly large scope may be to expect too much from one committee however expert. Reflecting the Roman Empire's "Tetrachy" it may be more appropriate to segment macroprudential risks by, for example, the immediacy of the potential threats or type of issue. There could be a committee concerned with leverage and asset prices, another committee could focus on protecting the payments systems and cyber-security and a third committee could consider long-terms issues such as demographics and climate change. Finally, a fourth committee would need to concern itself with identifying institutions and markets not currently subject to regulatory oversight and microprudential supervision where risks of instability may be forming. These committees would need to be coordinated both with each other but also with monetary, fiscal and microprudential policy. This increases complexity but, in turn, this acknowledges the complexity of the risks.

132 Questions to Sir John Gieve, (Deputy Governor Responsible for Financial Stability) regarding the Bank of England's role in failing to prevent the collapse of Northern Rock, (oral evidence on 20 September 2007 to the Treasury Select Committee), question 6–8.

133 Andrew Whittaker (FSA's General Counsel), 'The role of competition in Financial Services Regulation', (speech given on 21 April 2001, paragraph 16, "[having a competition objective] would not only mean that we had an unclear and confusing mandate."

134 Claudio Borio, 'Macroprudential frameworks: (too) great expectations?', (August 2014), 25th anniversary edition of *Central Banking Journal*, 4.

In addition to the "turbulent frontier" concept there are a number of other broad issues with macroprudential policy.

2.13 Limitations on the use of macroprudential policy

The issues with macroprudential policy generally arise if macroprudential policy is viewed simply as a grander version of microprudential regulation or solely as a branch of economic modelling. Specifically, they include:

- political and institutional legitimacy and the closely aligned concerns over accountability,
- the relationship with microprudential regulation,
- the limited consideration given to conduct of business regulation in the macroprudential context,
- the excessive expectations placed on macroprudential policy,
- the extent to which macroprudential policy can be "fine-tuned",
- failure of macroprudential policy to consider the wider economic and societal issues, and
- the effectiveness of some of the tools and the potential for unintended consequences arising from any regulatory intervention across all, or a sector, of the financial services industry.

2.13.1 Political and institutional legitimacy

Macroprudential policy can impinge on the political sphere and have political implications. For example, what appear to be technical changes at the microprudential level may have clear macroeconomic consequences as soon as their visibility is raised as macroprudential policy.

> Macroprudential policy may not be fully implemented due to political constraints and therefore during a crisis more stringent brakes are applied with consequent more political interference…[and it is] a balancing act to counter political headwinds and to retain democratic legitimacy.[135]

This issue is considered in more detail in Chapter 6.

In part, institutional and operational legitimacy rests on adequate accountability which in turn requires transparency and openness supported by reasoned arguments based on fair and consistent process.[136] However, this may pose severe problems for macroprudential policy which is designed to stifle "euphoric"

135 Viral Acharya, 'Financial stability in the broader mandate for central banks: a political economy perspective', (2015) Hutchins Centre on Fiscal and Monetary policy at Brookings, Working paper No. 11, 4 and 12.

136 Rosa Lastra, *Central banking and banking regulation* (London School of Economic, Financial Markets Group, London, 1996), 53.

booms. Consequently, there is a risk that it may be politically expedient to use less publicly obvious, highly technical macroprudential measures since they will attract the least public and political attention. It is less acceptable politically if the costs are seen to be immediate but the benefits of financial stability are less apparent.[137] Further, as this book argues more use should be made of conduct of business regulation employed in a macroprudential role since it is less likely to raise concerns over political legitimacy.

2.13.2 Relationship between microprudential and macroprudential policy

Almost all the macroprudential "tools" operate, in practice, at the microprudential level whether these are, as mentioned earlier, structural or cyclical. The macroprudential policymaker is dependent on the microprudential regulator for information on what is happening with individually regulated financial institutions and for the implementation of macroprudential policy. This level of dependency is a major reason influencing the appropriate regulatory structure and the co-location of the macroprudential and microprudential authorities, for the most significant firms, in the UK.

Macroprudential regulation could be undertaken by the microprudential regulator. However, as described at the start of this chapter, macroprudential policy is a state of perception. It requires a separate body to think differently, in the context of a set of broad macroprudential objectives, and to select the appropriate "tools" to be applied by the microprudential regulator. Further, as mentioned above, while microprudential regulators normally need to be taciturn and discreet, frequent and clear communication is an important element in role of the macroprudential regulator. This is an aspect that has still to be developed by all macroprudential authorities as will be seen in Chapter 3.

2.13.3 The limited consideration given to conduct of business regulation

Regardless of whether the discussion of macroprudential policy originates, for example, from the FPC, IMF or Bank of International Settlements, almost no mention is made of the policy's relationship with conduct of business regulation. For example, macroprudential policy is seen as reducing, or controlling, the supply of credit to an over-heating economy. However, there is little, if any, discussion of the use of conduct of business regulation to limit the availability of credit.[138] To a certain extent this can be seen as the role of monetary policy

137 Supra, note 131, (Barthold), 143.

138 For example, the Financial Policy Committee's (FPC) minutes are limited to noting that "tighter underwriting standards were also being introduced as part of the FCA's Mortgage Market Review (MMR)". 'Record of the Financial Policy Committee meeting held on 20 November 2013', paragraph 14, 5. There is also a reference to using the MMR interest rate

but, as will be seen later, the latter can best be described as a blunt instrument compared to a more nuanced approach applied by the use of conduct of business regulations. The FPC has briefly noted that the affordability test "constrains the size of mortgage obtainable relative to incomes".[139] Further, the FPC sees an important role for its power to designate the interested rate to be used in undertaking affordability calculations and its monitoring of economic indicators to identify structural problems early.[140] However, this fails to recognise that the conduct of business regulations require the lender to look, in detail, at the financial position of the potential borrower, going well beyond matters relating to their income, and FPC specified tests. The conduct of business regulations has the ability to act as a powerful macroprudential "tool" which both protects consumers by restricting their ability to borrow with the corollary of reducing demand for credit. The effect of this is to limit asset price and debt growth. Whether this is an appropriate macroprudential "tool" is central to this work. It is an issue which is addressed further later in this, and in subsequent chapters.

2.13.4 Excessive expectations

There are high expectations placed on the post-financial crisis regulatory structures both in preventing another crisis and mitigating the damage when a further problem develops. The macroprudential policymaker is the first line of defence with the task of identifying a potential issue at a very early stage and, using the apposite clichés, turning off the dance-music or taking away the punch-bowl.[141] The ability to do this in the face of what will be political, industry and popular sentiment is recognised but remains untested. There are likely to be many "false positives" where the metrics indicate the start of an asset price "bubble" which

---

stress tests to improve underwriting standards, 'Record of the Financial Policy Committee meeting held on 19 March 2013', paragraphs 10 and 11, 4.

139 FPC minutes 23 and 29 November 2016, 6.

140 Bank of England, 'Financial Stability Report', (June 2017), 13. Similar wording is contained in the FPC minutes of 21 June 2017, (4 July 2017), 9 and 10.

141 The "dance" analogy refers to comments by Chuck Prince (Citigroup CEO) on the eve of the recent collapse of global financial markets when he "dismissed fears that the music was about to stop for the cheap credit-fuelled buy-out boom", saying that Citigroup was "still dancing" in an interview with the *Financial Times.*

> The party would end at some point but there was so much liquidity it would not be disrupted by the turmoil in the US subprime mortgage market. When the music stops, in terms of liquidity, things will be complicated. But as long as the music is playing, you've got to get up and dance. We're still dancing.
>
> (*Financial Times*, 9 July 2007)

The 'punch-bowl' reference is attributed to a speech made in 1955 by William McChesney Martin, Chairman of the Federal Reserve Board, in which he said that the role of the Federal Reserve was to remove the punch-bowl at a party just when the party was really warming up because there are economic danger signals in sight. The quotation has been repeated many times by others over the years.

fails to develop in the classic Minsky/Kindleberger model. Macroprudential action may result in what may appear to be the premature demise of an economic boom to politicians, the financial services industry and the general public. It would be a severe test of the creditability and hence, perversely, of the legitimacy of the macroprudential policymaker. A financial crisis prevented will gain the latter little credit. This issue has been recognised but has not really been addressed.[142]

2.13.5 Regulatory "fine-tuning"

There is also a risk that targeted macroprudential actions would appear to be an attempt to replicate policies in the 1960s and 1970s to "fine-tune" the economy. This system of trying to manage the economy failed due to the complexity of the system.[143] Much of this failure was due to misconceived economic models and entrenched powerful interest groups.[144] It is likely that there are too many factors in macroprudential policy to be able, mathematically, to model all the interactions.[145] Haldane makes a broadly similar point in another area of financial regulation.[146] This is not a reason for failing to try to use macroprudential policy but the belief that it is susceptible to "fine-tuning" may only result in further unpredictable distortions to the financial system.

2.13.6 Failure of macroprudential policy to consider the wider economic and societal issues

Reading the extensive literature on macroprudential policy, mainly written after the recent financial crisis, one is struck by the narrow focus of almost all the documents.[147] There is a void when it comes to considering the possible interaction of macroprudential policy on wider economic and societal issues. In part, this is probably due, as mentioned above, to the approach taken by economists developing mathematical economic models.[148]

142 Supra note 3 (Goodhart, 'The macro-prudential authority'), 19 and supra note 2, (Haldane, 'Macroprudential policies'), 4.

143 G. C. Peden, 'New revisionists and the Keynesian era in British economic policy: a comment', (2003) *Economic History Review*, Vol. LVI, 1, 118, 122–123.

144 Kathleen Burk and Alec Cairncross, *Goodbye Great Britain: the 1976 IMF crisis* (Yale University Press, New Haven, 1992), 209–212.

145 These models have been heavily criticised for ignoring the important role of banks and their part in the intermediation process, Charles Goodhart, Dimitrios Tsomocos and Martin Shubik, 'Macro-modeling, default and money', (2013), London School of Economics, Financial Markets Group Special Paper 224, 3.

146 Andrew Haldane, 'The dog and the frisbee', at the Federal Reserve Bank of Kansas City's 36th economic policy symposium, 'The changing policy landscape', Jackson Hole, Wyoming, 31 August 2012.

147 Supra, note 94, oral evidence given by Jacques De Larosière to the House of Lords Committee.

148 Supra, note 145, (Goodhart, Tsomocos and Shubik), 3. See also Philipp Hartmann, 'Real estate markets and macroprudential policy in Europe', (May 2015) European Central Bank Working

This complexity is recognised by microprudential regulators who have started to view "their flock" of regulated firms not just as a set of accounting numbers but as complex organisations with operations and processes, systems of governance and interactions with other bodies. In addition, over-arching all this are the foibles and drivers of individual actions within these firms. To an extent, for banks, microprudential regulation derived from Pillar 2 of the Basel III regulatory regime, seeks to address these aspects of risks. Macroprudential policy has still to consider, evaluate and decipher this broader canvas. For example, the macroprudential policymaker needs to appreciate that the interaction between credit and housing is not just a narrow economic assessment but requires an understanding of the housing market, why demand for housing exists and how it might be satisfied.

By restricting regulation to simply limiting the provision of credit other financial instabilities may be generated with the potential to threaten financial stability: the steam will still escape from the pressure cooker. In practice this means that the macroprudential authorities need to widen their view by considering other relevant factors such as the supply of housing. This means employing experts who can provide information and advice on, for example, housing markets, derivative asset pricing, commercial property, etc. in a search for areas of potential financial imbalance that could result in financial instability. It requires macroprudential policy to take a wider perspective including providing advice on fiscal matters. These aspects are considered in more detail in Chapters 6 and 8. It would also be worthwhile to look at the approaches employed in other jurisdictions. Examples of this include the concept of the "qualified mortgage" and the role of the Veterans Administration in the US. These are both analysed in Chapters 4 and 7 respectively.

2.13.7 Effectiveness and unintended consequences

Macroprudential policy is so little understood that its collateral effects are largely unknown. In parallel, its effectiveness in open trading economies is still unclear. For example, macroprudential measures may have an effect on competition. They may increase barriers to entry and exit from the industry and hence reduce competition. There is some evidence that competition increases bank risk-taking as margins are restricted.[149] Conversely, other studies indicate that increased competition may reduce risk.[150] However, it is clear that the data supports the

Paper No. 1796, which advocates the use and effectiveness of LTV and DTI measures but fails to mention the legitimacy deficit issue.

149 Michael Bordo, Angela Redish and Hugh Rockoff, 'Why didn't Canada have a banking crisis in 2008 (or in 1930, or in 1907 or…)?', (2011), National Bureau of Economic Research Working Paper 17312.

150 John Boyd, Gianni De Nicolò and Abu Jalal, 'Bank risk-taking and competition revisited: new theory and new evidence', (2006) IMF Working Paper WP/06/297, 29.

hypothesis that when banks are faced with more intense competition, they gravitate towards higher levels of leverage.[151]

Although this is not evidenced, there is also a risk that business, subject to macroprudential constraints, may shift to non-regulated areas. There is a related risk that attempts to restrict the growth in credit will result in some of the demand being supplied by lenders beyond the jurisdiction of the macroprudential regulator, known as the risk of "leakage". In 2012 the Bank for International Settlements' Committee on the Global Financial System (CGFS) suggested that in order to prevent the risk of "leakages" to foreign lenders, "LTV caps [should be] deployed…through 'conduct [of business] rules'".[152] However, the CGFS did not develop this point. This perspective is a central to this work and is addressed in the next section and in subsequent chapters as part of an examination of macroprudential tools and their efficacy.

2.14 Consumer protection

The protection of consumers from over-borrowing benefits not just the individual but also helps to ensure the stability of the financial system. It is likely to reduce the rapid expansion of credit and the commensurate increase in asset values. At the same time as reducing the probability of financial instability it lessens the potential costs of an economic downturn since there will be fewer non-performing loans, reduced provisioning and assets prices will be stronger with less risk of property fire-sales. However, the use of conduct of business regulations is rarely mentioned, if at all, in the studies of macroprudential tools.[153]

Conduct of business policies are generally accepted, and they are not challenged on grounds that they lack public "legitimacy". Conversely, for example, Taylor makes the point that macroprudential policies, particularly in housing, would have taken "the [Federal Reserve] into political controversy".[154] This latter issue is a factor deterring the use of LTV and LTI macroprudential policies and is discussed in more detail in Chapter 6. Second, the conduct of business regulations applies to the mortgage as a transaction or product. However, LTV and LTI policies normally operate in respect of particular institutions and may be avoided by lenders outside the scope of regulation.[155]

151 Supra, note 100, (Hanson, Kashyap and Stein), 22.

152 Supra, note 45, (CGFS Papers No. 48), note. 29 and 38.

153 For example, conduct of business regulation was not mentioned by Jon Cunliffe (Deputy Governor Financial Stability at the Bank of England) in a speech on macroprudential policy options, 'Credit: can trees grow to the sky?', (9 February 2016 speech at the British Property Federation Annual Residential Investment Conference, London).

154 John Taylor, 'Simple rules for financial stability', Keynote address at the Financial Markets Conference 'Maintaining financial stability: holding a tiger by the tail', Federal Reserve Bank of Atlanta, 9 April 2013.

155 'Prudent mortgage lending standards help ensure financial stability', Luci Ellis (Head of Financial Stability Department), address to the Australian Mortgage Conference, Sydney, 23 February 2012, 6.

As already mentioned, as a property boom gets underway credit standards weaken for a number of reasons including the belief that asset prices will only continue to rise and if the borrower fails to service the debt, rising property prices will protect the lender from loss.[156] Most of the regulatory responses, as noted in this chapter, have been to consider the more conventional macroprudential policies. However, it is worth noting that both Australia and Germany have identified the importance of existing conduct of business regulations as macroprudential policies. The Reserve Bank of Australian's Head of Financial Stability considered the importance of conduct of business rules to protect financial stability

> in Australia, the previously state-based but uniform consumer credit code was reformed and brought under national control in 2009. The range of products covered was broadened, and the suitability tests that lenders must apply were tightened. However, this reform was not motivated by financial stability considerations, and the previous system already had the features needed to avoid a systemic deterioration of lending standards beyond the point of prudence.[157]

She saw the borrower's capacity to service their mortgages as more important than property prices and LTV ratios, and conduct of business regulation forming a "second line of defence" to assist macroprudential policies.[158] Moreover, LTV measures can also been seen as "indicators of relative risk" since high LTV levels can be viewed as both predictors of the probability of lenders mortgage losses and the extent of such loss levels.[159]

Similarly, the German Financial Stability Committee, in addition to LTV and LTI measures, recommended that lenders "conduct a credit assessment of potential borrowers by measuring their debt service capacity and the recoverable value of their collateral. This helps to reduce the probability of default on residential real estate loans".[160] However, it failed to pursue this line of reasoning since it considered that "such credit assessments are difficult to measure

156 William Bassett and others, 'Changes in bank lending standards and the macroeconomy', (2014) *Journal of Monetary Economics*, Vol. 62, 23, 38.

157 Luci Ellis, 'Macroprudential policy: what have we learned?', paper at the Bank of England's Centre for Central Banking Studies Workshop, London, 6 March 2013, 3. Ellis is sceptical about the ability of LTV limits to prevent financial instability due to the ease of avoidance, problems with ascertaining the value of property in a housing boom and the effect of LTV caps on first time buyers, 'Macroprudential policy: a suite of tools or a state of mind?', speech by Luci Ellis at Paul Woolley Centre for the Study of Capital Market Dysfunctionality Annual Conference, Sydney, 11 October 2012.

158 Supra, note 155, (Luci Ellis 'Prudent mortgage lending standards') 7.

159 Eric Kolpfer, 'A mortgage insurer's look at Basel II and residential mortgage credit risk', (September 2002) *Housing Finance International*, Vol. 17, No. 1, 22–32, 23.

160 German Financial Stability Committee, 'Recommendation on new instruments for regulating loans for the construction or purchase of residential real estate', 30 June 2015, AFS/2015/1.

or quantify precisely, which means they cannot be used as a macroprudential instrument".[161]

In summary, conduct of business regulations, if properly applied and enforced, like monetary policy, can "get into all the cracks". Regulation, such as the FCA's Mortgage Market Review, apply, considered in detail in Chapter 5, to the lending transaction. They do not depend on whether the lender is prudentially supervised. The regulations are "always on" and do not require activation. Moreover, as a consumer protection measure, it has inherent public support and consequent "legitimacy". However, its effectiveness depends on the adequacy of the conduct of business supervision and its enforcement. These issues are considered further in Chapters 4 and 5.

As mentioned earlier, there is a hierarchy of instruments which may be used to effect macroprudential policies. Monetary and fiscal policies may have the broadest consequences and these are considered in the next section. The focus of these policies increases with what may be termed the more "traditional" macroprudential "tools" followed by microprudential actions which target specific regulated organisations. As mentioned above, consumer protection policies fall outside the realm of traditional macroprudential policies but they should not be neglected since they may be very effective in curbing credit growth: at the same time protecting borrowers and delivering macroprudential policy objectives. However, it is worth noting that research by the Central Bank of Ireland indicates that affordability tests may, nevertheless, be undermined by periods of low interest rates and rapid rises in house prices.[162] In the Irish Republic, the number of new mortgages rose from 80,000 in 2000 to over 120,000 by 2005 with house prices rising on average by almost 65% over the same period.[163] Mandatory interest rate stress tests, as required by the MMR in the UK may reduce this risk.

2.15 Conclusion

As discussed, the importance of macroprudential policy can be seen in the clear linkages between credit growth, the housing market and financial instability. By limiting the escalation of credit in the economy, macroprudential policy can assist in protecting financial stability. However, macroprudential policy is predicated on its ability to identify, sufficiently early, potential risks to financial instability and root causes and to deploy the necessary macroprudential tools in time and to effect. The evidence that this would happen is not robust. Further, these concerns are increased by the possibility that the risks to financial stability may manifest themselves in areas beyond the regulatory perspective.

Moreover, there are a number of fundamental issues with macroprudential policy. These include: the political legitimacy of macroprudential policy; how

161 Ibid., (German Financial Stability Committee, 'Recommendation on new instruments'), 9.

162 Yvonne McCarthy and Kieran McQuinn, 'Credit conditions in a boom and bust property market', (October 2013), Central Bank of Ireland Research Technical Paper 8/RT/13, 5.

163 Ibid., (McCarthy and McQuinn), 6.

it relates to microprudential and conduct of business regulation; the need to manage excessive expectations; and to recognise that macroprudential policy cannot be "fine-tuned". Further, macroprudential authorities need to consider their ability to cooperate and the wider economic and societal issues and the effectiveness of some of the macroprudential tools and their potential for unintended consequences.

Although discussion of macroprudential policy goes back to at least the early 2000s, the difficulties inherent in this form of regulation, coupled with a reluctance to interfere when asset prices rose rapidly, meant that it took the recent financial crisis for its importance to be fully recognised. Again, as has been stated, macroprudential policy is at a very early stage. Nevertheless, there are dangers that it may become too narrowly focused or, alternatively, policymaking always needs to be on the move to subdue one more "turbulent frontier" after another. To avoid this happening its needs to address a range of issues both conceptual and operational. Those relating to the efficacy of the suite of macroprudential instruments is considered in the next chapter.

3 Macroprudential policy instruments

There are a range of macroprudential tools. These include those which are structural (e.g. capital and liquidity) and others which have a cyclical effect (e.g. countercyclical capital buffers and loan-to-value (LTV) and debt-to-income (DTI) limits). Broadly, the former works by increasing business costs and hence restricting credit while the latter imposes direct quantitative limits. There are other macroprudential measures such as fiscal and monetary policies and the full range of prudential regulatory requirements including stress testing, recovery and resolution planning, deposit protection insurance, etc. There are other actions which can be taken to enhance financial stability including requiring bank assets to be deposited at the central bank. There is a variant of this, sometimes called "narrow banking" where, for example, bank deposits can only be invested in government funds or deposited with the central bank.

Macroprudential policy may be seen as an enhanced version of microprudential regulation since many of the measures are similar. However, the objectives are different and in some cases these policies may work against each other. The focus of this work is on LTV and DTI policies, and there is a strong risk that those subject to them (i.e. borrowers, lenders and intermediaries) may seek to work around these types of macroprudential policies.

A number of studies, both cross-jurisdictional and within countries, have found that DTI and LTV measures are often circumvented and that these policies tend to work best when coupled with fiscal and direct government intervention in the housing market.

Finally, the potential for conduct of business regulations to assist macroprudential policymakers is central to this book.

3.1 Introduction

As discussed in the last chapter, macroprudential policy is heavily focused on controlling credit. But credit is also a highly political area and Adair Turner has said that the "amount of credit created and its allocation is too important to be left to bankers".[1] This is an issue considered in more detail in this and subsequent chapters.

1 Adair Turner, *Between debt and the devil* (Princeton University Press, Princeton, 2015), 104.

The danger is that it is tempting to see macroprudential policy as the answer to everything and macroprudential tools have been described as "a gleaming new armoury for policymakers".[2]

This chapter reviews the main macroprudential "tools": the instruments available to the macroprudential policymaker. These include monetary, macroprudential and microprudential policies. All have roles to play in implementing macroprudential policy, and it is possible to envisage these elements as three concentric rings forming an archery target. Monetary policy would provide the outer circle, followed by macroprudential policy as you move towards the middle with highly focused microprudential policy in the centre. These policies have also been described as a "hierarchy of instruments" with monetary policies employed before macroprudential measures.[3] The use of fiscal measures by government may sit outside this "hierarchy of instruments". Since there are aspects of fiscal policy, in particular, the use of taxation, which may function as macroprudential measures, these are also considered in this chapter.

At the same time, microprudential and macroprudential tools are often interchangeable. This chapter will include an assessment of the close, and often overlapping, relationship between macro and microprudential regulation.[4] Finally, this chapter examines the effectiveness of some of the tools, across an array of jurisdiction, and the potential for unintended consequences arising from any regulatory intervention across all, or a sector, of the financial services industry.

The key issue is the workings of the transmission system from macroprudential policies through the financial system and their effectiveness in reducing systemic risk, their efficiency in achieving this goal without a "significant adverse effect on the capacity of the financial sector to contribute to…economic growth" over the medium- to long-term and the transparency of the "nature and use" of the tools.[5] Understanding these mechanisms has been described as "still in its infancy".[6] However, the communication of macroprudential actions is recognised as salient since the management of market expectations is important and "signaling is the key transmission channel".[7]

All these instruments are capable of controlling the growth of credit since the lesson "for policymakers…[is that] history demonstrates that they ignore credit

2 Independent Economists Group Report, 'The role of macroprudential policy in the policy framework', (June 2014), 5.

3 Jaime Caruana and Benjamin Cohen, 'Five questions and six answers about macroprudential policy', (April 2014), Banque de France, *Financial Stability Review*, No. 18, 15–23, 19.

4 In the UK microprudential regulation refers to the need to "promote the safety and soundness of the firms it regulates, focusing on the adverse effects that they can have on the stability of the UK financial system", Prudential Regulation Authority', 'Approach to banking supervision', June 2014, 1.

5 Chapter 2, n. 9, (Bank of England 'Instruments of macroprudential policy').

6 Chapter 2, n. 35, (Aikman, 'Curbing the credit cycle'), 32.

7 Ibid., (Aikman and Haldane), 31. This papers states that macroprudential regulators need to act with "simplicity and humility" since macroprudential regulation "cannot be expected to eliminate the credit cycle". See also the paper presented by Andrew Haldane in which he makes a similar case for simplicity in financial regulation, Chapter 2, n. 146, ('dog and the frisbee').

at their peril".[8] Conceptually, these tools can be divided into two groups: first, those which work by increasing the cost of lending but leave it to the management of individual banks to decide how to manage and respond to these factors and, second, those which are more prescriptive such as the setting of LTV and DTI limits. Although this chapter considers a broad spectrum of macroprudential tools its focus is on policies relating to this latter group which operate via a form of macroprudential policy "diktat".

In particular, this chapter looks at the approaches taken in employing LTV and DTI policies, issues with their use and their effectiveness both generally and in selected jurisdictions. Depending on the economic conditions, it appears that LTV and DTI limits, on their own, do not work for long. This is due to what are known as "leakages" as both lenders and borrowers find ways around the restrictions. Some of these methods involve the use of overseas funding. This reinforces the need for macroprudential policies to be coordinated across borders. As considered later, a central theme of this book is that while LTV and DTI policies should not be dismissed they should be employed in conjunction with conduct of business measures to help restrict the growth of credit in order to avoid unmanageable financial instability.

3.2 Types of macroprudential instruments

This section considers the types of macroprudential instruments. Macroprudential tools fall into two main categories: structural (e.g. capital and liquidity) and cyclical (e.g. countercyclical capital buffers and LTV and DTI limits).[9] The former are aimed at "building structural resilience in the financial system throughout the business cycle".[10] The latter are aimed at "mitigating systemic risk that can build up over the business cycle".[11] As mentioned above, broadly, the former work by increasing costs while the latter imposes direct quantitative restrictions.

There are also broader macroprudential tools such as the "stress testing" programmes, which subject regulated entities to regular assessments based on standardised scenarios designed to test their resilience in the face of a variety of demanding economic contingencies. The ability of these institutions to withstand these stresses reinforces the stability of the financial system as a whole. Those that are found to be inadequate need to increase their capital and liquidity. In addition, there are a number of other actual and potential macroprudential

8 Chapter 2, n. 82, (Schularick and Taylor, 'Credit booms gone bust'), 1058.

9 José Viñals, 'Making macroprudential policy work', speech at the Brookings Institution, Washington, DC, 16 September 2013.

10 Loretta Mester, 'The nexus of macroprudential supervision, monetary policy and financial stability', speech at the Federal Reserve Bank of Cleveland and the Office of Financial Research 2014 Financial Stability Conference, 5 December 2014.

11 Ibid., Mester. This is sometimes known as the "Kindleberger cycle" where "optimism over asset price rises [which] leads to lower credit standards in which the lender relies on asset price growth to absorb any credit defaults".

tools. These include monetary policy, fiscal measures, in particular the use of taxation, and the use of central bank facilities to provide liquidity to institutions and markets as the "lender of last resort".[12] A number of Asian states have specifically combined macroprudential and fiscal measures to restrict the growth of credit. This raises important issues which are considered later in both this chapter and Chapter 6. Finally, there is the employment of conduct of business regulation as a macroprudential tool. The latter is often overlooked as a macroprudential policy tool, and its importance is a key theme in this book.

As discussed in the previous chapter, macroprudential tools can be widely defined to include a range of measures including stress testing, recovery and resolution planning, deposit protection insurance and the national and cross-border regulatory and supervision architecture as a whole. All of these help provide resilience to the financial system. There is a sweeping counter-argument which states, in a number of guises, that regulation, and in particular, deposit protection schemes, increase moral hazard because layers of safety-nets and protections encourage risk-taking and undermine prudence and caution.[13] There is extensive literature discussing this issue which, however, falls outside the scope of this work.[14]

It is also worth taking a broader perspective when considering possible macroprudential tools. For example, it is likely that the search for higher returns during a period of low inflation and interest rates encourages financial institutions to innovate. This may undermine financial stability.[15] It may be less costly for macroprudential policy if financial institution assets were "neutralised" by requiring a large proportion of them to be deposited at the central bank. This is a slightly less radical approach to those that advocate strict "narrow banking" where, for example, bank deposits can only be invested in government funds or deposited with the central bank.[16] However, these restrictions have a history

12 Andrew Campbell and Rosa Lastra, 'Revisiting the lender of last resort – the role of the Bank of England', in Iain MacNeil and Justin O'Brien (eds), *The future of financial regulation* (Hart, Oxford, 2010), 161–178, 163.

13 Charles Calomiris and Stephen Haber, *Fragile by design* (Princeton University Press, Princeton, NJ, 2014), 36–37, 461–462; Andrew Campbell, 'Designing a framework for protecting bank depositors', in James Devenney and Mel Kenny (eds), *Consumer credit, debt and investment in Europe* (Cambridge University Press, Cambridge, 2012), 234–252, 234. See also Charles Goodhart, *The regulatory response to the financial crisis* (Edward Elgar Publishing, Cheltenham, 2009), 42–44 who recognising the morale hazard risks but says that deposit protection needs to be balanced by heavy regulation.

14 Ben Bernanke, *Essays on the Great Depression* (Princeton University Press, Princeton, NJ, 2000) 89–97. See also Frederic Mishkin, *Prudential supervision: what works and what doesn't* (University of Chicago Press, Chicago, 2001), 6–7; Chapter 2, n. 126, (Freixas, Laeven and Peydró), 37, 112–113; Franklin Allen, Elena Carletti and Agnese Leonello, 'Deposit insurance and risk taking', (2011) *Oxford Review of Economic Policy*, Vol. 27, No. 3, 464–478.

15 Adair Turner, *The Turner review* (Financial Services Authority, London, 2009), 47–49.

16 Jaromir Benes and Michael Kumhof, 'The 'Chicago Plan' revisited', (2012) IMF Working Paper, WP/12/202, 4. This was a plan devised by Henry Simons of University of Chicago in the 1930s and publicised by Irving Fisher of Yale in 1936. The plan would require "100% backing

of being avoided.[17] There are also measures adopted in Canada and Australia which require the insurance, often by government agencies, of higher risk mortgage lending.[18] It has also been suggested that market forces could be harnessed by, for example, the Bank of England by increasing the liquidity requirements and paying higher rates of interest on bank reserve deposits and thus reducing the incentive for banks to develop new higher risk products.[19] This is a very broad subject and, again, outside the scope of this work.

It has also been suggested that microprudential supervision can be dispensed with for individual financial organisations that are not systemically important and reliance placed wholly on macroprudential policy.[20] Individually, these smaller firms may not be able to damage financial stability but collectively, as a "herd", they may threaten the stability of the system. Hence, macroprudential policy can substitute for microprudential supervision of these firms.[21] As can be seen macroprudential policy and its operational tools can cover a very wide spectrum. The next section narrows the scope of these measures to those that seek to limit the growth of certain types of bank balance sheet assets.

This chapter has already mentioned the role of counter-cyclical capital and liquidity, since, in particular, the former has been the main macroprudential policy used in the EU to date. As already noted, capital and liquidity requirements are also the mainstays of microprudential regulation and supervision. They operate by raising the costs of financial institutions and hence reduce short-term profitability and returns to shareholders. The main focus is on tools which have curbing the growth of credit as their objective since, as mentioned, this is viewed as at the core of most financial crises and a cause of financial instability.[22] It is worth noting that surges in the expansion of credit have also been blamed for

---

of deposits by government-issued money, and second" by ensuring that new bank credit was only financed by retained earnings. It would end fractional reserve banking since banks could only lend by borrowing money from the government.

17 For example, prior to the financial crisis in 1907 in the US national banks had been heavily regulated and had to keep 25% of deposits in cash and gold and were prohibited from making loans secured on land. Trust organisations, however, had quickly developed and only had to keep 5% of deposits in cash and had no restrictions on lending. The US financial system came close to collapse when almost all the trusts failed – leading to the establishment of the Federal Reserve, Ellis Tallman and Jon Moen, 'Lessons from the panic of 1907', (May/June 1990) Economic Review, Federal Reserve Bank of Atlanta, 11–12.

18 Ivo Krznar and James Morsink, 'With great power comes great responsibility: macroprudential tools at work in Canada', (2014) IMF Working Paper 14/83, 15–16.

19 Anil Kashyap and Jeremy Stein, 'The optimal conduct of monetary policy with interest on reserves', (2012) *American Economic Journal: Macroeconomics*, Vol. 4, No. 1, 266, 270.

20 Chapter 2, n. 26, (Brunnermeier), 28.

21 Note that there may be some rationality in such "herd" behaviour relevant to both macroprudential policy and microprudential supervision, Raghuram Rajan, 'Why bank credit policies fluctuate: a theory and some evidence', (1994) *The Quarterly Journal of Economics*, Vol. 109, No. 2, 399, 402.

22 Chapter 2, n. 74, (Reinhart and Rogoff), xxv; Chapter 2, n. 58.

the misallocation of national resources and high levels of inflation.[23] However, the main focus of the next sections will be on LTV and DTI measures which are perceived as exclusively macroprudential tools to control the growth of credit by limiting the quantity of the latter's use in financing property transactions.[24] These tools work best when operating "with the grain" of monetary policy and fiscal measures.[25]

3.3 Relationship between macroprudential regulation and monetary policy

The Bank of England's Monetary Policy Committee (MPC) has price stability as its objective, while the primary objective of its Financial Policy Committee (FPC) is to protect and enhance the stability of the UK's financial system.[26] The relationship between the two committees was considered at a hearing of the Treasury Select Committee in January 2016.[27] The Governor of the Bank of England provided an insight into the interaction between the MPC and FPC. He explained that the FPC usually meets just before the MPC's meeting and the FPC agenda includes consideration of the "overall risk environment". This allowed the MPC to include the FPC's assessment in its own deliberations on monetary policy "recognising that monetary policy is viewed in general as the last line of defence against financial stability issues".[28] Fisher, who has served both on the MPC and FPC, has acknowledged that although each committee is independent this is only "partial" since what one committee does may affect the other.[29] He described this effect as "policy spillover".[30] He saw three factors as important as ensuring good coordination between the committees: cross-committee membership, shared information and a "common understanding of the economy".[31] However, he was keen to stress that "coherence doesn't

23 Stacey Schreft, 'Credit controls: 1980', (November/December 1990) *Economic Review*, 26–27, www.richmondfed.org/~/media/richmondfedorg/publications/research/economic_review/1990/pdf/er760603.pdf considers the rationale for ending limits on war-time house purchase credit by Congress in 1953.

24 Andrew Haldane, 'Macroprudential policy in prospect', in George Akerlof, Olivier Blanchard, David Romer and Joseph Stiglitz (eds), *What have we learned?: macroprudential policy after the crisis*, (The MIT Press, Cambridge, MA, 2014), 67.

25 Hyun Song Shin, '*Macroprudential policies beyond Basel III*', (2010), Princeton University Policy Memo, 9–10.

26 The Bank of England was given its financial stability objective under 2 (2) (a) of the Financial Services Act 2012 and the same legislation established the FPC and its objectives (9C (1) (a)).

27 Oral evidence: Bank of England December 2015 Financial Stability Report, HC 780, 26 January 2016.

28 Ibid., (oral evidence) answer to question 104.

29 Paul Fisher, 'Microprudential, macroprudential and monetary policy: conflict, compromise or co-ordination?', speech at Richmond University, London, 1 October 2014, 5.

30 Ibid., 5.

31 Ibid., 6.

always mean agreement", and it is important that dissent is part of the culture of both committees.[32]

The MPC may maintain low interest rates in order to meet its objectives. However, the FPC will take action to

> ensure that a tail of highly indebted households does not emerge as a result of this...That is a fundamental point about the difference between macro-prudential policy and monetary policy. Monetary policy is [about] delivering averages. Macroprudential policy is about taking out the tail risks.[33]

Alex Brazier, Executive Director, Financial Stability Strategy and Risk at the Bank of England, gave, as an example, the action taken by the FPC in 2014 to limit high LTV lending.

> In the owner-occupied housing market...the action we took then was to prevent a tail of highly indebted households from emerging. At the time, we did not think that that action would bite, because the threshold we set for the proportion of mortgages that could be at high loan to income ratios was in excess of what was actually going on. It was an insurance policy against a risk building...it looked like it may have been contradictory with what the MPC was trying to achieve at that point, but in no sense was it contradictory. It actually helped the MPC to sustain the monetary policy stance.[34]

Clearly, Macroprudential policymakers are aware that they need to work closely with those responsible for both microprudential and monetary policy.[35] However, macroprudential policy cannot be successfully used to remedy issues with monetary policy where, for example, the latter is constrained by a currency union

32 Ibid., 10.

33 Supra note 27, (Oral evidence, 26 January 2016). See also the answer to question 139 by Brazier,

> Let us suppose we wanted to think about the housing market...You can look at rental yields, for example. You may take some comfort from the fact that rental yields...in most areas of the country, look in line with long-running averages. If you were trying to spot the central outlook for the cycle, [you are also looking at whether] yields are lower now than they were, on average, in the past. On that basis, your view of the tail event [c]ould be bigger than it was in the past. We are not just trying to assess how things look upon the face of it today. We are trying to ask the question: how bad could it be? That is where we use our risk appetite and why we try to specify what could happen. The most interesting thing I heard a senior policymaker say about the financial crisis...was that we spent far too long thinking about whether there was a housing bubble and not enough time thinking about what if there is a housing bubble.

34 Ibid., answer to question 118.

35 Donald Kohn, 'Comparing UK and US macroprudential systems: lessons for China', speech at the Global Financial Forum, Tsinghua University, Beijing, 11 May 2014, 5–6.

or where monetary policy lacks credibility.[36] There is evidence that loose monetary policy encourages less attention to credit quality assessments by lenders.[37] Greenspan's remarked that

> this vast increase in the market value of asset claims is in part the indirect result of investors accepting lower compensation for risk. Such an increase in market value is too often viewed by market participants as structural and permanent…But what they perceive as newly abundant liquidity can readily disappear…history has not dealt kindly with the aftermath of protracted periods of low risk premiums.[38]

However, it is hard to identify asset mis-pricing in time.[39]

Monetary policy can be used to deliver financial stability by increasing the cost of borrowing and reducing the value of assets that could be used as collateral for increased credit.[40] Consequently, higher interest rates tend to reduce the growth of financial intermediaries' balance sheets that often facilitate credit growth.[41] There is a trade-off between perceptions of asset value increases and risk, and on the other hand, the threats to lender liquidity – since asset financing is often based on short-term funding.[42] The effect is particularly strong depending on the level of liquidity weakness in the balance sheet.

It also has an immediate effect on financial institutions that watch their net interest margin (NIM) closely since these are likely to contract. Those lenders, however, betting on asset price rises may be impervious to NIM reductions. Contractions in the money supply will also reduce deposits which transmits itself through to a reduction in assets. However, there is a time lag of several months before these effects can be seen and bank balance sheets restabilise. This process may lead to a period of financial instability as banks become forced sellers of securities as they deleverage.[43] Monetary policy thus affects both sides of the lenders' balance sheet. The effect can produce a sudden shock to the financial

36 IMF, 'The interaction of monetary and macroprudential policies', (29 January 2013), 17 and 18.

37 Gabriel Jiménez and Jesús Saurina, 'Credit cycles, credit risk, and prudential regulation', (2006) *International Journal of Central Banking*, Vol. 2, No. 2, 64–98, 94.

38 Chapter 2, n. 41, (Greenspan, 'Reflections on central banking').

39 Jonathan McCarthy and Richard Peach, 'Are home prices the next "bubble"?', (2004) *Economic Policy Review*, New York Federal Reserve Board, Vol. 10, No. 3, www.newyorkfed.org/research/epr/04v10n3/0412mcca.html.

40 Ben Bernanke and Mark Gertler, 'Inside the black box: the credit channel of monetary policy transmission', (1995) *Journal of Economic Perspectives*, Vol. 9 No. 4, 27, 35–44.

41 Tobias Adrian and Hyun Song Shin, 'Financial intermediaries and monetary economics', (2009) Federal Reserve Bank of New York Staff Reports, No. 398, 64–65.

42 Claudio Borio and Haibin Zhu, 'Capital regulation, risk-taking and monetary policy: a missing link in the transmission mechanism', (2012) *Journal of financial Stability*, Vol. 8, 19, www.bis.org/publ/work268.pdf.

43 Ben Bernanke and Alan Blinder, 'The Federal Funds Rate and the channels of monetary transmission', (1992) *The American Economic Review*, Vol. 82, No. 4, 901, 919.

system with implications for financial stability.[44] However, it is worth noting that much depends on the institutions' perception of the risks and whether they actually perceive, for example, triple A rated collaterised debt obligations as high risk. "It is important to bear in mind that this behavior of banks is not irrational; simply they live in the same economic environment" as everyone else with which they share the "expectational climate...euphoric expectations pushing firms to expand their business during booms is the same optimism motivating banks to expand credit".[45]

Finally, there is a view that excessive central bank independence with its unrelenting focus on monetary policy can induce financial instability.[46] This may be due to a number of reasons including being isolated from political factors which may require a more balanced approach and the "creation of paradox of credibility" in which the belief permeates the market that the central bank will prevent financial problems.[47]

Further, financial stability and monetary policy concerns may not coincide so, for example, an increase in interest rates may damage the broader economy when a looser macroeconomic policy was more appropriate. This clearly would have social and political implications.[48] In addition, increased rates would increase the debt burden of financial services firms and weaken their asset base which could have the effect of increasing financial instability.[49] It also appears that investors may be impervious to higher interest rates in the short term if they remain convinced that asset prices will continue to rise since the benefits of the latter may substantially out-weigh the immediate higher interest rate costs.[50] There will also be a time lag before higher interest rates becoming effective, and it is possible that the credit boom may continue to expand for some time before the effect of the new borrowing costs are felt and financial instability increases in this interim period.[51] This suggests that the use of monetary and macroprudential policies may be complementary with the former used, for example, if there is evidence of serious avoidance of the macroprudential tools employed.[52]

44 Supra note 42, (Borió and Zhu), 17–18.

45 Eugenio Caverzasi, 'Minsky and the subprime mortgage crisis: the financial instability hypothesis in the era of financialization', (2014) Levy Economics Institute, Bard College, Working Paper No. 796, 14.

46 Wolfram Berger and Friedrich Kissmer, 'Central bank independence and financial stability: a tale of perfect harmony?', (2013) *European Journal of Political Economy*, Vol. 31, 109, 110.

47 Michael Bordo, 'Central bank independence and financial crises in history', (2010) Oesterreichische 38th Economics Conference 2010, 33–34.

48 Giovanni Dell'Ariccia, and others, 'Policies for macrofinancial stability: how to deal with credit booms', (2012) IMF Staff Discussion Note, No.12/06, 19–22.

49 Paolo Gelain, Kevin Lansing and Gisle Natvik, 'Leaning against the credit cycle', (2015) Norges Bank Research Working Paper, 04/2015, 19.

50 Giovanni Dell'Ariccia, Deniz Igan and Luc Laevan, 'Credit booms and lending standards: evidence from the subprime mortgage market', (2012) *Journal of Money, Credit and Banking*, Vol. 44, No. 2–3, 367, 377.

51 Supra, note 43, (Bernanke and Blinder), 919.

52 Chapter 2, n. 11, (Brunnermeier and Schnabel), 21–22.

Consequently, the better view may be that while monetary policy may be used as a last resort to protect financial stability there are more appropriate macroprudential tools available.[53]

Not all credit is of equal concern. The evidence suggests that different categories of credit are extended in the run-up to a financial crisis.[54] These can be divided into those which are considered "sound" in all circumstances, for example, lending to prime quality borrowers at LTVs of 70% or less and those mortgages which are provided to high-risk borrowers at high LTVs. The latter is speculative and depends on good economic conditions and rising property prices. It is unlikely that this latter type of lending will "be stemmed by changes in the monetary policy stance".[55] This also tends to negate the use of monetary policy for macroprudential purposes.

There is also a view that interest rates are too blunt an instrument to be used to address instability risks.[56] Nevertheless, Stein's view is that financial stability concerns should influence monetary policy decisions since the consequences of financial instability are likely to undermine monetary policy objectives if they are not addressed.[57] However, diluting clear targets for monetary policy with other objectives could undermine its effectiveness and threaten the creditability of an independent central bank.[58]

Monetary and financial stability polices have different objectives. "They are best conducted separately" even if the same authority is in charge of both.[59] "Price stability does not imply financial stability" and vice versa.[60] However, a failure to ensure financial stability is likely to undermine a central bank's price stability strategy.[61]

53 Daniel Tarullo, 'Monetary policy and financial stability', speech at the 30th Annual National Association for Business Economics Economic Policy Conference, Arlington, Virginia, 25 February 2014.

54 Chapter 2, n. 69, (Crowe 'Policies'), 12.

55 Chapter 2, n. 69, (Crowe), 12.

56 A. J. Hughes Hallett, 'Econometrics and the theory of economic policy: the Tinbergen–Theil contributions 40 years on', (1989) *History and Methodology of Econometrics*, Oxford Economic Papers, New Series, Vol. 41, No. 1, 189.

57 Jeremy Stein, 'Incorporating financial stability considerations into a monetary policy framework', speech at the International Research Forum on Monetary Policy, Washington, DC, 21 March 2014.

58 John Williams, President and Chief Executive Officer of the Federal Reserve Bank of San Francisco, 'Macroprudential policy in a microprudential world', (June 2015) Federal Reserve Board of San Francisco Economic Letter, 2015–18, 2, www.frbsf.org/economic-research/publications/economic-letter/2015/june/macroprudential-policy-in-a-microprudential-world/.

59 Lars Svensson, 'Monetary policy and financial stability', speech at 'Financial liberalization, innovation, and stability: international experience and relevance for China', the 3rd Joint Conference, People's Bank of China and IMF, Beijing, 16 March 2015.

60 Ibid., (Svensson), 4.

61 Andrew Levin, 'The design and communication of systematic monetary policy strategies', (2014), 13, Hoover Institution conference on 'Frameworks for central banking in the next century', at Stanford University, 29 and 30 May 2014.

> As Minsky demonstrated, price stability may even conflict with financial stability, rather than complement it. This is because a reduction in macroeconomic volatility may seem to reduce risk, and therefore make financial institutions raise their leverage, and reach for yield.[62]

Similar arguments apply to low inflation. During periods of continuing and expected low inflation, lenders are protected by monetary policy and with little or no risk of inflation are inclined to lend more.[63] Monetary policy does not target the key imbalances and "involves too much collateral damage to activity".[64] "Macroprudential instruments seem more appropriate which focused more directly on the source of the excessive exuberance. But we still have much to learn about how such instruments work in practice and how they interface with monetary policy".[65] In addition, while interest rate changes may moderate the business cycle there is no evidence that they affect the credit cycle.[66]

The problem is highlighted when there is a lack of clarity over the role of the macroprudential regulator. In recent years this is evident in Sweden. The central Riksbank is responsible for monetary policy. However, it has expressed considerable concern that the macroprudential and microprudential regulator, Finansinspektionen, has failed to control indebtedness and other areas of macroprudential policy.[67] Consequently, the Riksbank has kept interest rates higher than they should be with consequences for employment and growth.[68] This approach is sometimes described as "leaning against the wind" where monetary policy is used to set a higher interest rate than would be justified simply to meet the inflation target. The consequential adverse effect on the economy and employment is balanced against the threat to financial stability.[69]

> Monetary policy...can be one of several factors contributing to a build-up of financial imbalances...long periods of low interest rates can increase the risk that debt and asset prices will reach unsustainable levels...low interest rates tend to prompt financial market participants to intensify their search for yields from high-risk assets. Hence, even though the objectives and the

62 Chapter 2, n. 48, (Goodhart, 'Lessons for monetary policy'), 3.

63 Evan Koenig, 'Like a good neighbor: monetary policy, financial stability, and the distribution of risk', (2013) *International Journal of Central Banking*, 9, 57, 57–59.

64 Charles Bean and others, 'Monetary policy after the fall', Federal Reserve Bank of Kansas City Annual Conference Jackson Hole, Wyoming, 16 September 2010, 28.

65 Ibid., 28.

66 Chapter 2, n. 35, (Aikman, Haldane, Nelson), 27.

67 Sveriges Riksbank, 'Further measures are needed to manage household indebtedness', (Press release), 25 November 2015).

68 John Williams, 'Financial stability and monetary policy: happy marriage or untenable union?', (June 2014), Federal Reserve Board of San Francisco Economic Letter, 2014–17.

69 Lars Svensson, 'Cost benefit analysis of leaning against the wind: are costs larger also with less effective macroprudential policy?', (2016) IMF Working Paper, WP/16/3.

> instruments are different, monetary policy and macroprudential policy cannot be viewed as separate.[70]

However, there are strong arguments for what has been described as a "decoupling approach" with monetary policy solely targeted at price stability while macroprudential policy is used to ensure financial stability.[71] Therefore, there is a stronger case for employing monetary policy alongside other regulatory actions since the former "may reach into corners of the market that supervision and regulation cannot".[72] It remains uncertain which macroprudential tools are effective and how best they should be used. These issues are considered later in this chapter. Nevertheless, the evidence is that interest rates will "influence house prices, leverage, and maturity transformation", but it may be appropriate to adjust monetary policy to "get in the cracks" that persist in the macroprudential framework.[73] In addition, there are many traditional monetary policy tools such as banking reserve requirements which can also be used as macroprudential tools.[74] Nevertheless, it may be "helpful to distinguish between tools that primarily build through-the-cycle resilience against adverse financial developments and those primarily intended to lean against financial excesses".[75]

In conclusion, the proposition can be summarised by stating that

> [a] robust monetary policy should...take into account the risk of a build-up of financial imbalances.... At the same time, monetary policy must not be overburdened. Banking regulation and supervision must be the first line of defence against shocks to the financial system.[76]

Indeed, there are limits to both monetary and macroprudential policies and there may be market changes that cannot be detected and regulatory action may be too slow.[77] Nevertheless, it is likely that monetary policy actions may be

70 Øystein Olsen, 'Integrating financial stability and monetary policy analysis', speech at the London School of Economics and Political Science, 27 April 2015.

71 Jeremy Stein, 'Overheating in the credit market: origins, measurement and policy response', (2013), paper presented to a research symposium sponsored by the Federal Reserve Board of St Louis, 15.

72 Ibid., 17 and Claudio Borió and Mathias Drehmann, 'Financial instability and macroeconomics: bridging the gulf', (2009), paper presented at the Twelfth Annual International Banking Conference, 'The international financial crisis: have the rules of finance changed?', held at the Federal Reserve Bank of Chicago, Chicago.

73 Andrea Ajello and others, 'Financial stability and optimal interest-rate policy', (2015), Board of Governors of the Federal Reserve, Working Paper.

74 Stanley Fischer, (Vice-chairman of the Federal Reserve Board), 'Macroprudential monetary policy', speech at the 59th Economic Conference of the Federal Reserve Bank of Boston, Boston, MA, 2 October 2015.

75 Janet Yellen, 'Monetary policy and financial stability', Michel Camdessus Central Banking Lecture, IMF, Washington, DC, 2 July 2014.

76 Ibid., (Øystein Olsen, 'Integrating financial stability and monetary policy Analysis').

77 Ibid., 16–17.

responsible, at least in part, for some of the financial imbalances which threaten financial stability.[78] Low interest rates may encourage increased demand for credit and, at the same time, encourage a search by savers for yield and consequently greater risk.[79] Moreover, it is likely that it is "new" debt that may be destabilising and an increase in interest rates affects all debt and not just the issue of rapid credit expansion.[80] Consequently, using monetary policy to address macroprudential concerns may result in some new cracks being opened. Nevertheless, macroprudential policy cannot "substitute for monetary policy" and, as this work discusses, "the politics…are much more complicated than the politics of monetary policy".[81]

Therefore, it is important to consider other tools first and whether fiscal policy may provide better options for macroprudential policy.

3.4 Fiscal policy

Discussion has been limited on the role of fiscal levers in achieving macroprudential objectives. Fiscal policies may affect the two main aspects of microprudential policy: those actions that influence the cost structures of banks (e.g. requiring more and specific types of capital) and those that control the quantity and type of business.[82] There is a microprudential policy preference towards using the former since they leave the associated problems with the bank and are less overt than direct restrictions. How banks meet their capital requirements is likely to be strongly influenced by fiscal policy since taxation policies increase the propensity of banks to hold debt capital rather than equity and that this in turn increases credit growth.[83] However, there is no evidence that taxation policies were a direct factor in causing the recent financial crisis.[84]

There are a range of fiscal measures that could be used as part of a macroprudential policy to contain or restrict the growth of credit. These include

78 "I am also mindful of the potential for low interest rates to heighten the incentives of financial market participants to reach for yield and take on risk, and of the limits of macroprudential measures to address these and other financial stability concerns". Supra, note 75, Yellen, 'Monetary policy and financial stability'.

79 Chapter 2, n. 35, (Aikman, Haldane and Nelson).

80 Supra note 49, (Gelain, Lansing, and Natvik), 19.

81 Philipp Hildebrand, former head of the Swiss Central Bank, quoted in the Financial Times, 'Bank of England: crashing the party', (24 June 2014).

82 Beatrice Weder di Mauro and Ulrich Klüh, 'Reshaping systemic risk regulation in Europe', in Stijn Claessens, Michael Keen, and Ceyla Pazarbasioglu (eds), 'Financial sector taxation: The IMF's report to the G-20' (IMF, 2010), 90, www.imf.org/external/np/seminars/eng/2010/paris/pdf/090110.pdf.

83 Ruud de Mooij, Michael Keen and Masanori Orihara, 'Taxation, bank leverage, and financial crises', (2013) IMF Working Paper.

84 Julian Alworth and Giampaolo Arachi, *Taxation and the financial crisis*, Julian Alworth and Giampaolo Arachi (eds), (Oxford University Press, Oxford, 2012), 26.

restricting the deductibility of long-term debt interest from profits.[85] This would have the effect of increasing the cost of bank capital and probably result in de-leveraging assets.[86] There are proposals which differentiate between different sources of bank profits with high rates of taxation applied to profits from more risky activities.[87] One proposal is to levy a "Pigouvian tax" on bank lending to reduce the level of such lending and to reflect the externalities if subsequent problems with such bank assets results in public assistance to banks and to help reinflate the economy.[88] In addition, there are the straightforward imposition of bank levies based on balance sheets and, separately, transaction taxes.[89] An annual bank levy has been imposed on large UK banks since the financial crisis. However, research indicates that in response the more risky banks further increase their portfolio risk.[90]

There is also evidence that fiscal measures may be ineffective in preventing or containing an economic boom due to the time it takes for them to become effective.[91] There is the additional issue that fiscal "tools" are prone to political interference since they are a key element of most government policies. Moreover, as already mentioned, there are sufficient difficulties in coordinating monetary and macroprudential policies, and it is even more difficult to do this when it comes to influencing government spending and taxation strategies. However, it is interesting to note the coordinated actions taken by both the FPC and HM

85 This could be achieved by introducing an "Allowance for Corporate Equity" (ACE) which would allow a cost of equity deduction from corporation tax so that the cost of equity equated to that for debt capital. This can be contrasted with a "Comprehensive Business Income Tax" (CBIT) which taxes revenue with no deduction for the cost of capital, 'Written evidence submitted by Professor Michael Devereux and Dr. John Vella to the Parliamentary Commission for Banking Standards', 24 June 2013.

86 John Cochrane, 'Equity-financed banking and a run-free financial system', comments given at the 'Ending too big to fail symposium', Federal Reserve Bank of Minneapolis, 16 May 2016, 8. Cochrane considered that

> capital regulation should...take the form of Pigouvian taxes rather than a regulatory ratio. For every dollar of short-term debt that a bank or other intermediary issues, it has to pay...five cents tax per year. That tax could...decline smoothly with maturity, be larger depending on capital ratios and other measures of how run-prone the institution is [and] be larger for "systemically important" institutions, and could be varied over time as macroprudential policymakers sniff trouble.

87 Andrew Mullineux, 'Taxing banks fairly', (2012) *International Review of Financial Analysis*, Vol. 25, 154, 157–158.

88 Olivier Jeanne and Anton Korinek, 'Managing credit booms and busts: a Pigouvian taxation approach', (2010) National Bureau of Economics Research Working Paper No. 16377. The tax would reflect the costs of the business operation which are not internalised by the business and reflected in its costs, Arthur Pigou, *The economics of welfare*, (published 1920, McMillan, London, 1932), 138.

89 Michael Devereux, John Vella and Niels Johannesen, 'Can taxes tame the banks? Evidence from European bank levies', (2013) Oxford University Centre for Business Taxation, WP 13/25.

90 Ibid., (Devereux, Vella and Johannesen), 23.

91 Ibid., (Devereux, Vella and Johannesen), 22.

Treasury to restrict buy-to-let lending. The latter employed fiscal measures, increased stamp duty land tax (SDLT) and limited the set-off of mortgage interest against rental income thus reducing the attractiveness of this market.[92]

Nevertheless, it is important to consider the effectiveness of existing financial stability protection measures and to explore the use of microprudential capital and liquidity tools for macroprudential purposes.

3.5 Macroprudential and microprudential policies

It is possible to view macroprudential measures as microprudential policies writ large. In many ways macroprudential policy is an adjunct to microprudential regulation since they both use similar tools and a microprudential regulator would not be doing their job properly if they failed to "look at the big picture".[93] It is also possible to view risk as divided between that which is idiosyncratic and that which is subject to microprudential policy and, separately, market risk which falls to macroprudential oversight.[94] Further, the distinction between macro and microprudential policy gets blurred if the banking system is highly concentrated in the hands of a few large banks.[95] However, from my own experience, there is a rational tendency for microprudential regulators to try to place a boundary around their areas of responsibility to ensure focus and to best employ their finite resources. The microprudential regulator will attempt to avoid issues posed by "the turbulent frontier" where there is always pressure to attempt to regulate one further aspect or type of business.[96] It presents a significant risk to the microprudential regulator since resources and senior management focus are likely to be dissipated and in an attempt to control every area nothing is properly supervised. The result is that macroprudential policy needs to look over the horizon and must not be constrained by artificial regulatory boundaries.

Consequently, macroprudential policy can best be described more as "a state of mind than a suite of tools".[97] In part, macroprudential policy "creep" is a consequence of the migration of risk to new areas, either to avoid regulatory attention or simply due to market dynamics. The difference between micro and macroprudential policy is highlighted by the different questions asked. The microprudential supervisor may only ask if there is, for example, rapid growth in credit in the regulated institutions while macroprudential regulation needs to ask the broader question: where is credit growing? This could relate to a

92 See the Chancellor of the Exchequer's Parliamentary Budget speech on 16th March 2016. SDLT increases to 15% of the value of the properties over £1.5 million if bought as a buy-to-let investment or second home compared to 12% for a main residence.

93 Chapter 2, n. 157, (Ellis, 'Macroprudential policy: a suite of tools or a state of mind').

94 Malcolm Edey (Assistant Governor (Financial System) of the Reserve Bank of Australia), 'Macroprudential supervision and the role of central banks', remarks to the Regional Policy Forum on Financial Stability and Macroprudential Supervision, Beijing, 28 September 2012.

95 Chapter 2, n. 157, (Ellis, 'What have we learned?'), 5.

96 Chapter 2, n. 16, (Galbraith, 'The "turbulent frontier" as a factor in British expansion'), 150.

97 Chapter 2, n. 157, (Ellis, 'What have we learnt?') 8th paragraph.

particular market or group of institutions. As discussed later in this chapter it is this breath of view which harbours both the strengths and weaknesses of macroprudential policy.

The overlap in responsibilities and available tools may lead to tensions between macro and microprudential policies.[98] There are also strong cultural differences. The microprudential supervisor will be immersed in the detail of the institutions they supervise. They will have to be experts in the latest technical guidance and will need to consider issues posed by institutions attempting to interpret and implement the latest rules and other requirements. At any point in time they will be preparing for, or undertaking, a review of particular aspects of an institution and they will be caught up with the bureaucracy of regulation and supervision (e.g. preparing briefings, contributing to reports, providing daily, weekly and monthly progress information, etc.) and undertaking training and attending many coordination meetings. Microprudential policy considers not just the capital and liquidity and the financial numbers but also the institution's business plan and the "human element" since the culture and ethos generated by the board and senior management of a financial services firm may have a "profound effect" on the business and its operations.[99] All the time the microprudential supervisors will be attempting to avoid being "captured" by the regulated institutions or, at the other extreme, be corrupted by the exercise of power. Consequently, it is very difficult for the microprudential supervisor to take a broad perspective. Organisationally, the institution responsible for microprudential policy may seek to avoid this difficulty by having dedicated units responsible for key microprudential "themes" which affect a number of supervised institutions. However, at its heart, microprudential policy remains concerned with the safety and soundness of individual firms.

Macroprudential policy, as discussed in the previous chapter, knows almost no boundaries. It must consider the areas beyond the regulatory perimeter both domestically and internationally. It will be concerned with government policies and their implications, the role and development of markets, demographics, technology, climate change, etc.[100] It is possible that with this breadth to their scope macroprudential and microprudential policy may become uncoordinated particularly in view of their very different time horizons. Microprudential supervision may appear to lack perspective while macroprudential policy may be seen as too esoteric. The Bank of England has expressed concern that it "still has a long way to go to integrate micro and macroprudential" policies.[101]

98 Jacek Osiński, Katharine Seal, and Lex Hoogduin, 'Macroprudential and microprudential policies: toward cohabitation', (2013) IMF Staff Discussion Note 13/05, 6–9.

99 Katherine Braddick (Director of Prudential Policy at the Prudential Regulatory Authority), 'The changing face of prudential policy', speech at the Future of Financial Services Summit, London, 11 March 2014).

100 For example, Mark Carney, 'Breaking the tragedy of the horizon – climate change and financial stability', speech at Lloyd's of London, 29 September 2015).

101 Andrew Bailey's speech at the New York Federal Reserve Board conference on 'defining the objectives and goals of supervision', 18 March 2016.

The next section considers the use of quantitative limits on credit creation as a macroprudential tool. Their employment has been limited in practice. This may because there are concerns about the effectiveness of LTV and DTI restrictions on the growth of debt.

3.6 LTV and DTI tools: how they work and issues with their use

The new powers to employ these measures was granted to the FPC in 2015.[102] Consequently, there is still a lack of knowledge of how macroprudential tools generally work in practice.[103] However, there is some evidence from other jurisdictions on the use of LTV and DTI measures and these are discussed later in this chapter.

The use of quantitative restrictions such as those on LTVs and DTI may have a number of advantages over those macroprudential tools which try to increase the cost of capital and lower lender margins. For example, if capital and liquidity are freely available due to, for example, capital inflows, then quantitative limits may be more effective.[104] They can also be more effective than attempting to influence financial institution cost and profitability.[105] For example, during periods of intense competition for market share price signals are likely to be ignored by senior management and lending standards relaxed.[106] Based on my personal experience senior executives and boards may become obsessed with "the chase" seeking to keep up with, or to overtake, rival companies. During these periods of excitement and intense pressures, market signals are often ignored or their importance explained away. For example, in 2006–2007 Northern Rock, a small regional UK bank, expanded its mortgage book very rapidly and grew its new business market share to almost 19% in July 2007 just before it collapsed.[107] It

102 HM Treasury, 'The Financial Policy Committee's housing market tools', (October 2014), 5.

103 Many writers on macroprudential policy focus exclusively on those tools that raise bank costs and to ignore those that are quantitative in nature. For example, Tobias Adrian, Daniel Covitz and Nellie Liang, 'Financial stability monitoring', (2014) Federal Reserve Bank of New York Staff Reports No. 601.

104 Gianni De Nicoló, Giovanni Favara, and Lev Ratnovski, 'Externalities and macroprudential policy', (2012), IMF Staff Discussion Notes, No. SDN/12/05, 12.

105 Ibid., 8.

106 For example, Halifax Bank of Scotland (HBoS), in the years preceding the financial crisis, faced increasing competition in its core business of providing residential mortgages and in order to retain its market share and profitability "HBOS expanded its mortgage activities in less competitive areas, such as self-certification [where the borrower provided no evidence of their claimed income] and buy to let mortgages, where margins were higher… By 2007, 27% of mortgage lending exposure was in 'specialist lending' [i.e. self-certification mortgages at around £30Bn]". The "buy-to-let mortgage portfolio was the area of real growth, almost doubling to £27 billion between 2006 and the end of 2007, where maintaining market share also meant moving up the risk curve". Bank of England and Financial Conduct Authority, 'The failure of HBOS plc (HBOS)', (2015), 115.

107 'Northern Rock boasts 18.9% net market share', Mortgage Strategy, (25 July 2007), "Looking at residential mortgages, our gross lending for the year was 23% higher at £29.0 billion and net lending was 13% higher at £15.1 billion, again with a strong second half performance…

aimed to overtake Halifax Bank of Scotland, the market leader. There was considerable liquidity in the market with rapidly rising house prices and very high levels of mortgage lending. There were many new non-deposit taker entrants in the market and lending margins fell to zero or lower. The signs indicated a "Minsky moment" and the need for great caution. Some, with better management, heeded the warnings and left the market. However, others continued to fuel the market with increased lending in a dash for market share and positive recognition by the mortgage media.[108]

There were major failures of corporate governance.[109] The imposition of increased capital and liquidity requirements in the period before the recent financial crisis are unlikely to have been effective unless imposed very early on before the asset and credit boom was well underway. However, LTV and DTI limits would have had an immediate effect and would have provided a clear signal to lenders and the market. Moreover, these types of restrictions could be used to target the highest areas of risk such as lending to the speculative residential property market.

Nevertheless, it is important to note that measures such as LTV and DTI limits only apply to new lending and not to the "stock" or back-book of loans. Excessive risks may already exist in this part of the lender's balance sheet. Increased capital and liquidity requirements may be used to address these risks. The effect could be a search for more capital and liquidity or de-leveraging the assets portfolio or a mixture of both. This may result in systemic problems, risk contagion and "fire-sales" as lenders compete to sell loan books and other assets and thus "signal" concerns to the rest of the market. This could generate a need to revalue assets and could result in a threat to the solvency of lenders. Consequently, measures aimed at reducing systemic risk could precipitate it. This is the main reason why it is difficult to employ additional capital and liquidity requirements as short-term macroprudential tools. They work better at the microprudential level over longer periods. There are a number of other significant difficulties arising from the use of LTV and DTI tools, considered later in this chapter.

3.7 When to apply LTV and DTI restrictions and other options

More broadly, there are a number of issues with macroprudential tools, including LTV and DTI measures. These include problems with the accessibility of timely and accurate data, which may determine whether it is necessary to deploy macroprudential tools and their calibration. For example, as mentioned earlier,

economic fundamentals are set to remain supportive for the mortgage market – our core market.", Northern Rock, 'Annual report and accounts 2006', 8–9.

108 'Northern Rock has been voted best overall lender in the 2006 Alexander Hall awards', Mortgage Solution, 29 January 2007.

109 'The run on the Rock', House of Commons Treasury Committee, Fifth Report of Session 2007–08, HC 56–I [Incorporating HC 999 i–iv, Session 2006–07] Published 26 January 2008, 18–19.

rapid credit growth is often seen as an important factor in the development of systemic financial instability. Consequently, considerable reliance is now placed on credit growth data in relation to GDP.[110] A more qualitative method has been suggested using regular surveys of senior lender credit officers assessing levels of relaxations in lending policies.[111]

These data issues mean that it is very difficult to know when to apply LTV and DTI restrictions and how to calibrate them.[112] It appears, for example, that LTV limits applied at the peak of the property cycle have the most effect since these loans are the most vulnerable.[113] There are many other potential problems with the use of LTV and DTI tools. These include their social cost, their potential to distort the market, their social and political legitimacy, their effectiveness in restraining credit, the difficulties in measuring their effectiveness and their interaction with other policies including microprudential tools and macroeconomic and fiscal measures.

There are a number of measures that can be used to address these issues. These are considered both in this chapter and in Chapter 8 which considers the political aspects of credit and housing policy. These steps can be categorised into three groups with an additional fourth strategy with much broader implications. First, those that allow LTV and DTI tools to be precisely targeted with, for example, some reference to limiting the restrictions for young first-time buyers or only applying the restrictions to properties in certain geographical zones. Second, there are approaches which attempt to address the legitimacy issue by placing responsibility for how the tools are employed on the lenders. For example, allowing the latter to lend a fixed proportion of mortgages above the restricted level. This places the rationing decision in the hands of the lender and distances it from the macroprudential policymakers. It is, in many ways, akin to the operation of macroprudential tools that raise the cost of lending, mentioned earlier, where the effects of these measures are issues for the management of the regulated firm to resolve. Third, there are public policy actions that mitigate the effects of LTV and DTI limits, for example, by subsidising deposits and mortgage insurance. All of these work by manipulating the supply of credit. The final measure is even broader and has a central objective of increasing the supply of housing. This addresses a number of issues including reducing the cost of buying

110 Rochelle Edge and Ralf Meisenzahl, 'The unreliability of credit-to-GDP ratio gaps in real time: implications for countercyclical capital buffers', (2011) *International Journal of Central Banking*, Vol. 7, No. 4, 261, 262–264 and 296. Part of the problem relates to significant subsequent revisions made to GDP figures and the number of "false positives" which erroneously indicate large increases in credit.

111 Chapter 2, n. 156 (Bassett, 'Changes in bank lending standards and the macroeconomy'), 27.

112 Ian Christensen, 'Mortgage debt and procyclicality in the housing market', (Summer 2011) Bank of Canada Review, 35–42, 39 considers the use of automatic LTV restrictions linked to the rise of house prices but does not mention the risks of "leakages" and other forms of limit avoidance which appear to develop the longer LTV constraints apply.

113 Niamh Hallissey, Robert Kelly and Terry O'Malley, 'Macroprudential tools and credit risk of property lending in Irish banks', (2014) Central Bank of Ireland, Economic Letter Series, No. 10, 3.

a home through increased supply and hence reduces the demand for credit. It clearly has a number of socio-economic aspects some of which are considered in Chapter 8.

3.8 Other concerns

There are other concerns with the use of LTV and DTI tools. These include the ability of lenders and borrowers to evade their effects, known as "leakages", the failures of these measures to address root causes and the effects of unintended consequences.

3.8.1 "Leakages"

The Bank of England has looked at the issue of macroprudential "leakages" in relation to the use of capital tools, using overseas branches operating in the UK as a control group.[114] It found that a 1% decline in lending by UK authorised banks due to increased capital requirements lead to a 32% "leakage".[115] The effect is material but the Bank still determined that the macroprudential tools were effective.[116]

At the heart of the issue is that the two main protagonists: the borrower and the lender want to complete the transaction and, possibly, aided by an intermediary broker, may attempt to find ways around the restrictions. It may be undermined by a combination of high levels of housing sales and purchases in an escalating property market as borrowers increase their borrowing in frequent steps without breaching LTV limits. Some of these aspects are considered later as part of the analysis of how LTV and DTI restrictions have worked in other jurisdictions. Additionally, side arrangements between borrowers and property-site developers may provide some, or all, of the higher deposit required under a LTV macroprudential policy.[117] In another example, non-bank intermediaries and foreign financial institutions may become active and reduce the effect of the

114 Shekhar Aiyar, Charles Calomiris and Tomasz Wieladek, 'Does macropru leak? Evidence from a UK policy experiment', (2012) Bank of England Working Paper No. 445, 4.

115 Ibid., (Aiyar, Calomiris and Wieladek), 4.

116 Ibid., (2012), 28.

117 'The Council of Mortgage Lenders (CML) and the Royal Institute of Chartered Surveyors (RICS) in talks over bogus new build buy-to-let (B2L) valuations', (Mortgage Strategy, 23 December 2005),

> concerns over bogus new build buy-to-let valuations, as industry confidence in new build continues to waver. Two weeks ago Portman subsidiary The Mortgage Works made an official decision not to lend on new build properties as a result of concerns that some developers were doing deals on the price of the property outside of the formal contract.

See also The Telegraph, 'Five dirty tricks in today's rising housing market', (3 October 2013) refers to practices in 2006/7 of "'fake' discounts on newly built properties" and "no money down property deals with 'property clubs'".

macroprudential measures.[118] Further, deposits may be funded by unsecured loans perhaps backed by various forms of credit insurance or conditional ownership contracts.

The Bank of England is aware of these issues.[119] However, since LTV and DTI policies have only had limited application in the UK, it is not clear what the response may be if, and when, they are more fully applied. Other jurisdictions have had more experience of these issues and these are considered later in this chapter. All this emphasises the need for cross-border macroprudential cooperation.[120] This is not new since, for example, the methods used to avoid compliance with the supplementary special deposit scheme ("the corset") in the 1970s, included the use of overseas operations and "disintermediation of a purely cosmetic nature".[121]

3.8.2 Socio-economic root cause analysis

There is a concern that the focus of macroprudential tools, in general, and LTV and DTI measures, specifically, has been too numeric and formulaic.[122] Economic studies fail to consider the root cause of financial instability including behaviours that are evidence of "rent-seeking" and risk-taking (e.g. looser contractual terms, more new financial products, etc.).[123] These issues are bound up in wider economic concerns over the globalisation of capital flows, serious economic imbalances, social inequality and the reliance on debt.[124] These aspects go beyond the subject of this work, but are legitimate issues against which to assess macroprudential policy.

3.8.3 Possible unintended consequences of LTV and DTI macroprudential policies

There is a risk that uncoordinated macroprudential policies can "spillover" from one country to another. This is important since foreign bank branches in the

118 For example, although not directly in relation to a macroprudential interventions a lender based in the Czech Republic offered no-document mortgages in the UK via the internet.

119 Jon Cunliffe, remarks at the Alastair Ross Goobey Memorial Lecture, London, 26 April 2016, 5, describing how "nearly 15% of new mortgages...had loan to income ratios *just below* the FPC's threshold of 4.5 almost double the proportion in 2008/9".

120 Ignazio Angeloni, 'European macroprudential policy from gestation to infancy', (April 2014) Banque de France, Financial Stability Review, No. 18, 71–84, 81.

121 Bank of England, 'The supplementary special deposits scheme', (March 1982) *Quarterly Bulletin*, 74–84, 82, www.bankofengland.co.uk/quarterly-bulletin/1982/q1/the-supplementary-special-deposits-scheme.

122 Chapter 2, n. 157, (Luci Ellis, 'Macroprudential policy: What have we learned?'), 12.

123 Ibid., (Luci Ellis), 11.

124 Martin Wolf, *The shifts and shocks* (Penguin, London, 2015), 158–173 and Turner, *Between debt and the devil*, supra note 1, 94–97; governments have been too eager to use mortgage credit as a "costless answer enabling low-income citizens to finance consumption", (121). See also Raghuram Rajan, 'Let them eat credit', (New Republic, 27 August 2010), summarising the main argument in his book: *Fault lines: how hidden fractures still threaten the World economy*, (Princeton University Press, Princeton, NJ, 2010).

UK are an important factor in the latter's domestic economy; more so than in that of other developed nations.[125] However, in the run-up to the financial crisis overseas branches in the UK provided little credit to UK households.[126] The role of foreign bank branches is a particular concern when different jurisdictions use different polices to address similar risks. There is evidence that where one jurisdiction increases its lending restrictions that the "UK-resident affiliates owned in that jurisdiction expand...household lending in the UK".[127] However, another study could find no statistically significant evidence of any "spill-over" of increased lending when the home country increases lending standards regulation.[128]

The political legitimacy of using LTV and DTI policies is a more significant issue.

3.8.4 The legitimacy of LTV and DTI macroprudential policies

Very few of the studies of the macroprudential use of LTV and DTI limits consider, or even mention, issues concerning the political legitimacy involved in their use.[129] There are clearly groups who will be adversely affected by the application of LTV and DTI macroprudential policies. It is possible, when organised by pressure groups, politicians and the media that these measures, and those responsible for them, may be subject to intense scrutiny and questioning including the legitimacy of their actions.[130] This important issue is addressed in Chapter 6.

Consequently, political pressure may limit the effectiveness of macroprudential restrictions on mortgage lending. Nevertheless, jurisdictions operating under different political norms, such as Hong Kong, Singapore and South Korea, have consistently been able to apply more robust macroprudential policies in the mortgage market.[131] The use of LTV and DTI limits in specific jurisdictions is considered later in this chapter after a broader review of the effectiveness of these policies.

125 Robert Hills and others, 'Cross-border regulatory spillovers: how much? How important? What sectors? Lessons from the United Kingdom', (2016) Bank of England Staff Working Paper No. 595, 2, "foreign banks account for nearly half of total banking system assets in the UK, amounting to around 250% of GDP (of which around three-quarters is accounted for by branches, and the remainder by subsidiaries)".

126 Glenn Hoggarth, John Hooley and Yevgeniya Korniyenko, 'Which way do foreign branches sway? Evidence from the recent UK domestic credit cycle', (2013) Bank of England Financial Stability Paper No. 22, 12.

127 Supra, note 125, (Hills and others), 4.

128 Piotr Danisewicz, Dennis Reinhardt and Rhiannon Sowerbutts, 'On a tight leash: does bank organisational structure matter for macroprudential spillovers?, (2015) Bank of England Working Paper No. 524, 6, 13–14.

129 For example, Luis Jácome and Srobona Mitra, 'LTV and DTI limits – going granular', (2015) IMF Working Paper WP/15/154, appears to regard the use of such measures are purely a technical matter. The writings of Ed Balls and Paul Tucker are notable exceptions.

130 Supra note 48, (Dell'Ariccia, 'policies'), 27.

131 Salim Darbar and Xiaoyong Wu, 'Experiences with macroprudential policy – five case studies', (2015) IMF Working Paper WP/15/123, 4–9 and 24–29.

3.9 The effectiveness of LTV and DTI policies

There is evidence that lending based on high LTVs and DTIs is more susceptible to economic shocks.[132] Consequently, macroprudential tools that restrict high LTVs and DTIs may be more effective than other options.[133] However, there is a general paucity of data on which to base LTV and DTI decisions. As a result much of the policymaking in this area is based, in practice, on a set of best estimates.[134] This section looks at the effectiveness of the applications of these types of macroprudential measures; and their political acceptability.

There are a number of methods of applying LTV and DTI limits. For example, in Hong Kong LTV restrictions are set in the form of a "ladder" with different levels of LTV applied to a range of property values. This is considered in more detail below. In the UK, DTI limits may be applied to percentages of the lender's loan book.[135] Further, it has been suggested that LTV limits should be applied automatically, linked to a counter-cyclical macroprudential strategy.[136]

In the US the highest LTV and DTI levels were seen in the period 2005–2007 and it is the mortgages sold in these years that are the most likely to have resulted in financial difficulties or default.[137] The other predictor of financial difficulty is a correlation between those with first charge mortgages with an LTV over 80% supplemented by a second charge.[138] This suggests that borrowers had found ways of circumventing some lender restrictions by using loans from other less rigorous lenders. Further, it is possible that increasing LTV requirements, or higher interest rates, may deter better risk customers, with lenders subject to adverse selection.[139]

It is difficult to determine how effective quantitative limits on lending are in practice. In order to avoid regulatory arbitrage, the various limits need to apply to any financial service firm capable of offering mortgages and not just to banks

132 Owen Lamont and Jeremy Stein, 'Leverage and house-price dynamics in US cities', (1999) RAND Journal of Economics, Vol. 30, No. 3, 498, 514.

133 It is worth noting that, counter-intuitively, neither LTV nor DTI levels appear to affect borrower non-housing consumption expenditure as measured across a range of countries, Alessandro Calza, Tommaso Monacelli, and Livio Stracca, 'Housing finance and monetary policy', (2009) European Central Bank Working papers Series No. 1069, 8.

134 Stanley Fischer, 'Financial sector reform: how are we?', Martin Feldstein lecture at the National Bureau of Economic Research, Cambridge, Massachusetts, 10 July 2014, 11.

135 Financial Policy Committee, 'Statement on housing market powers of direction from its policy meeting, 26 September 2014', issued 2 October 2014, 60.

136 Caterina Mendicino, 'Collateral requirements: macroeconomic fluctuations and macroprudential policy', (2012) Banco de Portugal Working Papers 11/2012, 3.

137 Yuliya Demyanyk and Otto Van Hemert, 'Understanding the subprime mortgage crisis', (2008) Federal Reserve Board of St. Louis Supervisory Policy Analysis Working Paper, 1–7, with LTVs of between 84% and 86% and DTIs over 40%.

138 Manuel Adelino, Antoinette Schoar and Felipe Severino 'Credit supply and house prices: evidence from mortgage market segmentation', (2012) National Bureau of Economic Research Working Paper 17832. This is based on a large sample of transactions across ten US cities which indicates that this method of finance grew extensively in 2004–2006, (page 36).

139 Joseph Stiglitz and Andrew Weiss, 'Credit rationing in markets with imperfect information', (June 1981) *The American Economic Review*, Vol. 71, 393–410, 408–409.

and building societies.[140] I have discussed the effect of the DTI limitations, mentioned earlier, imposed by the Bank of England in 2014, with heads of mortgage credit at most of the major lenders.[141] They have all had to impose much lower restrictions on the percentage of business that can be undertaken at these high multiples to ensure that there is a sufficient buffer so that the lender did not fall foul of the Bank of England restrictions. The limit is imposed on drawdown rather than commitment so the various credit departments have had to develop forecasting models since there is normally a two- to three-month gap between these two dates. In practice, some lenders have had, suddenly, to cease offering these levels of mortgage with the result that mortgage brokers have directed all the business to competitors. This has had a cascade effect across the mortgage industry with a series of "stops and starts". However, from discussions with the mortgage brokers trade body, there has always been at least one lender able to meet borrower demand. The Bank of England has confirmed that after a short-term slow-down lending at high DTI levels has resumed with "nearly 15% of new mortgages" written, in the fourth quarter of 2015, at "ratios just below the FPC's threshold of 4.5 – almost double the proportion in 2008/9".[142]

One possible option would be to impose a limit on the enforceability of the mortgage security above a set LTV limit.[143] This would limit the risk of "leakage" since it would be difficult to avoid. However, lenders may, for example, be able to source low cost insurance for the excess amount or simply accept the risk for the unsecured potion of the loan, especially in a rising property price market. It is also possible that the microprudential supervisors may be concerned since this may complicate the capital risk weighting calculations and undermine part of the prudential security of lenders.

3.10 The effectiveness of LTV and DTI/LTI measures: the experience of other jurisdictions

3.10.1 Cross-border surveys

A few countries since the late 1990s have operated LTV and DTI/LTI (the terms are used interchangeably) restrictions. Analysis of their effectiveness has been limited. This is probably due to the idiosyncrasies of the housing markets in each jurisdiction and the complexity caused by other interventions including, government housing policies, taxation and macroeconomic actions. Nevertheless, there are some general lessons which may be drawn from the experience of others. This section looks at the five major cross-border surveys in this area. This is followed by a review of the results and issues found in five individual jurisdictions (i.e. Sweden, Korea, Israel, New Zealand and Hong Kong). Finally,

140 Chapter 2, n. 69, (Crowe), 20.
141 One major bank declined to be interviewed.
142 Supra note 119, (Cunliffe at Goobey Lecture, 2016).
143 Mark Stephens and Peter Williams, 'Tackling housing market volatility in the UK: a progress report', (2012), Joseph Rowntree Foundation Report, 7.

reference is made to the introduction of LTV and DTI restriction in the Republic of Ireland in 2015. The Irish central bank has tried to learn from other jurisdictions and to apply its policies in its own context although it is too early to analyse the results for these measures.

3.10.2 Multi-jurisdictional surveys

A review of some 2,800 banks across forty-eight countries over the period 2000–2010 found that LTV and LTI policies had a statistically significant effect on reducing bank balance sheet asset growth.[144] This is in contrast to countercyclical capital measures which had no such effect.[145] Another survey based on seventy-four banks in Asia across eleven economies between 2000 and 2014 found that macroprudential policy in Asian countries used housing based tools rather than other policies to curb credit growth. This review found that LTV and DTI limits, higher risk weights requirements on mortgage loans and the taxation of land and property had the biggest effects.[146]

Another survey of fifty-seven economies over some thirty years from 1980 found that policies limiting the supply of credit by increasing its cost had "little or no detectable effect on the housing market".[147] However, DTI measures were more effective in controlling the demand for credit than LTV policies probably because rising property prices negated the latter's effect.[148] It is interesting to note that neither set of actions had any clear effect on house prices.[149]

A survey of 119 countries between 2000 and 2013 found that LTV and LTI limits were "associated with reductions in the growth rates in credit and house prices".[150] These actions, together with leverage limits and dynamic provisioning, were particularly effective although the evidence of their effectiveness is weaker "in financially more open economies and those economies that have deeper and presumably more sophisticated financial systems, suggestive of some evasion".[151]

It has been pointed out that these multi-jurisdictional surveys fail to take account of important local characteristics, including the quality of microprudential

144 Stijn Claessens, Swati Ghosh, and Roxana Mihet, 'Macroprudential policies to mitigate financial system vulnerabilities', (2014) IMF Working Paper WP/14/55, 17.

145 Ibid., 17 (Claessens, Ghosh and Mihet).

146 Longmei Zhang and Edda Zoli, 'Leaning against the wind: macroprudential policy in Asia', (2014) IMF Working Paper WP/14/22, 9 and 30.

147 Kenneth Kuttner and Ilhyock Shim, 'Can non-interest rate policies stabilise housing markets? Evidence from a panel of 57 economies', (2013) BIS Working Papers No 433, 24–25.

148 Ibid., 24–25. Chapter 2, n. 45, (CGFS Papers No. 48), 56–57, which suggests that the DTI policies work better during periods of rapid house price inflation since income levels do not rise as fast.

149 Supra note 147, (Kuttner and Shim), 24–25.

150 Eugenio Cerutti, Stijn Claessens, and Luc Laeven, 'The use and effectiveness of macroprudential policies: new evidence', (2015) IMF Working Paper WP/15/61, 3.

151 Ibid., 3.

supervision, the phasing of local credit expansions and contractions, fiscal policies in relation to housing and the role of capital markets and non-bank financial institutions.[152] Moreover, the range of countries is very wide including a host of different political systems and economic conditions. In other words, there are probably too many variables to draw any useful conclusions. Consequently, it may be more helpful to consider a number of specific jurisdictions that have employed LTV and LTI measures in recent years.

I have examined a representative group of jurisdictions; some are selected both for the period of time over which they have deployed LTV and LTI policies and the intensity of their application and others because they display, clearly, some of the fundamental issues with the use of these instruments. Some jurisdictions have been excluded, since their residential property macroprudential policies are so entwined with their taxation systems that it is very difficult to assess the success or failure of the former. For example, the Netherlands introduced a cap on LTV lending in 2013 of 105%, set to decrease to 100% by 2018.[153] Not only is this a very high LTV but new mortgages qualify for interest tax deductibility, which has a distorting effect on the market.

Canada presents particular issues. It is difficult to discern what is happening in the Canadian housing market since there are a large number of factors influencing both the process and outcomes. First Canada is not one market but several with areas such as the Toronto metropolitan district, British Columbia and the other western provinces operating as distinct markets with very different dynamics to each and the rest of the country.[154] Moreover, the mortgage market is dominated by the big four federally regulated banks and almost all high-LTV mortgages must have credit insurance issued by the Federal Canada Mortgage and Housing Corporation (CMHC) or equivalent private sector insurer.[155] Since 2008 the government has changed its restrictions on LTVs and debt service ratios especially for investment properties and limited access to mortgages for those with poor credit scores.[156] In addition, limited competition among lenders, a high propensity for borrowers to pay down their mortgages as early as possible and the introduction of a very high foreign-buyer tax in 2016 in British Columbia, and, a year later, in Toronto make it further difficult to draw broad lessons from the Canadian experience of LTV measures.[157] These measures appear to have been effective for owner-occupied properties while "the growth of

152 Stijn Claessens, 'An overview of macroprudential policy tools', (2014), IMF Working Paper, WP/14/214, 17.

153 Supra, note 131, (Darbar and Wu), 15–16.

154 Lawrence Schembri, 'Housing finance in Canada: looking back to move forward', (November 2014) National Institute Economic Review, No. 230, 53.

155 Ibid., 48.

156 Jason Allen and others, 'The impact of macroprudential housing finance tools in Canada: 2005–10', (August 2016), Bank of Canada Staff Working Paper 2016-41, 1.

157 Ontario, Ministry of Finance, 'Fair Housing Plan: Non-Resident Speculation Tax, (16 December 2017).

residential investment recovered to levels above those before the first round of tightening…and that most effects have since dissipated".[158]

Both Korea and Hong Kong are included since they both adopted LTV and DTI limits following the Asian financial crisis in the 1990s and consequently have the longest history of the application of these policies and their effectiveness. I have included Sweden since it highlights the less than coordinated approach to macroprudential and monetary policies.[159] This chapter also considers Israel's macroprudential LTV policies since it highlights issues where LTV policies were challenged as part of the social and political process. New Zealand is included rather than Eire since the latter's LTV and LTI limits were introduced more recently in 2015 and are similar to those recently set by the Bank of England and are largely modelled on the New Zealand policies.[160]

3.10.2.1 Sweden

Swedish macroprudential policy is governed by the Swedish Council for Cooperation on Macroprudential Policy with joint representation by the Riksbank (the central bank) and the Finansinspektionen (the financial supervisory authority with the roles of promoting stability and efficiency in the financial system as well as ensuring consumer protection). The Council was concerned about increasing mortgage lending and especially the increase in new lending and higher LTVs.[161] Shortly afterwards, in 2013, the Council was replaced by the Financial Stability Council chaired by the Minister for Financial Markets with representatives from the Finansinspektionen, the Swedish National Debt Office and Sveriges Riksbank.[162] Macroprudential regulation is the responsibility of Finansinspektionen since it already undertakes microprudential regulation and it appeared convenient to have both areas covered by the same body. It is also possible that there was a political purpose in this arrangement, since Finansinspektionen is a government agency.

Nevertheless, the Riksbank, as an independent central bank, still issues its regular financial stability reports and, as mentioned earlier, has continued to express concern about the lack of clarity regarding who has responsibility for

158 Martin Kuncl, 'Assessment of the effects of macroprudential tightening in Canada', (August 2016), Bank of Canada Staff Analytical Note 2016–12, 5.

159 Wall Street Journal, 'Sweden plans tighter mortgage rules to tackle household debt – Swedish financial watchdog seeks to cool borrowing as interest rates remain low', (11 November 2014), "The central bank, the Riksbank, has long warned that Swedish private debt levels are rising too rapidly".

160 Irish Central Bank (Supervision and Enforcement) Act 2013 (Section 48) (Housing Loan Requirements) Regulations 2015 and 'Information note: Macro-prudential policy for residential mortgage lending'.

161 Council for Cooperation on Macroprudential Policy minutes, (1 October 2013).

162 Swedish Riksbanks website: The Council for Cooperation on Macroprudential Policy/Financial Stability Council (from 2013).

macroprudential regulation.[163] A LTV limited of 85% was introduced in 2010, but Finansinspektionen appears not to have the power to introduce a LTI restriction and Swedish households remains, paradoxically, one the highest savers and most indebted in Europe.[164] Finansinspektionen has also imposed requirements that all new mortgages with LTVs over 70% must be paid down to at least 50% of LTV at a rate of 2% each year.[165]

3.10.2.2 South Korea

Korea deregulated the financing of its housing market in the 1990s. Commercial banks were able to make mortgage loans and the Korean Housing Banks which had previously monopolised the mortgage market were privatised in 1997. Following the Asian financial crisis in the late 1990s, LTV limits were introduced in 2002 and DTI limits in 2005.[166] The Korean Financial Supervisory Service created a macroprudential supervision department to assess macroprudential risk which set LTV and DTI limits at different rates depending on where the mortgage properties were located, who the purchasers were, their age and marital status, etc.[167] Between their introduction and 2014, LTV and DTI have been adjusted some nine times with the LTV limits moving within a 40–70% range.[168] The picture is complicated by a number of government interventions, including taxation changes, financial support for both public and private home construction and government building of new houses and buying existing homes depending on market conditions and political expediency.[169] In addition, the Bank of Korea employs price-based tools (e.g. macroprudential stability levies) to promote financial stability.[170] However, the LTV and DTI restrictions seem to have had a number of unintended effects including, increases in non-bank mortgage lending, and a lengthening of the term of mortgages.[171]

163 Riksbanks, 'Financial Stability Report', (2015:2), 16–17. The report has also recommended changes to a variety of areas such as the level of mortgage interest allowed for tax deduction purposes and standardised affordability tests as part of the credit assessment by the lender, 20–21.

164 ESRB, 'Vulnerabilities in the EU residential real estate sector', (November 2016), 117–121.

165 Finansinspektionen, 'Amortisation requirement for new mortgages', (11 March 2015).

166 Deniz Igan and Heedon Kang, 'Do loan to value and debt to income limits work? Evidence from Korea', (2011) IMF Working Paper WP 11/297, 7.

167 Ibid., 24.

168 Choongsoo Kim, (Governor of the Bank of Korea), 'Macroprudential policies in Korea: key measures and experiences', (2014) *Banque de France Financial Stability Review*, No. 18, 125, www.banque-france.fr/fileadmin/user_upload/banque_de_france/publications/FSR18_Kim.pdf.

169 Supra, note 166, Igan and Kang, 7.

170 Supra, note 168, Kim C, 126.

171 Supra, note 168, Kim C, 126. In addition, Korea has its own form of rental market known as the "Chonsei system". Some 55% of homes are owner-occupied and over 20% of properties are rented on a conventional basis but over 22% nationally, rising to more than 33% in very high-value areas such a Gangnam in Seoul, are occupied using the Chonsei system. Under this

The results appear to demonstrate a reduction in housing transactions and a slowing in the growth of property prices in the months following an increased restriction in LTV and DTI limits as plans to buy a new home are postponed.[172] However, the main effect of these measures is to signal to market speculators reduced property price growth expectations.[173] This is particularly relevant since the growth in credit and property prices in Korea is blamed on in-flows of capital from outside the country and the macroprudential measures have reduced the attractiveness of Korea for these capital movements.[174]

3.10.2.3 Israel

Although Israel did not suffer a financial crisis in 2007/8, it has faced similar problems to other developed economies with low interest rates and rapidly rising house prices. Consequently, the central bank adopted a number of macroprudential policies including increasing the risk weights for loans secured on housing and higher capital requirements.[175] In addition, the Bank of Israel imposed LTV restriction in 2010. However, in the light of political pressure in 2012 the LTV limit was raised to 75% from 70%, for first time buyers and lowered to 50% for those buying a second home.[176] Stanley Fischer has said that the central bank was "subject to far more criticism" over its use of its LTV policies "than over [its] standard monetary policy measures".[177]

The LTV restrictions appeared to have worked for some six months following their introduction but house prices have continued to rise rapidly with none of the macroprudential measures being effective while interest rates were kept low for monetary policy purposes and capital was readily available.[178] Israel is an

arrangement between 50% and 90% of the value of the property is deposited with the owner by the occupier for two to three years. The owner then earns interest on this sum. At the end of the agreed period the deposit is returned. There has been a public sector version of the system since 2011. Many of the owners are themselves tenants who own a number of Chonsei properties to supplement their income, Soosung Hwang, Sanha Noh and Jinho Shin, 'The price impact of deposit in residential lease contracts: the collapse of Chonsei system in Korea', (2015), this paper argues that the system is in decline due to the prevalence of low interest rates.

172 Supra, note 166, Igan and Kang, 4.

173 Supra, note 166, (Igan and Kang), 14.

174 Valentina Bruno and Hyun Song Shin, 'Assessing macroprudential policies: the case of South Korea', (2014) *Scandinavian Journal of Economics*, Vol. 116, No. 1, 128, 129–131.

175 Stanley Fischer, 'Macroprudential policy in action: Israel' in George Akerlof, Olivier Blanchard, David Romer and Joseph Stiglitz (eds), *What have we learned? Macroprudential policy after the crisis* (MIT Press, Cambridge, Massachusetts, 2014), 93.

176 Ibid., 94. See also BBVA Research, 'Macroprudential measures on mortgage lending: country experiences', (2014) *Economic Analysis*, www.bbvaresearch.com/en/publicaciones/financial-systems-and-regulation-watch-macroprudential-measures-on-mortgage-lending-country-experiences/.

177 Supra, note 175, (Fischer), 95.

178 IMF Country Report No. 14/48 on Israel, 12. See also the Bank of Israel Financial Stability Report 2015, 4–5.

example of the difficulties of using macroprudential tools in the face of strong monetary policy headwinds and where LTV policies are challenged as part of the social and political process.

3.10.2.4 Hong Kong

Even before the Asian economic crisis in the 1990s, Hong Kong had used macroprudential measures to restrain credit growth and the "build-up in leverage".[179] During the Asian financial crisis Hong Kong house prices fell by 66% but defaults were low and there was no banking crisis.[180] Hong Kong has had LTV limits since the 1990s due to the importance of residential mortgages in the economy and the limits placed on its monetary policy as a result of the Hong Kong dollar's peg to the US currency. Residential property lending is a significant part of bank lending in Hong Kong. In 1991 LTVs were capped at 70%, and in 1996 this was restricted to 60% for what were deemed "luxury properties".[181] Over the years the LTV limits have moved up and down and a debt-service ratio was introduced in 1997 and by 2010 there was a complex LTV "ladder" depending on the value of the property being financed with mandatory credit insurance for loans with high LTVs.[182] Although LTV restrictions have dampened the growth rate of housing market activities and household leverage, it has had little effect on property price growth.[183]

It is worth noting that in 2010 the Hong Kong government introduced a special stamp duty of up to 15% on properties sold within two years of purchase. This was increased to 20% in 2012 for those resold within three years. In 2013 this tax was doubled for all property sales except to local first-time buyers.[184] This tax appears to have reduced both demand and, consequently, house price growth.[185] It may be that macroprudential policy needs both quantitative controls, such as LTV limits, as well as fiscal measures to be fully effective. This reinforces the view that LTV measures need to be coordinated with other macroprudential and fiscal actions.[186]

179 Dong He, 'Hong Kong's approach to financial stability', (2013) *International Journal of Central Banking*, Vol. 9, No. 1, 299, 301.

180 Ibid., Dong He, 302.

181 Supra, note 176, (BBVA Research), 16–17.

182 Ibid., 17.

183 Supra, note 179, (Dong He), 310.

184 Dong He, 'The effects of macroprudential policies on housing market risks: evidence from Hong Kong', (2014), *Banque de France Financial Stability Review*, No. 18, 107, www.banque-france.fr/fileadmin/user_upload/banque_de_france/publications/FSR18_DONG-HE.pdf.

185 Ibid., Dong He (2014), 107.

186 Eric Wong and others, 'Loan-to-value ratio as a macroprudential tool Hong Kong's experience and cross-country evidence', (2011), Hong Kong Monetary Authority Working Paper No. 01/2011, 22.

3.10.2.5 New Zealand

New Zealand first used LTV limits in 2013, setting a series of "speed limits" on high LTV lending requiring that no more than 10% of a bank's new mortgage lending could be with LTVs in excess of 80%.[187] There are a number of exemptions including high LTV loan refinancing and home-movers. In addition, capital requirements for residential mortgage loans were increased in September 2013.[188] The New Zealand central bank is concerned about "leakages" since it only regulates banks and is not responsible for other financial sectors and cannot influence funds coming in from overseas.[189] The latter is an important factor since the Reserve Bank wishes to avoid the New Zealand Dollar continuing to rise in value as more investments are attracted to the country.[190]

The approaches taken by these different jurisdictions illustrate the difficulties in using LTV and DTI measures for macroprudential policy objectives and the problems in attempting to draw generally applicable lessons for use in other countries. The issues are exacerbated by the variety of policymaking and implementing structures adopted by various jurisdictions.

3.11 Conclusions

As discussed, macroprudential policy is in the process of development and it operates in an area of considerable complexity combining the effects of microprudential regulation, fiscal measures and monetary policy. Moreover, while some macroprudential tools such as LTV and DTI limits are superficially attractive, in practice their robust use may generate questions about the legitimacy of these tools and the institutions employing them. It is possible that western style democracies may not be able to use them to full effect. Moreover, it is evident from other jurisdictions that LTV and DTI limits may simply not work in the face of market forces, political interference and the lack of any constituency willing to support such measures.

In summary, macroprudential policy needs to be subject to realistic expectations with limited "role responsibility creep" and the policymakers need to establish the public and political legitimacy of their use. Macroprudential policy must be coordinated with monetary and fiscal policy and with those undertaking similar responsibilities in other jurisdictions. Finally, it should not neglect the importance of conduct of business regulation in restricting the growth of credit in the economy. This is the subject of the next two chapters.

187 Lamorna Rogers, 'An A to Z of LTV ratio restrictions', (2014) Reserve Bank of New Zealand: Bulletin, Vol. 77, No. 1, 1.

188 Ibid., 6–7.

189 Ashley Dunstan, 'The interaction between monetary and macroprudential policy', (June 2014) *Reserve Bank of New Zealand Bulletin*, Vol. 77, No. 2, 19–20, expresses the view that LTV restrictions can only be temporary otherwise the incentives for "leakage" increase.

190 'The introduction of macro-prudential policy', speech by Graeme Wheeler, Governor of the Reserve Bank of New Zealand, to Otago University, Dunedin, 20 August 2013.

4 US mortgage conduct of business regulatory policy

As part of the financial reforms (known as the 'Dodd-Frank Act') following the recent financial crisis the US government set up the Consumer Financial Protection Bureau (CFPB). This is a marked change since regulation in this area was previously spread across a number of Federal regulators and was also the responsibility of individual states. The lax provision of credit for house purchases was at the heart of the debacle, and the aim was to have a single powerful regulator to supervise this area.

The CFPB has to work closely with individual state regulators who are responsible for credit intermediaries. This may be an area of both strength and weakness in the system. Much depends on how each state approaches this role, but at the same time it provides an opportunity to experiment and to learn from the best. The financial crisis was not uniform in its causes across the US, and the approach to setting policies and regulating needs to be fitted to the situation of each state working with Federal policymakers.

Through a process of historic 'path-dependency', the CFPB largely sees the provision of clear information to borrowers as central to protecting consumers ('Know before you owe'). However, at the same time the Bureau and Congress developed the concept of the 'Qualified Mortgage' which, on a risk-adjusted basis, may protect lenders from both regulatory sanction and private litigation, and, at the same time, provide a level of balanced protection to borrowers. This approach is innovative and may be a way forward for other jurisdictions.

Finally, the regulation of mortgages is highly politicised in the US, and many Republicans would like to see the CFPB abolished. As a consequence, President Trump has taken steps to reduce the effectiveness of the Bureau.

4.1 Introduction

As is well known, the US experienced a housing price boom fuelled by mortgage credit in the period leading up to the recent financial crisis. It is important to note that while there are substantial differences between the housing and mortgage markets in the US and other countries, there may well be lessons which each jurisdiction can learn from each other. This is the subject of this chapter and Chapter 7.

Chapter 2 on macroprudential regulation considered the wide range of reasons given for the 2007/8 financial crisis. This chapter focuses on the interaction between mortgage lender, intermediaries and their customers and Federal legislation and regulations used to protect borrowers both before and after the crisis. Attributing causation is difficult. Some consider that the US Federal government's intervention in the housing market was a substantial reason for the financial crisis, and this issue is considered in more detail in Chapter 7. It is unlikely that there was a single cause and it is more likely that there were a range of factors at work. The problems were compounded by poor financial supervision at all levels. This includes the unexplored aspects of the organisational structural and cultural reasons for the crisis. These issues apply to both the regulated businesses and the regulators. They can be grouped into four broad but overlapping areas: the desire of individuals and organisational departments to self-restrict their areas of responsibility to those aspects with which they feel comfortable and resourced to address; a short organisational "attention span" due to changes in personnel, re-assessed priorities, new initiatives, etc.; a reluctance to use all the powers and regulatory "tools" available and, often coupled with the latter, a "Hamlet-like" level of indecision and a hope that the problem will resolve itself.[1]

Nevertheless, at the heart of the crisis was the supply of credit which drove up property prices, and these increased values, in turn, provided more security for more lending.[2] Coupled with this is the view that inadequate underwriting by lenders together with "predatory lending" – where borrowers were enticed into taking out loans beyond their ability to repay – was fundamental to the creation of the housing credit crisis.[3] As discussed later in this chapter, the US Federal response was to create the Consumer Financial Protection Bureau. However, the actual institution and the concepts behind this polarised the US government with, for example, Senator Elizabeth Warren stating that

> thanks to the consumer agency's [Consumer Financial Protection Bureau (CFPB)] new rules, families will be safer...our whole economy will be safer...and the rules will reshape the mortgage market for the better. They will give people a better chance to buy homes and a better chance to keep

1 These factors will continue to exist, to a greater or lesser extent, no matter what systems of regulation and supervision operate. Aspects of these issues have been considered looking at organisation structure and management systems and compliance (e.g. Malloy, 'Regulation, compliance and the firm'), Chapter 2, n. 52, 451, (where the individual in the organisation can avoid making a decision to act by "redefining the situation so as to ensure that the norm is not activated, a cognitive process known as defensive denial").

2 Atif Mian and Amir Sufi, 'The consequences of mortgage credit expansion: evidence from the U.S. mortgage default crisis', (November 2009) *Quarterly Journal of Economics*, Vol. 122, No. 4, 1449–1496.

3 Rajdeep Sengupta, 'Alt-A: the forgotten segment of the mortgage market', (January/February 2010) *Federal Reserve Bank of St. Louis Review*, Vol. 92, No. 1, 55–71, 58.

those homes...These rules will help markets work better, and they will reduce the risk that the economy will crash again.[4]

Conversely, many Republicans want to abolish the CFPB: "the legislation that Rep. Ratcliffe and I are introducing today gives Congress the opportunity to free consumers and small businesses from the CFPB's regulatory blockades and financial activism, which stunt economic growth".[5] This bifurcation of views continues to influence much of the debate in the US.

There was also a significant element of speculative property buying in a number of key "housing bubble" states.[6] Shiller, echoing Minsky and Kindleberger considers that these types of bubbles are brought about by psychological factors driven by "herd" investing and leverage.[7] It is these aspects which are central to this chapter with a focus on the regulation of the interaction between borrowers, lenders and intermediaries as the development of mortgage conduct of business regulation in the US seeks to balance protecting consumers from overborrowing while maintaining access to the aspiration of homeownership.

As a consequence of the financial crisis and the need to reform the conduct of financial service providers towards consumers, the Dodd-Frank Act established the new CFPB.[8] This marked a significant change in US Federal regulation.[9] Previously, how lenders and intermediaries conduct their business with borrowers was largely a matter for individual states. There were Federal requirements governing the disclosure of information to borrowers but it was not clear which Federal agency supervised this aspect of regulation. This all changed when the CFPB started work. The role of the CFPB is considered further in this chapter. More recently, the administration of President Trump has sought to undermine the role and the effectiveness of the CFPB and aspects of these changes are considered later in this chapter.

In particular, there are five key themes to this chapter. First, it is necessary to understand the political and socio-economic context and the importance of homeownership as part of the "American Dream" and the bi-partisan political

4 Elizabeth Warren, US Senator for Massachusetts web-site, 'Sen. Warren praises new CFPB mortgage rules that make families, economy safer', (7 January 2014), www.warren.senate.gov/?p=press_release&id=309, (accessed 5 July 2019).

5 Ted Cruz, US Senator for Texas web-site, 'Sen. Cruz, Rep. Ratcliffe introduce legislation to abolish the CFPB', (14 February 2017), www.cruz.senate.gov/?p=press_release&id=3004, (accessed 5 July 2019).

6 Andrew Haughwout, Donhoon Lee, Joseph Tracy and Wilbert van der Klaauw, 'Real estate investors, the leverage cycle and the housing market crisis', (September 2011) Federal Reserve Bank of New York Staff Report No. 514, 1, 40.

7 Robert Shiller, *Irrational exuberance*, (2nd ed., Princeton University Press, Princeton, New Jersey, 2005), 149–153.

8 The Act's full title is: 'Dodd-Frank Wall Street Reform and Consumer Protection Act' (124 STAT. 1376 Public Law 111–203—July 21, 2010, H.R. 4173).

9 Timothy Geithner, *Stress test*, (Random House Business Books, New York, 2014), 427. The former US Treasury Secretary describes the establishment of the CFPB as "the most important new US regulatory body since the Environmental Protection Agency".

support this concept enjoyed. This theme is central to understanding the US approach to consumer mortgage protection where, as mentioned, the government has intervened to continue to provide access to credit to finance home loans and also set up the CFPB, as a powerful regulator, to protect borrowers. As discussed later the UK, culturally, shares aspects of this belief in the importance of homeownership. The cultural, political and socio-economic elements influencing popular aspirations towards owning a place of ones' own and how this is financed have a strong influence on both the regulatory approach and government policy. These aspects are considered in Chapter 7 on the role of the US Federal government and possible lessons from government interaction in the housing and mortgage markets and their regulation.

Second, in the US the quality of mortgage lending in the period leading up to the start of the financial crisis was uneven. This has implications for regulatory policy. Consequently, this chapter seeks to identify and consider what the problems areas were. This includes understanding who the problematic borrowers were and, specifically which mortgage products caused the most damage and the role of the intermediaries who often promoted these types of loans. This chapter then examines the regulatory changes both in terms of structure and content and how these changes have been implemented. This form of analysis will help determine whether the current solutions will work and what other steps can be taken.

Third, as a centralised Federal organisation the CFPB is too remote from the day-to-day operations of the mortgage market in such a large and diverse nation. It needs to persuade individual states to act, to set best practice and to monitor and report on what is happening and to act as a conduit to share both best practice and information on what is happening locally. It will also give individual states opportunities to experiment to find what works best and to avoid some attempt at operating a centralised "command and control" system.

Fourth, this chapter questions the extent to which reliance can be placed on providing customers with extensive disclosure material. Finally, this chapter considers the 'Qualified Mortgage' as a regulatory concept and whether it may be beneficial to adopt it in the UK.

4.2 The context: borrowers, lenders and products sold

It is important to consider what types of borrowers existed in the lead up to the housing boom in the late 1990s and early in the 2000s and their interaction with the lenders. This analysis will assist in determining whether the conduct of business actions taken after the crisis are likely to be effective. US homeownership rates were around 44% in 1935 (the end of the Great Depression).[10] They then rose steadily until reaching a plateau in 1970 at 64% before sharply rising again from 1997 to 69% just before the financial crisis.[11] The increase in

10 Carlos Garriga, William T. Gavin, and Don Schlagenhauf, 'Recent trends in homeownership', (September/October 2006) *Federal Reserve Bank of St. Louis Review*, Vol. 88, No. 5, 397–411, 398.

11 Ibid., (Garriga), 398.

homeownership was largest among "Hispanic, Black and Asian groups (16–17%) compared with an 8.6% increase for non-Hispanic Whites".[12] The stock of mortgages "lent by US banks to US households went from 15% of GDP in the 1970s to 96% in the 2000s. In the 1970s, one in ten Dollars lent out by US banks was towards a mortgage; but in the 2000s, this was one in three".[13]

Problems became evident in 2006. In 2005 only just over 1% of mortgages were classified as in default within their first two years of inception. This figure doubled in the period 2006–2008.[14] For sub-prime loans the default figures increased from 10% in 2006 to 40% in 2010.[15] The Triennial Survey of Consumer Finances found homeownership "rose from 63.9% in 1992 to 69% in 2004 and the share of households with a mortgage rose from 38.4% to 45%".[16] In 1998, almost 100% of mortgages were written as 30 year fixed rate loans.[17] This percentage had fallen to 35% by 2004 and did not rise much above 40% by 2007.[18] By the end of 2009, 40% of the subprime adjustable rate mortgages (ARM) policies were seriously delinquent.[19] This percentage rose to 53% for ARMs sold between 2005 and 2007 compared with 48% for fixed rate mortgages sold during the same period.[20] The delinquency rate for prime ARMs rose from "0.6% in 2005 to 18% by the end of 2009".[21] ARMs "by the end of 2007 represent 22% of outstanding mortgages but 62% of...foreclosures".[22] By "mid-June 2010 4.6% (about 2.2 million properties) were in foreclosure and another 4.8% (about 2.3 million) were 90 days past due". [23] Further, there is evidence that the increase in problem mortgages was skewed towards those with "cognitive limitations" and that "poor numerical ability correlates with missed payments and defaults".[24]

12 Ibid., (Garriga), 400.

13 Dirk Bezemer, 'Schumpeter might be right again: the functional differentiation of credit', (November 2014), *Journal of Evolutionary Economics*, Vol. 24, No. 5, 935–950.

14 CFPB, 12 CFR Parts 1024 and 1026, RIN 3170-AA19, 12–13.

15 Ibid., (CFPB, 12 CFR), 13, There are a variety of definition of "sub-prime" all of which attempt to capture the increased riskiness of the borrower. The measures include credit scores, high LTV and high interest rate loans, see Oren Bar-Gill, 'The law, economics and psychology of sub-prime mortgage contracts', (2009) *Cornell Law Review* Vol. 94, 1073–1151, 1087–1088.

16 Daniel Bergstresser and John Beshears, 'Who selected adjustable-rate mortgages? Evidence from the 1989–2007 Surveys of Consumer Finances', (2010), Harvard Business School, Working Paper 10 083, 2.

17 Supra, note 3, (Sengupta), 58.

18 Supra, note 3, (Sengupta), Table 1, 58.

19 The issue of adjustable rate mortgages is considered in more detail later in this chapter.

20 , Chapter 2, n. 53, (Bubb and Krishnamurthy, 'Regulating against bubbles'), 1606.

21 Supra note 3, (Sengupta) Table 1, 58.

22 Supra, note 16, (Bergstresser and Beshears), 6.

23 John Campbell and others, 'Consumer finance policy: Implementing two-tier mortgage regulation', (December 2010), Russell Sage Foundation, 1.

24 Supra note 16, (Bergstresser and Beshears), quoting research by Gerardi, Goette and Meier in 2009 on New England subprime mortgages, 5–6 (Kristopher Gerardi, Lorenz Goette, and Stephan Meier, 'Financial literacy and subprime mortgage delinquency: evidence from a survey matched to administrative data', (2010) Federal Reserve Bank of Atlanta, Working Paper 2010-10).

This data paints a picture of a rapid rise in homeownership starting in the late 1990s and accelerating in the final years leading up to the collapse in 2006/7. This rise was largest in the first-time buyer, minority and single-parent demographic groups.

It is worth noting that ARMs are not inherently problematic. They are a standard type of mortgage sold in the UK, Australia, Canada, etc.[25] The issue appears to be that ARMs were sold with low initial premium periods, which low-income borrowers were able to afford with a significant increase in the monthly repayment some years later. The position is further clouded by the development of the "Alternative-A" ("Alt-A") mortgage market. Traditionally those whose credit was impaired due to, for example, past unpaid debts borrowed in the sub-prime mortgage market. Alt-A mortgage products were normally used by those with good credit scores who were unwilling or unable to provide supporting documentation for their income declaration as part of the mortgage underwriting process. These individuals were normally self-employed and were often paid periodically in cash. Between 2001 and 2003 subprime mortgage origination grew by 95%.[26] The "comparable growth rates between 2003 and 2006 for the subprime and Alt-A segments were 94% and 340%, respectively".[27] Both sub-prime and Alt-A mortgages experienced very high default rates usually within the first twenty-four months after origination with significantly worse outcomes for those written after 2003.[28] Nevertheless, significant losses still came from the traditional fixed rate market.[29]

It is clear that the quality of lender underwriting declined in the early 2000s and more sharply after 2003 in all sectors. However, prospective borrowers' initial contacts were with intermediaries and not the lenders and many of the issues relate to this interaction.[30] By 2005, some 60% of sub-prime loans were

25 Emanuel Moench, James Vickery and Diego Aragon, 'Why is the market share of adjustable-rate mortgages so low?', (2010), *Current Issues in Economics and Finance*, Vol. 16, No. 8, www.newyorkfed.org/medialibrary/media/research/current_issues/ci16-8.pdf.

26 Supra, note 3, (Sengupta), 56.

27 Supra, note 3, (Sengupta), 56.

28 Supra note 3, (Sengupta), 65.

29 Michael Lea and Anthony Sanders, 'Government policy and the fixed-rate mortgage', (2011), *Annual Review of Financial Economics*, Vol. 3, 223–234, 230, "The 30-year fixed-rate mortgage remains the fool's gold standard for mortgages throughout the United States, offering superior stability for some homeowners and potential catastrophe for U.S. and global financial systems".

30 It is also worth noting that many of the mortgage "originators" were both mortgage brokers and lenders and often had parent companies that held mortgage securitisations. These groups in effect were "eating their own cooking" (Bubb and Krishnamurthy), Chapter 2, no. 53. For example, the largest mortgage originators besides New Century were Ameriquest (a savings and loan association) part owned from 1999 by Washington Mutual and closed in 2007, First Franklin bought by Merrill Lynch in December 2006 and wound-down in 2008; WMC bought by GE Money in 2004 and closed in 2007; Fremont Investment and Loans (a savings and loan association) closed when its parent company filed for bankruptcy in 2008; BNC bought by

originated by mortgage brokers.[31] Mortgage brokers have been described as being the "engines of the sub-prime market".[32] They were remunerated by lenders and were regulated, if at all, at the State level. For example, New Century Financial Corporation (New Century) had "more than 7,100 employees and 222 sales offices nationwide, and was one of the largest subprime mortgage originators in the United States".[33]

> In 1996, the company originated over $350 million in loans. In 1997, New Century went public and was listed on NASDAQ. In 2001, the company's subprime loan origination volume exceeded $6 billion. Volume continued to grow rapidly, and volume increased tenfold to over $60 billion in 2006.[34]

In April 2007, the company filed for Chapter 11 protection. Between 1997 and 2005, some 30–40% of all its loan applications were made with no documents to support the mortgage applicants' income declaration (with a figure of 42% in 2004: the high point of this practice).[35] For example, of the loans originated by New Century in 2005, 7% were in default within 15 months.[36] It is difficult to be precise about who was most at fault in writing such poor quality business. There was a congruence of interests: many borrowers, who would not normally have been able to do so, were able to buy and keep their homes, others were able to borrow against the equity in their properties to fund other expenses or to speculate in the housing market, brokers were remunerated by lenders dependent on the volume and profitability of the mortgages they originated and lenders used cheap funds to produce high returns.

Lehman Brothers in 2003 and closed in 2007; Countrywide Financial which demerged its savings and loan operation: IndyMac Bank in 1997, was sold in 2008 to Bank of America; Aegis owned by Cerebus Capital, a private equity firm filed for bankruptcy in 2007, and Option One, owned by H&R Block, a tax planning business, closed in 2009. In addition, a number of major banks had their own mortgage originators trading under their parents' names, for example, HSBC (formerly HFC), CitiMortgages, Wells Fargo and GMAC Residential Funding. All these businesses were either closed or filed for bankruptcy between 2007 and 2009, (Bubb and Krishnamurthy), and The Centre for Public Integrity website, www.publicintegrity.org (accessed 14 August 2019).

31 Mortgage brokers accounted for 59.3% of subprime originations in 2005. 'Brokers flex their muscle in 2005, powering record subprime year, inside B&C lending', (March 2006) reported in Ellen Schloemer and others, 'Losing ground: foreclosures in the subprime market and their cost to homeowners', (December 2006), Center for Responsible Lending.

32 Mark Fox and David Lane, 'Lessons from the US subprime mortgage crisis', (2008) *Journal of International Banking Law and Regulation*, 449.

33 Antje Berndt, Burton Hollifield and Patrik Sandas, 'The role of mortgage brokers in the subprime crisis', (2009), NBER Working Paper 16175, 5.

34 Ibid., (Berndt), 6.

35 Ibid., (Berndt), 33.

36 Ibid., (Berndt), 39.

The role of mortgage brokers has largely been overlooked. It is clear that brokers are "salesmen".[37] Many of the problems could have been prevented if adequate conduct of business regulations, backed by sound supervision, had been in place. This chapter will return to this aspect of the broad theme and how intermediaries should be regulated and supervised. After the crisis, as mentioned above, many borrowers, but not all, were evicted and the business of both lenders and brokers collapsed. The issues, as mentioned earlier, appear to be have been exacerbated by property speculation and the picture is not complete until this aspect is also considered.

4.3 "Bubble states" and investor borrowers

The role of four US "housing bubble" states and the rise of house-buying investors appears to be a little explored aspect to the recent financial crisis. The data indicates that in four US states (Arizona, California, Florida and Nevada) house prices doubled between 2000 and 2006 with most of the increase dating from 2004 and that this was significantly higher than in the rest of the country.[38] Most of this activity in these housing markets was generated by housing investors owning two or more properties and that these individuals were major drivers of growth in non-prime securitised mortgages.[39] The patterns of trading indicate that these investors were a mixture of those interested in buy-to-let operations and those looking for a quick resale of the properties into a rapidly rising market.[40] Some 25% of the Alt-A market was used to finance these types of investments.[41] The implications are that these borrowers would seek any finance they could and were largely impervious to interest rates and costs since they did not expect to hold the property for long. Again this aspect has implications for regulation.

4.4 The legislative approach: overview

As mentioned earlier, at the heart of the crisis there was poor mortgage underwriting. The common confusion between mortgage underwriting and mortgage affordability is addressed in Chapter 5. In the US these separate issues were conflated in two broad changes to consumer financial protection following the financial crisis. The first was to strengthen existing legislation and, the second, as mentioned earlier, was to adopt a new approach to consumer protection with the creation of the CFPB and the passage of the Wall Street Reform and Consumer

37 Susan Woodward and Robert Hall, 'Diagnosing consumer confusion and sub-optimal shopping effort: theory and mortgage-market evidence', (December 2012) The American Economic Review, 4.

38 Supra, note 6, (Haughwout and others), 1, 40.

39 Supra, note 6, (Haughwout and others), 25.

40 Supra, note 6, (Haughwout and others), 9–11.

41 Supra, note 15, (Bar-Gill), 1112.

Protection Act 2010 ("Dodd-Frank").[42] This Act also amended the Truth in Lending Act 1968 (TILA), covering disclosure of information on mortgage costs for customers and the Real Estate Procedure Settlement Act 1974 (REPSA) covered other aspects of disclosure and which prohibited undisclosed payments between intermediaries and lenders as well as misleading loan advertisements.[43]

The CFPB is responsible for most rule-making in these areas of legislation. For example, loan applications made after August 2015 are now subject to the "TILA-RESPA Integrated Disclosure Rule" or "TRID".[44] The CFPB was also given the role of enforcing these pieces of legislation. How this has been implemented in the "Know before you owe" initiative is discussed in more detail later. Of particular relevance is that Dodd-Frank now requires lenders to "make a reasonable and good faith determination, based on verified and documented information, that the consumer will have a reasonable ability to repay the loan".[45] There are also new requirements regarding the provision of information to consumers to improve their understanding of mortgage transactions and this aspect will be considered later in this chapter.[46]

4.4.1 Summary of the revised regulations

Dodd-Frank makes the CFPB responsible for setting detailed rules and enforcing a range of legislation including TILA, RESPA, the Equal Credit Opportunity Act (ECOA) 1974 (banning lenders discrimination on grounds of race, gender, etc.), Home Mortgage Disclosure Act ("HMDA") 1975 (requiring lenders to provide information, which is made public, on its lending practices to the CFPB).[47] Previously it was unclear which Federal agencies had responsibilities for enforcing these pieces of legislation.[48] These are now all the responsibility of the CFPB.

42 Title X. The CFPB was set up under the Consumer Financial Protection Act (CFPA) passed under the Dodd-Frank "umbrella" legislation.

43 Truth in Lending Act 1968 (TILA), 82 STAT. 146, Public Law 90-32. The regulations implementing the statute, known as "Regulation Z", are codified at 12 Code of Federal Regulations 226. Real Estate Procedure Settlement Act 1974 (REPSA) is codified 12 U.S.C. §§ 2601–2617.

44 TILA-RESPA Integrated Disclosure Rule: Guide to the Loan Estimate and Closing Disclosure forms (January 2015). As the name implies these rules combine the disclosure requirements set out in a number of earlier consumer protection regulations.

45 s1411 Dodd-Frank, codified as 15 U.S.C. 1639c.

46 CFPB, 'Final rule on simplified and improved mortgage disclosures', (November 2013) s1032f of Dodd-Frank codified as 12 USC 5532(f).

47 Equal Credit Opportunity Act (ECOA) 1974, 15 U.S.C. § 1691 and Home Mortgage Disclosure Act ("HMDA") 1975, 89 STAT. 1124 Public Law 94-200.

48 Leonard Kennedy, Patricia McCoy and Ethan Bernstein, 'The Consumer Financial Protection Bureau: financial regulation for the twenty-first century', (2012) *Cornell Law Review*, Vol. 97, 1141.

The CFPB also has responsibility for the SAFE Mortgage Licensing Act.[49] The latter required the Office of the Comptroller of the Currency, the Board of Governors of the Federal Reserve Board, the Federal Deposit Insurance Corporation, the former Office of Thrift Supervision, the National Credit Union Administration, and the Farm Credit Administration (collectively, the Agencies), to jointly develop and maintain a Federal registration system ("Federal Registry") for individual employees of Agency-regulated institutions who engage in the business of residential mortgage loan origination. Subsequently, the Federal Registry was established and has been operational since January 2011. Dodd-Frank Act transferred the authority to develop and maintain the Federal Registry from the Agencies to the CFPB. The SAFE Act statute requires individual mortgage loan originators employed by "Agency-regulated" institutions to be registered with the Nationwide Mortgage Licensing System and Registry (Federal Registry), a database established previously by the Conference of State Bank Supervisors (CSBS) and the American Association of Residential Mortgage Regulators to support the licensing of mortgage loan originators by the states.[50]

The CFPB has based its consumer protection strategy on improving the disclosure of information to consumers prior to them taking out a new loan. The disclosure rules existed before the financial crisis. They were augmented by the Federal Reserve in 2008 and amended by the Dodd-Frank legislation.[51] Previously there were two different disclosure documents required by two different pieces of legislation. As mentioned earlier, Dodd-Frank empowers the CFPB to combine these into a new document. As part of a "Know before you owe" initiative the CFPB consequently designed two new forms.[52] The first of these: "the Loan Estimate", provides information on the key features, costs, and risks of the mortgage. It must be provided to consumers within three business days after they submit a loan application. Second, "the Closing Disclosure" provides

49 The Secure and Fair Enforcement for Mortgage Licensing Act of 2008 (122 Stat. 2810 Public Law 110-289).

50 Bryce Gray, 'The Secure and Fair Enforcement for Mortgage Licensing Act of 2008', (2011) *Review of Banking and Financial Law*, Vol. 31, 51. The SAFE Act 2008 was enacted as part of the Housing and Economic Recovery Act 2008

> to set up a national licensing and registration system for individuals working as mortgage loan originators. Previously this was a matter for individual states. The aim of the legislation is to: facilitate responsible behavior in the subprime mortgage market place.

The responsibility for licensing is placed on each state. It exempts those employed by institutions supervised by a number of Federal bodies (e.g. Federal Reserve, FDIC, etc.). States had one year to pass their own legislation to implement the law. It specifies fingerprinting, examinations, training, background checks, etc. There are similar requirements imposed on Federal agencies for those they supervise.

51 Bureau of Consumer Financial Protection 12 CFR Part 1026 CFPB-2011-0008; CFPB-2012-0022] RIN 3170-AA17 Ability-to-Repay and Qualified Mortgage Standards under the Truth in Lending Act (Regulation Z) Bureau of Consumer Financial Protection 12 CFR Parts 1024 and 1026 [Docket No. CFPB-2012-0028] RIN 3170-AA19.

52 Supra, note 48, (Kennedy), 1161 and Michael Mierzewski and Jeremy Hochberg, 'CFPB proposes new mortgage disclosure rules', (2012) *Banking Law Journal*, Vol. 129, 809.

information on all the costs of the transaction. This document is five pages long combining two previous disclosure statements and came into effect from August 2015.[53] This latter document must be supplied at least three business days before the mortgage contract is completed. The CFPB has tested all these documents on nearly a thousand consumers to check that they are clear and understandable. However, this information is provided very late in the mortgage process. The effectiveness of information disclosure is considered later. The CFPB has also strengthened the mortgage affordability assessment.[54]

4.4.2 Ability to repay

This book does not attempt to describe, in detail, the full complexity of the ability to repay requirements set out in Dodd-Frank and subsequent legislation. The focus is to provide an analysis of the main themes in this important area.

In assessing a borrower's ability to repay the mortgage the CFPB expects the lender to consider a number of factors, including current or reasonably expected income, employment status, currently and proposed debt obligations, other obligations such as "alimony, and child support, the monthly debt-to-income ratio or residual income", and the consumer's credit history. This information must be verified with "reasonable third party sources".[55] It is worth noting that this calculation, unlike that operating in the UK, described in the next chapter, does not include a comprehensive affordability computation based on a detailed expenditure assessment. Nor does it include an affordability 'stress test' using regulatory mandated higher interest rate. However, the US version does include special calculations for variable-rate mortgages and "balloon and interest-only payments, or negative amortization".[56] The lenders' compliance with these regulations is now enforced by the CFPB.[57] This approach is not without controversy since there is a view that it may contravene the Fair Housing legislation since minorities seeking to become homeowners may have the most difficulty demonstrating their ability to repay.[58]

There are two arms to the CFPB's enforcement role and a third relating to contract enforceability. These are not mutually exclusive. The CFPB can take action itself or it can rely on private litigation based on CFPB regulations. The new private right of action provides special damages for borrowers who find

53 Mark Samra, 'New regulation under the CFPB', (2012) *Review of Banking and Financial Law*, Vol. 31, 545.

54 CFPB website, 'Summary of the ability to repay and qualified mortgage rule and the concurrent proposals', http://files.consumerfinance.gov/f/201301_cfpb_ability-to-repay-summary.pdf, (accessed 26 June 2019).

55 Ability-to-Repay and Qualified Mortgage Standards Under the Truth in Lending Act (Regulation Z), 78 Fed Reg. 6408 (30 January 2013) (codified at 12 C.F.R. pt. 1026).

56 Ibid., (12 C.F.R.), 1026.43f.

57 Truth in Lending (Regulation Z) 15 U.S.C, 1639c; 12 C.F.R., 1026.43.

58 Nicolas Cassidy, 'The Fair Housing Act, disparate Impact and the ability-to-repay: a compliance dilemma for mortgage lenders', (2013) *Review of Banking and Financial Law*, Vol. 32, 431.

themselves with an unaffordable loan.[59] For a three-year period following closing, borrowers may bring an action alleging the lender failed to make a reasonable good-faith determination of their ability to repay the loan. Failure to properly assess affordability can also be raised as a defence to foreclosure. There are limits set for calculating the damages.[60] The "mortgage originator" as well as the "creditor" can also be liable to pay these damages. The former includes individual loan officers and mortgage brokers, both individuals and businesses.[61] Consequently, there are now three separate but related risks faced by firms and individuals: direct action by a Federal agency, the threat of private litigation and the possibility that the lender may be unable to enforce a foreclosure. However, in parallel, lenders and intermediaries are encouraged to provide less risky, standardised "qualified mortgages".

4.5 The "qualified mortgage"

Dodd-Frank has created a "safe harbor and rebuttable presumption" for residential mortgages that satisfy a number of criteria described below.[62] These types of secured loan are termed "qualified mortgages" under the legislation.[63] If a mortgage satisfies the "qualified mortgage" requirements there is no need to carry out an ability to repay assessment. This element in the regulations is very different in concept to the approach taken in the UK. Dodd-Frank requires that a "qualified mortgage" meets certain requirements including no negative loan features (i.e. "negative amortization, interest-only payments, balloon payments, or terms exceeding thirty years"), no mortgages where fees paid by the consumer exceed 3% of the total loan amount and "no documentation" loans are excluded from being qualified mortgages.[64] Finally, "that monthly payments be calculated based on the highest payment that will apply in the first five years of the loan and that the consumer have a total debt-to-income ratio that is less than or equal to 43 percent".[65]

In conceptual terms, the "qualified mortgage" exemption establishes a level of legislative and regulatory risk tolerance. For example, UK conduct of business regulations place *sole* responsibility for ensuring that a prospective customer can

59 15 U.S.C., 1639b(d) and more generally 15 U.S.C. 1640.

60 Damages in these actions are limited to: "the greater of actual damages or an amount equal to three times the total amount of direct and indirect compensation or gain accruing to the mortgage originator in connection with the residential mortgage loan involved in the violation". (15 U.S.C., 1640(c). Action can also be brought by the State Attorney General, Germán Salazar, 'Mortgage lending', (2015) 51 March Arizona Attorney 18). Class action damages are available, as with other TILA actions, limited to the lesser of $1 million or one percent of the creditor's net-worth. (15 U.S.C. 1640(a)(2)(B)).

61 15 U.S.C. 1639b(d)(1).

62 15 U.S.C. 1412.

63 15 U.S.C. 1412(b)(2)(A).

64 Supra, note 55, 43 (e) (2).

65 Supra, note 55, 43 (e) (2).

afford the mortgage fully on the lender and the UK regulations do not contemplate any level of error tolerance. Under the UK's regulatory system, a lender is exposed to regulatory and compensatory action if a mortgage has been deemed to have been mis-sold. There is no equivalent "safe harbour" or public interest defence or safeguard. In contrast, the US regime accepts, for public policy reasons, linked to the benefits of homeownership that mortgage affordability assessments should reflect this objective. The regulators appear to have accepted that in due course some borrowers will not be able to service or repay these types of mortgage but that the public policy benefits of wider homeownership outweigh this risk. This properly leaves the issue of risk in the provision of housing finance and its relationship with consumer protection as a matter of public policy and not one solely determined by the regulator. This is important since if the issue is left to the regulator the latter, for understandable institutional and regulatory objective reasons, is likely to devise the most restrictive regulations. In practice, there are many more public policy issues at stake and these need to be considered as well. These include matters of housing policy and socio-economic factors. Consumer protection is an important element in these deliberations and needs to be considered and balanced against other objectives. Besides address regulatory issues the US legislation also looks at the important private law implications of the regulations.

In private law terms, the regulatory safe harbour for a "prime qualified mortgage" is almost invulnerable since the consumer will be deemed to satisfy the ability to repay test. For "sub-prime qualified mortgages" there will be a rebuttable presumption that the consumer has met the ability to repay requirements. The CFPB have interpreted this to mean that consumers would need to rebut this presumption for a "qualified mortgage" by showing that "at the time the loan was originated, the consumer's income and debt obligations left insufficient residual income or assets to meet living expenses".[66] Guidance accompanying the rule notes that

> the longer the period of time that the consumer has demonstrated actual ability to repay the loan by making timely payments, without modification...the less likely the consumer will be able to rebut the presumption based on insufficient residual income.[67]

However, the CFPB was concerned that the market for non-qualified mortgages might disappear, therefore it created a temporary rule permitting another category of qualified mortgages that do not need to meet all the qualified mortgage provisions and which will not require the ability to repay checks provided the various government agencies (e.g. U.S. Department of Housing and Urban Development, Department of Veterans Affairs) will purchase or insure these

66 Supra, note 55, 43b.
67 Supra, note 55, 43 (e) (I).

mortgages. The expectation is that these types of mortgages will be phased out within seven years, if not earlier.[68] It is important to note that the ability to repay assessment should not to be confused with a credit appraisal which is necessary for any lender and is required for prudential regulatory purposes. It is likely that lenders will in future concentrate on the provision of qualified mortgages as a means of defending themselves from future litigation.[69] It is also possible that the mortgage refinancing market may only accept "qualified mortgages" due to the risk of litigation and the difficulties in unwinding complex mortgage arrangements.[70]

In conclusion, the concept of the "qualified mortgage" is attractive in that it is "based on a vision of housing as a foundation for a stable life for homeowners and their families" and regulation consequently encourages lenders both to produce a simple, "vanilla" product and to avoid troublesome innovation.[71] The view is developing that while innovation may produce good mortgage products it is generally a malign influence.[72] Consequently, Dodd-Frank encourages lenders, by reducing the regulatory requirements for suitability and affordability assessments, to provide the standardised "qualified mortgage". This chimes in with the approach advocated by Barr and others mentioned earlier advocating a "standard mortgage product" which is "sticky".[73] Use of such products will prevent sub-prime lending and the use of noxious contractual clauses and charging arrangements. Nevertheless, much will depend on the effectiveness of the CFPB.

4.6 The CFPB in operation

Consumer financial protection existed before the CFPB regime but it was seen as severely "flawed with consumer protection as an 'orphan' mission that had no regulatory 'home' in any single agency and subordinated to regulatory concerns about [ensuring] bank profitability. [The regulators were seen as lacking] expertise in consumer financial issues" and with responsibility spread across many Federal and State agencies this "created regulatory arbitrage opportunities".[74]

68 Supra, note 54, CFPB summary 12 CFR.

69 Elizabeth McKeen and others, 'Mortgage underwriting: the qualified mortgage and the ability to repay', (2012) *Banking Law Journal*, Vol. 129, 829.

70 Stephen Ornstein, and others, 'CFPB ability to replay rule and qualified mortgage definition', (2012) *Consumer Finance Law Quarterly Report*, 66, 424.

71 Michael Barr and others, 'Behaviorally informed financial services regulation', (New American Foundation, October 2008).

72 Neil Seitz and others, 'Bank integrity: the case of subprime lending', (2009) *Company Lawyer*, Vol. 30, No. 9, 277.

73 Supra, note 71, (Barr), 8.

74 Adam Levitin, 'The Consumer Financial Protection Bureau: an introduction', (2013) *Boston University Review of Banking and Financial Law*, Vol. 32, 321, 329.

The call for a "Consumer Product Safety Commission" pre-dates the financial crisis and is, in part, based, on the work of Professor Elizabeth Warren.[75] The CFPB defines its two objectives as "helping consumer markets work" and "empowering consumers to take more control over their economic lives".[76] It mainly satisfies these objectives by a combination of consumer education and information provision and ensuring that regulated firms provide standard and consistent information to consumers. It also makes regulations and carries out regulated firm assessments. Additionally, the CFPB's also has enforcement powers but these are limited to banks with more than $10 billion in net assets, or only just over a hundred institutions out of over 16,000 banks.[77] Many of the latter are authorised by the states and not by Federal regulators. Consequently, the CFPB operates as a co-regulator with state authorities. Recognising this, their respective roles are governed by a memorandum of understanding (MoU) between the CFPB and the Conference of State Bank Supervisors.[78] While the issue of CFPB and State regulation of banks is covered by the MoU there is no equivalent arrangement for mortgage intermediaries. This issue is considered later in this chapter.

The regulator has already levied large fines using its enforcement powers in areas outside its mortgage remit.[79] John Coffee has considered the possible role of regulatory enforcement and private litigation in the development of the securities market in the US.[80] There is no equivalent research for mortgage markets. Paradoxically, prior to the establishment of the CFPB, there appears to have been a false confidence in the US mortgage market. The financial crisis changed this view and it now appears that regulatory action is very relevant and necessary to the mortgage industry where compliance is "dependent on supervisory

75 Elizabeth Warren, 'Unsafe at any rate', (Summer 2007), Democracy, Issue No. 5, "If it's good enough for microwaves, it's good enough for mortgages. Why we need a Financial Product Safety Commission". Her analysis paralleled that of earlier consumer product safety campaigners such as Ralph Nader and his criticism of the US car industry and the creation of the Consumer Product Safety Commission in 1972, Ralph Nader, *Unsafe at any speed*, (Knightsbridge Publishing, Mass, 1965).

76 CFPB website, 'Strategic Plan, 2013–2017', (April 2013), 5. The 2018–2022 Strategic Plan limits the Bureau to a more business orientated mission.

77 Supra, note 74, (Levitin), 338.

78 CFPB website, 'State supervisory coordination framework', (7 May 2013), http://files.consumerfinance.gov/f/201305_cfpb_state-supervisory-coordination-framework.pdf, (accessed 26 June 2019).

79 CFPB website, 'CFPB orders GE Capital to pay $225 million in consumer relief for deceptive and discriminatory credit card practices', www.consumerfinance.gov/about-us/newsroom/cfpb-orders-ge-capital-to-pay-225-million-in-consumer-relief-for-deceptive-and-discriminatory-credit-card-practices/, (accessed 26 June 2019).

80 John Coffee, 'Law and the market: the impact of enforcement', (2007), Columbia Law and Economics Working Paper No. 304. There is some correlation between enforcement and litigation on confidence in the market.

enforcement policy and record".[81] Any "knowing violation can result in a civil penalty of up to $1 million per day".[82] For example, in November 2013 Castle & Cooke Mortgages paid penalties and consumer restitution of over $13 million following CFPB action. The firm had broken CFPB regulations by paying "bonuses to loan officers who placed consumers with mortgage loans that had higher interest rates".[83]

Since these early days of the CFPB's existence there has been a change of administration heralding a significant different approach and style. To an extend this is evident in a report in 2019, in which the CFPB published the results of its assessment of the ability to repay and qualified mortgage requirements.[84] In a strangely worded section, the CFPB asserts that the introduction of the ability to repay rule did not result in "improvement in loan performance" due, in part, "to the fact that delinquency rates on mortgages originated in the years immediately prior to the effective date of the Rule were historically low, as credit was already tight at that time".[85] Further, there is no evidence that the start of the ability to repay rule caused any "significant break in the volume of mortgage applications or the average approval rate...This is attributable in part to the fact that, as noted, following the financial crisis and before the Rule took effect credit had tightened substantially".[86] The Bureau also "observed that most entities, depository or non-depository, examined by the Bureau are generally complying with the" the new rules.[87]

4.7 The effect of the 'qualified mortgages' and borrower ability to repay

There has been some back-testing of mortgages written in the run-up to the recent financial crisis to see what would have been the effect if they had been subject to the 'qualified mortgage' requirements. For example, home loans subject to qualified mortgage

> criteria have a lower probability of default than mortgages that do not meet the criteria. This pattern is most pronounced for loans originated near the peak of the housing bubble, when non-traditional mortgage products and

81 Vincent Di Lorenzo, 'Barriers to market discipline: a comparative study of mortgage market reforms', (2012), *Arizona Journal of International and Comparative Law*, Vol. 29, 517, 552.

82 Discussed in Laureen Galeoto and others, 'The Consumer Financial Protection Bureau: the new sheriff in town', (2012) *Banking Law Journal*, Vol. 129, 702.

83 CFPB website press release, 'CFPB Takes Action Against Castle & Cooke For Steering Consumers Into Costlier Mortgages', (7 November 2013), www.consumerfinance.gov/newsroom/cfpb-takes-action-against-castle-cooke-for-steering-consumers-into-costlier-mortgages/, (accessed 26 June 2019).

84 CFPB, 'Ability-to-Repay and Qualified Mortgage Rule Assessment Report', (January 2019).

85 Ibid., (CFPB Assessment report), 9–10.

86 Ibid., (CFPB Assessment report), 10.

87 Ibid., (CFPB Assessment report), 80.

> lax underwriting proliferated. For example, of loans originated from 2005 to 2008, 23 percent of those that met the [qualified mortgage] criteria experienced a spell of 90-day or more delinquency or a foreclosure by the end of 2012, compared with 44 percent of loans that did not meet the [qualified mortgage] criteria.[88]

In addition, a number of states have operated regulations that restrict access to non-standard mortgage terms (e.g. balloon payments, etc.). The effects of these laws have been studied and provide a form of control experiment on the effectiveness of qualified mortgage requirements. For example, at study considered the effect of the Office of the Comptroller of the Currency intervention in 2004 which over-rode ('pre-empted') state regulations which restricted non-standard mortgage terms.[89] This research found that in these 'pre-empted' states 'lenders increased their origination of loans with risky characteristics' and an increase default risk for certain types of securitised mortgages.[90]

By way of example, between 1999 and 2000 North Carolina's Predatory Lending Law ('NCPLA') came into force.[91] This prohibited certain forms of lending including lending deemed 'high cost', negative amortisation, the practice of repeatedly refinancing an existing home loan, etc.[92] The result was a pronounced fall in subprime lending compared to neighbouring states. However, the fall was concentrated in the re-financing of existing subprime loans.[93]

> These results also have policy significance beyond North Carolina...[they demonstrate] that a carefully crafted law can selectively filter out the most egregious kinds of subprime loans without having to resort to punitive enforcement provisions that increase the cost of securitization.[94]

These findings are also supported by the work of Acolin, An and Wachter.[95]

Another study looking at non-GSE securitised mortgages taken out between 1997 and 2009 found that certain mortgages (e.g. Alt-A, negative amortisation, balloon and interest-only payments, etc.) correlated with mortgage

88 Federal Register, Vol. 78, No. 183, 20 September 2013, Proposed Rules, 57989.

89 Lei Ding, Roberto Quercia, Carolina Reid and Alan White 'The impact of Federal preemption of state antipredatory lending laws on the foreclosure crisis, (Spring 2012) *Journal of Policy Analysis and Management*, Vol. 31, No. 2, 367–387, 383, 385.

90 Ibid., (Ding, Quercia, Reid and White), 385.

91 N.C. GEN. STAT. § 24-10 (2002); N.C. GEN. STAT. § 24-1.1E (2002).

92 C. Bailey King, 'Preemption and the North Carolina Predatory Lending Law', (2004) *University of North Carolina School of Law*, Vol. 8, No. 1, 377–397, 379–381.

93 Roberto Quercia, Michael Stegman and Walter Davis, 'Assessing the impact of North Carolina's anti-predatory law', (2004) *Housing Debate*, Vol. 15, No. 3, 573–601, 594.

94 Ibid., (North Carolina APL), 596.

95 Arthur Acolin, Xudong An and Susan Wachter, 'Lending competition and non-traditional mortgages', (December 2017). Working Paper, 1–38, 20.

non-performance.[96] The research found that of their sample 44% of the "loans became seriously delinquent. Filtering on loans meeting the definition of QM reduces the historical serious delinquency rate only modestly to 34%".[97] However, it is worth noting that there was a higher correlation with default using poor credit scores and high LTV ratios.[98] This suggests that the definition of a qualifying mortgage may need to include other factors such as high LTVs and the borrower's past credit history.[99]

A similar review, again, found that credit scores and high LTV ratios were "the most important determinants of the occurrence and timing of serious delinquency".[100] Additionally,

> states with strong loan regulations consistently experienced the largest reduction in risk for targeted loans relative to control states. Laws taking effect in Massachusetts (2004), New Mexico (2004), New Jersey (2003 and 2004), Georgia (2002 and 2003), and New York (2000 and 2003) all reduced their relative risk by 80 percent or more.[101]

4.8 The political legitimacy of the CFPB

The CFPB, as a regulatory institution has still to establish its claim to "institutional legitimacy". It is perceived as lacking both accountability in governance and financial terms since it is run by a sole director and not by a board and it takes its funding direct from the Federal Reserve not from a Congressional allocation of funds.[102]

Former Congressman Jeb Hensarling, a Texas Republican, who chaired the House of Representatives' Financial Services Committee from 2012 until he stood down from Congress in 2019, was highly critical of the CFPB. For example, he said that the CFPB is

> perhaps the most powerful and least accountable government agency in the history of the republic. The CFPB and its unelected director were given unbridled, discretionary power over everyday financial products….Not only

96 Ioannis Floros and Joshua White. 'Qualified residential mortgages and default risk', (2016) *Journal of Banking and Finance*, Vol. 70, 86–104, 87–88.

97 Ibid., (Floros and White), 87–88.

98 Ibid., (Floros and White), 87–88.

99 Ibid., (Floros and White), 102.

100 Wei Li and Keith Ernst, 'Do state predatory lending laws work? A panel analysis of market reforms', (2007) *Housing Policy Debate*, Vol. 18, No. 2, 347–391, 384.

101 Ibid., (Li and Ernst), 384.

102 David Carpenter, 'The Consumer Financial Protection Bureau: a legal analysis', (14 January 2014), Congressional Research Service.

> does this agency have the power to make these products less available and more expensive, it has the power make them completely unavailable.[103]

The administration of President Trump reflects this animosity towards the CFPB. Following the resignation of Richard Cordray, Mick Mulvaney took over as Acting Director in November 2017 followed by the appointment of Kathleen Kraninger as the permanent Director at the end of 2018. Nevertheless, the rules of the CFPB, relating to ability to repay mortgages, have largely remained unchanged. However, the new regime has reduced the level and extent of CFPB examinations and hence supervision of financial institutions and has significantly limited the use of the Bureau's enforcement powers.[104]

There are also concerns from a social cohesion perspective that the regulatory regime may result in "reverse redlining" with high-risk mortgages being concentrated in "low-income and minority communities" with a "confluence of public policy wishing to regenerate deprived areas and intermediaries and lenders keen to provide high margin loans".[105] It has been argued that during a downturn the process may go into reverse and these same areas are likely to be the worst affected.[106] In other words the increase in homeownership is illusionary.[107]

However, despite the establishment of the CFPB it is still not clear that the actions taken to date will be sufficient to prevent further problems in the retail mortgage industry. The over-reliance on information disclosure and role of mortgage brokers are considered later in this chapter. Nevertheless, it is worth noting that failures in the area of conduct of business happen quickly. It is apparent

103 Jeb Hensarling web-site, speech in Athens, Texas on 27 April 2014, https://hensarling.house.gov/media-center/in-the-news/the-monitor-hensarling-fights-for-east-texans, (accessed 14 July 2017). Similar views have been expressed by Patrick McHenry, the current Ranking Member of the Committee, "it is the American consumer—who cannot access a mortgage or basic banking services—that bears the true brunt of this law's failures, Five years later, Dodd-Frank has failed", 21 July 2015.

104 Mulvaney e-mail to CFPB staff, 23 January 2018, 'To everyone from the Acting director',

> bringing the full weight of the federal government down on the necks of the people we serve should be something that we do only reluctantly, and only when all other attempts at resolution have failed. It should be the most final of last resorts.

www.documentcloud.org/documents/4357880-Mulvaney-Memo.html, (accessed 3 July 2019). For the changes to the CFPB and the consequences see Patricia McCoy, 'Inside job: the assault on the structure of the Consumer Financial Protection Bureau', (2019) Minnesota Law Review, Vol. 103(6), 2543–2615.

105 Eric Belsky and Susan Wachter, 'The public interest in consumer and mortgage credit markets', (2010) Research Paper No. 10–05 Institute for Law and Economics, University of Pennsylvania Law School, 14. In 2009 mortgage lending to non-Latino whites fell by 17% while the equivalent fall for Latinos was 63% and African-Americans was 60%, Greg Jones, 'Mortgage lending: confusing in every language', (2012) *Loyola University of Chicago School of Law, Consumer Law Review*, Vol. 24, 661.

106 Ibid., (Belsky and Wachter), 15.

107 Ibid., (Belsky and Wachter), 23.

that underwriting standards in the US fell very quickly over a very short period mainly between 2005 and 2006.[108] Consequently, it is questionable whether supervisors, using data which may be several months old, will be able to identify issues and act quickly enough.

In addition, little work has been undertaken on the role of non-deposit taker mortgage lenders.[109] There may be a correlation between the entry of non-deposit takers into the mortgage market and the decline in underwriting standards.[110] Despite having a large share of the subprime market these lenders largely fell outside regulatory supervision since they did not accept deposits. It is possible that "innovative corporate structures and financial instruments" will again be designed to circumvent and to reduce active supervision.[111] Moreover, often it is the regulations themselves that drive lender strategies. For example, banning prepayment penalties may have encouraged borrowers to use their homes as cash-machines by taking equity from their property and increasing the LTV with no cost with the consequence that they were far more vulnerable to a property price downturn making default more likely.[112] Ultimately, borrowers will need to be equipped to look after their own interests and part of the regulatory strategy is to ensure that they are provided with sufficient information in an easy format to enable them to exercise their own best judgement

4.9 Behavioural economics and mortgage regulation

The foundation of US consumer mortgage policy is to provide borrowers with the information needed to let them choose. Similarly, as discussed in the next chapter, the regulatory approach in the UK was, initially, based on the understanding that the market for mortgage is competitive. Regulation in this, and other areas, assumes that markets are open and competitive and that a well-informed borrower is able to make rational decisions in their best interest. Regulation should be there to support but not to interfere in this process. The original conceptual approach to mortgage regulation in the UK, when mortgages first became regulated, was to encourage consumers to shop around for their mortgages by requiring lenders to provide standardised information which could be

108 Chapter 3, n. 137, (Demyanyk and Van Hemert), 33.

109 William Francis, 'UK deposit-taker responses to the financial crisis: what are the lessons?', (2014) Bank of England, Working Paper No. 501.

110 Yuliya Demyanyk and Elena Loutskina, 'Mortgage companies and regulatory arbitrage', (2013), ssrn 2051001, 4. This paper sets out the results of empirical research comparing the use of less regulated non-deposit taking banking group subsidiaries to write the high-risk mortgage loans.

111 Ibid., (Demyanyk and Loutskina), 29.

112 Todd Zywicki, 'The behavioral law and economics of fixed-rate mortgages (and other just-so stories)', (January 2014), *Supreme Court Economic Review*, Vol. 21, No. 1, 157–214 and Steven Laufer, 'Equity extraction and mortgage default', (2013) Finance and Economics Discussion Series Divisions of Research & Statistics and Monetary Affairs Federal Reserve Board, Washington, DC, 3, who estimated that borrowers of some 30% of homes purchased between 2000 and 2003 defaulted due to "equity extraction".

compared by the consumers before deciding. If prospective borrowers are given standardised information, they will have the tools to select the best product.[113] This would further benefit mortgage product development and distribution in favour of consumers and the market.

However, the reality is evidently very different, especially between those undertaking a re-mortgage, who have more experience, and those new to the process. FSA research found that the latter did not shop around but tended to rely on mortgage intermediaries to find the best deals.[114] The reasons for this included lack of time, inexperience in the mortgage market, and difficulties in understanding the information.[115] In addition, the research found considerable distrust of financial institutions but, in parallel, an understanding that they need to place their trust in someone and this tended to be an independent mortgage broker.[116]

This dependency, on intermediaries, is also clear from a CFPB survey in the US which found that borrowers failed to shop around and tended to rely on their existing lender or broker. The vendor's estate agent was the next most popular source of advice on finance.[117]

Consequently, borrowers tend to place their faith in the intermediary and focus on the immediate monthly cost of the mortgage measured against an approximate amount deemed affordable.[118] Complexity is ignored and borrowers are likely to be over-optimistic in their ability to make higher payments if interest rates rise due to changes in the economy or as introductory low interest rate periods come to an end.[119]

4.10 The failure of disclosure

A mixture of consumer inattention and 'bounded rationality', and lack of numeracy skills are at the heart of the failure of disclosure and challenge the underpinning of market-based regulation.[120]

113 FSA, 'Choosing a mortgage – Consumer Research 8, (June 2001), 3.

114 Ibid., (FSA, 'Choosing a mortgage), 6–7.

115 Ibid., (FSA, 'Choosing a mortgage), 6–7.

116 Ibid., (FSA, 'Choosing a mortgage), 32.

117 CFPB, 'Consumers' mortgage shopping experience', (January 2015), 10.

118 Oren Bar-Gill, *Seduction by contract*, (Oxford University Press, Oxford, 2012), 159.

119 Ibid., (Bar-Gill), 157.

120 "Bounded rationality" is used describes individuals who in undertaking economic decisions will not attempt all the necessary rational calculations to determine the best path but will instead use what information they have and employ a range of broad assumptions to make up their mind, in the time available, to come to a view that satisfies their immediate objectives but may not be the best objective approach and decision, Daniel Kahneman, 'Maps of bounded rationality: a perspective on intuitive judgement and choice', Nobel Prize Lecture, 8 December 2002.

4.10.1 Consumer inattention and 'bounded rationality'

In the US, there have been many initiatives, over the decades, to ensure that adequate information is provided to consumers in advance of their committing to a mortgage.[121] However, there is evidence that consumers presented with too many options will default to inaction and leave decision making to an intermediary.[122] As early as 2002 Engel and McCoy discredited consumer protection views' on disclosure which underpinned US legislation in this area going back to the 1960s and 1970s.[123] Similarly, Renuart and Thompson were critical of the ability of consumers to understand much of what is disclosed in mortgage literature, citing a number of studies including one in which a quarter of consumers were unable to identify the cheapest mortgage even after the disclosure requirement had been improved.[124]

Research indicates that due to "bounded rationality" and the dominating desire of consumers to buy their home they will discount information on the risks of borrowing.[125] In addition, mortgage applicants tended to pay less attention to future costs, ignore future risks and concentrate on the monthly payment element of a loan and exclude other aspects such as early repayment costs and various fees and other expenses.[126] There is also an over-emphasis on small numbers. For example, applicants focused on "differences between $100 and $200" but were less concerned by "differences between $1100 and $1200".[127] The "mental ruler" is closer to a "logarithmic scale" and does not allow for equal spacing between numbers.[128] There was also a belief that mortgages were subject to more regulation than was actually the case and this view appeared to be sustained by the level of mandated regulatory disclosure.[129]

In the UK, the Financial Services Authority's (FSA) research found that consumers tended to focus on the immediate mortgage payments making neither "long-term assessment of the suitability [or] the value of the product".[130]

121 This was originally set out in the Truth In Lending Act in 1968 and amended several times since (see supra, note 43) and supra, note 37, (Woodward and Hall), 4.

122 Ian Ayres, 'Homo economicus, homo myopicus and the law and economics of consumer choice: menus matter', (2006) *University of Chicago Law Review*, Vol. 73, 9.

123 Kathleen Engel and Patricia McCoy. 'A tale of three markets: the law and economics of predatory lending', (2002), *Texas Law Review*, Vol. 80, No. 6, 1255–1381, 1275.

124 Elizabeth Renuart and Diane Thompson, 'The truth, the whole truth, and nothing but the truth: fulfilling the promise of truth in lending', (2008) *Yale Journal of Regulation*, Vol. 25, 181–245, 196.

125 Andrea Boyack, 'Lessons in price stability from the US real; estate market collapse', (2010), 10.2139/ssrn.1665124.

126 Lauren Willis, 'Decision making and the limits of disclosure: the problem of predatory lending', (2006) *Maryland Law Review*, 65, 707, 738.

127 Ibid., (Willis), 739.

128 Ibid., (Willis), 739.

129 Ibid., (Willis), 740.

130 FSA, 'Mortgage Effectiveness Review: stage two report', (March 2008), 34. See Chapter 2 for further discussion.

However, the CFPB has also carried out consumer testing of its mortgage disclosure document: "Know before you owe" and found that consumers value this information.[131] Additional research supported the view of the CFPB.[132] It is worth noting however, that evidence suggests that the more complex mortgage were disproportionally used by sophisticated, high-income, prime credit score customers.[133] Nevertheless, recent research in cognitive psychology does not support the efficacy of product disclosure.[134]

4.10.2 Lack of numeracy

The evidence is that numerical problems challenge a significant number of people. Recent research found that across thirty-one OECD countries between half and three-quarters of the populations could not understand a simple financial line graph nor could they calculate discounts.[135] The researchers state that the issues "go beyond numeracy and require individuals to apply their numerical and literacy skill to a real world financial problem".[136] This is not a new issue. The 2002 US National Adult Literacy Survey found that 96% of adults could not work out the interest charge on a $10,000 mortgage with all the statutory information provided, and, yet, described themselves as financially literate and numerate.[137]

131 Cordray, Richard, 'Know before you owe', remarks at field hearings, Des Moines, Iowa, 23 November 2013.

132 Supra note 37, (Woodward and Hall).

133 Gene Amromin and others, 'Complex mortgages', (November, 2010) Federal Reserve Bank of Chicago, WP 2010–1017, 3–4.

134 Jessica Choplin and Debra Stark, 'Doomed to failure: a psychological analysis of mortgage disclosure and policy implications', (2013), Vol. 32, No. 10 Banking and Financial Services Policy Report, 1. The paper talks of the "Gricean norm of quantity", ("the assumption that all important things are included and all those that are not important are omitted as a conversational norm but mortgage brokers sometimes break this norm"). Consumers tend to "skim disclosure forms looking for info which confirms what they have been told ("confirmatory test strategy")." There is also "part-set cueing" where the consumer tries to recall a set of information which is made more difficult when they are given part of the list and has to remember the rest.

> The borrower knows that there are important items they have to check on a form (eg APR, monthly payments, adjustable rates, term and interest changes during the terms etc). If the broker mentions one or two of these things the borrow will have problems remembering the rest.

135 Aditi Bhutoria, John Jerrim and Anna Vignoles, 'The financial skills of adults across the world. New estimates from the Programme for the International Assessment of Adult Competencies (PIAAC)', (March 2018), 1, UCL Institute of Education web-site, www.ucl.ac.uk/ioe/news/2018/mar/england-has-one-lowest-levels-financial-literacy-study-says, (accessed 17 July 2019).

136 Ibid., (Bhutoria, Jerrim and Vignoles), 1.

137 Cited in Lauren Willis, 'Decision making and the limits of disclosure: the problem of predatory lending', (2006) *Maryland Law Review*, Vol. 65, 707, supra note 126.

4.11 The consequences of the failings of financial disclosure

As has been seen the evidence strongly indicates that many borrowers cannot be trusted to make correct borrowing decisions in their own interest. They struggle with simple arithmetic and place considerable reliance on lenders and brokers for advice. Focusing on TILA, it is possible that the disclosures required by regulation "commonly reflect politicians', lawyers', and economists' beliefs about solutions to problems" rather information that is meaningful to consumers.[138] It is possible that a more innovative approach can be taken using symbols and signs to convey important information.[139]

The establishment of the CFPB can be seen as evidence of the US catching up with some other countries.[140] It presents a number of conceptual challenges to the US approach to conduct of business financial regulation. US regulation now requires that one party to a contract has to look after the interests of another more weakly positioned contractor reflecting a "proto-fiduciary duty which changes the consumer debtor/creditor relationship".[141] There will consequently be two outcomes: an increasingly "paternalistic regulatory mindset...and [the] reduction/rationing [of] mortgage credit".[142] This perception may reflect a more "libertarian" and, possibly, financial services' industry view. It also reflects a view that Federal regulation may inhibiting the aspiration of homeownership, the importance of which was considered earlier in this chapter. Pottow quotes two Congressmen that the position will be that of the government saying to a potential homeowner that your access to the "American Dream" is denied since we the government are "smarter than you" and "we have to protect you from yourself".[143]

While the current approach in the US is still to rely on the provision of adequate information to the consumer the focus is more on establishing 'important guardrails' in the hope that these will 'prevent a return to ...risky lending practices'.[144] Nevertheless, in both the UK and US there is a growing emphasis on empirical research. This includes a 'functional' perspective on product risk which examines the risks and consequences arising from consumer mistakes. It considers what consumer needs the product is meant to satisfy and how a

138 Federal Trade Commission, 'Improving consumer mortgage disclosures: an empirical assessment of current and prototype disclosure forms', (2007), Bureau of Economics Staff Report, 121. There were similar findings in Nicholas Wonder, Wendy Wonder and David Fewings, 'The financial rationality of consumer loan choices: revealed preferences concerning interest rates, down payments, contract length and rebates', (2008), *The Journal of Consumer Affairs*, Vol. 42, No. 2, 243.

139 Luca Cian, Aradhna Krishna and Ryan Elder, 'A sign of things to come: behavioral change through dynamic iconography', (2015) *Journal of Consumer Research*, Vol. 41, No. 6, 1426.

140 John Pottow, 'Ability to pay', (2011), *Berkeley Business Law Journal*, Vol. 8, 175–208, 193.

141 Ibid., (Pottow), 205.

142 Ibid., (Pottow), 205.

143 Ibid., (Pottow), 205, quoting Representatives Neugebauer and Hensarling.

144 CFPB, 'Consumers' mortgage shopping experience', (January 2015), 3.

product is used in practice and why there may be a significant mis-match and how this can be best addressed.[145]

In conclusion, clear and concise consumer information is important and should be a regulatory objective. However, it may be an error to place much reliance on this aspect of regulation as a bulwark of consumer protection.[146]

4.12 Regulatory paternalism

The US State of Illinois attempted to apply a paternalistic approach to mortgage lending in 2005 requiring sub-prime mortgage borrowers to undertake debt counselling if they wished to borrow using a high-risk mortgage product.[147] The independent counsellors were required to check the ability of individual borrowers to afford the mortgage. However, the legislation only applied to state-licensed lenders and was limited to a four-year pilot in parts of metropolitan Chicago.[148] Over the course of the pilot some 1,200 borrowers were counselled and the results assessed. In almost 10% of cases there were indications of fraud and in approximately half of all cases customers were advised that they clearly could not afford the loan or were on the cusp of affordability.[149] The vast majority of sub-prime lending was undertaken by the state-licenced lenders and there was a significant correlation between the reduced volume of lending in areas subject to the pilot and those outside its operation.[150] The pilot was ended abruptly after only twenty weeks following litigation and protests by community activist groups and residents on the grounds that it was racially discriminatory.[151] This pilot tends to support the view that market discipline cannot be relied upon and even with all the information clearly presented there are limits to which individual borrowers can be trusted to make responsible decisions.

As discussed in the next chapter, the FCA has already come to this conclusion and adopted a paternalistic regulatory approach. The UK approach could be seen as going beyond paternalism and moving towards a form of "consumer infantilism" where the borrower takes little or no responsibility. The US approach is

145 FCA, 'Applying behavioural economics at the Financial Conduct Authority' (April 2013), 31.

146 Hooman Estelami, 'An ethnographic study of consumer financial sophistication', (2014) *Journal of Consumer Behaviour*, Vol. 13, 328, 335, with empirical evidence of the "bandwagon effects" where consumers based their financial decisions on what others had done: a form of "following the herd" and including "unidimensional decision making" where the consumer focused on only one element in making a financial decision as a means of dealing with complexity. See also Gregory Elliehausen, 'Implications of behavioral research for the use and regulation of consumer credit products', (2010) Finance and Economics Discussion Series, Federal Reserve Board, Washington, DC, 31.

147 Sumit Agarwal and others, 'Do financial counseling mandates improve mortgage choice and performance? Evidence from a legislative experiment', (October 2009) Federal Reserve Bank of Chicago Working Paper 2009–2007, 6.

148 Ibid., (Agarwal), 7–8.

149 Ibid., (Agarwal), 9.

150 Ibid., (Agarwal), 19. See Chapter 7, n. 44 for the Di Maggio and Kermani research.

151 Ibid., (Agarwal), 9.

more balanced, albeit buttressed by the threat of severe enforcement and private litigation risk. Yet, at the same time, the regulations steer all parties toward the "safe harbour" of standard term and lower, but not risk free, mortgages. However, this approach rests on the adequate supervision of mortgage intermediaries.

4.13 The regulation and supervision of mortgage intermediaries

As already mentioned, mortgage intermediaries have a central role in the mortgage sales process. For some 60% of mortgages sales, borrowers will primarily deal with the intermediary not the lender. It is likely that the first evidence of serious failures in the underwriting process or gaps in the ability to repay assessment will be found in the mortgage intermediation system. As mentioned earlier the current US regulatory system divides the regulation and supervision of mortgage intermediaries between states and the CFPB. The latter sets minimum standards on disclosure of information, non-discriminatory policy and ability to repay regulations. Everything else, including the licensing of intermediaries, is a matter for individual states.[152] Too often this is restricted to basic licencing procedures covering criminal record checks and training requirements with little proactive supervision of individual broker conduct.[153] The CFPB appears to have limited its own role in this area and has not sought to become involved with how intermediaries interact with borrowers.[154] Moreover the CFPB does not appear to seek information from State supervisors on what is happening at a local level in the mortgage origination market.[155] It is possible that this approach has been adopted to make the best use of limited resources.[156] In addition, the conceptual structure of US regulation leaves local regulation and supervision to individual states while regulation at a national level falls to Federal agencies.[157] Clearly there are risks; for example, states working in their own interest contrary to the national objectives, the "capture" of states by local interest groups, uncoordinated actions and the expectation that the nation state will

152 Mortgage Nationwide Licensing System, 'Mortgage industry report', (Q2 2015 Update), 402,468 individuals and 10,149 companies were licensed by Federal bodies (e.g. Federal Reserve, Office of the Comptroller of the Currency and FDIC while at State level 36,563 companies, 45,873 branches and 351,940 individuals were licensed as mortgage originators).

153 Keith Ernst, Debbie Bocian and Wei Li, 'Steering wrong: brokers, borrowers and subprime loans', (8th April 2008), Centre for Responsible Lending, 8.

154 CFPB, 'Supervisory highlights', (Fall 2015), Issue 9.

155 CFPB, 'Semi-annual report', (Spring 2015).

156 As discussed in Chapter 5, the FCA have adopted a similar approach and concentrate almost all their supervision resources on few lenders rather than the many intermediaries.

157 James Madison, Alexander Hamilton and John Jay, 'The Federalist Papers', (published 1788, Penguin Books, London, 1987), 296. Here the authors state that the

> powers delegated ... by the Federal government are few and defined. Those which are to remain in the State governments are numerous and infinite...The powers reserved to the several states will extend to all the objects which...concern the lives, liberties and properties of the people [of that State].

pay for local individual State failures. Nevertheless, State-level experimentation is a missed opportunity.[158] It is possible that states are experimenting with innovative forms of regulation and supervision which may be usefully employed more widely and states may well have information on market practices which could be disseminated across the country. For example, Washington State's Department of Financial Institutions, which supervises aspects of the operations of mortgage originators, issues regular "best practice" statements on mortgage intermediaries.[159] Other states do the same. The CFPB is in a unique position to undertake this coordination role and to assess the efficacy of each approach without stepping on State prerogatives.

4.14 Conclusion

This chapter primarily considers the importance of understanding the recent major changes to mortgage conduct of business regulations in the context of the overwhelming desire in the US to support a broad popular aspiration to own ones' home. This approach to regulation seeks to balance supporting widespread homeownership, and all the civic benefits this brings, with the need to protect both borrowers and the wider financial system from over-borrowing. The context is a high-level of government intervention supporting access to homeownership.

First, built into the conduct of business of regulations is a level of "risk tolerance" in the interest of promoting wider homeownership for public policy reasons. It accepts that borrowers and lenders will make mistakes. This is evident in the regulatory protection given to the standardised "qualifying mortgage". Some 23% of this type of mortgage, written just before the financial crisis, defaulted.[160] Ultimately, it is a political and regulatory decision balancing the risks to the individual of over-borrowing and the costs to the financial system against a range of socio-economic and political beneficial objectives. Whether this approach could be transferred to other jurisdictions may be difficult. It requires both political and regulatory will. In the US, the benefits of homeownership are a bi-partisan objective and embedded in the legislation and form part of the "American Dream". Regulation follows this underlying concept.

Second, the CFPB places too much faith on the efficacy of mortgage information disclosure. It is important that the potential borrower is informed in the most effective manner possible of the mortgage's key points. However, the behavioural evidence suggests that only limited reliance can be placed on disclosure regulations.

158 Federalism is often seen as encouraging economic development via competition between states within the federalist system. See Friedrich Hayek, 'The economic conditions of interstate federalism' and Charles Tiebout, 'A pure theory of local expenditures', quoted in Barry Weingast, 'The economic role of political institutions: market-preserving federalism and economic development', (1995) *Journal of Law, Economics and Organization*, Vol. 11, 1, 5.

159 Department of Financial Institutions, 'FYI financial news – updates from DFI's Consumer Services', (Winter 2014).

160 Supra, note 88, (Federal Register), 57989.

Finally, as mentioned above, the best documentation and information may be undermined by the actions of lenders and intermediaries. The US regulatory and supervisory system attempts to balance both State-level and Federal perspectives'. Whether or not the balance is struck in the right place, it nevertheless, provides opportunities for information and best practices to be shared between states and the Federal authorities. The new regulatory approach contains built-in known risks. These need to be monitored and reported regularly to check that balanced judgements remain sound.

5 Conduct of business mortgage regulation in the UK

The UK's approach to the regulation of mortgages marketing is 'path-dependent' since it is largely derived from regulatory steps taken in the 1980s to protect the clients of stockbrokers. However, in the shadow of the recent financial crisis the UK moved towards a much more paternalistic approach following what was known as the 'Mortgage Market Review (MMR)'. It requires almost all potential borrowers to seek advice from a 'trusted adviser' and the ability of consumers to understand and act upon information provided has been downgraded. The advisor now has to assess and evidence that the loan is not only suitable but also affordable to a level of certainty, over the term of the mortgage. The broad aim is to protect consumers from themselves. However, there has been little reflection on the potential socio-economic consequences of this approach to the regulation of mortgages.

The steps now required to be able to take out a mortgage are complex and time consuming, and the tests to be able to demonstrate that the mortgage is affordable are onerous. The effectiveness of this new approach has yet to be tested in a property boom. In addition, there is an extensive history in the UK of conduct of business regulations failing. There is also a real risk that an extensive failure by lenders to properly assess mortgage affordability could potentially threaten the financial viability of lenders, since the costs of restitution would be extensive. It is unclear if this aspect has been considered by either the conduct of business or prudential regulators.

A better, more targeted approach is suggested, possibly adopting a more risk-focused policy similar to the US 'Qualified Mortgage'.

5.1 Introduction

The regulation of financial services' conduct of business governs how firms in this sector market and sell their products and generally engage with their customers. Although it is an area which is frequently the subject for the personal finance media, it has been, comparatively, little studied. It can be seen as the "poor relation" of the more glamorous prudential and capital markets forms of regulations. It lacks the "theatre" of the trading floor and the larger-than-life personalities and inhabits the world of the ordinary. Its business is a mundane and drab milieu devoid of mystery. Its very ordinariness means that everyone believes that they understand it and consequently, it has merited only limited study. This lack of research interest is particularly true of the residential mortgage market. However, unrestrained mortgage credit has triggered a series of financial crises in the UK, and other countries, over the last fifty years. In the most recent financial collapse "ordinary" home lending was at the centre of events that almost destroyed the global financial system. Consequently, it is important that regulators at all levels: macroprudential, microprudential and conduct of business, pay attention to the residential mortgage market.

This chapter will demonstrate that there is nothing "ordinary" about the conduct of business regulation of homeowner mortgages. It is difficult to enforce and has a wide range of societal consequences which deserve particular policy-making attention. Nevertheless, conduct of business regulation is central to this book as a major component of macroprudential regulation with its ability to limit the access to credit in a manner generally understood and more acceptable to politicians, the media and general public than more conventional tools.

Residential housing markets are very specific to each jurisdiction. They have developed as a result of history, culture, economics, taxation policy, land tenure and political drivers. Access to housing in the UK has been an issue of major public concern in the 20th and 21st centuries. Consequently, the ability to secure a mortgage is closely bound-up with the aspiration of homeownership. Nevertheless, extending credit brings with it the risk of default and repossession. This has both significant consequences for individuals, their families and, more widely, for society. How those at risk and the wider economy are protected is the theme of both this chapter and this book.

There are a wide range of approaches to regulating this area. They are not mutually exclusive. They include industry codes of conduct, consumer education and information campaigns, the application of selective taxation and subsidies, political control over the planning process to control what can be built and where, central control over what institutions may lend, to whom and how much, monetary policy using interest rates, macroprudential and microprudential controls on lending and conduct of business regulation. Later chapters will consider some of the political aspects of regulation and other options. This chapter looks at the conduct of business regulation of mortgages in the UK and the scope for employing it as a significant macroprudential tool.

In May 2009, the Financial Services Authority (FSA) launched its review, known as the MMR, of the regulation of the marketing and distribution of domestic mortgages in the UK. The FSA believed

> that irresponsible borrowing has been just as much a part of the problem in the mortgage market as irresponsible behaviour by firms. Our policy approach to date has been underpinned by a view that mortgage consumers will act rationally to protect their own interests. We believe that we need to change that approach … and be more interventionist to help protect consumers from themselves.[1]

1 FSA, 'Discussion paper: mortgage market review', (October 2009), 9/3, 14.

The result was that in April 2014 new regulations came into force. The FSA considered that its

> existing regulatory framework has been shown to be ineffective in constraining irresponsible high-risk lending and borrowing and there is a general consensus that substantial regulatory policy reform is needed to reduce the probability and dampen the severity of future financial crises.[2]

At the heart of the new regulations was the wish to ensure that consumers could afford their loans both at inception and over the term of the mortgage and are able to repay them. Broadly, this is achieved by providing information to the consumer at various points before the loan is concluded and placing responsibility on the lender to check that the loan is both suitable for, and affordable by, the consumer. It is these elements and their implications that are considered in this chapter.

Section 5.2 of this chapter considers a number of key concepts in understanding the UK conduct of business regulation in the context of the mortgage market including the mortgage distribution structure and the common failure to distinguish between issues relating to mortgage affordability and credit risk by both international and domestic regulatory policymakers. Sections 5.3 and 5.4 looks at the origins of the regulation of mortgage advice in the UK, since the history of regulation in this area over a period of almost a quarter of a century has set the foundations for the current approach to regulation. The strong element of path-dependency was responsible for closing off other regulatory options. This is particularly relevant since the current UK conduct of business regulatory model has changed little from that developed in the late 1980s by the regulators set up under the Financial Services Act 1986.[3] This approach seeks, as far as possible, to remove risk to the consumer by developing the path-dependent form of regulation adopted to regulate investment business.[4] It is based on the concept, which can be summed up, as that of the "trusted adviser". Section 5.5 summarises the "affordability" assessment aspects of new regulations. Sections 5.6 and 5.7 examine the key issues and concepts underlying conduct of business regulation in the area of mortgages. This includes the conceptual confusion embedded in the

2 Ibid., (FSA, 'Discussion paper', October 2009), 9.

3 Conceptually, the rules looked at how the customer would interact with the investment provider (i.e. via marketing literature and advertising and interacting with a financial adviser and if things went wrong through the firm's complaints handling system). The firm must provide standardised information about the product and all its marketing must be fair, clear and not misleading. Financial advisers must be honest and properly trained and provide suitable advice while the complaints process must be fair and timely and provide recourse to the independent Financial Ombudsman Service if the customer still considers that they are not satisfied with the result. Key elements of this model were considered by Alan Brener, 'The golden threads of compliance', (1995) Journal of Financial Regulation and Compliance, Vol. 3, No. 4, 344–349.

4 This form of analysis is borrowed from economic work by Paul David and Brian Arthur demonstrated that often consideration of a possible course of action is "locked-in" by historical events, Brian Arthur, 'Competing technologies, increasing returns, and lock-in by historical events', (1989) Economic Journal, Vol. 97, 642–665.

mortgage advice process of whether regulation in this area is designed to protect lenders or borrowers. The same section also examines the role of consumer information and Section 5.8 reviews the pronounced regulatory move towards a more paternalistic approach to regulation of mortgage business with the "new paternalism" operating at the heart of the MMR while Section 5.9 considers the socio-economic implications of the new regulation and the consequential effects on access to secured loans. This latter aspect is considered in more detail in Chapter 8 on the housing markets in relation to mortgage regulation.

Sections 5.10 and 5.11 question the level of confidence that regulators can reasonably place on measures designed for consumer protection where parallel regulation has proved generally inadequate in the insurance and investment business sectors. In support of this proposition this chapter considers the past failures of UK conduct of business regulation and the potential consequences if there is a similar failure following the introduction of more prescriptive recent mortgage regulations in 2014. Finally, Sections 5.12 and 5.13 set out the argument that a more targeted approach could achieve the consumer protection objectives without the need to deploy blunt-edged regulation. In summary, regulators may be placing too much faith on mortgage conduct of business regulations to protect consumers at the expense of wider socio-economic consequences while the consumer protection and socio-economic requirements could be better balanced by a different approach.

5.2 Key concepts relating to conduct of business regulation

5.2.1 Manufacturer and distributor structure

The investment business regulatory structure is based on business practices which draw a distinction between the "manufacturers" and the "distributors" of financial products and services. For example, the "trusted adviser" with access to the client may assemble a number of investment funds suitable for their client from a range of fund managers. The latter can be described as the "manufacturers" of these funds while the adviser acts as the distributor. As explained earlier financial services regulation imposes a range of different obligations on each business. For example, the advisor has to understand their clients' needs and to provide suitable advice.[5] The fund manager, for example, has to look after the clients' money left with it for safe keeping pending investment in a fund.[6] The subsequent regulation of investment business has highlighted a continuing tension between "manufacturers of products" and "distributors" who sell the investments, all measured in levels of market share, commission payments, "ownership" of the

5 FCA Conduct of Business Rules 9.2.2.
6 FCA Client Assets Rules: Principle 10 and Guidance 5.2.7.

client relationship, with the customer coming last.[7] This conceptual approach to the conduct of business regulation of the investment business industry is important in understanding the later regulation of mortgage business which, in many ways, not only adopted the same approach to regulation but also a similar market structure and comparable battle for access to customers. Finally, in this area it is important to distinguish between the important credit and affordability assessments both of which need to be undertaken by the lender. These often cause considerable confusion. Nevertheless, they are central to both macro and microprudential policy as well as conduct of business regulators.

5.2.2 The issue of credit and affordability assessments

Many of the issues relating to mortgage regulation hinge on a failure to distinguish between the "credit" and "affordability" assessments. The former is part of the prudential steps aimed at protecting the lender. It involves assessing the creditworthiness of the borrower and their ability to meet the servicing costs of the loan and their ability to repay the principle. If, for any reason, the borrower fails to meet their obligations some, or all, of the security may become forfeit and, in the UK, they can be pursued for any outstanding balance through the courts. The assessment of the borrower and the security they are able to provide to cover the lender's risk, coupled with the lender's "risk appetite", have formed a fundamental element of banking since the business was first developed in its modern form in medieval Italy and Flanders.[8] However, although closely related to aspects of the credit appraisal, the "affordability assessment" is different in concept, origin and consequence. It is important to emphasise that the latter is regulated in order to protect the borrower, often from their own inclinations, intuitions and folly. The microprudential supervisor will focus on credit while affordability falls within the purview of the conduct of business supervisor.

Credit and underwriting departments, within banks and other well-established lenders, have long been familiar with their traditional role of protecting their employer's business. However, they have had to go through a period of process and cultural adjustment to implement the affordability regulations first promulgated in 2004 in the UK. The requirements have become more onerous and they now need to carry out two separate assessments often using different data, for two different purposes. First protecting the lender from financial loss due to customer default and inadequate security and second, protecting the customer from over-borrowing contrary to the financial services regulations. This can often result in cultural confusion. Organisationally, compliance and credit staff have worked in separate "silos". Credit staff are likely to be highly experienced credit officers with little exposure to others areas of regulation. Secured lending

7 Discussed more fully by Kit Jebens, Lautro, a pioneer regulator 1986–1994, (private printing, 1997).

8 James Murray, 'The Bruges credit and payments systems', in Bruges: Cradle of Capitalism (Cambridge University Press, Cambridge, 2005), 210–258.

credit staff will normally concentrate on the value and adequacy of the security in relation to the risk exposure in order to ensure that the lender is protected. However, compliance staff come from a variety of backgrounds often with a legal or an operational perspective. In a commercial bank their objective can be summarised as consumer protection and hence protecting the organisation from regulatory and reputational damage. Credit staff will use a specialist language of statistical analysis, determining levels and risks of probability of default, loss given defaults and exposure at default. The credit teams will be part of the business generation process and will work closely with the marketing, distribution and pricing units. Compliance, on the other hand, is exclusively a control function. In the UK it is generally kept separate from the Risk and Legal function.[9] This often makes for poor communication and understanding between credit and compliance staff who have different objectives, reporting lines and measures of success. These aspects have neither been addressed in the policy deliberations nor in the regulations themselves. This confusion may be seen in regulatory responses to the concerns expressed by the Financial Stability Board (FSB).

5.3 FSB and the regulatory response

The FSB is a transnational body operating through the medium of "soft" law but nevertheless commanding great authority and excising considerable influence. In its March 2012 publication on the results of its thematic review of domestic underwriting and sales processes the FSB expressed concern that poor underwriting of mortgages could affect global financial stability through the mechanism of international securitisation.[10] Consequently, in April 2012, the FSB issued its Principles for Sound Residential Mortgage Underwriting Practices.[11] This document has multiple aims, including protecting borrowers and investors and "limit[ing] the risks the mortgage markets pose to financial stability".[12] The Principles cover areas such as debt security and mortgage insurance. However, the Principles also include ensuring that lenders adopt prudent LTV ratios. They went onto state that lenders should verify the income of borrowers and "that lenders … assess borrowers; ability to service and fully repay their loans without causing the borrower undue hardship and over-indebtedness".[13] The FSB's focus is, appropriately, on the narrow issue of poor quality mortgage lending "infecting" the global securitisation markets and hence international financial stability. However, there are almost no, or only limited, references to the role of consumer protection in either macro or microprudential policy. Based on this it is not clear that other regulators appreciate the difference between "sound

9 Iris H-Y Chiu, Regulating (from) the inside, (Bloomsbury, Oxford, 2015), 51.

10 FSB, 'Thematic review of residential mortgage underwriting and origination practices', (March 2011).

11 FSB, 'Principles for sound residential mortgage underwriting practices', (April 2012).

12 Ibid., 2.

13 Supra note 11, (FSB Underwriting Principles), 2–7.

underwriting" which protects the lender, and which consequently supports microprudential regulation, and mortgage affordability and repayability policies which protect the consumer and may, only as a secondary outcome, protect the lender.[14] These two different types of assessment and the organisational and cultural challenges they pose need to be kept in mind when viewing the history and implementation of mortgage regulation.

The protection of the borrower is at the heart of mortgage conduct of business regulation and it adjusts the relationship between two parties; imposing a set of obligations on each with rights and duties. These factors are all within the purview of legal assessment and understanding. In contrast the protection of a lender from financial distress and collapse is fundamentally a question of economic assessment and modelling. As mentioned later these different conceptual positions are often reflected within the organisational structure of lenders with the areas responsible for protecting customers lodged within the Compliance department while those responsible for managing credit risk form an important part of the Risk function. Each has different reporting lines and are subject to different organisational expectations.[15] These issues, not normally the subject of regulatory analysis, coupled with an increasingly disconnected distribution system, indicate potential structural flaws in the regulatory model.

5.4 The origins and concepts behind UK mortgage conduct of business regulation

5.4.1 The relationship between mortgage and investment advice regulation

In order to understand the conduct of business regulation of mortgages in the UK it is necessary to understand how these regulations originated. It is important to appreciate that the conceptual structure of current mortgage regulation follows those determined as appropriate some thirty years ago to protect the clients of stockbrokers; a wholly different financial services sector. As argued later in this chapter this may not be the right approach. The concept of the trusted adviser – acting in the best interests of their client – underlies much of UK's conduct of business regulation. Its origins can be seen in the reaction to the collapse of the stockbroking firms Hedderwick Sterling and Gumbar, and Halliday Simpson in 1981 and 1982.[16] These two failures revealed failings in

14 For example, the Bank of England's press release of 22 March 2017 setting out the FPC's statement from its policy meeting of that date refers to the risks of increased household indebtedness representing "a risk to lenders if accompanied by weaker underwriting standards". The FPC propose to counter this risk, and others, using annual cyclical stress tests and countercyclical capital buffers.

15 Supra note 9, (Chiu), 90–92.

16 The report by Professor Gower was prompted by the failures of a number of stockbrokers and the debate in Parliament on this report largely focused on the role of stockbrokers and, to some

the existing limited regulation of investment business and the inadequacy of the Prevention of Fraud (Investment) Act 1958; the only piece of regulation protecting clients at the time. Consequently, the Secretary of State for Trade and Industry, in the newly elected Conservative government, asked Professor Laurence Gower to consider what could be done to improve the regulation of investment business. The need for action was reinforced by the extensive fraudulent activities of the investment business of Barlow Clowes which came to light in 1987. In Gower's final report in 1984, he outlined a "transactional model" for regulating investment business.[17] In Gower's opinion "regulation should be no greater than is necessary to protect reasonable people from being made fools of".[18] Caveat emptor would be replaced by adequate disclosure and reliance on trusted advisers backed by monitoring and enforcement under a new regulatory structure. Gower was, however, clear that "regulation should not seek to achieve the impossible".[19] In his view "the task of regulation was not to protect fools from their own folly".[20] However, as will be explored later, the proposed model for regulating the financial services was narrowly drawn and is based on what I term the "trusted investment adviser" concept.

5.4.2 Path-dependency of mortgage conduct of business regulation

There are a number of types of path-dependency.[21] This work focuses on rules-driven path dependence where initial structures determine legal rules which in turn determine subsequent arrangements. It is possible that these subsequent developments may not be efficient but as a result of sunk cost, costs of switching or change may not be cost effective. Change may also not occur due to the actions of those who want to maintain "rent-seeking" embedded in the existing

---

extent, Lloyds of London (e.g. towards the end of the debate Anthony Nelson MP, previously a City merchant banker and asset manager and later Economic Secretary at the Treasury said "I regret that, unlike some of my colleagues, I cannot start my speech with a declaration of some enormous shareholding in a profitable firm of stockbrokers. I rise with some temerity as one of the first non-stockbrokers to speak from the Conservative Benches". Hansard, HC Deb, 16 July 1984, Vol. 64, 49–114, 87)

The subsequent structure of the rules envisaged the client meeting and discussing their affairs with a trusted investment adviser (supra note 5). The initial regulatory framework was based on a "self-regulatory" model with a regulatory "club" of investment advisers devising their own rules, within limits and subject to independent review, and applying these rules to its members using contract law.

17 Mads Andenas and Iris Chiu, The foundations and future of financial regulation', (Routledge, London, 2013), 22.

18 Laurence Gower, Review of Investor Protection: Report, Part 2, (H M Stationery Office, London, Cmnd 9125, 1984), 6.

19 Ibid., (Gower), 6.

20 Ibid., (Gower), 7.

21 Lucian Bebchuk and Mark Roe, 'A theory of path dependence in corporate ownership and governance' in Jeffrey Gordon and Mark Roe (eds), Convergence and persistence in corporate governance (Cambridge University Press, Cambridge, 2004), 68.

structures and interest group politics. All this results in an "imperfect Coasian world".[22] It can also be due to simple "habit" where simple lassitude inhibits change or pride and insularity which rejects innovations that were "not invented here". There is also the old civil service rationale of wanting to avoid change since it may increase risk and that it may be safer to retain what is known.[23] The importance of these behavioural and institutional factors should not be ignored. Policymakers are very conscious of the effect of unintended consequences and the need for what has been described as the "short-sightedness of evolution" where the rationality of risk-aversion out-paces innovation.[24] For these reasons rules established to govern investment conduct of business largely formalised existing industry structures.[25] Statutory conduct of business regulation of mortgages followed a similar path. As mentioned above, there are many reasons for this. No single factor dominated other than an "endowment effect", (i.e. the need to protect existing large players in the market by avoiding too much disruption).[26] This influenced the development of investment business, and hence mortgage, conduct of business regulation in the UK.

It is clear that in the 1984 Parliamentary debate on the Gower Report, the proposed regulations were to be aimed at a narrow group of the public who could afford the services of stockbrokers and investment managers and it appears that most of the speakers in the Commons debate had either been stockbrokers or had close family who were stockbrokers.[27] The subsequent structure for the regulation of conduct of business largely followed the pattern set out by Gower. It revolved around a series of transactions between the client and the regulated firm: the style and content of marketing and disclosure material, the provision of "suitable advice" by honest and competent advisers who had a duty imposed on them to act in the best interests of their clients, how the investment was cared for on behalf of the client and, if matters went wrong, a process for addressing client complaints.

It is this high cost approach that was used, subsequently, as the model for conduct of business mortgage regulation affecting a much wider section of society. This model may be appropriate for a financial services business which foresees a long-term "transactional" relationship, for example, in personal banking or asset management. However, mortgages are largely "commodity" products and often processed by the computer systems of lenders with little actual human contact or

22 Ibid., 71.

23 Supra, note 4, (David and Arthur).

24 Reinhard Schmidt and Gerald Spindler, 'Path dependence and complementarity in corporate governance', in Jeffrey Gordon and Mark Roe (eds), Convergence and persistence in corporate governance (supra note 21), 119.

25 Supra note 7, (Jebens), 8.

26 Lucian Bebchuk and Mark Roe, 'A theory of path dependence in corporate ownership and governance', (1999) Stanford Law Review, Vol. 52, No. 2, 127, 141.

27 Supra note 16, (Commons debate, 16 July 1984), 49–114.

intervention.[28] Consequently, a regulatory approach designed with, for example, a stockbroker or private banker in mind, may not be appropriate for the mortgage "mass market".[29]

Conduct of business regulation is designed to clarify the distinction between those whose role it is to advise customers and businesses which provide financial products.[30] It is possible to view it in class terms with the professional adviser using their skill to select the appropriate financial products provided by the "financial tradesman", particularly bankers, who manufacture them.[31] For example, stockbroking, with the right cultural background, was an acceptable profession for a gentleman.[32] The barrister and financial adviser were much higher up the social scale than, for example, the solicitor and certainly well above the commercial banker. This was especially true since much of the banking and insurance industry in England has its origins in the trade of goldsmiths and foreign exchange dealers largely established and run by non-conformists and foreigners, and mutual societies based around skilled trades and self-help associations.[33] The socially acceptable professional used their professional skill and vocation to advise their clients and did not deal with money, "the scale of professional prestige was largely determined by distance from flagrant 'money grubbing'".[34] Professionals keeping their own house in order was the underlying concept behind the Gower Report, the subsequent Parliamentary debate and the self-regulatory system enshrined in the Financial Services Act 1986.

As mentioned earlier this view of how financials services are, or should be structured, has been applied by regulation to the mortgage market. Consequently,

28 The term "commodity product" in this context refers to those financial products that cannot be differentiated other than by price.

29 Financial services firm, and other types of business, will attempt to segment customers into different categories in order to match costs and income. This can range from private banking and bespoke high-value lending (e.g. the "black credit card") and asset management to more "mass-market" products and services with lower costs and charges. As explained above, mortgages, for the most part, are commoditised products and available to all who can satisfy the credit and affordability assessments mentioned later.

30 For example, the distinction is maintained in the FCA Handbook in which the major division is between "Conduct of Business" (COBS) regulation largely governing financial advice and information disclosure and the "Client Assets" (CASS) rules designed to protect client money from misuse.

31 The economist Sir William Petty, spoke of the "trade of banking", Collected Works of William Petty, (published 1899, Charles Henry Hull (ed) as the Collected economic writings of Sir William Petty, Terrance Hutchinson (ed), Routledge, London, 1997), Vol. II, 447.

32 David Ward, 'The public schools and industry in Britain after 1870', (1967) Journal of Contemporary History, Vol. 37, 46, notes that before the First World War the "acceptable" future professions for boys from, for example, the great public school, Wellington were the military, clergy, civil service, academia, teaching and stockbroking. Banking and insurance were not mentioned.

33 Geoffrey Elliott, The Mystery of Overend and Gurney, (Methuen Publishing, London, 2006), 44–55.

34 Martin Wiener, English culture and the decline of the industrial spirit, 1850–1980, (published 1981, 2nd ed, Cambridge University Press, Cambridge, 2004), 15, 14–16.

how the latter is structured has influenced, and in turn been influenced by, conduct of business regulation.[35]

5.4.3 The development of UK conduct of business mortgage regulation

This section sets out the legislative and regulatory background to the development of UK conduct of business mortgage regulation. Key factors influencing this were: the malign effects of the recession in the early 1990s on house prices and interest rates coupled with the misuse of a number of financial products by insurance companies, banks, building societies and various financial advisers in the late 1980s and early 1990s.[36] It is arguable that the UK recession in the early 1990s had a greater effect on the general population compared with the much milder recession of 2007/8. The former had a significant effect on unemployment and, consequently, on housing with high levels of both "negative equity" (where the amount outstanding on the mortgage exceeded the value of the property and made selling the home to pay off the mortgage an impossible option) and home repossessions.[37] In total there were 340,500 repossessions between 2008 and 2012. This was substantively much lower than 556,300 repossessions during the earlier crisis between 1990 and 1994.[38]

The housing and unemployment problems during the crisis in the early 1990s were exacerbated by the practices of many of the trusted investment advisers. They had developed new ranges of investment products in the 1980s and early 1990s and coupled these with mortgage lending. These took two main forms: mortgage endowment policies ("MEPs") and home income plans ("HIPs").

35 For example, prior to the introduction of conduct of business regulation it was often unclear whom the financial adviser represented. In almost all the instances, they were creatures of the asset manager, insurance company or bank with few duties owed to the customer. Conduct of business regulation placed specific requirements on the adviser in order to protect customers. In the realm of investment business, RDR has had the effect of changing the structure of the industry with the cost and risks of regulation resulting in the number of advisers falling (from over 40,000 in 2011 before the regulation came into force to just over 30,000 in 2014) as banks exited the advice market. The market is now dominated by independent financial advisers who largely restrict their business to high-net-worth customers reflecting this cost and risk effect, (HM Treasury and FCA, 'Financial advice market review: final report', (March 2016), 18–20). The report contains recommendations to try to amend the regulations to reverse this effect (e.g. by encouraging the development of automated "robo" advice for the mass market, 27–30). There are similar developments in the mortgage advice market, (FCA, 'Embedding the mortgage market review: advice and distribution: thematic review', (July 2015), TR15/9, 31–34).

36 Matthew Watson, 'Constituting monetary conservatives via the 'savings habit': New Labour and the British housing market bubble', (2008) Comparative European Politics, Vol. 6, 285–304, 295–296.

37 Over 70,000 properties were repossessed in the UK in each of the years 1991 and 1992 (0.75% of all mortgages) compared to just over 40,000 in each of years 2009 and 2010 (0.38%), Library of the House of Commons, 'Repossessions and mortgage arrears: statistics', (February 2011), SN/SG/179.

38 Ibid., (House of Commons Library), 5.

MEPs involved the adviser using a life insurance equity-based investment product known as an "endowment policy", which for part of the 1980s was subsidised through the tax system, and an interest only mortgage. The customer only paid the interest on the mortgage and the insurance premiums. The scheme involved the insurance investment policy maturing at the same time as the mortgage had to be repaid and rested on the proceeds of the redemption of the investment policy being sufficient to pay off the mortgage. The products were often sold on the basis that even after the mortgage had been repaid there might be a surplus for the customer. The HIP was designed for older customers who borrowed against the equity in their home and invest some of, or all, the proceeds of a remortgage in an investment product. The mortgage interest was rolled up and the proceeds of the sale of the investment policy would be available to pay off the mortgage and the accrued interest on the death of the mortgagee/investor. This product was sometimes known as a "lifetime" or "equity release" mortgage. However, each of these types of product involved a gamble, which in most cases failed, on interest rates, equity growth and the health of the general economy.

Due to high interest rates, a fall in equity values in 1987 and in the recession in the early 1990s customers were unable to repay their mortgages and homes were repossessed. Customers had difficulty holding anyone responsible because the financial advisers, regulated under the Financial Services Act 1986, often turned out to be "men of straw" with no, or insufficient, assets and the investors compensation scheme limits were too low to help. The mortgage lenders were not subject to conduct of business regulation. Some legal actions against lenders were successful but only after the cases had been pursued through to the House of Lords.[39] Consequently, political and consumer groups called for investment business regulation to be extended to include mortgages sales. The issue was taken up by the Labour Party and its 1997 election manifesto proposed to introduce mortgage conduct of business regulation. The new government also started the process of dismantling the existing regulatory structure and combining a range of regulatory bodies covering both prudential and conduct of business regulation into a single regulator: the Financial Services Authority (FSA).

5.4.4 *The response by the lending industry and the cautious approach by the new regulator*

In an attempt to pre-empt detailed regulation of the mortgage distribution conduct of business, in 1996, the Council of Mortgage Lenders (CML), a trade body, developed and implemented a voluntary code of practice, based on the investment business regulatory model, known as the "Mortgage Code" for the mortgage industry.[40] It was an important development since much that was

39 For example, Investors Compensation Scheme v. West Bromwich Building Society, House of Lords, 19 June 1997, Session 1997–1998, 2All ER 98 [1998].

40 Michael Coogan, Director General, Council of Mortgage Lenders, 'Recent developments in the UK housing and mortgage market', (Housing Finance International, March 1998).

contained in this Code was subsequently transposed into the final regulations that came into force in 2004. Following Labour's election victory in 1997, HM Treasury launched the first regulation of mortgages consultation in July 1999.[41] This proposal was also mentioned in the Treasury consultation paper on creating the FSA.[42] The new FSA issued a cost-benefit analysis for mortgage regulation in October 1999.[43] The Treasury undertook a further consultation before it issued a Regulated Activities Order (RAO) in February 2001 covering pre-sale mortgage information. However, in deference to the industry's Mortgage Code of 1996, mentioned above, the Order did not include mortgage advice, which was left subject to the CML's Mortgage Code.[44]

How regulation would be implemented was set out, at a high level, in the FSA's Consultation Paper (CP) 70 in November 2000 followed by more detailed proposals in CP 98 in July 2001.[45] The regulations mirrored those for investment business and were based on a number of broad areas including the FSA's high level principles (e.g. treating customers fairly, transparency with the regulator, adequate systems of control, which were largely carried over from the previous regulatory regime established by the Financial Services Act 1986), providing information to customers, training and competence of staff, etc. This approach was consistent with the concept of "transaction regulation", which as mentioned earlier, conceptually envisaged conduct of business regulation as encompassing a series of interactions between customers and their trusted advisers and the firms that employed them or they represented. Nevertheless, conduct of business mortgage regulation was a new challenge for the FSA and its response was uncertain.

5.4.5 FSA concerns and its "diffident" approach

The FSA remained uncertain how to regulate mortgage conduct of business and expressed concerned about the effect of regulation on the mortgage market. Nevertheless, as explained earlier, there were certainly issues with business practices. In their 2000 consultation the FSA explained its own twofold concern: that they had found evidence of consumer detriment in the mortgage market based on the sale of endowment insurance policies alongside mortgages.[46] The FSA equivocated about whether the adequacy of the borrower's security should

41 H M Treasury, 'Regulation of mortgages, a discussion document', (July 1999).

42 H M Treasury, 'Financial Services and Markets Bill: A Consultation Document, overview of financial regulatory reform', (July 1998).

43 FSA, 'A cost-benefit analysis of statutory regulation of mortgage advice', (October 1999).

44 H M Treasury, 'Regulating mortgages', (October 2000); H M Treasury, 'Response to the Consultation Paper: regulating mortgages, October 2000', (February 2001).

45 FSA, 'Mortgage regulation: The FSA's high level approach', (CP 70), (November 2000), and 'The Draft Mortgage Sourcebook, including policy statement on CP70 (CP98)', (July 2001).

46 Ibid., (CP70), 4. See also, for example, FSA's enforcement action against Abbey life Insurance (part of Lloyds Bank) for mis-selling mortgage endowment policies between 1995 and 1999, (2002).

be a sufficient basis on which to lend.[47] However, the FSA appeared to conclude that "… it is not prudent to lend on the basis of security alone" and that the FSA needed to reflect its "Principle 6" (the need to "pay due regard to the interests of its customers and treat them fairly").[48] However, the FSA saw that it was important to "strike a balance when considering Principle 6…. [since] any restrictions to lending practices introduced by the FSA may simply limit access to the mortgage market".[49] Conversely, the FSA were concerned that without some restrictions lenders might "exploit consumers by lending in circumstances where it is self-evident that they would be unable to repay through income".[50]

It is worth contrasting this approach with the regulatory stance some nine years later where the regulator, and regulation, took a much more "dirigiste" form adopted by the MMR and Mortgage Conduct of Business section of the FCA rule-book. In the early 2000s the FSA was content to regulate with a mixture of industry "self-regulation", under the auspices of the CML Mortgage Code, mentioned earlier, buttressed by limited FSA rules. The FSA's ambivalence was shortly afterwards altered by EU action which sought to bring "intermediation activities" within the scope of financial services regulation. This formed part of the EU Commission's strategy to develop a single market in financial services. The consequence was to incorporate the Mortgage Code within the FSA's own regulations.

5.4.6 The end of "self-regulation" and the move to a solely statutory based regulatory regime

As mentioned above, there was a change of plan and timetable with the proposed EU Insurance Intermediaries Directive which widened regulation to include advice and intermediary regulation.[51] As a result the effective date for mortgage regulation was set back to October 2004. The FSA consultation in August 2002 (CP 146) set out its revised plans to regulate the mortgage advice process and advisers who would be subject to the new regulations.[52] The regulation of investment advice remained the model. The Feedback Statement on the consultation's draft rules appeared in May 2003 (CP 186).[53] Final rules known as "MCOB" were published in October 2003. Much of the debate at the time was focused on

47 Supra note 45, (CP 70), 24.

48 Ibid., It is worth noting that the Office of Fair Trading had carried out its own review in 1995 on mortgage advice and concluded by simply publishing a guidance leaflet for consumers, 'Annual report of the Director of Fair Trading', (1995), 16. See also House of Commons Library, 'Endowment mortgages', (8 June 2015), Briefing Paper 570.

49 Supra note 45, (CP 70), 24.

50 Ibid.

51 Insurance Mediation Directive 2002/92/EC of the European Parliament and Council (9 December 2002) Official Journal L 009, 15/2/2003 P. 3–8.

52 FSA, 'Approach to regulating mortgage sales', (2002), CP 146.

53 FSA, 'Mortgage regulation: draft conduct of business rules and feedback on CP146', (2003), CP 186.

mortgage disclosure requirements and adapting the path-dependent approach for investment business for mortgage distribution.[54]

The 2003 rules, which came into force in October 2004, required the mortgage adviser to advise the customer "which mortgage contract will be suitable ... [and] to have reasonable grounds to conclude that the customer can afford to enter into the [mortgage contract and that it] is appropriate to the needs and circumstances of the customer".[55] As part of the affordability assessment the adviser should "give due regard" to the "information the customer provides about his income and expenditure and any other resources ... any likely changes" to these areas and any increase in interest charges after the initial mortgage introductory offer expires.[56] As already mentioned the rules are a mirror of those relating to investment business. Shortly after the new rules came into effect the FSA carried out a series of reviews, the results of which, combined with the start of the financial crisis led to a regulatory change of policy.

5.4.7 The financial crisis and the effect on mortgage conduct of business regulation

This section considers the FSA's new approach and the origins of its MMR. The FSA acted quickly after the new regulations came into force to assess how they had been implemented. To an extent these reviews were overtaken by the start of the financial crisis. The FSA, under new leadership, adopted a much more assertive tone.[57] There was an FSA thematic review of the implementation of the new regime in 2005 which was published in 2006 as part of "phase 1". This was focused on disclosure, advice and selling standards in the prime mortgage market. However, the "phase 2" review, which looked at higher risk areas, was more influential since it straddled the start of the financial crisis, with the review starting in April 2007 and reporting in March 2008.[58] As a result of this, and deficiencies revealed by the financial crisis, the FSA launched its MMR in May 2009.[59]

54 Kevin Littler and Robert Hudson, 'The impact of regulatory change on retail financial product distribution in the UK', (2003) Journal of Financial Regulation and Compliance, Vol. 11, No. 2, 76.

55 Rule 4.5.4, (CP 146), supra, note 53.

56 4.5.7 Evidential section, (CP 146), supra, note 53.

57 Hector Sants became chief executive officer in July 2007. The change in style is clearly stated in his speech, 'Delivering intensive supervision and credible deterrence',

> There is a view that people are not frightened of the FSA. I can assure you that this is a view I am determined to correct. People should be very frightened of the FSA ... The FSA has been seared by recent events but it is tougher and better as a result,
>
> at the Reuters Newsmakers event, 12 March 2009

58 FSA, 'Mortgage effectiveness review: stage 2 report', (March 2008).

59 Supra note 2, (Discussion paper: Mortgage Market Review, 2009).

The FSA considered that a review was necessary since they believed that potential consumer detriment existed since consumer incomes were not verified in 49% of mortgage applications and 32% of mortgages were provided on an interest only basis.[60] The FSA's view was that it was only the existence of low interest rates and lender forbearance that had prevented problems crystallising.[61] The new rules placed responsibility for ensuring the suitability and affordability of the mortgage solely on the lender no matter who provided the mortgage advice; affordability had to be evidenced and documented; the effective banning of interest only mortgages and specifying what factors needed to be taken into account in determining affordability. The FSA briefly considered adopting other paths to mortgage regulation. Its 2009 consultation considered the use of higher capital requirements to constrain mortgage lending but concluded that "...increasing capital requirements would not be an effective mechanism for deterring high-risk lending and that using prudential levers to achieve objectives relating to consumer detriment is subject to significant uncertainty".[62] The FSA also considered applying LTV, DTI and loan-to-income (LTI) ratios but conclude that

> capping ratios is a blunt approach ... it would lead to a reduction in access to credit for some people able to afford high LTVs but not having access to means (such as parental support) by which others may afford high deposits.[63]

However, a form of product regulation was developed as a possible way forward but only to be used in a number of limited circumstances. These included prohibiting high LTV loans to those customers who display a number of "high risk factors" such as "credit impaired borrowers who have an unstable income or other 'toxic' mixes".[64]

5.4.8 Borrowers not properly advised

According to the FSA's own information in 2007 about 1.9% of mortgages, by number, were made to those who were "credit impaired" and just over 14% were made to those whose future income may be irregular or "unstable".[65] The FSA was also concerned that products designed for the self-employed, where the

60 Ibid., 20.

61 FSA, 'Mortgage Market Review', (December 2011), CP 11/31, 15.

62 Supra note 2, (Discussion Paper, Mortgage Market Review, 2009), 9 and 30–31. It is worth noting that the Financial Policy Committee has imposed LTV restrictions on high debt to income mortgages (Bank of England, 'CP11/14 Implementing the Financial Policy Committee's recommendation on loan to income ratios in mortgage lending', (June 2014).

63 Supra note 2, (MMR 9/3) 11 and 37–44. It is worth noting that the FPC has recently been granted powers to set LTV and LTI limits as part of its macroprudential set of "tools", (The Bank of England Act 1998 (Macroprudential Measures) Order 2015).

64 Supra note 2, (MMR 9/3), 12.

65 Supra note 2, (MMR 9/3), 46.

borrower "self-certified" their income, were being abused and that this type of lending should be prohibited.[66] More generally, the FSA's key issue was the "lack of proper affordability assessments".[67] Specifically, the FSA's concern was that customers were not being properly advised as this required a full "affordability and appropriateness" assessment for all mortgage sales.[68]

5.5 The main elements of the new regulations in relation to mortgage "affordability"

5.5.1 The issue of who should be responsible for assessing the ability of customers to afford a mortgage

The intermediaries are also subject to regulation and are authorised and supervised by the FSA/FCA. However, "to remove any uncertainty about the respective responsibilities of lenders and intermediaries" the regulations were amended to place on the lender "ultimate responsibility for assessing and verifying affordability in every sale".[69] Consequently, the borrower would need to meet the intermediary face-to-face and provide information on their income, spending and prospective outgoings together with documentary evidence. The intermediary would, in due course, pass all this information to the lender for the latter to carry out a full affordability assessment.[70] It is pertinent to consider, in more detail, how the regulator expected this to be undertaken.

5.5.2 Verifying income and expenditure

The requirements for verifying income and spending, both current and future, were very prescriptive with some three layers of calculation and evidence.[71] The expenditure "can be verified against publicly available sources (e.g. level of income tax and national insurance) or documentation provided by a consumer (e.g. bank account statements and [utility bills]) … or accept consumer

66 Supra note 2, (MMR 9/3), 12. FSA thematic work found many examples where brokers had not been able to justify recommending a "self-certified" mortgage. There were also widespread cases of failures demonstrate customer mortgage affordability: 'FSA mortgage regulation – one year on', Callum McCarthy, Chairman of the FSA, speech to the Council of Mortgage Lenders Annual Conference, 6 December 2005.

67 Supra, note 2, (MMR 9/3), 12.

68 Supra note 2, (MMR 9/3), 62. It is possible that the regulatory focus on lenders is deliberate so as to enable the FCA to use its resources more efficiently on a small number of large lenders rather than several thousand mortgage brokers.

69 Supra, note 2, (MMR 9/3), 63. Although not discussed by the FSA in their MMR papers, there may be acceptable technology methods to assess and verify income and expenditure using, for example, authenticated tax record filings and models based on Office of National Statistics (ONS) and in-house lender data. The former would require approval by the UK tax authorities and both approaches would need to be acceptable to the FCA.

70 Supra, note 2, (MMR 9/3), 63.

71 Supra, note 2, (MMR 9/3), 53.

provided data (e.g. food expenses)".[72] "Some of this data can be checked against national averages [using Office of National Statistics information] so that any non-credible outliers can be identified and investigated".[73] The result of all of this, and the requirements to provide advice, was to place the process firmly back in the hands of a "trusted adviser".

5.5.3 New regulations come into effect in April 2014: a summary

The FSA was replaced by the Financial Conduct Authority in April 2013. As mentioned, the draft rules went through a number of consultations before the final rules were issued in December 2012, coming into effect in April 2014.[74] The MMR 2012 rules were designed as "anticipatory regulation".[75] The objective of the 2012 rules is to prevent a future crisis.[76] Although the approach became more paternalistic it, nevertheless, continued to reinforce the concept of the "trusted adviser". The approach is "paternalistic" in that, for behavioural reasons, the FCA considers that borrowers are generally not able to take care of their own interests. This subject is considered in more detail later in this chapter. The regulatory view that borrowers are largely myopic and unengaged is addressed by requiring them to consult a "trusted adviser" before entering into a mortgage contract.

As mentioned earlier, the FSA issued its final MMR Policy Statement and Rules in October 2012.[77] Much of the Policy Statement was concerned with areas such as the definition of "advice", the ability of high-net-worth customer to opt-out of the affordability assessment requirements and the application of the rules to business customers. The regulations also included mandating the provision of advice to customers to be provided either face-to-face or over the telephone. Allowing customers to proceed without advice (i.e. "execution only") was largely restricted to mortgages arranged over the internet.

There were also new prudential requirements for non-deposit taker mortgage lenders and new rules for arrears management and forbearance. The key rules on assessing the affordability, repayability and suitability of the loan are set out in Sections 11.5–11.7 of the new Mortgage Conduct of Business ("MCOB") rules.[78] These restrict the provision of interest only mortgages by requiring that the consumer has a repayment strategy and that this is evidenced.[79] There are detailed rules regarding the need for the lender to be able to demonstrate that

72 Supra, note 2, (MMR 9/3), 55.
73 Ibid.
74 FSA, 'Policy Statement 12/16 Mortgage Market Review Feedback on CP11/31 and final rules'.
75 Karen Harris, 'Anticipatory regulation for the management of banking crises', (2005) Columbia Journal of Law and Social Problems, Vol. 285, 38.
76 Supra, note 2, (MMR 9/3), 22.
77 Supra, note 74, ('MMR Policy Statement').
78 FCA, 'Mortgage Conduct of Business Rules', (MCOB) 11.5–11.7.
79 Ibid., 11.6.

the customer is able to afford the mortgage. This needs to be based on verified income from a source other than the customer (e.g. from tax returns, payslips, etc.).[80] The customer's level of expenditure must be ascertained and analysed into committed and basic essential expenditure (e.g. food, washing, utility payments) and basic quality of living costs which are "hard to reduce and [give] a basic quality of life" (e.g. holidays, entertainment).[81] The lender also needs to consider potential changes in income and expenditure (e.g. planning a family or retirement date).[82] It is interesting to note recent anecdotal reports on potential borrowers suppressing information to avoid problems with the new affordability calculations.[83] The latter need to include a future interest rise stress test over at least the first five years of the loan.[84] The new rules place responsibility on the board of the lender to set policies and to arrange for the monitoring of, and reporting on, a range of these detailed policies relating to mortgage affordability.[85] These policies need to include:

a details of the types of income which are acceptable;
b the proportion of different income streams which is acceptable;
c how variations in income over time, of which the firm is aware, are to be considered;
d what is acceptable evidence of income (including the time period to be covered by the evidence);
e how committed expenditure, basic essential expenditure and basic quality-of-living costs are taken into account when assessing affordability;
f how future interest rates are taken into account when assessing affordability; and
g the calculations used to determine whether the … mortgage is affordable.[86]

80 Supra note 78, 11.6–11.8.
81 Supra note 78, 11.6.10.
82 Supra note 78, 11.6.14–11.6.15.
83 Business Reporter, 'Many young female home-buyers "hide family plans from mortgage lenders"', (8 October 2015),

> A survey from uSwitch.com among more than 2,000 women aged 25 to 45 who had applied for a mortgage found that 25% had intentionally kept their family plans from lenders in case they missed out on the best mortgage rate or were rejected.

Daily Telegraph, 'How borrowers are tricking mortgage lenders', (5 December 2015)

> Prospective mortgage borrowers are resorting to desperate measures to hide their personal spending in an effort to pass lenders' tough affordability checks, according to new research [by MoneySuperMarket]. One in five of those planning to apply for a mortgage in the next three years is planning to withdraw and spend cash rather than use credit or debit cards so that lenders can't see what they spend their money on.

84 Supra, note 78, 11.6.18.
85 Supra, note 78, 11.6.20.
86 Ibid.

The board of the lender is required to have an independent monitoring and reporting programme in place usually undertaken by the firm's Compliance or Internal Audit functions, which have their own responsibilities and regulatory accountabilities.[87] This is part of a wider series of regulatory actions to increase board and individual accountability in regulated firms.[88] There are extensive evidential record keeping requirements which may be used by the FCA's supervision teams for their own monitoring of lenders and in referrals to the FCA's Enforcement Division.[89]

The rules place particular importance on the ability of the lender to be able to demonstrate the affordability of the mortgage after the borrower has reached retirement.[90] It is important to note the FCA's guidance since it is very specific and has attracted significant criticism during the consultation process and subsequently. It states that:

> If the term [of the mortgage] would extend beyond the date on which the customer expects to retire (or, where that date is not known, the state pension age), a firm should take a prudent and proportionate approach to assessing the customer's income beyond that date. The degree of scrutiny to be adopted may vary according to the period of time remaining to retirement when the assessment is made. The closer the customer is to retiring, the more robust the evidence of the level of income in retirement should be. For example, where retirement is many years in the future, it may be sufficient merely to confirm the existence of some pension provision for the customer by requesting evidence such as a pension statement; where the customer is close to retirement, the more robust steps may involve considering expected pension income from a pension statement.[91]

The result is that it may be very difficult for a lender to provide a mortgage which extends into a borrowers' retirement.[92] In contrast, it may be easier to borrow once a potential borrower has retired and their post-retirement income is known since this makes it easier to carry out the affordability assessment.

5.6. Mortgage regulation: key issues

5.6.1 The FCA's assessment of the consequences

As already mentioned, the rules place all the responsibility on the lender for assessing the affordability of the mortgage.[93] There is no regulatory responsibility

87 Supra, note 78, 11.6.22–11.6.24.
88 FCA, 'Consultation Paper 15/22 Strengthening accountability in banking', (July 2015).
89 Supra, note 78, 11.6.60–11.6.61.
90 Supra, note 78, 11.6.15.
91 Supra, note 78, 11.6.15(2).
92 Daily Telegraph, 'Forty-somethings "too old to get a mortgage"', (11 July 2014).
93 Supra, note 78, 11.6.2.

placed on the intermediary mortgage adviser to undertake this assessment. In other respects, the new requirements are very similar to previous rules. However, they are set out in much greater detail and are expressed in more prescriptive terms. As mentioned above, areas such as interest only mortgages, which were typically used by first time buyers, are effectively banned. The same applies to "self-certification" mortgages (where the borrower states their income and this is not verified objectively) which may have encouraged some consumers to over-inflate their incomes, and are now also prohibited. As part of their cost-benefit assessment, the FSA estimated that only some 2% of affordable mortgages, in a depressed property market, and 11%, in a booming market, would now be declined under the new rules.[94]

5.6.2 *Who may be affected by the MMR regulations*

The FSA considered this effect on those who could afford a mortgage is an acceptable consequence of the new regulations.[95] However, there is anecdotal evidence from some lenders that the adverse effect on "good" consumers is much higher and much more significant. The FSA stated that the effect on prime borrowers would be close to zero.[96] However, this fails to take account of the likely impact on mortgages, which run beyond the consumer's likely retirement date and the effect of income verification, particularly on the self-employed. The FSA considered that most of those affected will be interest only borrowers who use this type of loan to enter the housing market and who later switch to a repayment mortgage as their household income increases as they advance in their careers.[97] Certainly, consumer mortgage application interviews have lengthened to over three hours or more and they have become much more intrusive in terms of their personal questions and information requirements.[98] Consequently, "giving advice" may have important societal and financial consequences.

5.6.3 *The long-term implications of "giving advice"*

Compliance with the regulations will be assessed by the FCA's monitoring teams who are required to exercise their judgement in determining whether the lender has met both the letter of the rules and the spirit of the FCA's Principles. There is considerable fear among lenders how this judgement will be exercised and this is acknowledged by the FCA.[99] The concern of lenders is reinforced by the potential cost of not achieving the right standard. The cost of restitution would certainly dwarf any regulatory fine. The "trusted adviser" is required to understand

94 Supra, note 74, FSA, 'Mortgage Market Review', (December 2011), CP 11/31, A3:2.
95 Supra, note 74, A2 27–28.
96 Supra, note 74, A2:25 and A2: 42.
97 Supra, note 74, A2:54–62.
98 The Guardian, 'Applying for a mortgage? Prepare for the third degree', (2 June 2014).
99 Supra, note 74, (FSA, 'MMR Policy statement and feedback on CP11/31').

the needs of the customer and to provide "suitable advice". If the adviser fails in this regulatory duty, they expose themselves to a claim for compensation. The standard basis for this is calculated on the cost of putting the customer back in the position they would have been in if the investment had not been made and includes an element for "loss of opportunity".[100] With loans of tens of thousands of pounds covering long-term contracts the lender could be required to reduce the outstanding balance or the interest rate or both to ensure that the mortgage is affordable.[101] Spread over many thousands of mortgages this has the potential to threaten the financial soundness of the lender. Of course, the PRA has the power to direct the FCA to refrain from taking any action, which the PRA believe may "threaten the stability of the UK financial system, or result in the failure of a PRA authorised person in a way that would adversely affect the UK financial system".[102]

The degree of input by the FCA into the deliberations of the PRA and FPC appears to be limited and it is not clear that conduct of business matters impinge over-much on the PRA's concept of prudential regulation.[103] This is unfortunate since the FCA will have information which may be relevant to the prudential regulator concerning, for example, ethics and culture within dual-regulated firms and insights into business models. In all the many mis-selling scandals (e.g. mortgage endowments, pension opt-out and transfers, split capital investments, payment protection insurance, etc.) none have threatened the failure of a systemically important firm. However, it is possible, for the reasons described above, that a major mortgage mis-selling problem relating to mortgage affordability may threaten one or more such firms. It is an aspect which does not appear to have been the subject of much prudential regulatory, industry or political concern.

5.6.4 The effect of EU mortgage credit directive on the MMR

It is worth noting that in parallel to the MMR, the EU Commission developed its own Mortgage Credit Directive (MCD), which was implemented in the UK in 2015 and came into force on 21 March 2016.[104] The only significant change

100 Financial Ombudsman Service, 'On-line Technical Resource: Compensation for being "deprived" of money and for investment loss'.

101 The Financial Ombudsman Service reported in 2014 the largest increase in mortgage related complaints (13,659 in 2013/14 compared to 12,845 in 2012/13. This is Money web-site 14 May 2014). These mainly related to problems involving financial difficulties. See also a successful compensation claim reported in The Guardian, 'Key repossession ruling opens door to mortgage mis-selling complaints', (22 March 2009).

102 s3I, Financial Services Act 2012.

103 This is based on non-attributable conversations with regulatory staff.

104 2014/17/EU. It has been implemented by Statutory Instrument: Mortgage Credit Directive Order 2015 and FCA rule changes, 'PS15/9: Implementation of the Mortgage Credit Directive and the new regime for second charge mortgages, feedback to CP14/20 and final rules', (March 2015).

to UK regulation is the requirement to replace the current Key Facts Illustration (KFI) sheet with the European Standardised Information Sheet (ESIS). The FCA's view is that this latter document is much less useful for customers compared to the existing KFI. Member states are obliged to use the ESIS without amendment. However, it includes terminology that is unfamiliar in the UK (e.g. "exit charges" rather than "early repayment costs"). It also requires a second "annual percentage rate of charge" (APRC) calculation based on the highest level of interest rate on a product in the last twenty years which is likely to cause confusion and not be helpful. As part of the FCA's commitment to behavioural testing, the KFI was tested on a range of customers and changes made to ensure clarity and understandability before being implemented.[105] The EU Commission has not carried out any such testing on the ESIS.[106]

5.7 UK regulation, information disclosure and behavioural economics

As a result of market and regulatory changes the proportion of UK mortgages sourced from intermediaries rose from 35% in 2000 to almost 65% by 2007, with an additional 18% undertaken on an "execution only" basis by post and the internet.[107] The likelihood was that the consumer expected the intermediary to do the research for them and to find the best mortgage deal available. Prior to 2007, when credit was freely available, lenders would offer attractive one or two year low interest deals before the borrower moved onto higher "standard variable rate" terms.[108] However, borrowers, assisted by intermediaries, would move before the low rate offer expired to another lender's low interest rate mortgage and so the process would continue. Consequently, due to high levels of competition for borrowers coupled with the growth of mortgage intermediaries there was little incentive for consumers to spend too long shopping around nor to read mortgage disclosure material.

105 For example, 'Smarter consumer communications, DP15/5', Christopher Woolard, Director of Strategy and Competition, speech, 25 June 2015.

106 This is based on my own discussions with EU Commission staff in 2013 and confirmed by subsequent conversations with FCA staff. The EU Commission launched a Green Paper in December 2015 on 'Retail financial services' looking at the barriers to expanding cross-border retail financial services.

107 Supra, note 74, (FSA CP 11/31, 'Mortgage Market Review', December 2011), 147. The market share for mortgage brokers continues to rise and was expected to reach 75% by the end of 2016 (Mortgage Solutions (a trade paper), 28 August 2015) and this has been confirmed by the regulator in 2019, FCA, 'Consultation on mortgage advice and selling standards', (CP19/17), 7.

108 David Miles, The UK Mortgage Market: Taking a Longer-Term View: Final report and recommendations, (HM Treasury, London, 2004), 37,

> 4.41 The great majority of mortgage intermediaries' remuneration is paid in the form of commission from the lenders to which they refer business ... intermediaries have some financial incentive to sell short-term discounted products with the prospect of a resale in the near future.

5.7.1 FSA research findings

This view is supported by FSA research, which found that consumers did not use disclosure documentation as expected.[109] "Our consumer research suggests that [the] disclosure documents are not being used in the way we intended".[110] The main disclosure document was being used by consumers "as a record of their purchase [rather] than as a tool to inform their decision on a product ... [it was] only ... used to compare products by a small proportion of consumers".[111] Consequently, building on this research, the FCA has reduced its faith in the effectiveness of information provided to consumers and instead placed more reliance on the role of the lender to ensure affordability.[112] This approach appears to be part of a much broader regulatory strategy, which regards consumers as rarely capable of looking after their own interests. It places a duty on the adviser and lender to "act in the best interests of the consumer".[113] Evidence from behavioural economics does appear to support the interventionist FCA attitude which may be appropriate in this area.[114] Indeed the FCA are looking more generally at behavioural biases in mortgage lending.[115]

5.7.2 FCA work on behavioural economics

The FCA has set up a Behavioural Economics Unit, which published its first report in 2013.[116] The FCA now look at four sets of behavioural tools: controlling information provided to consumers, determining the methods used to distribute products, how choices are presented to consumers and banning or restricting particular products.[117] The FCA has adopted all four sets of tools as part of their approach to regulating the mortgage market. Consequently, less emphasis is now placed simply on the provision of information to consumers. Instead, the FCA focuses on the provision of "key messages at the key points in the mortgage sales

109 Supra, note 74, (FSA CP 11/31, 'Mortgage Market Review', December 2011), 168.

110 FSA, 'Consultation Paper 28/10: Mortgage Market Review: Distribution & Disclosure', (November 2010), 23 and supra, note 58, (FSA Effectiveness review), 5.

111 Ibid., (FSA CP 28/10), 23.

112 Supra, note 74, (FSA CP 11/31), 169. This is supported by research undertaken on behalf of the FCA, Oxera, 'Review of literature on product disclosure', (October 2014), 3–4.

113 Supra, note 74, (FSA CP 11/31), 162.

114 Behavioural economics, in the field of conduct of business regulation, provides valuable insights. Consequently, the FCA has set up a behavioural economics team to look at how consumers actually behave and how regulatory policy should be adapted. The work on how consumers use information as mentioned in the main text is of particular relevance to mortgage conduct of business regulation. FCA's 'Applying behavioural economics at the Financial Conduct Authority', (April 2013).

115 Speech by Linda Woodall, (Director of Mortgages and Consumer Lending at the FCA) 'Building a common language in the mortgage market', (November 2013).

116 Supra, note 114, ('Applying behavioural economics'), 24–25 and a speech by Martin Wheatley, former Chief Executive of the FCA, 'The human face of regulation', 10 April 2013.

117 Supra, note 114, ('Applying behavioural economics'), 43.

process", and, as mentioned above, information is presented in a standard format to aid the consumer.[118] As already mentioned, certain mortgage products such as "self-certification" mortgages have been banned. Further, FSA research indicates that consumers do not understand the distinction between being provided with information and receiving advice.[119] Consequently, the FCA MMR rules have abandoned trying to draw a regulatory distinction and all interactions with customers are now described as "giving advice".[120] The result has been a greater propensity towards regulatory paternalism.

5.8 The new regulatory paternalism

5.8.1 Paternalism, politics and consumer financial regulation

UK conduct of business regulation is founded on the concept of correcting market failures.[121] However, this technocratic approach may be viewed as somewhat disingenuous since determining regulatory policy involves making a number of "political judgements".[122] This has developed into the FCA becoming a "surrogate citizen" deciding what level of protection to prioritise and who should be protected, in what manner and to what extent.[123] The FCA may consequently set out how much individuals can afford to spend and how much financial risk they should each be exposed to. This can be seen in the regulatory policy governing the UK mortgage systems and the latter's exposure of consumers to high levels of debt. Jane Ball notes that individual indebtedness in the UK was 86% of GDP (by 2017 this had increased to almost 140%) compared with, for example, only 48.3% in France.[124] It may be that lenders are more likely to make a loan in the UK since it is relatively easy to evict a mortgagee. In contrast, there are no mortgage eviction figures available in France.[125] The legal eviction process in France also takes account of social issues not least that someone evicted is likely

118 Sheila Nicholl, (Director of Conduct Policy at FSA/FCA) speech, 'Developing regulatory policy on mortgages at the national, European and international Level', 3 November 2011.

119 Supra, note 58, ('Mortgage Effectiveness Review'), 19–20. See also Christine Jolls and others, 'A behavioral approach to law and economics', (1998) Stanford Law Review, Vol. 50, 1471.

120 FCA, MCOB 4.7A2 and 4.8A. Recently, the FCA has tried to expand the number of 'execution-only' transactions from the current level of around 3%, supra note 108, (FCA, 'Consultation on mortgage advice'), 6–9.

121 For example, this approach is clearly set out in the FCA's 'Economics for effective regulation', (2014), Occasional Paper 13, 5 and it is embedded in the FCA's statutory strategic objective to "ensure that markets function well", FCA, 'Our future mission', (October 2016), 4.

122 Harry McVea, 'Financial services regulation under the Financial Services Authority: a re-assertion of the market failure thesis?' (2005) Cambridge Law Journal, Vol. 64, No. 2, 413–448, 445.

123 Ibid., (McVea), 445.

124 Jane Ball, 'Using banks: the effect of national attitudes to public intervention in mortgage lending and eviction in French and English law', (2010) International Journal of Law in the Built Environment, 122.

125 Ibid., (Ball) 125.

to have difficulty finding even rented property to live in since eviction carries a high level of social stigma. Consequently, because of the difficulty in evicting defaulters, banks are reluctant to lend unless they can be certain that there is no risk of needing to seek an eviction order.[126]

5.8.2 "Structured paternalism"

The MMR's approach is for the regulator to take greater control of the market and to determine what is best for consumers. Sigal Ben-Porath considered this form of state paternalism, and in her evaluation quoted both Kant's view of "paternalism" as "degrading of men" and Isaiah Berlin's contention that paternalism always leads to some form of coercion no matter how well intentioned.[127] Ben-Porath, however, believes that the proper functioning of the state requires it to act in a "structured paternalistic" manner by allowing the individual freedom of choice within set boundaries and that discussion should focus on where those boundaries should be.[128] However, the UK may be moving closer to the French model with a much more paternalistic approach to protecting borrowers.

5.8.3 "Libertarian paternalism"

Libertarian paternalism aims to influence "the choices … in a way that will make choosers better off" since "in some cases individuals make inferior decisions in terms of their own welfare decisions that they would change if they had complete information, unlimited cognitive abilities, and no lack of self-control".[129] It is based on the concept that it is right and proper for the state to act to protect the consumer from themselves and it is only a matter of deciding which are the best tools for this role in "the toolbox of libertarian paternalism".[130] This form of "soft paternalism" can include regulations which seeks to educate the

126 Supra, note 124, (Ball) 124.

127 Sigal Ben-Porath, Tough choices: structured paternalism and the landscape of choice, (Princeton University Press, Princeton, NJ, 2010), 25–28.

128 Ibid., (Ben-porath), 28.

129 Cass Sunstein and Richard Thaler, 'Libertarian paternalism is not an oxymoron', (2003) University of Chicago Law Review, Vol. 70, 1159.

130 Ibid., (Sunstein) 1174, From the examples given by the authors the approach adopted for mortgage advice, by the FCA, lacks the "libertarian" element they envisaged. The authors consider that the "bounded rationality" of people means that in some instances a form of "guiding" or "nudge" is necessary. People, generally, are not the rational calculating machines of classical economic theory. Herbert Simon (a Nobel economics prize-winner) first coined the phrase "bounded rationality" to describe "Man, faced with complexity beyond his ken, uses his information processing capacities to seek out alternatives, to calculate consequences, to resolve uncertainties, and thereby … to find ways of action that are sufficient unto the day, that satisfice". 'Rational decision making in business organizations', Nobel Memorial Lecture, 8 December, 1978.

borrower but still leaves them with the ultimate choice.[131] These could take the form of procedural constraints or default choices for consumers.[132] However, Wright challenges this view, believing that rational lenders will always take sufficient steps to protect themselves without the need for regulatory interference.[133] However, he was writing on the cusp of the financial crisis and there is substantial evidence of lenders mis-pricing risk contrary to their own interests, those of their customers and the financial system in general.[134] Consequently, the approach adopted by the FCA more or less ceases to treat consumers as consenting adults and places responsibility on the lender to act as the consumers' guardian and guarantor. This develops a form of "Coasian Theorem".[135] It implicitly views the lender as best placed not only to undertake the affordability and suitability assessments but also to shoulder any losses if the assessment turns out to have been wrong viewed with hindsight many years hence.[136] The key issue is whether the FCA's approach may prove to be beyond the capabilities of mortgage lenders both in terms of the risk that they make the wrong judgements about consumer mortgage affordability and, consequently, that their balance sheets prove too weak to sustain the cost of remediation work and consumer compensation at some future date. This issue could develop in a number of ways including higher cost mortgages to reflect this increased risk, a reduction in the provision of mortgages except to high-net-worth customers, or a subsequent taxpayer funded bail-out of broken mortgage lenders. All of these potential outcomes may have serious socio-economic and political consequences.

5.9 Socio-economic issues with the current approach

5.9.1 Socio-economic issues

The new MMR regulations protect those refused a mortgage from getting into unaffordable debt but the new rules may also prevent those who could afford the loan from obtaining their own home. This may well be of concern since, in

131 Emilios Avgouleas, 'Reforming investor protection regulation: the impact of cognitive biases', in Michael Faure and Frank Stephen, (eds), Essays in the law and economics of regulation in honour of Anthony Ogus, (Intersentia, The Hague, 2008), 143–166, 146.

132 Supra, note 129, (Sunstein), 1174.

133 Joshua Wright, 'Behavioral law and economics, paternalism, and consumer contracts: an empirical perspective', (2007) New York University Journal of Law & Liberty, Vol. 2, 476.

134 Chapter 3, n. 15, ('Turner Review'), 35.

135 Ronald Coase, 'The problem of social cost', (1960) The Journal of Law and Economics, Vol. 3, 2. In essence the theory states that losses between various parties are best distributed between them based on economic efficiency rather basing them on concepts of "fairness" and tortious or contractual rights.

136 Robert Cooter and Thomas Ulan, Law and economics, (6th Edition, Pearson, London, 2012), 81–102. There is a view that government regulatory intervention to correct market imperfection aimed at increasing market efficiency often only focusses on the "active" participant which in turn may produce consequential market imperfections, Richard Posner, Economic analysis of law, (8th Edition, Aspen, Wolters Kluwer, New York City, 2010), 64.

the UK there is a powerful aspiration for homeownership and this issue and its implications for regulatory policy are considered in later chapters. The effect of regulatory decisions can be very wide-ranging since they are likely to have political and socio-economic consequences.[137] In many instances the results may only emerge slowly over time while regulators receive little praise if a potential crisis is averted. There are also a number of other socio-economic issues to be resolved.

Separately, as mentioned earlier, there is also an increased risk that the new rules will encourage deceptive behaviour. It is likely that some otherwise honest consumers and intermediaries will attempt to work around the new rules and that some lenders may tolerate these contrivances.

5.9.2 Access to mortgage lending

It is possible that UK mortgage regulations may start to restrict access to mortgages, especially after the first few heavy enforcement actions. Coupled with the high price of houses the average age of the first time home-buyer has risen to around 35 or 37 compared with 28 ten years ago.[138] The MMR now makes it difficult to lend where the term may extend past the individuals retirement date due to the need to evidence affordability. This indicates that home buying may be limited to those between their mid-30s and 50, and those already retired drawing their pensions. High-net-worth individuals are largely exempt from these restrictions.

The significant issue at stake here is that while regulation may remedy one problem it invariably results in unintended consequences. There needs to be a balance struck between competing harms. Consequently, there is a need for regulations to be subject to continuous monitoring in order to assess the effects they are having, especially when operated in combination with other regulatory measures and as demographics, economic conditions and markets change.[139] The FCA is well aware of all these concerns and, as a result, has initiated a review

137 Eilis Ferran and others, The regulatory aftermath of the global financial crisis, (Cambridge University Press, Cambridge, 2013), 199.

138 Daily Telegraph, 'Average first-time buyer is now 35', (11 September 2012). However, the government's "Help to Buy" scheme may have reduced this figure for some borrowers (see Daily Telegraph, 'Help-to-Buy 2 shaves six years off first-time buyer age of 37', (5 February 2015).

139 Many have analysed this problem, however, the classic statement of the issue can be found in Friedrich Hayek's, New Studies in Philosophy, Politics, Economics and the History of Ideas, (published 1967, Routledge, Oxford, 1978), 80, "Man does not so much choose between alternative actions according to their known consequences as prefer those the consequences of which are predictable over those the consequences of which are unknown". Other examples include Donald Langevoort, 'The human nature of corporate boards: law, norms, and the unintended consequences of independence and accountability', (2000) Georgetown Law Journal, Vol. 89, 797, 818, which considers the effect of increased regulation on the composition and actions of corporate boards and the so called "Peltzman effect" where the danger of road accidents for pedestrians increased as vehicle drivers felt safer with the introduction of compulsory seat-belt wearing regulations, Sam Peltzman, 'The effects of automobile safety regulation', (1975) Journal of Political Economy, Vol. 83, No. 4, 677–726.

of competition in the mortgage sector including the difficulties of switching products and suppliers.[140]

Regulation has an important role and the regulators need to bear in mind the socio-economic effect of their actions. Aspects of these issues are considered in Chapter 8 based, in part, on my discussions with UK politicians and regulators.

5.9.3 Market effects

The new UK mortgage rules have substantially increased the barriers to entry for new lenders, not least by introducing capital requirements for non-deposit takers for the first time. This may be seen as part of a deliberate strategy to control lending since much of the property boom before 2007/8 was generated by a substantial influx of non-deposit taker lenders.[141] Finally, in this area mortgage regulation does not happen in a vacuum. The government is keen, for political, economic and social reasons, for mortgage lending to increase in order to reinvigorate the housing market and has employed a number of initiatives such as "New-build" and "Help to buy". While regulators need to be cognizant of government policy, they clearly have their own objectives which, for the most part, push in the opposite direction and restrict mortgage lending. The messages can be confusing. For example, FSA/FCA cost-benefit analysis of the proposed UK regulations estimated that only some 11% of good quality new mortgages would be prevented even in a booming market by the application of the new regulations.[142] The introduction of the MMR rules in April has coincided with a 5.5% fall in mortgage approvals compared with the same period in 2013 and a 17% fall compared with January 2014.[143] The Bank of England speculated that this may have been due to the introduction of the new regulations.[144] The reductions are substantially higher than those predicted by the FSA.[145] However, cause and effect is impossible to determine since there are too many social and economic factors involved. In more recent years the level of mortgage approvals has recovered.

5.10 Relying on conduct of business regulation

Finally, there is a significant question over how successful mortgage conduct of business rules have been and will be in the future. An FSA 2007 thematic review of the post-2004 regulations, as mentioned above, disclosed significant

140 FCA, 'Call for Inputs on competition in the mortgage sector', (October 2015).
141 Supra, note 2, ('Discussion paper, Mortgage Market Review', 2009), 11. In the US context see Purnanandam, Amiyatosh, 'Originate-to-distribute model and the subprime mortgage crisis', (2010) University of Michigan.
142 Supra, note 74, (CP 11/31), 12.
143 Bank of England, Monetary Policy Committee Minutes 4 and 5 June 2014, 4 and 5.
144 Ibid., (MPC minutes), 4 and 5.
145 Supra, note 74, (CP 11/31, A3:2).

regulatory failings by lenders and intermediaries.[146] The FCA has started to review the operations of the MMR regime but it is too early to say how effective it has been. In the short period since the new MMR rules came into effect in April 2014 the FCA undertook 134 "mystery shops" across both lender and intermediaries and 40 customer interviews and six customer focus groups. The results were published in July 2015.[147] 59% of mystery shops resulted in suitable mortgage recommendations; in 3% (four cases) the advice was demonstrably unsuitable and in 38% the FCA was unable to determine whether the advice was suitable since the firm had failed to obtain sufficient information.[148]

Based on the experience of investment business advice there is little reason to believe that these figures will improve significantly as time passes. However, it is possible to assert that some conduct of business mortgage regulation, no matter how flawed is better than none. Nevertheless, it is also difficult to establish the counter-factual of what would have happened if the 2004 MCOB rules had not been in place in the lead up to the financial crisis. However, it is possible to look at the effectiveness of the parallel investment business regulations, which have been in place largely unchanged from 1986 until the introduction of Retail Distribution Review (RDR) in 2013. This has been the subject of considerable regulatory enforcement action over the decades. For example, in the period leading up to the introduction of the RDR there were five major FCA enforcement actions relating to the mis-selling of such products.[149] The effect of RDR is still to be determined but anecdotal indications are that the banning of commission payments combined with the higher cost of training investment advisers has led to the reduction of advisers operating in the "mass-market".[150] It may be that investment business mis-selling has finally been cured by, in effect, closing, or significantly reducing, the market. After some thirty years, investment business may once again be the privilege of those in society who were wont to rely on the trusted family stockbroker. The mortgage market is still some distance away from this but its parallel, albeit lagging, regulation does not suggest that compliance with the conduct of business regulations will be any better.

146 Supra, note 58, ('Mortgage effectiveness review: stage 2 report', March 2008).

147 Supra, note 35, ('Embedding the MMR', July 2015).

148 Ibid., 3.

149 Combined Insurance Company of America (£2.8 million), HSBC (£10.5 million), Coutts (£6.3 million), Credit Suisse (£5.9 million), and Norwich and Peterborough Building Society (£2.4 million), FSA, 'Fines Table', (2011).

150 Supra, note 140, ('Call for input'), 6,

> Currently not all consumers may be able to find the form of advice that they want … at a price they are prepared to pay … There are a number of reasons why advice gaps may exist. There are barriers to people seeking advice; including, but not limited to, the cost of taking advice, lack of trust and lack of knowledge. There are also barriers to firms providing advice; including … regulatory costs, ongoing liability for sub-standard advice and potential lack of clarity about regulatory expectations.

5.11 Conduct of business regulation may not be effective

While it is too early to express a view on the revised mortgage conduct of business regulation, as mentioned earlier, the history of investment business conduct of business regulation has been one of failure. The history of conduct of business regulation is scattered with the debris of widespread product mis-selling activities. These included mis-selling personal pension and pension transfers in the early 1990s, mortgage endowments from the late 1980s to the end of the 1990s, split capital trusts in the 1990s and early 2000s, structured capital at risk products ('scarps') in the early 2000s, payment protection insurance (PPI) in the mid-2000s, credit card protection, interest rate swaps in the mid-2000s and "packaged" bank accounts in the late 2000s. It is worth noting that banks in the UK fell outside the main application of the conduct of business regime until the introduction of statutory regulation in this area with the Financial Services and Markets Act 2000. Moreover, these examples, exclude problems with individual institutions which often transgressed.

There are a variety of reasons for all these failures over the couple of decades regulation in this area has been in place. They include incompetence at all levels, a failure by senior management to understand key elements of the business, misaligned targets and incentives, very poor culture and ethics and self-delusion as to what was in the interest of customers, carrying on traditional unethical practices without any self-reflection on whether they were right (e.g. "industrial business" savings schemes) and so on. In many cases, the failures were due to boards setting, or maintaining, inappropriate business models often copying the behaviour of competitors in order, for example, to gain, or maintain, market share.

Some companies thought that they could distance themselves from misconduct by operating through "appointed representatives" (APs) who were not employees but this also failed since the actions of the APs were simply thought to be those of the regulated firm. The regulators tried many initiatives to improve matters over the years and the scale and level of the fines increased with no discernible effect. For example, in 2003/4 the FSA launched its "treating customers fairly" initiative in an attempt to improve conduct of business in regulated firms.[151] However, the mis-selling scandals continued as before with PPI looking like it will cost the financial services industry around £55bn or more in compensation. The introduction of the senior management and certified persons regime is the most recent approach. Additionally, the FCA's Retail Distribution Review (RDR) has reduced the risk of investment business mis-selling by effectively reducing investment product selling by raising the cost of training and employing staff as financial advisers and prohibited the payment of commission.

A major premise of this work is that mortgage conduct of business regulation can substantially strengthen macroprudential policy. However, if this is to be effective there needs to be a better approach.

151 FSA, 'Treating customers fairly – towards fair outcomes for consumers', (July 2006).

5.12 A smarter approach to affordability assessment

The current system for assessing mortgage affordability is based on the original methods for preparing personal financial investment advice for a client. As mentioned, it is laborious and time consuming and prone to abuse. Income information is collected, normally, now by an intermediary and verified against some form of third-party documentation. However, expenditure figures are largely dependent on what a customer discloses in order to provide an estimate of "surplus" income available to service and repay the mortgage. Much of the affordability assessment process is automated and at least one major lender outsources this work to an IT service provider. Some lenders use either their own data or those provided by credit scoring agencies to carry out reasonableness assessment on the income and expenditure figures.[152] It is necessary, at all times, to maintain rigorous records for each decision in order to pass regulatory inspections and, possibly, to defend the lender against future customer litigation and complaints.

However, with the rapid development of financial technology ("fin-tech") it should be possible for both intermediaries and lenders to use data access provided by the customer under, for example, the Payments Services Directive II. This could be used to assess mortgage affordability more accurately and with greater confidence and without the need for extensive customer interviews.[153] This may require the regulator to take the initiative since lenders are apparently too fearful to move in this direction themselves without regulatory approval due to the cost and potential regulatory risk.[154]

5.13 A more targeted approach

The FSA/FCA's approach to the MMR has been to ensure consumer protection with a form of "anticipatory" regulation. However, it is unlikely to suppress demand and it is likely that market pressures and the demand for credit to finance home purchases will put pressures elsewhere in the system. Moreover, regulation needs to be integrated into wider policymaking. At the heart of the problem is the failure in the UK to build sufficient housing to meet anything approaching the level of demand. The issue of housing supply is central to financial regulation in this area and is considered in Chapter 8. In addition, there are possible lessons from the US and, as seen in the last chapter, the UK should consider developing the US concept of the "qualified mortgage" and other options such as the

152 For example, Experian's web-site, 'Affordability check: better insights for more informed affordability decisions', (accessed 28 June 2019).

153 Directive 2015/2366 dated 25 November 2015 on payment services in the internal market.

154 FCA's web-site, 'FCA sets out progress and next steps in promoting innovation in financial services' (29 April 2019), (accessed 28 June 2019).

"unitised mortgage" where the home is bought in incremental steps without the need to take on excessive debt at the out-set.[155]

5.14 Conclusion

In the UK for the last ten or more years, the financial position of mortgagees has been relatively benign. Interest rates have been very low, in most areas house prices have risen and employment levels, even during the financial crisis have remained strong.[156] However, under different economic conditions, for example, closer to those experienced in the early 1990s, the effects on borrowers and hence the economy, as a whole, could be very severe. Mortgage conduct of business regulation has an important role to play in ensuring the provision of meaningful information to prospective borrowers and in ensuring that marketing is fair, clear and not misleading. In addition, conduct of business regulation can help mould the approach taken by both lenders and intermediaries towards protecting consumers (e.g. the setting of targets and incentives, product design, etc.). Central to the regulations introduced in 2014 the affordability test seeks to protect consumers from over-borrowing. It adopts a paternalistic point of view aimed at protecting consumers from themselves.

This may have a number of possible effects. For example, as evidenced by the FCA's thematic review in 2015, as an unfulfilled demand for mortgages builds up the result may be that many consumers in their desperation to achieve a home of their own may be driven to fabricate or conceal information to be able to demonstrate that they can afford the loan they seek.[157]

Second, mortgage conduct of business regulations have socio-economic implications. For example, homeownership and the aspiration of homeownership has a spiritual attraction. It provides an element of social stability with the homeowner having a financial stake in the well-being of the country and can embed them in the community. It has helped engender a willingness to save for the future if only to ensure that the outstanding mortgage is finally paid-off and many see the home as a method of saving for retirement. Much of this can be summarised in the phrase that the home forms both the major portion of a households "store of wealth" and a repository of hope for the future. The possession of the home may help ensure a good school and future career for the children; it may help provide for a comfortable retirement and may assist the next generation forming their own household and buying their own home in years to come. It demonstrates a firm belief in the future and a level of continuity and prosperity. The mortgage conduct of business regulations does not seek to address these concerns. The

155 Atif Mian and Amir Sufi, House of debt, (University of Chicago Press, Chicago, IL, 2015), 218.

156 i.e. Interest rate, employment levels and house prices.

157 Supra, note 35, (FCA Thematic review, 2015). For example, Evening Standard, 'Trapped in a mortgage cage', (13 October 2015), reports a survey by uSwitch that a quarter of young female borrowers "lied about plans to start a family" for fear of having their application rejected.

UK's FCA has consumer protection as one of its statutory objectives but this is not balanced by any need to consider the long-term socio-economic implications of its actions. The latter has a strong political dimension but ministers and the departments of state have tended to regard UK financial services regulation as a technical matter best left to the experts within the FCA. This demonstrates a failure to grasp the strategic issues binding regulation with socio-economic policy. More work is needed to see how consumer protection in the mortgage market, in the face of potentially very powerful market forces, can best operate taking account of socio-economic concerns.

Third, UK regulators have failed to consider the full implications of the new regulations. The all-encompassing rules will be breached at some point. Due to the sums involved mortgage remediation costs could potentially run into the tens of billions of pounds.[158] This could destroy the capital of lenders, forcing them into regulatory resolution with the possibility of taxpayer support.

Finally, it should be possible to redirect and target conduct of business mortgage regulation so that it better protects consumers but at the same time works with the grain of the socio-economic housing policy. This could include better targeted regulation since the assessment of mortgage affordability should lend itself to financial technology developments. Additionally, UK regulators could also look at US policy and the "qualified mortgage" concept considered in the last chapter.

158 The potential size of the issue can be seen from the total value of all UK mortgages outstanding at the end of Q3 2018: £2,430 Bn, (Bank of England and FCA Mortgage Lenders and Administrators Statistics for Q3 2018).

6 The political legitimacy of using macroprudential policy instruments

As part of the Bank of England, the Financial Policy Committee (FPC) has the potential to have a significant influence on individual lives. In part, its role includes a substantial political function as it decides how the scarce resource of credit is distributed across the populace. Consequently, this raises questions regarding its political legitimacy. It may be taken as given that the FPC has 'formal' legitimacy. It has been properly established, and operates within a normative framework including legal procedures and institutional accountabilities and transparency.

However, there are deeper issues. The concept of political legitimacy is based on the underlying ideas which sustain democratic accountability and the conventions and understandings that govern the use of power. Public acceptance cannot be taken for granted. It is ultimately governed by the world of politics, media, and public attention and criticism. The political legitimacy of organisations such as the FPC are often fragile and based on a mixture of technocratic expertise, concepts of independence, and transparency of both policymaking and its operation balanced with the "mystic" of authority. Bodies, such as the FPC, exist in the grey area of unwritten conventions and understandings balancing "sentiment and reason". It requires a strong and compelling "emotional" narrative to engage these sensibilities.

6.1 Introduction

This chapter considers the issue of the threat to political legitimacy of the Bank of England's FPC and its employment of macroprudential policies. It is important to consider Edmund Burke's view that we should

> not dream that your letters of office, and your instructions…are the things that hold together the great contexture of the mysterious whole. These things do not make your government. Dead instruments, passive tools as they are, it is the spirit of the [common] communion that gives all their life and efficacy to them… without any mutual relation, the cement is gone – the cohesion is loosened – and everything hastens to decay and dissolution.[1]

1 Edmund Burke, Speeches on America, on conciliation with America (published 1775, Arthur Innes (ed), Cambridge University Press, Cambridge, 1906), 160–161.

The concept of political legitimacy is based on the underlying ideas which sustain democratic accountability and the conventions and understandings that govern the use of power. These in turn have their roots in the development of the concept of national sovereignty. This latter element and its relationship with political legitimacy are considered in this chapter.

Further, this analysis assesses the division of political legitimacy into its formal or "dignified" aspect established by "black-letter" law and the "efficient" parts used to get things done and accepted.[2] Both concepts are necessary. The first sets out the normative framework including legal procedures and institutional accountabilities and transparency. These aspects are particularly important where authority is delegated to an independent institution such as the Bank of England and the FPC. The second establishes the basis, in societal and empirical terms, of how power is exercised.

This chapter examines the issues posed, in particular, by the delegation of policymaking and implementation powers to public organisations. Further, in the context of political legitimacy it also considers the balance that needs to be struck between public transparency and maintaining the "mystic" of authority.

Besides considering these aspects this chapter examines the socio-legal perspectives of political legitimacy including the limitations imposed by unwritten conventions together with an imprecise, grey area which contains an understanding of what is societally acceptable. The term "acceptance" is used here rather than, for example, "support" or "endorsement" since the bar is a low one: endorsement is not required; acceptance is sufficient – to do otherwise would raise issues of degrees of endorsement; "acceptance" has no voice; it is passive.

Nevertheless, public acceptance cannot be taken for granted. It is ultimately governed by the world of politics, media, and public attention and criticism. It may be that the FPC and the Bank of England are "but the 'dry trustees' of a fealty given to others" or, alternatively, their role and independence, in practice, reinforces the concept of their sovereignty.[3] These issues are considered later but first it is important to understand that they do not exist in a vacuum but have a wider context.

This chapter assesses the importance of both political and operational independence and the possession of technical expertise as factors in securing and maintaining political legitimacy. However, these are insufficient since in a number of areas, such as housing, the policymaker needs to ensure high levels of both popular and emotional engagement. This is particularly relevant since macroprudential powers are likely to have a significant influence on the aspiration of people to own their own home. Consequently, the FPC cannot rely on the usual tenets of political legitimacy. As this chapter discusses, it needs to be conscious of the power of "sentiment and reason" and the Rousseauian influence

2 Walter Bagehot, The English constitution (published 1865–1867, Oxford University Press, Oxford, 2001), 7.

3 Ibid., (Bagehot), 194.

of the "general will" as part of the development and maintenance of political legitimacy. Consequently, the FPC will need to provide a strong and compelling "emotional" narrative to engage these sensibilities.

6.2 Context

As mentioned in earlier chapters, rapid increases in credit are frequently the cause of financial instability. Preceding almost all financial crises there has been a close relationship between excessive lending and a rise in property (normally retail housing) values.[4] An increased availability of mortgages drives up the price of homes which in turn provides greater security for more lending.[5]

As set out in the introduction, this book has three broad themes. First that macroprudential policies have been developed, in part, as potential instruments to suppress market forces and the demand for credit. The ease of access to credit increases demand for property. Mortgages can be said to provide the "fuel" which powers the demand for housing.[6] However, the underlying economic pressures in the system and the demand for housing remain. As discussed in earlier chapters the evidence suggests that quantitative policy measures set by the FPC, such as LTV and DTI limits, are only likely to succeed, at best, for a short period of time in the face of these economic forces which encourage the subversion of these measures. The objective of lending restrictions such as LTV and DTI limits is not to reduce demand but to limit the means by which such demand may be put into effect. It is important to note that the demand remains. Other sources of finance, abetted by willing sellers, brokers and other agents, may be sought. Consequently, market forces may defeat macroprudential policy as more credit "leaks" into the system. This is reinforced by the evidence given by Goodhart and Buiter to the Treasury Select Committee:

> everyone loves [a boom] and the idea that you are going to have a regulator saying, "I am sorry, we are not going to have 100% or 125% loan to value ratios; Northern Rock, you are not allowed to behave that way, you are not allowed to do subprime mortgages based on nothing except the expectation that housing prices will go on rising, you are not allowed to do that," runs counter to the wishes of the lenders, the borrowers, and virtually every politician at the time during the boom.[7]

4 For example, Chapter 2, n. 84 (Borio and Lowe), 27.

5 Chapter 2, n. 87 (Waldron and Zampolli), 3–4.

6 Kathleen Scanlon and Marja Elsinga, 'Policy changes affecting housing and mortgage markets: how governments in the UK and the Netherlands responded to the GFC', (2014) Journal of Housing and the Built Environment, Vol. 29, No. 2, 335–360, 336–337.

7 Charles Goodhart and Willem Buiter, Oral evidence to the TSC, 'Run on the Rock: oral and written evidence', (House of Commons, Fifth Report of Session 2007–08, Vol. II), answer to Question 694, 90.

The second related theme of this work is that macroprudential policies only address the demand side of the economic equation. Unless the supply side of providing more housing is undertaken, macroprudential policies are likely to fail.

This chapter considers the third theme of this book and the concern that the use of LTV and DTI macroprudential tools may be challenged as lacking political legitimacy. This work is not intended to be a comprehensive analysis of the various forms of "legitimacy" but it is important to understand the concerns relating to political legitimacy which may undermine the use of quantitative macroprudential policies and the authority of the Bank of England as a policymaker.

As mentioned in the introduction political legitimacy is based on a superstructure the foundations of which rest on the concepts of sovereignty and, in particular, political sovereignty.

6.3 Political sovereignty

The concept of political sovereignty can be seen as early as the 14th century with the statement that a "king...does not recognise any superior" and does not require Papal sanction.[8] This was also evident shortly afterwards in 1414 at the Council of Constance with the recognition of national states with representatives from France, Italy, Germany and British Isles voting and working as national bodies.[9] At its centre is a question of who has the power to sanction executive actions; whether these be the raising and allocation of taxes or the making of appointments to episcopal benefices. This power is not fixed but moves through a "vertical ladder" and "horizontally" from, and through, different power-bases.[10]

The concept of sovereignty has mutated over time and as explained by Heller, "all conceptions of law are fundamentally political and tied to particular historical and social contexts".[11] Sovereign power does not just exist at the pinnacle of the society since for there to be a ruler there must also be those that are ruled: leaders require followers.[12] This was evident, for example, to the Spanish thinkers at the so-called School of Salamanca in the 16th century who saw that absolute power cannot successfully constrain market forces and that subjects will often seek, successfully, to evade, for example, price-control edicts, that affected

8 Len Scales, The shaping of German identity: authority and crisis, 1245–1414 (Cambridge University Press, Cambridge, 2012), 216–217, quoting Bishop Lupold of Bebenburg's 'Treatise on the rights of the Roman Kingdom and Empire', 1339.

9 Caspar Hirschi, The origins of nationalism (Cambridge University Press, Cambridge, 2012), 82.

10 John Jackson, 'Sovereignty-modern: a new approach to an outdated concept', (2003) American Journal of International Law, Vol. 97, 782–802, 791–792.

11 David Dyzenhaus, 'Hermann Heller', in Arthur Jacobson and Bernhard Schlink (eds), Weimar: a jurisprudence of crisis (University of California Press, Berkley, 2000), 249–279, 250.

12 Robert Wolff, In defense of Anarchism (University of California Press, Berkeley, 1998), 5–6.

their well-being.[13] Similarly, Bodin recognised that sovereignty did not confer absolute power in that the ruler was still bound by some constraints whether these be customary law or "some basic laws of the body politic".[14] Consequently, sovereignty requires that it is exercised "through institutions which knitted the government and community together".[15] The foundation of sovereignty is trust which confers legitimacy and is evidenced by "acceptance".

The need for the ruled to, at least, acquiesce to laws made by those that purport to exercise authority over them was developed further by Grotius with his concept of sovereignty as a form of trust so that "sovereignty is not a power that rulers have over subjects but one that they exercise on behalf of the body corporate".[16] Hobbes went further with the possibility of replacing the ruler with an "assembly of men" following "men agree[ing] amongst themselves to submit... voluntarily" to a "Commonwealth by Institution".[17] This applies equally to government agencies. Hobbes gave as an example the administration of the treasury charged with the "economy of the Commonwealth" which "in a Democracy" acts in "the quality of a Minister of the People".[18]

As the concept of sovereignty developed, Locke saw the government thus established as subject to specific "bounds" and operating under a trust on behalf of society.[19] In contrast, Rousseau saw the social contract as one that "gives the body politic absolute command over the members of which it is formed; and it is this power, when directed by the general will, that bears...the name of 'sovereignty'".[20] Moreover, "the sovereign knows no person but the body of the nation".[21] Indeed, a legitimate government is defined as one that will "follow the general will in all things".[22]

In Britain administrative complexity increased through the 17th century with significant fiscal requirements, largely due to the need to finance wars. Consequently, more powers had to be delegated to growing administrative functions. For example, the Long Parliament's administration of fiscal policy in England included establishing a network of public offices "to raise and spend money" and to audit the various treasury functions.[23] These administrative operations

13 Marjorie Grice-Hutchinson, The School of Salamanca, readings in Spanish monetary theory (Clarendon Press, Oxford, 1952), 93, 111, 116.

14 Francis Hinsley, Sovereignty (Cambridge University Press, Cambridge, 1986), 124.

15 Ibid., (Hinsley), 124.

16 Knud Haakonssen, 'Hugo Grotius and the history of political thought', in Knud Kaakonssen (ed), Grotius, Pufendorf and modern natural law (Dartmouth, Aldershot, 1999), 35–61, 40.

17 Thomas Hobbes, Leviathan (published 1651, Penguin, London, 1985), Part II, Chapter 18, 228.

18 Ibid., (Hobbes), Part II, Chapters 23 and 24, 290, 294.

19 John Locke, Second treatise of government (published 1689, Cambridge University Press, Cambridge, 1960), Chapter XI, 142, (363, CUP).

20 Jean-Jacques Rousseau, Social contract, Chapter IV (published 1762, Hafner Press, New York, 1947), 27.

21 Ibid., (Rousseau), (29 in the Hafner edition).

22 Jean-Jacques Rousseau, Discourse on political economy (published 1755, Hackett, Indianapolis, 2011), 128.

23 James Scott Wheeler, The making of a world power (Sutton Publishing, Stroud, 1999), 199.

continued after the Restoration and, in due course, the Bank of England became part of a "smoothly running fiscal state".[24]

Moreover, for the Federalists, sovereignty did not rest in anyone person or institution but rather in the "people".[25] The latter have a "general spirit" which is shaped by history, "mores and manners".[26] However, the idea of popular sovereignty was, in 1920s Germany, subsumed by Schmitt into the concept of the "state" itself becoming the sovereign body as if it existed as an organic, living entity with its own special "geist" and conferred with absolute power sustained by a "complete homogeneity of its people" coming with "the integration of this mass into a unified whole".[27] However, this analysis leads towards a totalitarian rather than a democratic state since it denies fundamental tenets of pluralistic democracy braced by bonds of earned trust.

Trust is particularly important since, as mentioned earlier, sovereign powers usually operate through a process of granting delegated authority. If authority is delegated those in power "are weaker and exposed to greater risks" since everything depends on those to whom elements of power have been delegated.[28] This aspect is considered further later in this chapter. While in a Lockian sense there are limits to sovereign power so the possessors of delegated authority operate under a form of trust "bound by positive law" and in accordance with an understanding or set of conventions "for fear that it may offend the bulk of the community".[29] Consequently, there are limits placed on what may be undertaken either by the democratically elected government or an agency appointed by it and these limits change over time depending on a number of factors including "economic and political circumstances".[30]

The need for public consent, or at least, acceptance, is a central element to this consideration of sovereignty and legitimacy. It goes beyond the formal role of a "sovereign" legislator and is influenced by a range of factors including the media. It is certainly not homogeneous since the "public consent" may contain a number of conflicting, unresolved issues. It is nebulous but at some point the general view may crystallise in opposition to a particular policy.

The underlying concept of political legitimacy in the context of public administration is a form of trust bound by explicit law setting out the objectives,

24 Ibid., (James Scott Wheeler), 214.

25 Joshua Miller, 'The ghostly body politic: the Federalist papers and popular sovereignty', (February 1988) Political Theory, Vol. 16, No. 1, 99–119, 113–114.

26 Charles-Louis de Secondat, Baron de Montesquieu, The spirit of the law (published 1748, Cambridge University Press, Cambridge, 1989), Book 19, Chapter 4, "What the general spirit is", 310.

27 Carl Schmitt, 'Der bürgerliche Rechstaat (1928)', in Weimar: a jurisprudence of crisis, supra, note 11, 299.

28 Niccolò Machiavelli, The Prince (published 1532, Penguin, London, 2011), 41.

29 John Austin, The province of jurisprudence determined (published 1832, Cambridge University Press, Cambridge, 1995), 193–194.

30 Claus Zimmermann, A contemporary concept of monetary sovereignty (Oxford University Press, Oxford, 2014), 23.

scope and processes. It governs an institution's establishment and operations and include its responsibilities to be both accountable and transparent. In addition, as already mentioned, these laws are augmented by conventions and understandings which place further limits on those operating with delegated authority.

6.4 The political legitimacy, the societal compact and its application to delegated agencies

An institution's political legitimacy may be described as "having two aspects, the one formal or normative and the other social".[31] The former requires compliance with an accepted legal process while the latter "refers to a broad, empirically determined societal acceptance".[32] It is difficult to determine "societal acceptance". In practice a number of political and non-political actors stand in as representatives of "societal acceptance".

Consequently, it is clear that "those who hold or seek political power have made a far-sighted bargain comparable to...Locke's social compact; they have surrendered control over the nation's validation process to various others" such as judges and an "inquisitive press".[33]

In addition, as mentioned earlier, democratic government, will also hold delegated agencies to account. This includes both how public resources have been used and how the exercise of public trust has been discharged.

6.5 Democratic accountability by those holding delegated powers

In the context of those holding delegated powers, democratic institutions accountability can be defined "as an obligation owed" by the former to "account for, explain and justify [their] actions or decisions against criteria of some kind and [to] take responsibility for any fault or damage".[34] Policymaking by an agency with delegated powers almost certainly needs to be undertaken by an independent, technocratic body working in the broader public interest. It would be expected to provide expertise, free from political influence and to ensure

31 Amaryllis Verhoeven, The EU in search of a democratic and constitutional theory, (Kluwer Law International, The Hague, 2002), 10–11.

32 Ibid., (Verhoeven), 11.

33 Thomas Franck, 'The emerging right to democratic governance', (1992) American Journal of International Law, Vol. 86, 46–91, 50.

34 Fabian Amtenbrink and Rosa Lastra, 'Securing democratic accountability of financial regulatory agencies – a theoretical framework', in Richard Victor De Mulder, Mitigating risk in the context of safety and security. How relevant is a rational approach? (Erasmus School of Law & Research School for Safety and Security, Rotterdam, 2008), 120.

continuity and flexibility as economic, social and political changes occur.[35] Nevertheless, an independent agency forms part of the general public administrative process and a balance needs to be struck between its autonomy and the need for "political oversight".[36]

Consequently, the expectation is that such agencies will be accountable to the elected representatives for meeting their statutory objectives and how they carry out their mandates. These will be factors in establishing their democratic legitimacy and it may be said that "democratic legitimation in some respects is mediated through democratic accountability".[37] In a Montesquieuian structure, accountability will be to both Parliament and the executive and, additionally, to the courts through the process of judicial review. This is the formal structure of accountability.

Accountability may take several forms including *ex ante* and *ex post* review and be supplemented by a requirement to provide regular and frequent explanations of the agency's decisions and actions.[38] This latter aspects require high-levels of transparency; setting out the short- and long-term objectives and the tools to be used.[39] This information helps permit democratic oversight. For example, *ex ante* accountability includes some degree of influence on who is appointed to head the agency and a requirement to publish and explain its plans. Conversely, *ex post* accountability is closer to the organisation rendering account for what it has done and what has, or has not, been achieved. It runs parallel to corporate governance stewardship theory and is based on a high level of trust with readily measurable objectives and outcomes.[40]

The chain of accountability is based on reason-giving, consultation and conformity with formal guidance and procedures. However, formal accountability may not be sufficient to sustain political legitimacy.[41] In addition, as mentioned earlier, there is a less formal level of accountability to the general public; intermediated by the media, public interest groups, etc. These aspects are considered later in this chapter. We live in an age of waning deference to authoritative institutions and a "distrust of authority and official discretion".[42] Consequently, in

35 Chiara Zilioli, 'Accountability and independence: irreconcilable values or complementary instruments for democracy? The specific case of the European Central Bank', in Georges Vandersanden and others (eds), Mélanges en hommage à Jean-Victor Louis (University of Louvain, Brussels, 2003), 395–422, 397.

36 Thomas Sargentich, 'Contemporary debate about legislative-executive separation of powers', (1987) Cornell Law Review, Vol. 72, 430–487, 441.

37 Supra note 35, (Zilioli), 398.

38 Supra note 35, (Zilioli), 401.

39 Supra note 35, (Zilioli), 404.

40 Beata Glinkowska and Boguslaw Kaczmarek, 'Classical and modern concepts of corporate governance (Stewardship Theory and Agency Theory)', (2015) Management, Vol. 19, No. 2, 84–92, 87.

41 Robert Baldwin, Martin Cave and Martin Lodge, Understanding regulation (2nd ed., Oxford University Press, Oxford, 2012), 340–343.

42 Ibid., (Baldwin), 349.

the context of limiting credit expansion, it is not clear, from the perspective of an ordinary borrower, why the agreement with a willing lender to borrow money to honour a contract to purchase a home should be prohibited for no reason that relates to the individual, personally, but based, instead, on some esoteric economic theory which, in any event, may well be wrong.

These concerns may be further aggravated if the policy comes from an obscure committee in a body remote from the perspective of democratic accountability:

6.6 Machinery of government actions to improve accountability and transparency

As mentioned earlier, in a Lockian sense all government operates under a form of trust and accountability. Most commonly this is backward looking; considering how the institution exercised the trust bestowed on it. However, it is likely to include some form of public and formal review of its plans and intentions, often in the form of public consultations.

Departments of state are subject to a number of controls. First, they are headed by government ministers. They are directly accountable to Parliament, normally via the over-sight of dedicated select committees and, in addition, the formidable Public Accounts Committee (PAC) which "since Gladstone's time" has been "known as the queen of the select committees...due to its cleansing effect in all government departments".[43] It holds the latter to account for the use of public funds and resources and the PAC's investigatory and assessment work is undertaken by the assiduous National Audit Office (NAO).

In a democratic system the delegated agency policymaker will be a creation of democratic processes. Its role, objectives, governance and accountabilities will be set out in statute. In the UK, central government's executive functions are carried out by both departments of state and a large penumbra of assorted agencies collectively known as "non-departmental public bodies" (NDPBs).[44]

Independent government agencies are often "established for reasons of political expediency" but they may possess advantages, over traditional departments of state due to their particular "focus, expertise and insulation from political pressure".[45] Delegated agencies tend to have a narrower, more focused set of objectives and, since there is less ministerial control of them, the level of "tinkering" and interference is reduced. The relevance of expertise and political insulation are considered later in this chapter. However, while NDPBs are formally legitimate their continuing "perceptional" legitimacy depends both on external factors and how they undertake their roles. Accordingly, they will be subject to both formal requirements and assessments and some form of conformance with societal expectations.

43 Peter Hennessy, Whitehall (Secker and Warburg, London 1989), 332.

44 Sometimes known as "arms length bodies".

45 Geoffrey Miller, 'Independent agencies', (1986) The Supreme Court Review, 41–97, 75–76.

6.7 The practice and problems of overseeing organisations with delegated powers

The oversight of NDPBs is difficult. There are ad hoc reviews, such the Cabinet Office 2015 review of aspects of NDPB accountability and transparency.[46] There is also government guidance on how NDPBs should be established and managed including procedures to ensure their formal accountability.[47]

The control can also take the form of H M Treasury determining the allocation of public resources as part of the public expenditure control process. As an anonymous official of this department is reported to have said the Treasury operates under a form of "delegated democracy…Parliament is incapable of exercising its financial responsibilities. We must do it for them".[48] However, NDPBs, such as the Bank of England, as a nationalised industry, may have their own resources.[49]

Finally, the ability of Parliament, or one of its committees, to hold an agency to account, *ex ante*, should not be overstated. This may be because "political accountability is incident-driven" and "focused on a limited number of issues and guided by political priorities and political saliency".[50] Moreover, a recent Public Accounts Committee (PAC) report indicates that there are "unclear lines of accountability between departments and such bodies [so that] it is not clear who to hold to account".[51] Additionally, Parliamentary committees are likely to find that many issues may be too conceptual and devoid of hard evidence and, consequently, not amenable to committee assessment. Further, they may lack sufficient time, resources, inclination and expertise to undertake the work.

Accountability may also operate through a process of "Institutionalisation" which "implies that all the participants in a political process understand and accept the rules of that process" and all operate within unspoken limits.[52] This has been developed further into a "dialogue model" between independent agencies and political institutions, where the former inform themselves about "the intentions, wishes and opinions of the political leadership" and use this information

46 Cabinet Office, Public bodies 2015, (2015).

47 GOV.UK website, 'Organisation types: a user guide', (updated June 2014), https://insidegovuk.blog.gov.uk/2014/01/13/gov-uk-organisation-types-a-user-guide/, (accessed 26 June 2019).

48 Supra note 43, (Hennessy), 397.

49 Bank of England Act 1946. The NAO has recently been granted powers to assess the Bank of England, s11 Bank of England and Financial Services Act 2016.

50 Madalina Busuioc, European agencies: law and practices of accountability (Oxford University Press, Oxford, 2013), 252.

51 House of Commons Committee of Public Accounts, 'Departments' oversight of arm's-length bodies', Twenty-first Report of Session 2016–17, published 21 October 2016, HC 488, 5. There currently some 460 such bodies in the UK described as arising through "accidents of history", (4 and 8 of PAC report).

52 Michael Gorges, 'The new institutionalism and the study of the European Union: the case of the social dialogue', (2001) West European Politics, Vol. 24, No. 4, 152–168, 155.

to conform their approach to policymaking by setting self-imposed limits.[53] All parties have a collective interest in, and a wish to maintain, the political and institutional structure and understand the boundaries around the exercise of their power. Consequently, they will avoid saying or doing anything that seriously challenges these constraints.[54]

Finally, accountability also rests on the adequate provision of information and the transparency of the institution and its decision making. However, there may be limits in these areas.

6.8 Preserving the "mysteries": the argument against transparency

Accountability is buttressed by the provision of information, which helps render the agency, and its actions and decisions, transparent and capable of scrutiny.[55] However, transparency may not always be a virtue and may hinder the work of financial supervision.[56] Ensuring financial stability and the detailed supervision of banks and other significant financial institutions forms the central part of the Bank of England's regulatory policy role. How these policies and powers operate is both transparent and are, at the same time, hidden behind a facade of omniscient expertise sustained by all the attributes of authority. It is based on a certain aloofness and is surrounded by an aura of mystery.

As Bagehot explains, in a similar context, symbols are important in sustaining legitimacy and that it is important that "we must not let in daylight upon magic".[57] It may threaten the "mystic" of the policymaking institution. In many ways it forms an "arcana imperii" or "the unspoken concepts behind the exercise of authority".[58] There are two forms of symbolism important in sustaining political legitimacy: that which accrues to the organisation itself and the "power of symbolic process".[59] Both the process and the entity itself need to maintain and enhance their "mystery". Indeed, Lipset saw the principal factors determining

53 Udaibir Das and Marc Quintyn, 'Financial crisis prevention and management: the role of regulatory governance', in Robert Litan, Michael Pomerleano and Vasudevan Sundsrarajan (eds), Financial sector governance: the roles of the public and private sectors (World Bank/IMF/ Brookings Publications, Washington DC, 2002), 163–208, 166.

54 Marc Quentyn and Michael Taylor, 'Regulatory and supervisory independence and financial stability', (2002) IMF Working Paper WP/02/46, 30.

55 Rosa Lastra and Heba Shams, 'Public accountability in the financial sector', in Eilís Ferran and Charles Goodhart, (eds), Regulating financial services and markets in the twenty-first century (Hart Publishing, Oxford, 2001), 165–188, 172.

56 Oral evidence by Mervyn King to the TSC, answers to questions 21 and 62, supra, note 7.

57 Supra, note 2 (Bagehot), 54.

58 Tacitus, The annals of Imperial Rome, Book II.36 (Michael Grant (tr), Penguin, London, 1956), 94.

59 Benno Netelenbos, Political legitimacy beyond Weber: an analytical framework (Palgrave Macmillan, London, 2016), 132.

political legitimacy as a mix of history and the "continuities of symbols and statuses".[60]

The esoteric world of macroeconomic policy and microprudential supervision help sustain the "mystery". However, while the requirement for legal process, accountability and transparency cannot be doubted they may not be sufficient. All this reinforces the concern that political legitimacy is always finely balanced and cannot, at any point, be taken for granted. There needs to be more; whether it be broad public support, or at least, acceptance of the political legitimacy of, in this case, the delegated policymaker.

6.9 Political legitimacy: a socio-legal perspective

As mentioned earlier the classical explanations of political legitimacy, expressed notably by Hobbes and Locke, are based on a social contract or agreement buttressed by democratic accountability.[61] Weber analysed this further and developed a concept of societal legitimacy. He viewed legitimacy based both on an objective need for conformance with, for example, legal procedure and, additionally, a subjective "belief in the legitimate authority of the source imposing" the obligation.[62] Others, such as Beetham conclude that political legitimacy needs to be founded on "shared beliefs" as well as compliance with legal process stating that "political legitimacy [is] based on: legal process, expressed consent and via shared belief".[63] Additionally, it requires an understanding of moral obligation and the concepts of reciprocity or "fair play".[64] It includes corresponding, beliefs grounded on "an ideal of fraternity" and based on a general desire of "well-being" for all.[65]

In the area of regulation, Weber's concept of political legitimacy, which focuses on the subjective psychological connection between authority and obedience, may be too limited.[66] In sociological terms "legitimacy" has been defined as meaning a "generalized perception or assumption that the actions of the entity are desirable, proper or appropriate".[67] However, this form of definition is too broad and requires a high degree of subjectivity to be useful. Moreover, it is unclear who provides this "generalized perception" and how it is ascertained, measured and preserved and whether it can only be judged with hindsight.

60 Seymour Lipset, Political man (Mercury Books, London, 1959), 83.

61 See, for example, Heinrich Triepel, 'The law of the state and politics', in Weimar: a jurisprudence of crisis, supra note 11, 187.

62 Max Weber, The theory of social and economic organization (published 1925, The Free Press, New York, 1947), 131–132.

63 David Beetham, The legitimation of power (Macmillan, London, 1991), 20–21.

64 Ronald Dworkin, Law's empire (Hart Publishing, Oxford, 1998), 190–200.

65 John Rawls, Theory of justice (Oxford University Press, Oxford, 1999), 90–91.

66 Roger Cotterrell, Law's community: legal theory in sociological perspective (Oxford University Press, Oxford, 1997), 157–158.

67 Mark Suchman, 'Managing legitimacy: strategic and institutional approaches', (1995) The Academy of Management Review, Vol. 20, No. 3, 571–610, 574.

6.10 The "sluice gate" or structuralist approach to political legitimacy

Habermas, quoting Johannes Winckelmann's development of Weber, did not see that legal procedure was sufficient to establish political legitimacy but rather that the latter needed to be "grounded" on a "general consensus".[68] Developing the views of Berhard Peters, Habermas saw public policy legitimacy as dependent on the responsiveness of the policymakers to external, public views and that these are controlled by a system of "sluice gates" which open to allow public pressure to bear on policy formation.[69] He took a "structuralist" view of political legitimacy where decisions are based on negotiations. It contains within it the unspoken assumption that by following this procedure political legitimacy is established and that there is no room for further dissent.[70]

6.11 The additional need for shared values and beliefs

All these models accept that political legitimacy must be based on legally accepted processes. However, they require something else which, in many ways, is closer to the views of Hobbes and Locke and the need for a broader level of public consent or, at least, acceptance. In addition, there are those who consider that political legitimacy also requires a level of "shared beliefs and values" since these are also necessary to establish "substantive legitimacy" above and beyond compliance with "procedural legitimacy".[71]

To an extent this develops Rousseau's view that while law is "a 'celestial voice' that dictates the precepts of public reason to every citizen" there also needs to be a "unity of sentiment and reason…as a condition of the possibility of forming a genuine general will".[72] Rousseau also draws a sharp distinction between general laws which express "la volonté générale" and decrees promulgated by the executive and its agencies. The latter "may be considered to be an indirect expression of the general will so long as the people as a whole do not thwart them".[73]

Evans describes legitimacy in this context as being based on the "ability to combine a Weberian bureaucratic insulation with [an] intense connection to

68 Jürgen Habermas, Legitimation crisis (published 1973, Polity Press, Cambridge, 1988), 99.

69 Jürgen Habermas, Between facts and norms: contributions to a discourse theory of law and democracy (Polity Press, Cambridge, 1996), 354–359.

70 James Bohman, 'Complexity, pluralism and the constitutional state: on Habermas's Fraktizität and Geltung ['Between facts and norms']', (1994) Law and Society Review, Vol. 28, 897–930, 921.

71 Michael Barnett and Martha Finnemore, Rules for the World: international organisations in global politics, (Cornell University Press, Ithaca, New York, 2004), 166–167.

72 David James, 'Rousseau on needs, language and pity: the limits of "public reason"', (2011) European Journal of Political Theory, Vol. 10, No. 3, 372–393, 374, 389.

73 Ethan Putterman, Rousseau, law and the sovereignty of the people (Cambridge University Press, Cambridge, 2011), 28.

the surrounding social structure".[74] Seabrooke sees this "social embeddedness" through the lens of "economic constructivism" where individuals and institutions in society determine political legitimacy based on an "interaction between ideas, norms and interests".[75] This is developed by Blyth into a need for "causal stories" or narratives to cement new ideas into the beliefs of society to justify and legitimate the actions of government agencies.[76] While Schmidt was concerned with how public policies "resonate with citizens' substantive values and identity as well as how they fit with their interests".[77]

The need to satisfy both the process of law-making and public values and expectations need to be analysed.[78]

6.12 "Input and output" and "foreground and background" political legitimacy

Scharf described a distinction between "legitimacy as based on inputs" including the process used to create laws and regulations and "output legitimacy [which] is instead concerned with the problem-solving quality of the laws and rules, and has a range of institutional mechanisms to ensure it".[79] Both elements were "necessary for democratic legitimization".[80] Similarly, Seabrooke describes two types of legitimacy: "foreground", based on process and law, and "background" which is found in the "political realm" with legitimacy conferred by a "social constituency".[81]

Schmidt develops Scharpf's views on political legitimacy further. Her view of political legitimacy

> relates to the extent to which input politics, throughput processes and output policies are acceptable to, and accepted by, the citizenry, such that citizens believe that these are morally authoritative and they therefore voluntarily comply with government acts even when these go against their own interests and desires.[82]

74 Peter Evans, Embedding autonomy: states and industrial transformation (Princeton University Press, Princeton, 1995), 50.

75 Leonard Seabrooke, The social sources of financial power: domestic legitimacy and international financial orders (Cornell University Press, Ithaca, New York, 2006), 34.

76 Mark Blyth, Great transformations: economic ideas and institutional change in the Twentieth Century (Cambridge University Press, Cambridge, 2002), 37–38.

77 Vivien Schmidt, 'Democracy and legitimacy in the European Union revisited: input, output and "throughput"', (2013) Political Studies, Vol. 61, 2–22, 11.

78 In Rousseau' view public "opinion" was paramount ("sur-tout de l' opinion") and "legislators should be highly circumspect" of such opinion, supra, note 73, (Putterman).

79 Fritz Scharpf, Governing in Europe: effective and democratic? (Oxford University Press, Oxford, 1999), 7–21.

80 Ibid., (Scharpf),11–13.

81 Leonard Seabrooke, 'Legitimacy gaps in the World economy: explaining the sources of the IMF legitimacy crisis', (2007) International Politics, Vol. 44, No. 2, 250–268, 253.

82 Supra note 77, (Vivien Schmidt), 9–10.

For Schmidt "output legitimacy requires policies" to resonate "with citizens' values and identity".[83] While for Seabrooke a "legitimacy gap" occurs when "the claims made by an institution or organisation with a specific policy function are rejected... [by] those being governed".[84] Moreover, public opinion may be influenced by how its expectations are satisfied.

6.13 Political legitimacy based on satisfying demands and "facilitating expectations"

Easton sees political legitimacy as based on an ability to satisfy stakeholder "demands" and public opinion as "influential in stimulating and shaping demands".[85] Considering this further it is possible to envisage government organisations not simply as a static structures but rather as agencies subject to the stress of constant demands with their authority being tested as these demands are considered and satisfied, or not, as they flow through the system.[86]

The political legitimacy of an institution and its actions is not solely an objective assessment; once achieved good for all times and circumstances. Instead the "concept is functionalised so that the question of the belief in validity can be treated as a variable" where legitimacy is dependent on circumstances and events and flows to and from the organisation.[87]

Consequently, political legitimacy may depend on the ability of an organisation to "facilitate expectations".[88] However, "expectations" are highly subjective and poses the question of whose expectations and when and in what context? The legitimacy of political actions appears to depend on the circumstance, the skill with which it is communicated and that it is "presented in a plausible way".[89] Easton went on to say that the sense of political legitimacy may be built up and augmented among stakeholders over time and acts as a reservoir of support until the reserve is exhausted.[90]

In conclusion, macroprudential policy is an aspect of public policy and consequently falls within the political domain. It requires, at least, public acceptance if not active support. However, some balance needs to be struck between clear communication and maintaining a certain level of reserve as a means of protecting the institution's continuing authority. Nevertheless, the degree of political legitimacy invoked by an institution remains fragile, dependent on all these

83 Ibid., Schmidt, 7–8.
84 Supra, note 81, (Seabrooke, 'Legitimacy gaps'), 258.
85 David Easton, A systems analysis of political life (John Wiley, New York, 1965), 38–42.
86 Ibid., (Easton), 69.
87 Niklas Luhmann, A sociological theory of law (published 1972, 2nd ed., Routledge, London, 2014), 205–206.
88 Ibid., (Luhmann), 78.
89 Andreas Philippopoulos-Mihalopoulos, Niklas Luhmann, law, justice, society (Routledge, Abingdon, 2010), 147.
90 David Easton, 'An approach to the analysis of political systems', (April 1957), World Politics, Vol. 9, No. 3, 383–400, 399–400.

factors as well as the swell of events and the demands of the public. It can also be damaged by the actions of opinion formers such as the media and politicians. Consequentially, there appear to be two sets of boundary lines: one governing who may intervene in public policy and, second, how such interventions are carried out. This issue is considered further in this chapter in the context of macroprudential policy.

6.14 Political legitimacy based on managing "disappointment"

There is a further element to sustaining political legitimacy bound-in with the economic process of allocating resources. Since not all demands for mortgage credit, housing or other social needs can be satisfied under a process of rationing scarce economic resources politics has an important role in "absorbing" or diverting unfulfilled expectations.[91] It is this ability to "process disappointment" that may be seen as a true test of whether society has bestowed political legitimacy on an institution.[92] The construction of a "narrative" is important in at least explaining, if not satisfying, these requirements and achieving and retaining societal endorsement. The theme of weaving a legitimacy narrative is considered later in this chapter but before that a number of other threads need to be drawn together.

6.15 Drawing together the threads

This section draws together the threads considered earlier and employs them to assess the extent to which aspects of macroprudential policy satisfy the requirements of political legitimacy. At its heart is the contention that macroprudential policymakers form part of a "headless fourth branch of the government" which is itself "a haphazard deposit of irresponsible agencies and uncoordinated powers".[93] By its very nature macroprudential policy is political. Consequently, it must be accountable to elected lawmakers. These establish the scope of macroprudential policymaking and set its objectives. The policymaker operates under the oversight of Parliament; it renders account to the legislature and it provides regular and frequent consultations and information to ensure transparency and to engage all stakeholders in assisting in its deliberations.

In addition, as discussed above in relation to concepts of sovereignty, there needs to be an element of public consent, or at least, acceptance above and beyond that provided by the assembly of the elected representatives. This contradicts the

91 Supra note 59, (Netelenbos), 113.

92 Ibid., 113.

93 'Administrative management of the Government of the United States: report of the President's commission on administrative management', (1936) known as the "Brownlow Committee", quoted in James Fessler, 'The Brownlow Committee fifty years later', (1987) Public Administrative Review, Vol. 47, No. 4, 291–296, 292.

views expressed by Woodrow Wilson in his "Study of administration", that after the legislature has set the objectives and legal framework officials are responsible for the results and the "public must not meddle with their choices...the cook must be trusted with a large discretion as to the management of the fires and ovens".[94] The exercise of discretion is central to concerns about political legitimacy: the broader and more wide-ranging the discretion the greater the risk of political challenge. This is core to macroprudential policymaking.[95] Operating close to the political legitimacy frontier macroprudential policymakers risk awakening public opposition.

6.16 Economics and social policy and macroprudential interventions

Macroprudential policy blurs the boundaries between economics, sociology, law and politics.[96] Such policymaking is founded on law but underpinned by economics. It does not exist as an "autopoietic system".[97] It needs to engage and communicate with other systems based on political and socio-economic assessments and in turn influence them.[98]

Macroprudential policy may, as a consequence, be undermined by political, media and interest group pressures and all these factors may, in turn, threaten the authority and the legitimacy of the macroprudential policymakers. Consequently, policies which, for example, restrict the growth of credit, may not work in the face of economic, political and social forces.

Moreover, in the socio-political sphere there is a danger that an active macroprudential policy, whether limiting access to credit or in advocating an increase in the supply of housing, may be perceived as having entered the world of political redistributional public policy. However, more broadly, almost all macroprudential or macroeconomic policy is very likely to have a social redistributive effect even if such an outcome was not intended. Nevertheless, the view is that once a perceived socio-political line had been crossed, "decisions involving significant redistributions of resources from one social group to another cannot be taken by independent experts but only by elected officials or those that report

94 Quoted in Marshall Breger, 'Thoughts on accountability and the administrative process', (Summer 1987) Administrative Law Review, Vol. 39, No. 3, 399–415, 400.

95 The Group of Thirty, Enhancing financial stability and resilience: macroprudential policy, tools, and systems for the future (The Group of Thirty, Washington DC, 2010), 62–63.

96 Colin Scott, 'Regulation in the age of governance: the rise of the post-regulatory state', in Jacint Jordana and David Levi-Faur (eds), The politics of regulation (Edward Elgar, Cheltenham, 2004), 145–174, 146.

97 Niklas Luhmann, 'Operational closure and structural coupling: the differentiation of the legal system', (1992) Cardozo Law Review, Vol. 13, 1419–1441, 1426.

98 Dimitris Michailakis, 'Law as an autopoietic system', (1995) Acta Sociologica, Vol. 38, No. 4, 323–337, 328.

directly" to them.[99] It is bound-in with "the existence of public aspirations... current distribution of wealth...and the inevitable role of law... in allocating entitlements and wealth".[100] The macroprudential policymaker is vulnerable since a popular mandate is absent; they were never elected to office and cannot be voted out. Procedural legal compliance and accountability may not be sufficient for the macroprudential policymaker to be able to justify their authority in areas of distribution that may appear properly to belong to the political world.

6.17 The role of the Financial Policy Committee and political legitimacy

An institution such as the Bank of England does not exist in a vacuum. It is shaped, and in turn, shapes the political, economic and social environment in which it exists. The political legitimacy of the FPC is more difficult to evaluate. It is likely to be perceived as an obscure committee and its claims to political legitimacy are fragile being based on adherence to formal processes and on a limited level of accountability to a Parliamentary select committee. However, its actions have a very direct effect on the lives of individual citizens. The key issue is that the people that are adversely affected by, for example, the imposition of LTV and DTI restrictions are readily identifiable while the broader group who may be protected by these measures from harm arising from financial instability are not. Moreover, the causation links between the risks of a systemic failure and the actions of the committee may be seen as remote and unclear.

Moreover, the central issue is that macroprudential policy is "fundamentally a politico-economic concept".[101] There is a very close relationship between the economic regulatory policies embedded within the macroprudential framework and the effect on societal objectives. Consequently, as mentioned earlier, macroprudential policies have, by their very nature, "redistributive consequences" and thus, "cannot rely on a firm foundation of legitimacy".[102] Indeed, "the question of legitimacy, in spoken or unspoken form, haunts much of the debate".[103]

Governments will seek blame avoidance and this has been expressed as a major reason for the creation of non-governmental agencies to devise and execute executive policies.[104] The legislature "is always willing to deal rhetorically with problems requiring regulation...but real decisions...will undoubtedly raise the

99 Giandomenico Majone, 'Regulatory legitimacy', in Giandomenico Majone (ed), Regulating Europe (Routledge, London, 1996) 284–301, 295.

100 Cass Sunstein, After the rights revolution (Harvard University Press, Cambridge, MA, 1990), 228.

101 Anthony Ogus, Regulation: legal form and economic theory (Clarendon Press, Oxford, 1994), 1.

102 Supra, note 99, (Majone), 295, 299.

103 Tony Prosser, The regulatory enterprise: government, regulation and legitimacy (Oxford University Press, Oxford, 2010), 4.

104 Kent Weaver, 'The politics of blame avoidance', (1986) Journal of Public Policy, Vol. 6, No. 4, 371–398, 391.

ire of powerful pressure groups on one side or the other that are affected by government regulation".[105] Consequently, setting up an independent policymaking agency is a better method of addressing these issues at the risk that these agencies may become political forces in their own right with their own constituencies and influence. The FPC, as part of the Bank of England has an agency role. It may need to take politically unpopular decisions so placing it at least one remove from central government may have the effect of ensuring that it acts as a lightning rod by diverting popular anger away from politicians.[106]

Moreover, there were institutional factors leading to the delegation of macroprudential policy to the Bank of England. It would have taken some time to have created a brand-new macroprudential policymaker while the Bank had the infrastructure in place to undertake the role. Moreover, placing responsibility for macroprudential policy elsewhere is likely to have resulted in a lack of coordination with the Bank of England's macroeconomic functions ensuring friction between the Bank and the neophyte organisation. Finally, in this area, the Bank of England already had an international presence and standing with bodies such as the Financial Stability Board and Bank of International Settlements. This is an important aspect bearing in mind the former's leading position in determining global macroprudential strategy.

There are also political symbolic reasons for locating the FPC within the Bank. It provides an element of symbolism in that an institution with authority, fixed with clear responsibility has ownership and accountability for macroprudential policy.[107] In addition, it acts as a "signal" both internationally and domestically, following the financial crisis, that the important role of preserving financial stability has been given to a recognised authoritative body. This allows the FPC to work within the shadow of the Bank's own "mystic" and provides immediate political legitimacy to a new organisation.

The technical expertise of the Bank of England is another significant reason for allocating it macroprudential policymaking powers. This may help secure its political legitimacy.

6.18 Technical expertise and political legitimacy

As mentioned earlier it may be possible to found political legitimacy on technocratic power operated by a "technocracy" of experts.[108] Moreover, there is

105 Peter Woll, American bureaucracy (2nd ed., W.W. Norton, New York, 1977), 10–13.

106 Morris Fiorina, 'Legislative choice of regulatory forms: legal process or administrative process', (1982) Public Choice, Vol. 39, No. 1, 33–66, 47.

107 Domenico Lombardi and Manuela Moschella, 'The symbolic politics of delegation: macroprudential policy and independent regulatory authorities', (2016) New Political Economy, 7–8.

108 For an example of the "technocratic ethos" see Lamoma Rogers, 'A new approach to macroprudential policy for New Zealand', (September 2013) Reserve Bank of New Zealand Bulletin, Vol. 76, No. 3, 12–22, 16, which discusses macroprudential LTV limits in purely technical terms with no mention of socio-political implications.

a belief that this provides a "naïve notion of escape from politics and substitution of the voice of the expert for the voice of the people".[109] Reliance on "expertness" may be "incompatible with the democratic political process".[110] In addition, the UK has traditionally had an ambivalent perspective on technical expertise with a view that "experts should be on tap but not on top".[111] It is this claim to political legitimacy by "rule of the knowers" or "epistocracy" that is considered next.[112]

6.19 "Rule" by technicians and the Promethean struggle

One possible view is to see the FPC as a group of expert technicians who employ their independence and expertise for the common good. Haldane, and others, have described the FPC is "technocratic".[113] This suggests an omniscient macroprudential priesthood, akin to Die Zauberflötes' Sarastro, "der göttliche Weise" ("the divinely inspired wise man") and Haldane poses the rhetorical question if only "there were a benign enlightened regulatory planner, able to redirect competitive forces, this could potentially avert future tragedies of the financial commons. Fortunately there is".[114] However, as Veblen warned, "popular sentiment…will not tolerate the assumption of responsibility by the technicians, who are in popular apprehension conceived to be a somewhat fantastic brotherhood of over-specialised cranks, not to be trusted".[115]

Baker saw the rise of macroprudential policy as some form of promethean struggle between central banker technocrats and the forces of bankers and politicians with the final "macroprudential ideational shift" resulting from "an 'insiders coup d'etat', which displaced the prior efficient markets orthodox".[116] Similarly, Tucker has described the Bank of England's move towards macroprudential policy as a "Gestalt flip to thinking of markets as inefficient, riddled with preferred habitats, imperfect arbitrage, regulatory arbitrage, herding,

109 Marver Bernstein, Regulating business by independent commission (Princeton University Press, Princeton, 1955), 493.
110 Ibid., (Bernstein), 493.
111 Randolph Churchill, Twenty-one years (Weidenfeld & Nicolson, London, 1965), 127 quoting his father Winston Churchill. It is a phrase I often heard during my time working in the Civil Service.
112 David Copp, 'Reasonable acceptability and democratic legitimacy: Estlund's qualified acceptability requirement', (January 2011), Ethics, Vol. 121, No. 2, 239–269, 241.
113 Andrew Haldane, 'Central bank psychology', speech at the 'Leadership: stress and hubris conference', hosted by the Royal Society of Medicine, London, 17 November 2014, 8.
114 Andrew Haldane, 'Financial arms races', speech at the Institute for New Economic Thinking, Berlin, 14 April 2012, 10.
115 Thorstein Veblen, The engineers and the price system (published 1921, Viking Press, New York, 1954), 150–151.
116 Andrew Baker, 'The new political economy of the macroprudential ideational shift', (2013) New Political Economy, Vol. 18, No. 1, 112–139, 127.

and inhabited by agents with less than idealised rationality".[117] However, this reasoned state of mind may be challenged during a crisis. Baker believes that after a period of "crisis politics when prior orthodoxies were overturned... a more normal phase of conventional interest-based politics and contests between regulators and regulated can be expected to emerge".[118] Looking beyond this revolutionary change of view Baker believes that politicians, acting on behalf of the bankers, will try to restrain the Jacobins within the Bank of England.[119] The zeitgeist will return to a Humean "higher-rationality".

Baker describes a paradox in that

> efforts to depoliticise macroprudential policy by allocating power and responsibility to unelected central banks, whose claims to authority are based on technical expertise, actually runs the risk of not only politicising macroprudential policy, but also politicising central banks themselves. In other words, depoliticisation begets politicisation.[120]

Moreover, technocrats in this role are likely to "become convinced of the correctness of their own prescriptions (and so grow over-confident) and can become divorced from popular sentiments", therefore to avoid this trap technocratic regulators must carefully monitor their actions against the changing "wider public moods and concerns".[121] This is echoed by Tucker who believes that macroprudential policy decisions which have a direct distribution effect on individual citizens should be left with elected politicians.[122] However, all central bank policies, whether these relate to monetary or macroprudential ends, are likely to have economic redistribution effects. Much depends on how obvious are their effects and how best the Bank employs the levers of legitimacy.

In view of concerns about the political legitimacy of its actions, the FPC has been inclined to set its policymaking within boundaries it believes are acceptable to the general will. The latter may not always be apparent and may change depending on the political, social and economic context.

117 Paul Tucker, remarks at Clare Distinguished Lecture in Economics, Cambridge Friday on 18 February 2011 discussing Lord Turner's Lecture, 'Reforming finance: are we being radical enough?', 3–4.

118 Supra, note 116, (Baker, 'New political economy'), 132.

119 Andrew Baker, 'The gradual transformation? The incremental dynamics of macroprudential regulation', (2013) Regulation & Governance, Vol. 7, 417–434, 429.

120 Andrew Baker, 'The bankers' paradox: the political economy of macroprudential regulation', (April 2015), LSE Systemic Risk Centre Discussion Paper No. 37, 26–27.

121 Andrew Baker and Wesley Widmaier, 'The institutionalist roots of macroprudential ideas: Veblen and Galbraith on regulation, policy success and overconfidence', (2014) New Political Economy, Vol 19, No. 4, 487–506, 502–503.

122 Paul Tucker, 'The design and governance of financial stability regimes: a common-resource problem that challenges technical know-how, democratic accountability and international coordination', (September 2016) Centre for International Governance Innovation, Vol. 3, 53–54.

6.20 The politics of political legitimacy and macroprudential policy: a "Pufferstaat" boundary

For the most part the actions of a policymaking institution are accepted and not challenged on grounds of legitimacy. Indeed, as mentioned earlier, institutions such as the Bank of England have a certain level of protection against attacks on its legitimacy enhanced by its tradition and symbolism which put it beyond the "ordinary". In many ways the Bank of England is preserved by an element of Gurvitchian "magic".[123] However, at some point that legitimacy may be eroded and it is then that the soundness of its foundations become important.[124]

The Bank of England is conscious that a reputation built-up over centuries may be squandered and, consequently, the Bank may be reluctant to employ macroprudential policies which may call into question its legitimacy.[125] As a result, its "scope for strategic action may be bounded" by what may be described as a "legitimacy boundary line".[126] This may be a "region" rather than a bright-line. Moreover, the extent of this area may change over time and depend on political, social and economic circumstances.

6.21 The legitimacy boundary

The boundary may be at the point at which macroprudential policy is directed at the individual. For example, Mervyn King described his experience in 2005 in his response to the Treasury Select Committee in 2009:

> Let me explain the nature of the problem. I did speak about house prices. I gave a speech in 2005 which had quite a big impact; it was all over the front pages of the usual tabloid press. I got a lot of letters saying 'How dare you talk about house prices!'...There were a lot of comments that I should not be intervening and making comments about house prices.[127]

Macroprudential policy may restrict what an individual may do; not because of anything they have done wrong (they are applying for a mortgage) but because it is in the interest of society's greater good. As a consequence the economic and regulatory policy systems are "fractured" and need "a specific mechanism of

123 "Mystic experience penetrates all archaic social institutions", George Gurvitch, Magic and law, (1942) Social Research, Vol. 9, No. 1, 104–121, 104.

124 Rodney Barker, Political legitimacy and the state (Clarendon Press, Oxford, 1990), 161.

125 Financial Times, 5 April 2012, 'Bank avoids role in limiting mortgages' quoting Tucker that "it is for the government to decide on borrowing caps", highlighting "unease among unelected technocrats at the BoE".

126 Julia Black, 'Constructing and contesting legitimacy and accountability in polycentric regulatory regimes', (2008) Regulation and Governance, Vol. 2, No. 2, 137–164, 162.

127 Mervyn King, answer to question 2354 on 26 February 2009 before the Treasury Select Committee, House of Commons Treasury Committee, Banking crisis, Vol. I, Oral evidence, (HC 144–I [Incorporating HC 1167 i–iv, Session 2007–08]), 281.

structural coupling" which can communicate a link between the private contract and the public economic interest.[128] A public/private line is "blurred" and it "unsettles our understanding of where" to locate the legitimacy of this action.[129]

This can be clearly seen in the response by Adair Turner before the Parliamentary Treasury Select Committee:

> I have to say that I think if we were to roll back and the FSA had come out in 2004 and had started aggressively challenging the mortgage banks to cut back on lending, I suspect that the predominant reaction of many people, including perhaps many people in this House, would have been to tell us that we should not be holding back the extension of mortgage credit to ordinary people; that we were preventing the democratisation of home ownership....we would have been pushed back politically if we had.[130]

As the Governor of the Bank of England at that time said to the same Committee, "Westminster and the Government would have been lobbied; it would have been a pretty lonely job being a regulator".[131] It is likely that macroprudential policies may infringe the political legitimacy boundary which directly limited the aspiration of those who wish for their own home.

6.22 The aspiration of home ownership: acceptable and unacceptable interference in public policy

As discussed in earlier chapters housing is an emotional as well as political subject which may merit public policy interference in what is perceived to be a free market. Moreover, housing may have, in a Durkheimian sense, a social cohesion role.[132] As already noted access to a home of ones' own is central, at least, to modern society and the aspiration to this goal provides a sense of hope for the future. In a Hegelian sense it is recognised as a source of individual freedom.[133] These are all important factors in a society's concept of social solidarity. Consequentially, as mentioned above, Habermas held that it is possible to determine

128 Supra note 97, (Luhmann, 'Operational closure'), 1435. See also Gunther Teubner, Law as an autopoietic system, (Blackwell, Oxford, 1993), 61–62.

129 Julia Black, 'Critical reflections on regulation', (2002) Australian Journal of Legal Philosophy, Vol. 27, 4, 35.

130 Adair Turner, answer to Question 2168 on 25 February 2009 before the Treasury Select Committee, House of Commons Treasury Committee, Banking crisis, Vol. I, Oral evidence, (HC 144–I [Incorporating HC 1167 i–iv, Session 2007–08]), 281.

131 Ibid., Mervyn King, answer to Question 2354 on 26 February 2009.

132 Steven Lukes and Andrew Scull, Durkheim and the law (Martin Robertson, Oxford, 1983), 5–8. Durkheim saw no issue with "frustrated aspiration" provided the individual was still bound to society by wider ties and beliefs, (Emile Durkheim, The division of labour in society (published 1893, Macmillan, London, 1984), 315).

133 Colin Tyler, 'The liberal Hegelianism of Edward Caird', (2010) International Journal of Social Economics, Vol. 37, No. 11, 852–866, 861.

a "boundary" between what is acceptable and unacceptable state interference when, for instance, there is an overwhelming desire by consumers for individual ownership of an object.[134]

For example, the aspiration for home ownership in the UK could be described as a cultural tradition, albeit a relatively recent one that only started to develop after the First World War as the soldiers returned. It was seen as so important that the boundary governing state interference in the market was breached with the Housing and Town Planning Act 1919, ("the Addison Act") and is evident in the debate introducing the Second Reading of this Bill. "These men who left our shores as youths return as grown-up men. In large numbers they are seeking independent homes. We cannot offer these men hovels. We want them to have the homes which they desire".[135] The MP then moved on from demobilised soldiers to the need for homes for miners

> if he [the Housing Minister] will enable any miner who wants it to have a suitable home, a home in the real British sense, a home which is really the Englishman's castle, a home reflecting the taste of the occupants of the home, as every home should do... We ask him to appeal not to cupidity but to imagination. We ask him to abandon the gospel of sops...I appeal to him to believe that the virtues of self-respect and independence are not the privilege of a class, but are the common and great inheritance of a great people.[136]

By way of context this legislation, which introduced housing regulation and state investment in house building, was introduced following the first UK general election with almost a modern suffrage with women having the vote for the first time, albeit only for those aged thirty or older, and against a background of revolution across much of Europe and Russia, turmoil in Ireland and global economic dislocation. It produced the first governmental large-scale housing construction programme and established good quality housing as a right and the legislation increased taxation to pay for house building subsidies.[137] Lloyd George is reported to have said that even if this cost of £100 million "what was that compared with the stability of the State".[138] This underlines that economic and political crises may produce a shift in the boundary between public policy

134 Supra, note 68, (Habermas, Legitimation crisis), 30.

135 James Kidd MP for Linlithgowshire, House of Commons debate on the Housing Bill, (7 April 1919) Hansard Archive, Vol 114, 1713–1820, 1754.

136 Ibid., Kidd MP, who was a lawyer and a Coalition Unionist MP serving in Lloyd George's government. He fought twice for his seat against Manny Shinwell. In his autobiography the latter described Kidd as "an exceptionally able man", Manny Shinwell, Leading with the left (Cassell, London, 1981), 69.

137 David Mullins and Alan Murie, Housing policy in the UK (Palgrave Macmillan, Basingstoke, 2006), 22. See also Mark Swenarton, Homes fit for heroes: the politics and architecture of early state housing in Britain (Heinemann Educational, London, 1981), 78–79.

138 Brian Lund, Understanding housing policy (2nd ed., Policy Press, University of Bristol, Bristol, 2011), 49.

regulation and the unregulated market, "not only into the economic system but also into the socio-cultural system".[139]

6.23 Applying the concept of "political legitimacy" to the FPC

The political legitimacy of an institution or action is not fixed in time, once and for all. Political legitimacy inhabits a spectrum containing degrees of acceptance which fluctuate depending on circumstances and events. It is complicated by the role of intermediation by, for example, the media and lobbying groups. These issues present the FPC with a number of policy problems and options. These could include a form of "self-denying ordnance" in which the committee limits its actions to the relatively obtuse areas of counter-cyclical buffers, etc. which tend to attract less intermediation attention. However, if the FPC employs high-profile macroprudential tools such as LTV and DTI limits it will have to engage in the political debate and be able to explain its actions. This would mean applying a new perspective. This may be culturally difficult since

> decision-makers have their own frames of reference, their own world views... the very topics under discussion may themselves challenge their own perceptions and frames of reference. Indeed, it may be...so bound up in its own rationality that it is incapable of seeing beyond it.[140]

6.24 Possible options

It is clear from interviewing senior Bank of England staff and other policymakers that the Bank is aware of these concerns. As part of a set of options to help improve the democratic accountability of the Bank of England one suggestion has been that while the Chancellor of the Exchequer continues to appoint the chairman of the Bank, some of the other senior appointments are made directly by Parliament.[141] Another option may be to attempt to "borrow" Parliamentary legitimisation by passing the measures through some form of Statutory Instrument process. However, HM Treasury may be reluctant to support such measures for the converse reasons that it exposes politicians to criticism and takes them into technical areas beyond their expertise and, moreover, it would negate a key reason for delegating responsibility for taking unpopular actions to an independent Bank of England. A former Treasury minister has suggested that

139 Supra, note 68, (Habermas, Legitimation crisis), 47.

140 Julia Black, 'Proceduralization of regulation', (2000) Oxford Journal of Legal Studies, Vol. 20, 597–614, 599.

141 Terence Daintith, 'Between domestic democracy and an alien rule of law? Some thoughts on the 'independence' of the Bank of England', in Mads Andenas and others (eds), European economic and monetary union: the institutional framework (Kluwer Law International, London, 1997), 357–372, 370–371.

there should be a government chaired "systemic risk oversight body…responsible for identifying and prioritizing systemic risk and making (non-binding) recommendations" with the central bank holding "operational independence" for macroprudential policymaking.[142] Finally, there is a tactical option under which the FPC avoids raising difficult issues and only employs macroprudential policies with a level of "low visibility" and does so in a manner which is a "conflict-minimize[r]".[143] Nevertheless, part of an institution's legitimacy is based on influencing opinions.

6.25 Weaving a "legitimacy narrative"

The actions of the FPC, combined with the circumstances at the time, may reinforce or undermine its legitimacy. The FPC needs continuously to weave a "legitimacy narrative", explaining clearly what it is doing and why in terms that will resonate with the various stakeholders. In the bardic tradition it needs to publicise its struggle to ensure financial stability as if it was contesting the great mead-hall against Grendel, drawing on examples from history, its own lineage and supported by a chorus of engaged politicians and media.

6.26 A broader scope for the Financial Policy Committee

Some have stressed the need to focus on the use of macroprudential tools such as LTV and LTI limits and a "greater control of non-banks" lenders.[144] However, this book goes further and suggests that, in addition, to attempting to use macroprudential policy to suppress the demand for credit the FPC should consider what steps may be taken to increase the supply of housing. Action in this area will, of necessity, be long-term and involve a range of bodies responsible for housing policy. If undertaken on a large enough scale over a sufficient period of time such a policy would increase housing supply substantially, reduce the price of both new housing and the existing stock and help to meet demand. Borrowers would, consequently, not need to borrow as much to acquire a less scarce asset.

The FPC has expressed its view that "the persistent gap between the supply of homes and the natural growth in demand was the underlying driver of the rate of UK house price inflation".[145] Nevertheless, the FPC have not given much prominence to this view nor taken a more active stance.[146] However, activity by

142 Ed Balls, James Howat and Anna Stansbury, 'Central bank independence revisited: after the financial crisis, what should a model central bank look like', (2016) Mossavar-Rahman Centre Working Paper Series No. 67, Harvard Kennedy School, 48–49.

143 Supra note 79, (Scharpf), 23–24.

144 Tony Dolphin and Matt Griffith, 'Forever blowing bubbles? Housing's role in the UK economy', (May 2011), Institute for Public Policy Research Report, 46–47.

145 FPC meeting minutes of 20 September 2016, published on 3 October 2016, 5.

146 Martin Čihák and others, 'Financial stability reports: what are they good for?', (2012) IMF Working Paper WP/12/1, 16, an international survey of such reports indicates that market developments are limited to a descriptions rather than any analysis or discussion.

the FPC in this area would trespass on the fiscal preserve of politicians and the nuanced decisions on the allocation of scarce resources. Nevertheless, there is probably scope for the FPC to review the data on the supply side and to publish its thoughts both on the short- and longer-term prospects on housing policy and its implementations. At the very least, the FPC could give emphasis to this work and provide authoritative information and views for Parliamentary select committees to consider, question and influence and for Parliament to debate.[147]

6.27 Conclusion

The foundations of political legitimacy rest on a democratic consensus. It requires a certain level of trust and understanding in democratic government and its institutions reinforced by democratic accountability and transparency. In additional to laws setting out legal processes establishing and maintaining this accountability, there needs to be a set of understandings and conventions governing the exercise of macroprudential policymaking and which set boundaries governing the use of such powers. These will change over time and vary depending on circumstances.

Sustaining political legitimacy may not be easy since, in some circumstances, it may be fragile as power flows to and from institutions. It does not exist in a vacuum but will depend on socio-economic and political factors. It is also subject to social "sentiment". This is particularly true in many areas where strong aspirations and expectations operate which influence the acceptance of institutional and policymaking political legitimacy. This is especially relevant to the potential use of LTV and DTI macroprudential tools by the FPC.

This chapter does not dismiss the possible employment of such instruments but it argues that a different approach is necessary in view of the concerns surrounding their political legitimacy. Moreover, this work seeks to provide other options including developing the application of conduct of business regulation both to protect borrowers and individual lenders but also for wider macroprudential purposes. These aspects have been covered in earlier chapters.

In addition, this chapter highlights the need for the FPC to address the aspirational desire for homeownership and the need for the committee to take a broader view of its role in supporting the need for a significant increase in housing supply. The FPC also needs to develop a longer-term approach to explaining its role and operations to a general audience. The search for political legitimacy by the FPC cannot be based solely on rational, cold argument. It needs to engage the hearts as well as the brain and be based on a narrative with emotional appeal.

147 For example, the Netherlands Central Bank published the conclusions of a meeting of its Financial Stability Committee of 12 May 2012 in which it commented on the failure to increase the supply of homes for rent in relation to macroprudential policy.

7 US Federal intervention in the housing market and possible lessons from the Veterans Administration

The aspiration of owning a home of ones' own is important in both the US and UK. This is particularly true in America where it forms part of the 'dream'. Financing this desire has bi-partisan support, and this has strongly influenced both the regulatory approach and government policy towards mortgage provision.

The Federal government housing policy has operated in a series of 'waves', since the 1930s, each with significant socio-economic effects. These measures have been both progressive and reactionary. Each intervention has contained serious failings. Often the process was one of reform followed by periods of stagnation influenced by the pressure of various powerful interest groups.

The flaws in the US mortgage market, both in the private and public sectors, are frequently identified as proximate causes of the recent financial collapse. However, there are areas of hope and good practice. In particular, there may be lessons from the approach taken by the US Veterans Administration ("VA"), guardians of the "G.I. Bill of Rights". While the VA provided generous support to home buyers, it also applied strict loan affordability criteria and an independent property valuation regime. Consequently, the VA avoided the problems of the financial crisis and may help set a model approach for both the US and other jurisdictions

7.1 The homeownership aspiration

Both the US and UK share similar views on the need for home ownership, but each has approached trying to achieve this objectives very differently. This chapter sets out the common themes and significant differences and highlights what the UK could learn from what appear to be the effects of sound conduct of business measures at the VA in performing a macroprudential task.

How a state views home ownership may say something about its ideology and is emblematic of what countries consider important. For example, in the US the government view is that housing is an "economic good", a "human right" and a "bulwark of democracy", tracing this back to the Jeffersonian "yeoman farmer".[1] In the view of President Calvin Coolidge "no greater contribution

1 David Reiss, 'Message in a mortgage: what Dodd-Frank's "Qualified Mortgage" tells us about ourselves', (2012), Brooklyn Law School Legal Studies Research Paper 264, 2.

could be made to the stability of the Nation and the advancement of its ideals, than to make it a nation of homeowning families".[2] Homeownership forms part of the "American Dream".[3] The ideological roots of homeownership in the US are deep but "first gain prominence as a moral issue" in the 1920s as a bulwark against "socialism and communism".[4] However, the modern Federal support for homeownership dates from the Great Depression with the creation of the Federal Housing Administration and subsequent legislation.[5]

The US is unique among western nations in the level of government intervention in the housing market. Much of this is focused on the residential mortgage market. Since the 1930s, in a series of actions, the Federal government has both encouraged and deterred residential mortgage lending.[6] These interventions have had both economic and social-engineering purposes, and consequences, and both aspects can be seen closely intertwined in what can be described as the three main waves of Federal intercession.

The Federal government first initiated steps in 1933 to save the US from financial collapse and to preserve social cohesion. However, at the same time, the actions taken resisted social change and maintained, and may even have strengthened, racial segregation.[7] A second, and even more intense, wave of Federal intervention in the housing market started in 1944 and continues both through legislation and the operations of the Government Sponsored Enterprises (GSEs). This established the "American Dream" of homeownership and turned it into a reality for millions of service men and women returning from World War II and the Korean War. In a few decades, it created a large middle class and extended city suburbs across the country.

A third intervention wave, started in the late 1960s and strengthened in the late 1990s and early 2000s. It sought to continue the process of economic redistribution to US minorities to help ensure social fairness and cohesion. Some, as described later in this section, have claimed that it was an intervention too far and have blamed it, in whole or part, for the recent financial crisis. However, others have defended the Federal role in this area and instead criticised loose

2 President Calvin Coolidge, quoted in Kenneth Jackson, *Crabgrass frontier: the suburbanization of the United States* (Oxford University Press, Oxford, 1985), 362.

3 Jim Cullen, *The American Dream: a short history of an idea that shaped a nation* (Oxford University Press, Oxford, 2004), 133.

4 Lawrence Vale, 'The ideological origins of affordable homeownership efforts', in William Rohe and Harry Watson (eds), *Chasing the American Dream* (Cornell University Press, Ithaca, New York, 2007), 19–20.

5 The National Housing Act 1934, Public Law 84-345, 48 Stat. 847. The Federal National Mortgage Association ("Fannie Mae") was established in 1938 to fund lenders providing mortgages under an amendment to the National Housing Act 1934 (Ch.13, §1, 52, Stat. 8). This created a market-based solution to ensuring a continuous supply of mortgages even in times of economic contraction.

6 Douglas Elliott, Greg Feldberg, and Andreas Lehnert, 'The history of cyclical macroprudential policy in the United States', (2013) Office of Financial Research Working Paper No. 8, Department of the Treasury, Washington DC, 1–74.

7 For example, Federal Housing Administration, *Underwriting Manual*, 'Rating of location: protection from adverse influences, Part II', (1936) discussed later.

monetary policy and the actions, ethics and mis-aligned innovations of lenders. The arguments on both sides have become politically partisan.

This section looks at aspects of these three waves of Federal intervention in the US housing market. It briefly sets out the history of these actions and highlights both the economic and, especially, the social purposes behind each phase. Each of these steps were both revolutionary for its time and necessary, but each contained serious flaws which fell to the next generation, and next intervention wave, to attempt to correct. It could be said that the process continues but reform appears to have been halted by the pressure of various powerful interest groups.

However, hope of positive change exists in what some might view as an unlikely quarter. This section highlights the approach taken by the US "VA", guardians of the "G.I. Bill of Rights". The VA were unusual among all the GSEs in the US in operating an approach to mortgage lending which is both generous, requiring no deposit by the borrowers, and by applying strict loan affordability criteria and an independent property valuation regime. Consequently, the VA, and those that it helped, avoided the problems of the financial crisis and may help set a model approach for both the US and other countries seeking to maintain the aspiration to have a place called home.

7.2 A brief history of US Federal intervention

Although a number of State chartered banks could lend against real property until 1913 US national banks were not permitted to make loans secured on land.[8] It was the Federal Reserve Act 1913 which first allowed this in very limited circumstances, for farm land.[9] Subsequent legislation in 1916 and 1927 extended this to residential real estate but subject to very tight limits including a maximum five year loan term.[10]

Both Federal and State policies contributed to a number of residential property bubbles. For example, there was a residential property boom in the 1920s which reached its zenith in 1926 followed by similar "irrational exuberance" in commercial property and equity stocks leading to the Great Crash.[11] However, the 1920s property collapse had only been based on limited amounts of credit. Banks had been relatively cautious in their levels of home mortgage lending and debt-to-asset ratios never rose above 25% compared to over 60% in 2006.[12]

8 Carl Behrens, 'Legal framework of urban mortgage lending by commercial banks', in Carl Behrens (ed), *Commercial bank activities in urban mortgage financing* (National Bureau of Economic Research, 1952), 16.

9 S24, Public Law 63-43 63d Congress H.R. 7837.

10 Supra note 8, (Behrens) 17–18.

11 Gregg Turner, *The Florida land boom of the 1920s* (McFarland, Jefferson, North Carolina, 2015), 165. However, there were extensive bank failures in both Florida and Georgia in the late 1920s due to fraud and commercial lending linked to the residential property boom, Raymond Vickers, *Panic in paradise: Florida's banking crash of 1926* (The University of Alabama, Tuscaloosa, 1994).

12 Chapter 2, n. 68, (Field), 72–73.

Prior to the Great Depression, housing mortgages were issued with very short maturities and subject to variable rate interest with low LTV ratios.[13] Every five years or so the borrower refinanced the mortgage. The banking crisis in 1932 and 1933 prevented this happening and properties were increasing foreclosed and sold onto a sharply falling market as banks struggled to maintain their solvency and, more importantly, their liquidity as depositors rushed to withdraw their money.[14] In 1933 the new administration sought to alleviate the panic by employing a number of measures including the creation of Federal deposit insurance and the establishment of the Home Owners Loan Corporation (HOLC). The aim was to halt, the epidemic of home foreclosures and to inject liquidity into the housing market to get lending going and housing built, and hence, employment restarted.

Using highly liquid government backed bonds the HOLC bought over a million problem mortgages from the banks and other financial institutions allowing the borrower to remain in their home and it converted these short loans into long-term fixed-rate repayment mortgages.[15] The latter carried a lower rate of interest and coupled with the longer period to maturity made the loan more affordable and reduced the probability of default. Nevertheless, the HOLC still ended up foreclosing on nearly 20% of the refinanced loans by 1940.[16]

The New Deal led to the creation of a number of other Federal housing support agencies including the Federal Savings and Loan Insurance Corporation (FSLIC) created to guarantee deposits at savings and loans organisations. The Federal Housing Administration (FHA) was established to provide government insurance to support the sale of mortgages into the general financial market and thus to generate more liquidity in the housing markets. In 1938 the emergency HOLC was replaced by Federal National Mortgage Association ("Fannie Mae"). The Federal Home Loan Mortgage Corporation ("Freddie Mac") was created in 1970 to provide some competition in this secondary market.

These Federal bodies were conceived in a period which admired soviet central planning.[17] This needs to be seen in the context of social and financial collapse in the 1930s, amid calls to nationalise the banking system and the deployment of Federal and State troops across the country. Initially, the steps taken in this

13 Chapter 4, n. 112, (Zywicki), 3.

14 Richard Green and Susan Wachter, 'The American mortgage in historical and international context', (2005) *Journal of Economic Perspectives*, Vol. 19, No. 4, 93–114, 95.

15 Ibid., (Green and Wachter), 95.

16 Price Fishback and John Wallis, 'What was new about the New Deal?', in Nicholas Crafts and Peter Fearon (eds), *The Great Depression of the 1930s: lessons for today* (Oxford University Press, Oxford, 2013), 318.

17 Many New Deal policies were influenced by Upton Sinclair and his "End Poverty In California" (EPIC) programme which envisioned a state-wide disability and pensions scheme and the state ownership of the means of production, including land, to provide work and the establishment of workers cooperatives, George Rising, 'An EPIC endeavor: Upton Sinclair's 1934 California Gubernatorial Campaign', (1997) Southern California Quarterly, Vol. 79, No. 1, 101–124, 111. Harry Hopkins, who went onto run many of the major New Deal programmes including the Federal Emergency Relief Administration, was supportive of the EPIC programme, Ibid., 117.

area in the 1930s did not distinguish between actions needed to preserve the economy and those required to maintain social cohesion. In time the latter objective grew in priority with housing and its finance used to effect socio-political objectives including support for veterans, farmers and minority ethnic groups.

The 1960s saw Federal intervention in the housing market focus on low-income housing projects. However, the on-budget cost of these projects and "the association of many of these with violence and drug use" increasingly turned Federal intervention towards using GSEs to finance homeownership.[18] In addition, the Federal government continued to provide direct support for residential housing through tax subsidies for homeowners, including permitting the deductibility of mortgages interest and the exemption of homes from capital gains taxation.[19]

7.3 Supporting minority group

As mentioned in Chapter 4, there is cross-party support in the US for public policy measures aimed at ensuring a ready supply of mortgage lending. In part, this is an ideological concept based on the home as part of the "American Dream" coupled with sociological evidence that home ownership appears to support improvements in householder civic engagement and improved outcomes for children. Homeownership also supports the housing development and construction industry, those marketing and selling residential property and all those involved in maintaining properties and related services. Most importantly, in the US context, the aspiration of owning a home of one's own allowed ethnic minorities to play their part in society.

Racial segregation runs deep in the US and a mixture of price barriers and restrictive covenants preventing the sale of residential properties to "non-caucasian whites" was widespread until the latter part of the 20th century.[20] For example, all the extensive housing developments during the 1920s Florida property boom contained these restrictions.[21] In 1926, the US Supreme Court upheld these covenants.[22] Indeed, "in some cities restrictive covenants were estimated to cover as much as 80% of residential property".[23] In 1921 the "Chicago Real Estate Board threatened to expel any member who sold a property" in an all-white area to a non-white.[24]

18 Nolan McCarty, Keith Poole and Howard Rosenthal, *Political bubbles: financial crises and the failure of American democracy* (Princeton University Press, New Jersey, 2013), 128.

19 Michael Carliner, 'Development of Federal homeownership 'policy', (January 1998) Housing Policy Debate, Vol. 9, No. 2, 299–321, 300.

20 Supra note 2, (Jackson), 133.

21 Supra note 11, (Turner), 143.

22 *Corrigan v. Buckley*, 271 U.S. 323 (1926).

23 Christopher Bonasta, *Knocking on the door: The Federal Government's attempt to desegregate the suburbs*, (Princeton University Press, Princeton, 2006), 60.

24 Ibid., 60.

From the start, the Federal housing agencies supported and developed segregation. For example, the Federal Housing Administration's 1936 "Underwriting Manual" said that Federal support would be restricted in order to ensure that properties "continued to be occupied by the same social and racial groups".[25] The process of Federal intervention in favour of segregation continued until the 1960s and had a significant effect on the social structure of many US cities. For example, in the late 1930s the expansion of Detroit led, in the view of the FHA, to some white property acquisitions coming too close to black owned homes. The result was that Federal mortgage guarantees were unavailable due to their "proximity to an 'inharmonious' racial group".[26] Prior to the 1960s, Federal housing support largely went to white middle-class borrowers and, in part due to Federal policy, the white population was able to flee to the suburbs and cities such as St Louis became a "premier example of urban abandonment".[27]

However, the 1960s introduced significant changes in the Federal position on civil society and desegregation. As seen in Chapter 4, homeownership was viewed as having a major role in this process and this view led to the Housing and Community Development Act 1974 which allowed greater flexibility in mortgage lending with the objective of increasing home ownership and community development for those formally excluded.[28] The chairman of the Senate Committee on Banking, Housing, and Urban Affairs claimed "that this legislation is the most significant in the field of housing legislation since the 1930s".[29]

The social upheavals, rioting and arson in US inner cities in 1967 lead to President Johnson, as part of his "Great Society" programme, to propose the Housing and Urban Development Act of 1968, with a goal of constructing 26 million homes over ten years, including those to 'replace the shamefully substandard units of misery where more than 20 million Americans still live'.[30]

> Homeownership is a cherished dream and achievement of most Americans. But it has always been out of reach of the nation's low-income families. Owning a home can increase responsibility and stake out a man's place in his community. The man who owns a home has something to be proud of and good reason to protect and preserve it. Today I propose a program to extend the benefits of homeownership to the nation's needy families…let us

25 Supra note 7, (Federal Housing Administration, *Underwriting Manual*), (1936), Part II, para 233.

26 Supra note 2, (Jackson), 209. The HOLC commissioned a study in 1933 which developed the original "red-lined" city maps designating "hazardous" lending zones, Glenn Alschuler and Stuart Blumin, *The GI Bill: the New Deal for veterans* (Oxford University Press, Oxford, 2009), 200.

27 Supra note 2, (Jackson), 285–286.

28 12 U.S.C. 1706e, Public L. No. 93-383, 88 Stat. 633.

29 Quoted in President Gerald Ford's, 'Remarks on signing the Housing and Community Development Act of 1974', on 22 August 1974.

30 Lyndon Johnson, 'Special message to the Congress on urban problems: *the crisis of the cities.*' 22 February 1968.

go forward, as one nation in common purpose joined, to change the face of our cities and to end the fear of those – rich and poor alike – who call them home.[31]

7.4 Recent history and influences

Through the 1980s, 1990s and early 2000s, there were a number of parallel and self-reinforcing initiatives by those supporting a homeownership socio-political agenda, legislators, lenders and financiers devising innovative financial products and those seeking to protect borrowers. During this latter period the increase in home-buying was led by first time buyers aged under 35 (15.5%) compared with a 2.7% increase by those in 45–54-year-old age bracket.[32] A range of legislative changes promoted lending to disadvantaged groups of citizens. These included legislation which expanded the range of products and changes in regulations (e.g. the Depository Institutions Deregulation and Monetary Control Act of 1980) which allowed all federally insured banks and thrifts to raise mortgage interest rates on all home loans pre-empting State usury laws. There was also the Alternative Mortgage Transactions Parity Act (1982) (AMTPA) which allowed all "lenders to issue adjustable rate, mortgages with large end 'balloon' payments and non-amortising mortgages".[33] There was also other legislation which provided additional incentives to lend to low income group (e.g. the Federal Housing Enterprise Financial Safety and Soundness Act 1992 and Community Reinvestment Act 1977). It is important to understanding the context in order to better elucidate the problems and solutions. As mentioned above, some consider that this series of laws were instrumental in persuading lenders to extent credit to those who should not have borrowed.

In 1995 President Clinton's administration issued its National Homeownership Strategy.[34] Nevertheless, even as late as 2003 there were still significant disparities in homeownership rates.[35] Consequently, in 2002 President Bush

31 Ibid., (Johnson).

32 Chapter 4, n. 10, (Garriga and Schlagenhauf, 'Recent trends in homeownership'), 398.

33 Chapter 4, n. 123, (Engel and Patricia), 1275.

The full titles of each Act are:

The Depository Institutions Deregulation and Monetary Control Act 1980 (H.R. 4986 Public Law 96–221),

The Alternative Mortgage Transaction Parity Act 1982 contained within Title VIII of the Garn–St Germain Depository Institutions Act 1982 (H.R. 6267 Public Law 97-320).

The Federal Housing Enterprises Financial Safety and Soundness Act 1992, (Public Law 102-550) contained within Title XIII of the Housing and Community Development Act 1992, (H.R. 533 106, Statute 3941, 12 U.S.C § 4501),

The Community Reinvestment Act (Public Law 95-128, 91 Statute 1147, contained within Title VIII of the Housing and Community Development Act 1977 (12 U.S.C. § 2901).

34 The objective of this strategy was to create up to 8 million new homeowners by 2000 using a range of mechanisms including expanded Federal down payment assistance and other forms of direct funding. See Rohe and Watson, *Chasing the American Dream*, 8, supra note 4.

35 75% of whites owned their own homes compared with 48% for black and 47% Hispanic households ('State of the Nation's Housing', (2003), Harvard University Joint Centre for Housing Studies, Fig. 17, 17.

launched his "Blueprint for the American Dream".[36] The objective of this plan was to increase minority homeownership by 5.5 million by 2010, by providing assistance with funding and down payments and increasing the supply of affordable housing.[37] There can be few Federal strategies that have commanded such broad support across political parties, the financial services industry, social change campaigners and the property and construction sectors.[38] It is symbolic that in 2002 a Presidential Proclamation declared that the month of June would be known as "National Home Ownership Month".[39] The Proclamation on 4 June 2002 announcing this described "Homeownership [as] an important part of the American Dream…a home provides…a source of great personal pride and an important part of community stability".[40] The Proclamation extolled the benefits of homeownership as it "encourages personal responsibility and the values necessary for a strong family. Where homeownership flourishes, neighbourhoods are more stable, residents more civic-minded, schools better and crime rates decline".[41] The President pledged the resources of the Federal government to help people to buy their own homes and to "pursue a better quality of life".[42] Further, the homeownership aspiration was "politically popular, in part, because it has a myriad of constituencies" including "developers, the financial services industry, planners, road-builders", etc.[43] This was encouraged by regulatory changes.

In 2004 in support of increased homeownership lending the Office of the Comptroller of the Currency (OCC) enacted a pre-emption rule preventing individual states applying laws which restricted the terms of mortgage lending, including borrower ability to repay verification.[44] This applied to all national banks supervised by the OCC. Research indicates that while controlling for other factors this resulted in an annual increase of between 11% and 15% in mortgage lending between national banks and those solely subject to State supervision which restricted lending to customers at risk of default.[45] These

36 A presidential announcement: *A blueprint for the American Dream: a public/private partnership to increase minority homeownership by 5.5 Million by the end of the decade*, (archive of the Department of Housing and Urban Development).

37 Ibid., (*Blueprint*), 2.

38 Calomiris and Haber describe it as a "grand banking bargain" to benefit all interested parties, *Fragile by design*, 216–255, Chapter 3, n. 13.

39 'Recognizing national homeownership month and the importance of homeownership in the United States', House of Representatives, Motion 477, 110th Congress (6 November 2007).

40 *National Homeownership Month, Presidential Proclamation*, (June 2002) White House Archive, George W. Bush, press releases.

41 Ibid., (*Homeownership Month*).

42 Ibid., (*Homeownership Month*).

43 Anne Shlay, 'Low-income homeownership: American dream or delusion?', (March 2006) *Urban Studies*, Vol. 43, No. 3, 511–531, 512.

44 Marco Di Maggio and Amir Kermani, 'Credit-induced boom and bust', (2016) Harvard Business School Working Paper 17-010, 2–3. See also Chapter 4, n. 147, (Agarwal and others), on the Illinois lending pilot.

45 Ibid., (Maggio and Kermani), 4.

regulatory were bound-in with political views and supported by socio-economic factors encouraging homeownership.

7.5 Socio-economic evidence

A considerable amount of socio-economic academic research supports the benefits of homeownership. For example, renters appear to have much less civic engagement with only 52% of renters saying that they had voted in local elections compared with 77% of homeowners.[46] Without owning your own home achieving upward social mobility is more difficult.[47] In addition, there is evidence that a family owning its own home "predicts positive outcomes for children" with continued school attendance and reduced teenage pregnancies.[48] Although the evidence is not conclusive there do appear to be public policy benefits supporting homeownership.[49] However, although causality may be difficult to determine, at the very least, homeownership is a symbol of a family's aspiration to prosper and to put down enduring roots.[50] It is important to understand the aspirational and socio-economic public policy context in order to make sense of what happened in the years leading up to the financial crisis. The GSEs were some of the chosen instruments to effect these housing policies.

7.6 Role of GSEs and the Community Reinvestment Act 1977 in the recent financial crisis

Following on the creation of the "Great Society" in the 1970s, the socio-economic purpose of the GSEs was amended and coupled with anti-discrimination legislation. This had the effect of embedding the financial and economic structures, which originated in the 1930s, in the US mortgage and financial markets of the last decades of the 20th and early part of the 21st centuries. The combination of the latter legislation with the role of the GSEs, magnified by financial innovation, has been blamed by many for the recent financial crisis. Further,

46 Denise DiPasquale and Edward Glaeser, 'Incentives and social capital: are homeowners better citizens?', (1999), *Journal of Urban Economics*, Vol. 45, No. 2, 354–384.

47 Will Paxton and John Brynner, *The asset effect* (The Institute for Public Policy Research, London, 2001) and developed by Alex Nunn, 'Factors influencing social mobility', (2007) Department for Work and Pensions Research Report No 450, 39. In essence the argument is that owning assets, not necessarily only housing, gives an individual a stake in society and promotes better citizenship.

48 Richard Green, Gary Painter and Michelle White, 'Measuring the benefits of homeowning: effects on children redux', (2012), Research Institute for Housing America: Special Report, 33.

49 William Rohe, Shannon Van Zandt and George McCarthy, 'The social benefits and costs of homeownership: a critical assessment of the research', (October 2001) Low-Income Homeownership Working Paper Series 01.12, Harvard University Joint Centre for Housing Studies, 23.

50 Julie Isaacs, Isabel Sawhill and Ron Haskins, 'Getting ahead or losing ground: economic mobility in America', (2008), The Brookings Institute, Washington DC, 50.

the GSEs were implicated in the Savings and Loan crisis in the 1980s.[51] In summary, it is claimed that the two largest GSEs, Fannie Mae and Freddie Mac, between the 1990s and 2006, motivated by hubris and politically driven socio-economic targets, relaxed their underwriting standards and financed unsustainable borrowings.[52] Further, additional obloquy is attached to the Community Reinvestment Act 1977 (CRA).[53]

The CRA had little effect between its introduction in 1977 and 1992 with only some $43 Bn lent by banks under this legislation in total during this period.[54] President Clinton said in 1999 that the CRA was "pretty well moribund until we took office…".[55] In parallel, many banks sought to merge and national banks needed Federal Reserve Board approval to do so. CRA activist groups set up the National Community Reinvestment Coalition as an umbrella group to promote their interests. This group in turn issued a guide on how to negotiate with banks seeking merger permission.[56] Banks judged as "good citizens" by CRA activist groups were more likely to have the latters' support for their merger plans.[57]

Again, the perception was that in the early 1990s, with a change in administration, there was renewed political interest in helping disadvantaged ethnic groups buy their own homes. This resulted in private sector lenders seeking political credit for meeting their CRA objectives.[58] The latter new lending objective arose in reaction to studies evidencing racial discrimination in granting

51 George Benston and George Kaufman, 'FDICIA after five years', (Summer 1997) *Journal of Economic Perspectives*, Vol. 11, No. 3, 139–158, 140. The GSEs preference for long-term fixed rate mortgages opens the risk of interest rate mis-match with other lenders, such as the Savings and Loan associations, exposed by their short-term variable rate deposits and money market funds finance. This issue coupled with deregulation in the early 1980s is largely blamed for the Savings and Loan crisis in that decade.

52 See, for example see Chapter 3, n. 13, (Calomiris and Haber), 252–255.

53 12 USC § 2901.

54 Chapter 3, n. 13, (Calomiris and Haber), 216–226.

55 Chapter 3, n. 13, (Calomiris and Haber), 217.

56 The National Community Reinvestment Coalition (NCRC),

> NCRC encourages its members and other neighborhood organizations to offer their comments on the CRA performance of banks…changing a rating from Outstanding to Satisfactory…can motivate a bank to increase the number of loans, investments, and services to low- and moderate-income communities.

'A brief description of the CRA', NCRC web-site, 16 November 2008, https://ncrc.org/a-brief-description-of-cra/, (accessed 25 June 2019).

57 The Financial Crisis Inquiry Report, (January 2011), The Financial Crisis Inquiry Commission, 97–99.

58 U.S. House of Representatives Committee on Oversight and Government Reform, chaired by Darrell Issa, 'The role of Government affordable housing policy in creating the global financial crisis of 2008', released July 2009 and updated May 2010), 9, House of Representatives,

> Although the annual value of CRA home mortgage lending increased some 250% between 1996 and 2008, CRA lending never exceeded about 3% of total originations. While CRA cannot be directly blamed for the huge volumes of risky nonprime mortgages…CRA continued a pattern of behavior of lowering mortgage underwriting standards.

mortgages coupled with a need to re-inflate the US economy after the recession in the early 1990s.[59] Moreover, there is an argument that regulators encouraged banks in the 1990s and 2000s to relax their credit standards to increase lending to poor areas subject to the CRA and that this piece of legislation was a major contributor to the financial crisis in the US.[60] There were also warnings of the potential effect of "anti-redlining" regulations "imposing substantial costs [of default] on financial institutions and the public" as early as 1980.[61] This view has taken on a political complexion with allegations that regulation has been "captured" by the political process.[62]

These issues were reviewed by the Congressional Financial Crisis Inquiry Commission which issued its report in 2010. However, all the Republican members of the commission dissented and one member of the commission, Peter Wallison, a fellow of the American Enterprise Institute (AEI), issued his own report.[63] In this document, he laid the blame for the financial crisis on the CRA and support for affordable housing. This view was based on an earlier paper by Edward Pinto, another fellow of the AEI and, until the late 1980s, an executive vice president and the chief credit officer for Fannie Mae.[64] However, a number of subsequent papers have criticised both the statistics and the analysis in this latter paper.[65] Other research concludes that while it is possible that CRA compliant lending did have some effect on poor credit decisions the results were not significant and were "not a significant contributor to the financial crisis".[66]

59 Alice Munnell and others, 'Mortgage lending in Boston', (1992) Working Paper No. 92-7, Federal Reserve Bank of Boston, 2, "after controlling for financial, employment, and neighborhood characteristics, black and Hispanic mortgage applicants in the Boston metropolitan area are roughly 60 percent more likely to be turned down than whites".

60 Rajan Raghuram stated that while

> irrational exuberance played a part...perhaps more important [factors] were the political forces distorting the markets. The tsunami of money directed by a US Congress, worried about growing income inequality, towards expanding low income housing, joined with the flood of foreign capital inflows to remove any discipline on home loans.
>
> 'Bankers have been sold short by market distortions' (Financial Times, 2 June 2010)

61 James Barth, Joseph Cordes and Anthony Yezer, 'Financial institution regulations, redlining and mortgage markets', (October 1979), The Federal Reserve Bank of Boston Conference Series on 'The regulation of financial Institutions', 101–143, 134.

62 John Campbell and others, 'The regulation of consumer financial products: an introductory essay with four case studies', (September 2010) Harvard Kennedy School Faculty Research Working Paper, 10-040, 37.

63 Peter Wallison, *Dissent from the Majority Report of the Financial Crisis Inquiry Commission, (AEI Press, Washington D.C., 2011)* blames the financial crisis on US government housing policy and Edward Pinto, 'Acorn and the housing bubble', *Wall Street Journal*, 12 November 2009.

64 Edward Pinto, 'Triggers of the financial crisis', (2010) a memorandum to staff of the Financial Crisis Inquiry Commission.

65 For example, David Min, 'Faulty conclusions based on shoddy foundations', (2011), Paper for the Centre for American Progress.

66 Neil Bhutta and Daniel Ringo, 'Assessing the Community Reinvestment Act's role in the financial crisis', (2015) Federal Reserve Board, FEDS Notes.

One research paper looked at the period around which banks were assessed for CRA compliance in the period 1999–2009 and found that CRA lending rose by 5% compared with banks not assessed at the same time.[67] This is seen as evidence that the CRA influenced the quality of credit assessments since there was a 15% increase in defaults in loans made during this period.[68] However, three other sets of research found that the effect of CRA compliant lending was much smaller and that this aspect of the provision of mortgage credit had not been responsible for the financial crisis.[69] Nevertheless, there is evidence from a pilot study in Chicago that paternalistic legislation to protect sub-prime borrowers was effective and that this form of protection was only removed after litigation and protests by community activists and residents on the grounds that it was discriminatory.[70] However, the facts about the type and quality of GSE supported lending, prior to the financial crisis, are unclear and disputed.

Estimating the level of subprime business is impossible for this period because, for example, Fannie Mae only classified loans as sub-prime if they originated from a lender specialising in this sector.[71] This probably understates the level of such lending. Moreover, the view that the GSEs restricted themselves to acquiring only prime mortgages is wrong, since, for example, the GSEs entered into extensive agreements with various mortgage originators to provide secured loans to low and moderate income households.[72] This compounded the general decline in lending standards. For example, the Office of the Comptroller of the Currency's 2005 report found that banks continued "to ease retail [underwriting] standards primarily because of increased competition".[73]

There are wildly different views on the extent of the subprime problem depending, largely, on individual political perspectives. For example, one version claims that by mid-2008 there were almost 27 million subprime mortgages; about 50% of the total number of mortgages (55 million).[74] "Two-thirds of these (16.8 million) were held or guaranteed by the FHA and the GSEs and by

67 Sumit Agarwal and others, 'Did the Community Reinvestment Act lead to risky lending?', (2012) National Bureau of Economic Research, Working Paper 18609.

68 Ibid., (Agarwal), 24.

69 Neil Bhutta and Glenn Canner, 'Did the CRA cause the mortgage market meltdown?', (2009) Federal Reserve Bank of Minneapolis Community Dividend looked at mortgages written in 2005-6 and found that only 6% were related to CRA requirements. Further work indicated that CRA related lending held-up well and few went into default, Neil Bhutta and Glenn Canner, 'Mortgage market conditions and borrower outcomes', (2013) Federal Reserve Bulletin, Vol. 99.

70 Chapter 4, n. 147, (Agarwal and others).

71 Oonagh McDonald, *Fannie Mae and Freddie Mac* (Bloomsbury, London, 2012), 244.

72 Ibid., 251–252. For example, in 2003 Fannie Mae agreed with Washington Mutual to finance $85 Bn of home loans over five years to such families.

73 Office of the Comptroller of the Currency National Credit Committee, 'Survey of credit underwriting practices', (June 2005), 5–6.

74 Peter Wallison, 'Government housing policy and the financial crisis', (Spring/Summer 2010) *Cato Journal*, Vol. 30, No. 2, 397–406, 402.

US banks (2.2 million)".[75] Somewhere between 8 and 13 million of these were foreclosed.[76] These figures are based on research by Pinto at the American Enterprise Institute and this work has been criticised by the Centre for American Progress:

> Pinto's estimate that there are 26.7 million subprime and Alt-A loans outstanding (roughly half of all outstanding loans) is an enormous outlier among analysts. The nonpartisan Government Accountability Office (GAO) found that as of December 31, 2009, there were only 4.58 million outstanding subprime and Alt-A loans out of roughly 55 million total loans. In other words, Pinto's estimate of subprime and Alt-A exposure throughout the mortgage system is more than five times greater than the GAO's estimate.[77]

However, it is clear that to reform the GSEs both prior and subsequent to the financial crisis has proved very difficult. The combination of social interest groups, lenders, mortgage brokers, construction firms and the GSEs themselves have thwarted change. It is reported that between

> 1998 and 2008, Fannie Mae and Freddie Mac spent over $176 million on lobbyists. They paid lobbyists to influence Members of Congress to block legislative proposals that would have stripped them of their preferential advantages. The GSEs even paid lobbyists just so they would not lobby against them.[78]

Reportedly, GSEs could act very determinedly: "Fannie has this grandmotherly image, but they'll…tie you up and throw you in the Potomac. They're absolutely ruthless".[79]

As already mentioned in earlier chapters the housing bubbles were significantly more pronounced in four states (Arizona, California, Florida and New Mexico) in the run-up to the financial crisis.[80] The crisis followed the pattern described by Minsky due to the ready availability of credit, low interest rates and a speculative housing mania. The process was further fuelled by additional credit provided by financial innovation and politically supported GSEs. Aspects of this latter element could be seen in cross-party and Presidential support for home-ownership as an aspiration for all and reinforced by the work of, in particular Freddie Mac and Fannie Mae.

75 Ibid., 402.
76 Supra, note 71, (McDonald), 334.
77 Supra note 65, (Min), 4.
78 Supra note 58, (Issa), 14–15.
79 Owen Ullmann, 'Crony capitalism: American style', (July/August 1999) *The International Economy*, 7.
80 Chapter 4, n. 6, (Haughwout and others, 'Real estate investors, the leverage cycle and the housing market crisis').

7.7 Opposition to reforming the GSEs

Following the crisis, the US GSEs remain largely unreformed and large amounts of their securities are held by the Federal Reserve.[81] Any change is opposed from a number of sides.[82] Support for the GSEs comes from a broad front of interested groups. For example, since the increase in the availability of credit produced higher house prices, the main beneficiaries were "real estate brokers, builders, building labor, the suppliers of building materials and speculators".[83] For example, the website of the National Association of Realtors states, "Fannie and Freddie, despite their flaws, are helping the housing recovery. Getting rid of them doesn't solve the problem...Making sure future homeowners have access to affordable home loans is good for the economy, and it's good for home values".[84] There appears to be a large enough coalition to prevent any significant changes to the GSEs with reform seen as a "common enemy".[85] As has been said "there is certainly more than enough blame to go around".[86]

Nevertheless, the VA was one GSE which came out well from the financial crisis. There is no definitive answer to why this was the case but it may be that it was due to its regime of applying strict affordability criteria and tests to applications for its support and its use of independent property valuers. The VA's approach to lending may show a potential way forward for continuing Federal support of homeownership and reinforce the major theme of this book on the importance of conduct of business regulation in helping to ensure financial stability.

7.8 The "G.I. Bill" and the VA's promotion of homeownership

In order to avoid the economic disruption and the domestic political agitation among veterans experienced after the First World War the US government took a number of steps as the Second World War came to a close. These included the creation of the VA mortgage insurance program as part of Servicemen's

81 Almost 40% of total balance sheet assets, ($1,736 Bn out of total balance sheet assets of $4,454 Bn) Quarterly Report on Federal Reserve Balance Sheet Developments, (November 2016), 4.

82 Supra, note 65, (Min), 4–5.

83 Edward Pinto, 'Fifty years of housing policy failure: how housing policies make homes unaffordable', (October 2015) American Enterprise Institution's International Centre on Housing Risk, 12.

84 National Association of Realtors web-site, 'The Future of Fannie Mae & Freddie Mac and What It Means for You', http://homeownershipmatters.realtor/issues/the-future-of-fannie-mae-freddie-mac-and-what-it-means-for-you/, posted 19 March 2014, (accessed 25 June 2019).

85 Lorraine Woellert, 'The real estate lobby Is ready to rumble',

> The housing lobby is mobilizing against its common enemy: a Republican plan to eliminate the federal government's guarantee of mortgages. 'It's a coalition that's going to be very difficult for our adversaries to beat,' says Jerry Howard, president and chief executive officer of the National Association of Home Builders. 'We're preparing for one hell of a fight.'
>
> Bloomberg Businessweek, 7 February 2011.

86 Supra, note 18, (McCarty), 126.

Readjustment Act of 1944 ("G.I. Bill").[87] The key purpose of this part of the legislation was set out in the preamble to the 1949 Housing Act stating the aim of providing "a decent home in a suitable living environment for every American family".[88] This provided mortgage repayment insurance to veterans borrowing to buy or refurbish a home and essentially allows no-deposit loans.[89] The rationale was that service personnel would not have been paid enough during their period of service to afford a house deposit.

This important measure both increased house building and, as part of a much larger scheme, carried out a programme of social engineering with free university education and vocational courses and subsidised housing for some 4 million returning service men and women.[90] The Act has been amended over the years but its structure remains in place and its benefits continue to be available for veterans.

The results of the G.I. Bill are seen as transformational. Besides the access to free university and technical training the legislation permitted millions of men and women in their early twenties to buy their own homes and start families. A home of their own and the independence it provided became a mark of their new status and created "social capital" providing an inheritance for their children. "The G.I. Bill helped to engineer physical revolutions that ushered in a new 'middle class'".[91]

"Between 1940 and 1960, the fraction of all households that own the home they occupy increased from 44 to 62 percent".[92] The pattern of VA mortgage guarantees increased significantly until 1954 with the return of veterans from both the Second World War and the Korean War so that between 1949 and 1953 the VA had a share which averaged 24% of the new mortgages market.[93] Consequently, the VA programme played an important part in the growth of home ownership. However, there was a marked change in the period preceding the recent financial crisis.

The number of VA loan guarantees continued each year at between 250,000 and over 300,000 in 2004. Then at the height of the housing boom, the annual numbers fell sharply to around 150,000 in 2005 and 2006 in marked contrast to that of Freddie Mac and Fannie Mae.[94] For example, the latter financed, in various forms, some 3.5 million homes in 2005.[95] Further, following the financial

87 Public law 346, Chapter 268, S.1767.

88 Alex Schwartz, *Housing policy in the United States* (Routledge, New York, 2006), 1.

89 Veterans Administration Loan Guarantee Guide, 1.

90 Kathleen Frydl, *The GI Bill* (Cambridge University Press, Cambridge, 2009), 263.

91 Ibid., (Frydl), 302.

92 Matthew Chambers, Carlos Garriga and Don Schlagenhauf, 'The New Deal, the GI Bill and post-war housing', (2012), Society for Economic Dynamics, Meeting Papers, No. 1050, 2.

93 Ibid., (Chambers), 7.

94 Libby Perl, 'VA housing', (4 February 2013), Congressional Research Service, 10.

95 Fannie Mae, Securities and Exchange Commission 10-K report for the year to 31 December 2005, 3.

crisis, the VA's delinquency rates were very low at levels close to that for prime mortgages.[96]

7.9 Assessment and conclusion

There appear to be a number of possible reasons for the VA's success including the VA's oversight of lenders and its selection of property appraisers.[97] However, the VA's loan underwriting process is the most likely reason for both the significant decline in housing guarantees in 2005 and 2006 and the low level of delinquency. Unlike the other GSEs the VA required both evidence of "reliable monthly income" and applied a detailed affordability test to determine whether the veteran had sufficient disposable income to meet both the mortgage costs and living expenses.[98]

It is possible that the decline in underwriting standards in 2005 and 2006 by other GSEs and private sector lenders attracted veterans away from VA loan guarantees. Consequently, there may have been a process of positive selection with the more fragile borrowers seeking help elsewhere. There may also be factors relating to the personal characteristics of former service staff. In addition, in some parts of the country the housing bubble inflated prices beyond the limits permitted by the VA. It may also be due to the activities of incentivised real-estate and mortgage brokers and the "targeted advertising" of subprime loans.[99] The whole issue is unexplored. Nevertheless, I submit that the application of documented affordability assessments coupled with sound property valuations were important factors in the success of the VA's approach to providing Federal assistance in the no-deposit mortgage market. The work of Di Maggio and Kermani tends to support this view.[100]

If this hypothesis is correct for the VA, then it reinforces the importance of conduct of business regulation as a macroprudential tool in reducing the expansion of residential housing credit.

96 US Congress, Evidence of Thomas Pamperin, Associate Deputy Under Secretary for Policy and Program Management, Veterans Benefits Administration, US Department of Veterans Affairs on 20 May 2010 to the House Committee on Veteran Affairs, Sub-committee on Economic Opportunity.

97 US Military, Veterans Administration, 'A look at the VA loan appraisal process'. See also Pamperin's evidence in supra, note 96,

> VA's adherence to sound credit and underwriting principles prohibited the program from engaging in risky or subprime lending practices. Our strong lender oversight ensured that VA's mortgage-industry partners complied with these policies. Additionally, VA's panel of fee appraisers, who are assigned on a rotational basis and monitored by VA, ensures that home values are reasonable in light of market conditions.

98 Veterans Administration, Lenders Handbook – VA Pamphlet 26-7, Chapter 4.

99 US Congress, Testimony of Tim Embree, (Iraq and Afghanistan Veterans of America, Legislative Associate) on 20 May 2010, to the House Committee on Veteran Affairs, Sub-committee on Economic Opportunity.

100 Supra, note 44.

8 Housing markets

The political and macroprudential policy implications

A number of national and regional housing markets across the world do not function well. Some, such as that in the UK, are broken. This is important for financial stability since the failure to build sufficient homes leads to an increased demand for more credit to buy what is available resulting in higher prices for housing. The consequent rise in value of homes provides the security for more borrowing and so on. This has the potential to form an economic 'bubble' which, when it bursts, may undermine the financial position of individual lenders and the financial sector as a whole and this can spread across the whole economy. Thus, it can be said that "almost every financial crisis has political roots" due to the failure to build sufficient housing. In many ways, increased debt is used as a 'palliative' by governments. Additionally, it is politically satisfying that existing homeowners are pleased that their property continues to rise in value.

Consequently, financial stability, housing policy and access to mortgages are socio-political issues of great importance whether this be in, for example, California, Toronto, Sydney or England. There are a number of methods of addressing chronic housing shortages, including reducing the cost of building by taking land for development into public ownership at current use values, changing taxation and certain land tax exemptions and amending local regulations restricting land use and others specifying minimum housing plot sizes.

Macroprudential policymakers are reluctant to intervene in the highly political area of housing policy since it may be seen to compromise their political legitimacy. However, there are steps they can take. These include highlighting and publicising the financial stability aspects of the problem and providing information to demonstrate progress, if any, in addressing these issues.

8.1 The issue

The politics of housing has been clearly stated:

> the housing market is at the core of much of our work on financial stability... To own the house you live in is of great value to most Norwegians. Owning a house can give a sense of safety and security...Strong public interest in housing market developments illustrates the important role housing plays

in the economy. Not a day goes by without the housing market being mentioned in the news.[1]

At the heart of the problem has been the failure to build sufficient housing: "better housing supply could also play a part in reducing economic volatility. Most major cycles in the UK economy over the past 30 years have been associated with instability in the housing market".[2]

"Almost every financial crisis has political roots".[3] This is true of a number of countries, including the US and UK. In the course of interviewing a number of senior staff at mortgage lenders and other policymakers, many have commented that the UK housing market is "broken". Similarly, a report issued in 2009 described the housing market as "dysfunctional".[4] The lack of suitable housing may be spread across a country but the severest problems are more likely to occur in local pockets. In the larger countries, the lack of suitable housing is evident at city, state and provincial levels. For example, Vancouver has seen the price of housing race ahead of income 'creating a crisis situation across the spectrum'.[5] A series of political acts of commission and omission have produced this result with severe implications for financial stability and macroprudential policy.

The rapid growth in new households is central to a number of global housing 'hot-spots'. For example, between 2005 and 2018 the population of Melbourne in Australia grew by almost 50% from 3.4 million to 5 million, while in Seattle, USA the population increased between 2010 and 2018 by 22.4%.[6] In the UK household formation is currently running at approximately, 214,000 per annum for England alone.[7] A projection in 2012 estimated that "the number of households in England will increase from 22.1 million in 2011 to 27.5 million in 2037".[8] This is an increase of 5.4 million, or 25%. "This implies that in 2037 we will need one additional home for every four that were in existence in 2011".[9] Another estimate states that the UK needs over 240,000 each year.[10]

1 Siv Jensen, Norwegian Finance Minister, 'How to ensure financial stability in a European environment?' speech at the Policy Exchange, 6 April 2018.
2 Kate Barker, 'Delivering stability: securing our future housing needs', (March 2004) Barker Review Final Report, 18.
3 Chapter 3, n. 124, (Rajan, *Fault lines*), 7.
4 Building and Social Housing Foundation (BHSF), *The future of housing* (BSHF publication, Coalville, 2009) Report of a consultation meeting held between 23–25 June 2009 chaired by Lord Best, 6.
5 City of Vancouver, Canada, 'Housing Vancouver Strategy', (November 2018), 3.
6 Population Australia web-site, Melbourne, www.population.net.au/melbourne-population/, (accessed 12 July 2019). US Census Bureau web-site, Seattle City, www.census.gov/quickfacts/fact/table/seattlecitywashington,US/PST045218, (accessed 12 July 2019).
7 Department for Communities and Local Government, '2014-based Household Projections: England, 2014–2039', (12 July 2016), 1.
8 Neil McDonald and Christine Whitehead, 'New estimates of housing requirements in England, 2012 to 2037', (November 2015), Town & Country Planning Tomorrow Series Paper 17, 18.
9 Ibid., (McDonald and Whitehead), 18.
10 Alan Holmans, 'New estimates of housing demand & need in England, 2011 to 2031', (2013) Town & Country Planning Tomorrow Series Paper 16, 5.

The current view is that the UK needs to build some 290,000 homes each year until, at least, 2031 to address the back-log in house building and to meet future demand.[11] In addition, another study used the terminology of "concealed households" to describe the existence of potential demand for housing including those living in overcrowded accommodation, older adults living with their parents, those in "unsuitable homes" (e.g. caravans, winter-let properties and the elderly and disabled unable to leave the accommodation due to access issues, etc.) in addition to those actually homeless.[12]

In the UK, in 2018 some 165,000 new homes were build; 135,000 by the private sector and 30,000 by housing associations and local authorities.[13] This compares, for example, with over 240,000 build in 1980 and some 426,000 homes build in 1968, the highest number of dwellings constructed in any post-war year.[14] Some 50% of these homes were built by local authorities and housing associations. This level of construction is much lower than in other developed countries. For example, the UK constructed "only 3.6 homes each year per thousand people, between 1975 and 2013 compared with over 6 in France and the Netherlands and 5.4 in the USA".[15]

In the UK, private sector building has not met the gap left by the demise of local government building which never recovered from a sharp decline in building in 1982 due to changes in central government policy. There have been earlier house building peaks. For example, between the two World Wars 4 million high-quality local authority homes were built together with a further 400,000 constructed by the private sector subsidised by taxpayers with an additional 2.5 million homes privately built without subsidy.[16] This represents some 350,000 houses constructed each year on average. There were further large-scale home building programmes immediately after the Second World War under the Attlee government and again in the 1960s as part of a programme of inner-city slum clearances (see Figure 8.1).[17]

Across the globe, housing shortages have resulted in a significant growth in house prices. However, there is little evidence, in the UK, that current

11 Wendy Wilson, 'Housing supply and demand: key issues for the 2010 Parliament', (May 2010) House of Commons Library Research: Key issues for the new Parliament, 2010, 76–77.

12 Glen Bramley and others, 'Estimating housing need', (November 2010), Department for Communities and Local Government, 42–54.

13 Department of Housing, Communities and Local Government, 'House building', Table 244, (updated 4 July 2019), www.gov.uk/government/statistical-data-sets/live-tables-on-house-building, (accessed 23 July 2019).

14 Ibid., Table 244.

15 Thomas Aubrey, 'The challenge of accelerating UK housebuilding', (January 2015) Policy Network Paper, 4.

16 Derek Fraser, *The evolution of the British welfare state* (Palgrave Macmillan, Basingstoke, 2009), 238.

17 For the 1930s see Crafts and Fearon, 'The 1930s: understanding the lessons', 57, Chapter 7, n. 16.

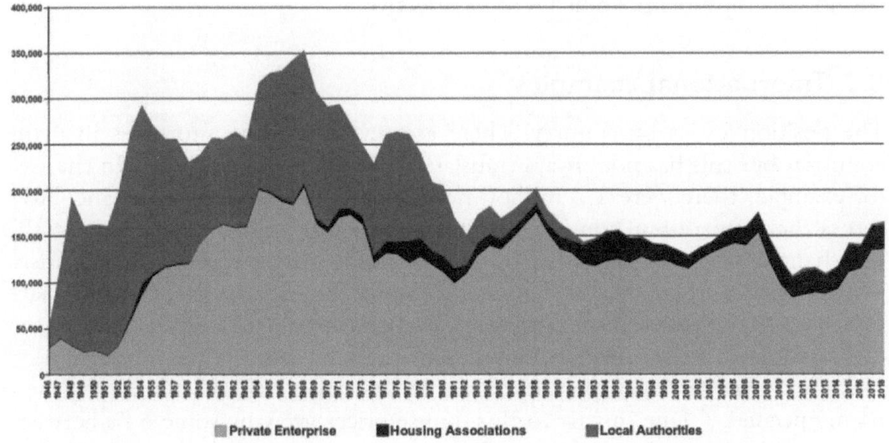

Figure 8.1 UK house building.

Source: Number of permanent dwellings completion in England Table 244. https://www.gov.uk/government/statistical-data-sets/live-tables-on-house-building, (accessed 29 July 2019).

government ministers are over-concerned about this.[18] In evidence to the House of Lord Select Committee the then Housing Minister said "that 'an awful lot of existing home owners will be very pleased' that [house] prices will continue to rise...the government's aim is not to stop house prices rising, rather their priority is to encourage home ownership without cost to existing owners".[19] Instead the rise in prices has been fuelled by increased debt and "easy credit has been used as a palliative... by governments" and exemplified by the cynical phrase of "let them eat credit".[20]

At the same time, UK government policy has been to support increased demand for housing by a range of means including schemes to increase access to mortgages and taxation subsidies with capital gains and inheritance tax exemptions. In addition, the significant increase in the payment of housing credit has helped develop the private letting market. The consequence is that when a future

18 Miguel Castro Coelho, Vigyan Ratnoo and Sebastian Dellepiane, 'Housing that works for all: the political economy of housing in England', (October 2014) Institute for Government, 10,

> Property prices soared in England between 1982 and 1989 – approximately 80% growth in real terms. They fell sharply but briefly from 1989 to the mid-1990s (about 40% in real terms), and then increased again dramatically till the great recession in 2008 (about 150% in real terms). With soaring house prices came large increases in wealth for a vast number of homeowners. This experience is likely to have contributed to disseminating the idea that homeownership is a ticket for individual prosperity.

19 House of Lords Select Committee on Economic Affairs, *Building more homes*, (15 July 2016), 1st Report of Session 2016–17, HL Paper 20, 29.

20 Chapter 3, n. 124, (Rajan, *Fault lines*), 9 and 21 and repeated by Mark Carney, 'Three truths for finance', remarks at the Harvard Club UK, Southwark Cathedral dinner, London, 21 September 2015.

housing bubble returns government action such as these will make it more difficult for macroprudential policies to be effective.

8.2 International examples

The position varies by country. There are severe housing shortages in many countries but this has not always translated into financial instability. In the US, for example, there were 1.2 million new households between 2016 and 2018 across the country but housing supply has kept up.[21] This may be due to the over-hang of empty homes from the collapse following the recent financial crisis.

Nevertheless, there are large areas with severe housing shortages which have driven up house prices and mortgage debt. For example, in California, between 2010 and 2018 the number of households grew by 600,000 (4.4% growth).[22] However, the housing supply increased by less than half the number of new homes needed.[23] Due in part to this, house prices grew by some 64% between 2010 and the end of 2018.[24] The substantial increase in the incidence of homelessness correlates with an increase in the high cost of housing. This can be seen in, for example, California where 'unsheltered' homelessness (i.e. those living on the streets or in makeshift shelters (tents, boxes), etc.) increased by 25% between 2014 and 2018 (to almost 90,000 people) and Washington State by 80% to over 10,000 and Oregon up almost 50% to 9,000.[25]

In Toronto, Canada, between 2011 and 2016 the city's population increased by 35,000 each year and is projected to grow by 2041 by over 1 million averaging 41,000 each year.[26] Annual construction in Toronto appears to be well short of satisfying this demand.[27] Moreover, the vast majority of new-build properties over recent years have been single bedroom condominium apartments.[28] Consequently, between 2008 and 2018 the median price of buying a home in Toronto, in constant prices, has risen by some 60% while median earnings have fallen by 15% over the same period.[29]

21 Harvard University, The Joint Center for Housing Studies, 'State of the Nation's Housing report', (2019), 1–2.
22 US Census web-site, www.census-charts.com/HF/California.html, https://factfinder.census.gov/faces/tableservices/jsf/pages/productview.xhtml?src=bkmk, (accessed 12 July 2019) In 2010 there were 13.7 million households compared with 14.3 million in 2018.
23 Sarah Mawhorter, 'Housing Policies in Californian cities', (March 2019), Terner Center for Housing Innovation at UC Berkeley, 3.
24 Zillow web-site, www.zillow.com/ca/home-values/, (accessed 12 July 2019), (median price $334k in 2010 and $547k in 2018).
25 Supra, note 21, (State of the Nation's Housing), 5.
26 Canadian Centre for Economic Analysis, 'Toronto housing market analysis -from insight to action', (January 2019), 5.
27 Canada Housing and Mortgage Corporation web-site, www03.cmhc-schl.gc.ca/hmip-pimh/#Profile/2270/3/Toronto, (accessed 15 July 2019).
28 Supra, note 26, (Toronto housing market analysis), 44–45.
29 Supra, note 26, (Toronto housing market analysis), 46.

Similarly, in Seattle, Washington State, the population has grown from some 575,000 in 2008 to 750,000 in 2019; an increase of more than 30%.[30] However, the owner-occupied housing stock has only risen by 25,000 over this period with most of the growth in housing coming from the rented sector.[31] Median house prices in constant dollars has risen over 70%.[32] In Australia, the population in the Sydney metropolitan area is expected to grow by 18% between 2011 and 2021 (1.7–2 million) with a similar increase in household numbers.[33] However, home building only increased by some 8% between 2011 and 2016 in the same area.[34]

Despite rising housing costs and mortgage debt, jurisdictions such as Canada and Australia have been able to manage their financial stability. This has not been the case in the UK.

8.3 A possible way forward

The lack of housing in the UK presents a significant and continuing risk to financial stability. The scarcity of supply and property price inflation is coupled with increasing credit and it may be an area suitable for macroprudential review and intervention. The FPC lacks the statutory powers and, almost certainly, the political legitimacy, and hence will, to employ macroprudential policy to reduce the rapid growth in credit by increasing the supply of housing. Such a policy would be highly political since a significant rise in the number of new homes build over a number of years would have the effect of reducing the value of both new and the existing stock of homes. Nevertheless, this issue needs to be addressed since, as mentioned earlier, it goes to the very heart of the macroprudential risks within the economy.

However, the FPC could, in meeting its statutory objective, highlight this issue and the macroprudential consequences of failing to build sufficient homes over a long period and call for a serious long-term house construction strategy. This would send a signal to the markets and indicate the required direction of travel and progress, if any, would be clearly measurable. The FPC could provide an independent report on developments by the government of the day, over several Parliaments, to undertake the work to meet the objective.

In practice the scale of the problem is so large that that it would require significant political intervention, probably involving some form of government

30 US Population web-site, https://theuspopulation.com/seattle-population/, (accessed 15 July 2019).

31 2018–2022 Consolidated Plan for Housing and Community Development City of Seattle, (July 2018), 10.

32 Ibid., (Consolidated Plan), 93, between 2000 and 2013.

33 New South Wales Government Research and demographics web-site, www.planning.nsw.gov.au/Research-and-Demography/Demography/Population-projections, (accessed 16 July 2019).

34 id Community web-site, https://profile.id.com.au/australia/dwellings?WebID=250, (accessed 16 July 2019).

established "National Housebuilding Agency".[35] This could be financed by issuing government backed bonds. The Bank of England might deem these securities as acceptable for microprudential liquidity purposes and treat them favourably for risk weighted asset calculations. Further, the Bank might purchase such bonds as part of any future quantitative easing programme.

A combination of market failures and government actions in the UK housing market has had significant social and macroeconomic effects. These issues have been central to the strains placed on macroprudential and conduct of business policies. These are seen, in particular, in the areas of housing affordability and the levels of homeownership.

8.4 Home affordability

The increase in housing costs, including rent, has had a significant macroeconomic effect. As with the examples mentioned above, in other jurisdictions, in the period 2002 to 2015 UK housing costs have "effectively wiped-out most if not all the...income gains made by the bottom 56% of working age households", although this picture is subject to wide regional variations.[36] For households with the oldest person aged 25–44 over the same period real income growth has been on average £12 per week (2%) while housing costs have risen by £25 (25%).[37] In 1994 1.6 million UK households (10%) spent more than a third of their income on housing, both renting and paying mortgages, compared to 3.3 million (17%) in 2013.[38] As mentioned earlier the percentage of households owning their own home has fallen from almost 70% just before the financial crisis to around 63% and continues to decline.

This has put a strain on both homeownership and rental affordability. As an approximation, housing costs that exceed 33% of household income are viewed as being on the cusp of affordability.[39] For example, in London, in 2013–2014, over 30% of household housing expenditure exceeds this limit compared only 9% in the lowest cost area of North East England.[40] The North West, Midlands and Wales formed a middle band of just under 15% of household housing expenditure exceeding a third of income.[41] UK household indebtedness levels

35 There are many other social benefits with type of programme. For example, the scheme run by Triodos Bank in the UK employs several hundred current and former prisoners, learning building skills constructing and renovating homes across the country and is financed by the sale of these buildings, The Scotsman, 'Barlinnie inmates to build Glasgow social housing', (25 July 2015). Triodos is a Dutch commercial bank which also operates in the UK with a social and environmental purpose.

36 Stephen Clarke, Adam Corlett and Lindsay Judge, *The housing headwind: the impact of rising housing costs on UK living standards*, (June 2016), Resolution Foundation, 6–7.

37 Ibid., (*The housing headwind*), 8.

38 Lindsay Judge, *Housing affordability in the UK*, (April 2016) Resolution Foundation, 5–6.

39 Christine Whitehead and others, *Measuring housing affordability: a review of data sources*, (April 2009), Cambridge University Centre for Housing and Planning Research, 7–9.

40 Ibid., (*Measuring housing affordability*), 25.

41 Ibid., (*Measuring housing affordability*), 25.

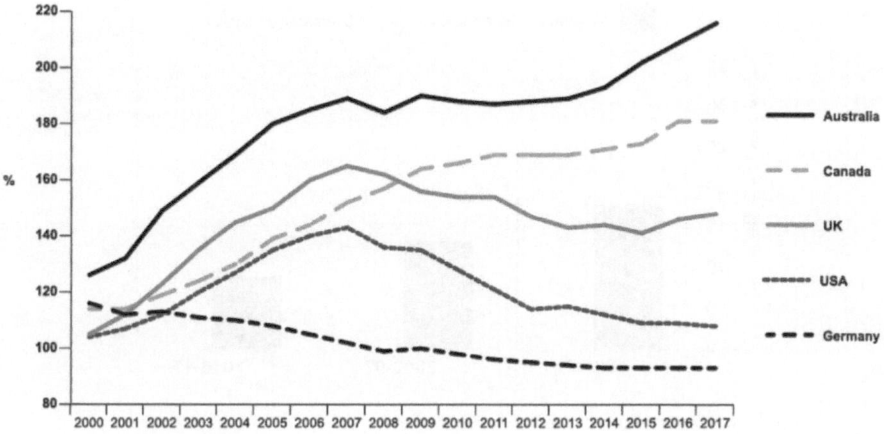

Figure 8.2 Indebtedness.
Source: OECD: Household debt as a% of net disposable income, 2000–2017. https://data.oecd.org//hha/household-debt.htm, (accessed 31 July 2019).

remain very high at over 140% of disposable income.[42] This compares with 105% in 2000 although there has been some deleveraging from 2007 when the equivalent figure was over 160%.[43] However, debt continues to expand in both Canada and Australia. Canada's household indebtedness rose from 144% in 2006 to 181% in 2017 (a 26% increase) while in Australia the equivalent figures were 185% in 2006 and an astronomic 216% in 2017.[44] Australia's economy has now had an unbroken run of growth for almost thirty years.[45] This like Canada, is based on low interest rates and high immigration (see Figure 8.2).[46] Moreover, as discussed in earlier chapters, despite high levels of household debt domestic lenders have been resilient and were not seriously affected by the recent financial crisis.

House price inflation coupled with stagnant employment earnings has put homeownership beyond the aspiration of most younger UK citizens. For example, it has been estimated that a single person in their twenties earning an average wage would take almost thirty years to save for a 20% deposit in London, compared with, for example, over eleven years in the Midlands.[47] Depending on the assumptions used, it is estimated that first time buyers would need annual

42 Daniel Harari, *Household debt: statistics and impact on economy*, (December 2018) House of Commons Briefing Paper, No. 7584, 10.
43 Ibid., (Harari), 9.
44 OECD web-site, OECD data, Household debt, https://data.oecd.org/hha/household-debt.htm, (accessed 17 July 2019).
45 OECD web-site, Australia economic snapshot, www.oecd.org/economy/australia-economic-snapshot/, (accessed 17 July 2019).
46 Trent Saunders and Peter Tulip, 'A model of the Australian housing market', (March 2019) Reserve Bank of Australia, Research Discussion Paper RDP 2019-01, 1.
47 Shelter, *A home of their own*, (January 2015), 10.

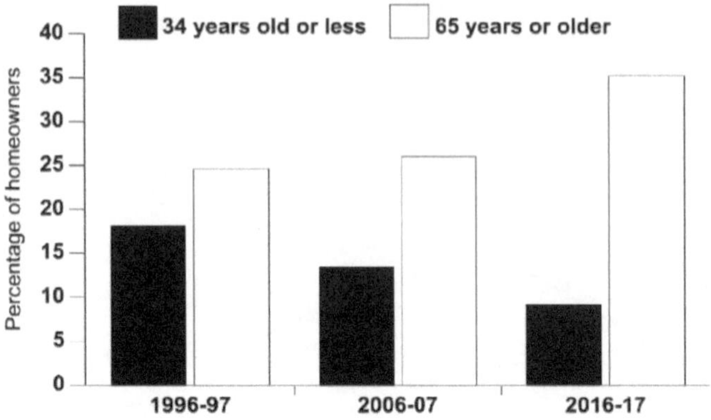

Figure 8.3 UK homeownership rates by age.
Source: English Housing Survey 2016–2017, Annex Table 1.1. Age of HRP, by tenure, 1996–97, 2006–07, 2016–17. https://www.gov.uk/government/statistics/english-housing-survey-2016-to-2017-private-rented-sector, (accessed 28 July 2019).

household salaries of approximately £45,000 by 2020 outside London and the South East in order to afford a deposit and mortgage.[48] This is some £20,000 in excess of where household income is now. In London, the equivalent household salary would need to be over £100,000 per annum.[49] There are similar concerns in a number of other jurisdictions.[50]

In summary, the continued rise in house prices and the growth of the rental sector and the increased share of household incomes used to pay for the cost of housing appears to constitute a misallocation of economy resources from more productive and societal beneficial employment.

8.5 Homeownership rates

The age profile of UK homeownership has fallen steeply. For example, in 1991 almost 70% of those aged between 25 and 34 owned their own home. This fell by half to 35% in 2013/2014.[51] Figures for 2016/2017 continue to show a downward trend to under 9% (see Figure 8.3).[52] The National Housing Federation reported that "20% of all households own 64% of total housing wealth in Britain…and 63% of all housing wealth is owned by those aged 55 and over".[53]

48 Shelter, *What salary will a typical first-time buyer need in 2020*, (April 2016), 4.
49 Ibid., (Shelter, *What salary*).
50 For example, Matthew Thomas and Alicia Hall, 'Housing affordability in Australia', (2015) Parliament of Australia Briefing.
51 Office of National Statistics, 'UK Perspectives 2016: Housing and home ownership in the UK', (25 May 2016).
52 Department of Housing, Communities and Local Government (MHCLG), English Housing Survey Home ownership, 2016–17, Table AT1.1.
53 National Housing Federation Research Paper, 'Intergenerational perspectives on housing wealth', (September 2016), 1.

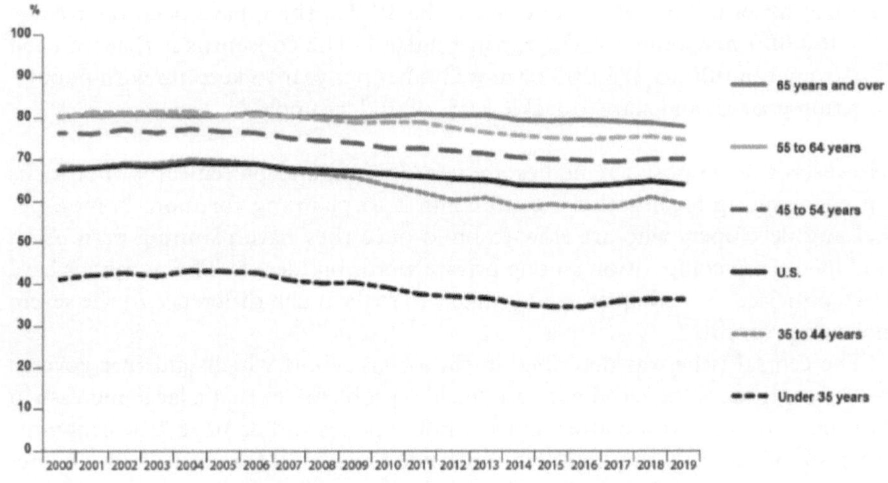

Figure 8.4 US homeownership rates by age.

Source: U.S. Census Bureau. Current Population Survey/Housing Vacancy Survey, July 25, 2019. US Census data: Table 19_Annual/quarterly homeownership rates by age of householder https://www.census.gov/housing/hvs/data/histtabs.html (accessed 31 July 2019).

The inequality of asset distribution in the UK tends to support the view that "for unto every one that hath shall be given, and he shall have abundance…".[54]

Nevertheless, the aspiration to own a home of ones' own remains high. There remains a "deep-seated sentiment towards home-ownership".[55] Some 80% of adults aspire in the UK to own their own home within the next ten years.[56] Since these surveys started in 1993 this aspiration has not changed.

In other major jurisdiction homeownership rates have held-up well. For example, even Vancouver and Toronto, with major housing issues, still have high homeownership rates of 73% and 66% respectively.[57] Homeownership rates remain high in Australia (approximately 66%).[58] However, in Australia this masks a steady reduction in the percentage of homeowners aged 34 or younger.[59] The downturn in US homeownership is most marked for those under 35 and those between 35 and 44 (see Figure 8.4)

8.6 Government intervention

The government has accepted that the UK's housing market is not functioning properly and in February 2017 it issued a White Paper stating that

54 Matthew 25, 29, King James' Version

55 Council of Mortgage Lenders, 'Still aspiring', (10 April 2013) YouGov survey report.

56 Ibid., (CML survey).

57 Royal Bank of Canada, Economic Research, February 2019, 1.

58 Australian Bureau of Statistics, 4130.0 – Housing Occupancy and Costs, 2017–18, (July 2019).

59 Reserve Bank of Australia, Submission to the Inquiry into Home Ownership House of Representatives Standing Committee on Economics, (June 2015), 5.

> our housing market is broken and the cause is very simple: for too long, we haven't built enough homes. Since the 1970s, there have been on average 160,000 new homes each year in England. The consensus is that we need from 225,000 to 275,000 or more homes per year to keep up with population growth and start to tackle years of under-supply.[60]

However, the proposed remedies are very limited and piecemeal with a focus on encouraging local authorities to commit to planning for more homes, penalising developers who are slow to build once they have planning permission and increasing competition among private sector builders.[61] The proposals have been criticised as inadequate and unlikely to make much difference to the severe housing problem.[62]

The central issue was described in the Lyons report which said that governments continue to be faced with an "insider problem" in that a large increase in housing provision would affect current house prices and damage "the economic interests of existing householders and landowners".[63] Moreover, "older owner occupiers are more likely to vote than those in socially or privately rented housing meaning they have often had a louder voice".[64]

The then Housing Minister, Brandon Lewis, said that by 2020 the UK would seek to build around a million extra homes.[65] However, a Parliamentary report in 2016 said that this target would be insufficient and that "to address the housing crisis at least 300,000 news homes are needed annually for the foreseeable future".[66]

Much of the housing development industry came close to financial collapse during the recent financial crisis due to a combination of heavy gearing and a sharp decline in asset values. This resulted in the government providing extensive financial support to the industry. Following the recent financial crisis, the government has initiated twenty-one schemes specifically to support the housing market.[67] These have provided almost £32 billion in grants, loans and

60 Department for Communities and Local Government White Paper, 'Fixing our broken housing market', (Cmd 9352, February 2017), 9.

61 Ibid., (White Paper), 16–17.

62 The Guardian, 'The Guardian view on the housing white paper: it won't fix a broken market', (7 February 2017), "such is the crisis that cabinet ministers call for ambitious, radical reforms to "turn things around". The trouble is, there aren't any in the white paper".

63 The Lyons Housing Review, 'Mobilising across the nation to build the homes our children need', (October 2014), 15.

64 Ibid., *Lyons Review*, 15. See also Herman Schwartz and Leonard Seabrooke, 'Varieties of residential capitalism in international political economy: old welfare states and the new politics of housing', (2008) *Comparative European Politics*, Vol. 6, 237–261, 239 which discusses "asset-based welfare".

65 The Architect's Journal, 'Housing minister targets 1 million new homes by 2020', (21 September 2015).

66 Supra, note 19, House of Lords, 'Building more homes', 5.

67 Shelter, 'Achieving the ambition: building one million homes this Parliament', (August 2016), 10.

guarantees of which the vast majority (£25 billion) has been allocated to supporting demand for housing in the form of "Help-to-Buy" loans and tax incentive schemes.[68] The balance has been used to increase housing supply by, for example, encouraging developers to restart "stalled" housing developments ("Kick Start 1 and 2") and providing finance to developers and builders ("Get Britain Building").[69] These initiatives appear to have helped large developers and builders through the financial crisis.[70] Large firms were generally better able to navigate the application process for these funding schemes and this may have been one of the reasons for the demise of many small builders and a widespread consolidation in the construction industry.

The housing development and building market has been described as "oligopolistic" with the eight largest firms building over 50% of homes and continuing to expand by acquiring small businesses.[71] However, an Office of Fair Trading study in 2008 concluded that there were no significant competition issues or barriers to entry.[72] It stated that

> on a national basis, concentration in the industry is low by comparison with that in many other consumer goods manufacturing industries. In 2006, the single largest firm supplied 11 per cent of the market and the top ten firms supplied 44 per cent of total supply. The 75 largest firms (all of whom produce 100 units a year or more) supplied about 63 per cent of output and roughly a quarter of supply was accounted for by a long 'tail' of about 5,000 firms.[73]

In addition, access to land is central to the housing development business model. Land is acquired by direct purchase and, more importantly, by a complex and opaque system of options. The scale and the obscurity of these contracts may, in themselves, pose a threat to financial stability and, consequently, would be worthy of study by the Financial Policy Committee. Moreover, a significant reason for consolidation in the development and building industry is the ability to access both current and strategic land banks.[74] This is considered in more detail later.

68 Ibid., ('Achieving the ambition'), 10–11.

69 Home & Communities Agency, 'Kickstart' web-site, http://webarchive.nationalarchives.gov.uk/20140805133148; www.homesandcommunities.co.uk/ourwork/kickstart, (accessed 16 July 2019). The aim of this scheme was to building 16,000 houses. See also Home and Communities Agency, 'Get Britain Building: programme prospectus', (December 2011). This scheme ended after building 12,000 homes.

70 Supra, note 67, (Shelter, 'Achieving the ambition'), 10.

71 Supra, note 19, (House of Lords report), 8.

72 Office of Fair Trading, 'Homebuilding in the UK: a market study', (September 2008), 6.

73 Ibid., (OFT study), 57.

74 KPMG, 'Homebuilding market study: Annex E – Study investigating financing for homebuilders' in the OFT's 2008 survey, 39, supra note 72.

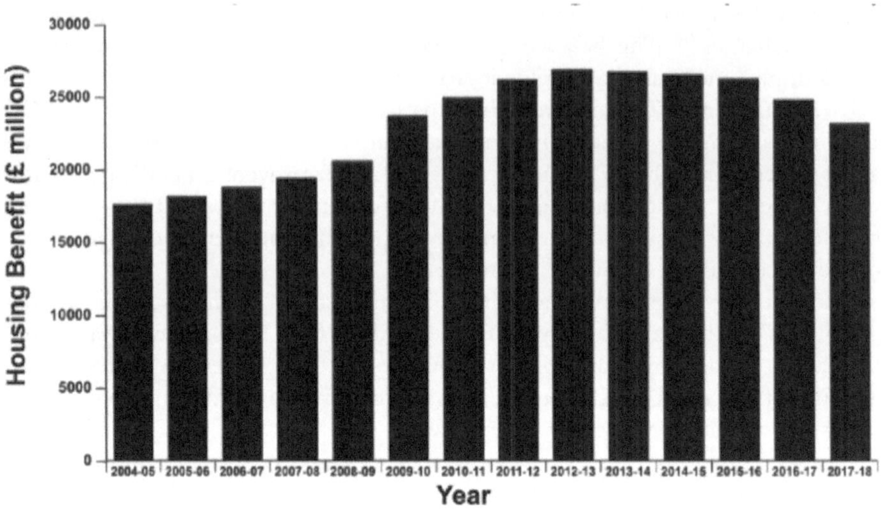

Figure 8.5 UK housing benefit.

Source: Ministry of Housing, Communities and Local Government Budget 2016, UK Housing benefit–£ million, real terms (2016/17 prices) – Table 1b: Expenditure by benefit https://www.gov.uk/government/statistics/housing-benefit-caseload-statistics, (accessed 28 July 2019).

8.7 Government housing benefit

Government intervention in the housing market also takes the form of housing benefit payments (rent payments) for those with very low incomes with minimal savings and in rented accommodation. Approximately £22.3 billion was paid out in government housing benefit in 2017/2018 (see Figure 8.5).[75] Of this, some £7.7 billion (35%) was paid to private landlords.[76] "Using 2013/14 prices, spending on housing benefit has risen from £16.5 billion in 1996/97 to £24.4 billion in 2012/13 – a 48 per cent real terms increase".[77] The point has been made by a number of people and organisations that this latter sum could be used to construct some 100,000 houses each year.[78] This can be summarised as a move away from investment in house building to an ongoing process of rent subsidies.

75 Department of Work and Pensions (DWP), 'Housing benefit expenditure' in 'Benefit expenditure and caseload tables 2019', (April 2019), www.gov.uk/government/publications/benefit-expenditure-and-caseload-tables-2019, Table 1b, (accessed 16 July 2019).

76 Ibid., (DWP data for 2017/8).

77 Chartered Institute of Housing, 'Ticking the box for a welfare system that works', (September 2014), 4.

78 Ibid., ("Ticking the boxes"). See also Nick Pearce, 'Housing benefit is out of control, but there is an alternative', (*The Guardian*, 21 June 2012) and Hilary Benn MP, Housing debate, House of Commons, 8 January 2014, column 328.

8.8 The role of developers and construction firms

The Office of Fair Trading have said that "large homebuilding businesses are driven by their land acquisition units with key corporate decisions on expansion, mergers and financial structuring most heavily influenced by the need to acquire land" and it is more appropriate to think of the industry as consisting of "land developers who have integrated downwards into home construction rather than housebuilders who have ventured into land development".[79] Besides the issue of industry consolidation, mentioned above, there are significant concerns that the housing development sector severely restricts construction in order to maintain its profitability. It does this by acquiring options on large amounts of development land and rations the building of homes on land even where planning permission exists with a consequential effect on house prices. For example, it has been reported that over "475,000 homes with planning permission still waiting to be built".[80] About a third of all successful planning applications for homes are never built.[81]

Nevertheless, the industry remains high-risk due to the amount of gearing it requires to finance land acquisition and construction work. Development and building firms have different gearing levels depending on their ownership. For example, those which are publicly listed have gearing levels which vary between 10% and 40% of total capital compared with those which are financed by private equity where the average is around 100%.[82] There is also evidence that "year end net debt is typically lower than average net debt".[83] This could be due to management performance targets which result "in a push for completions at year-ends to achieve bonus targets and meet investor expectations".[84] As mentioned the housing development industry suffered very badly during the financial crisis. Following the financial crisis Taylor Wimpey, Persimmon, and Barratt all, it was reported, had to renegotiate debt terms with their bankers.[85] Due to the lack of public information it is difficult to say what happened to those developers owned by private equity operations but their higher levels of gearing are likely to have hit them even harder. It is estimated that land write-downs for the big six publicly quoted developers in total was approximately £15 billion.[86]

In other jurisdictions, the issues relating to land development vary. In the US the rise in land prices coupled with an increase in the cost of labour has slowed

79 Supra, note 72, (OFT Study), 84.
80 Local Government Association web-site, www.localgov.co.uk/The-number-of-unbuilt-homes-reaches-record-high/40098, (accessed 25 July 2019).
81 Supra, note 19, (House of Lords report), 23.
82 Supra, note 74, (KPMG survey), 63–69.
83 Ibid., (KPMG survey), 71.
84 Ibid., (KPMG survey), 71.
85 Financial Times, 'Rate cuts fail to lift house sales, says Bellway', (4 December 2008), 'Bellway is the only volume developer that has not scrambled to its bankers to beg for understanding'.
86 Matt Griffith, 'We must fix it: delivering reform of the building sector to meet the UK's housing and economic challenges', (December 2011), Institute for Public Policy Research, 19–20.

home building.[87] There are also issues staffing construction sites. A third of construction trade workers are immigrants and the industry carries many staff vacancies.[88] Further, across all the metropolitan areas in Canada, US and Australia there is fierce local resistance to new development in areas close to where the objectors live. In addition, tax policies have favoured, or have not sufficiently restricted, speculative property development of, for example, single bed-room condominiums rather than family housing.[89]

8.9 Land options and the possible threat to financial stability

The land market is one of the key elements to increasing the supply of housing. Currently, the land options system is completely opaque. It is unclear who owns what options at what price. This is an area that has been little studied. It is possible that the extent of these options, their cost and financing may constitute a threat to financial stability. Similarly, without government intervention it is likely that a number of large developers would have collapsed as the recent financial crisis spread with consequential effects on lenders and the value of housing land and developments. This may constitute a significant threat to future financial stability and, at the very least, this is an area which would be worthy of review by the FPC.

8.10 The profitability of developers

UK housing developers depend on a business model largely dominated by the cost of land and financed with debt. With an ability to limit housing supply coming onto the market it is able to produce high returns on equity. Consequently, the model has been described as "dysfunctional [and] broken", relying "on ever growing credit" and the rise in value of the underlying land.[90] The view is that the most profitable part of "residential property development is land ownership rather than the construction of houses".[91] In addition, it is difficult to determine what level of funding is provided by "land creditors" where developer payments to landowners or option holders is deferred and thus provides a form of debt development finance.[92]

87 Supra, note 21, (State of the Nation's Housing), 8–9.

88 Supra, note 21, (State of the Nation's Housing), 9.

89 Thomas Cetrino and Gerald Benjamin, 'Classification of property for taxation in New York State: issues and options', (Fall 2014), Centre For Research, Regional Education and Outreach, State University of New York, Discussion Brief No. 13, 14.

90 Alex Morton, *Cities for growth: solutions to our planning problems* (Policy Exchange, London, 2011) 69.

91 Supra, note 15, (Aubrey), 4.

92 Supra, note 74, (KPMG survey), 70–71.

Most developers "prefer to concentrate on smaller levels of controlled output at larger margins" rather than increase the level of building.[93] This is a rational strategy for the companies concerned in view of the risks they run, as seen during the recent financial crisis. "As one housebuilder put it when interviewed about its growth strategy: 'We'll double in size, but halve the margins, so what's the point?'"[94]

The importance of the cost of land can be seen in the costing model in which it is estimated that land acquisition costs account for about 30% of a house developer's income, with construction costs accounting a further 40% with interest payments and overheads taking up a further 10% of the total leaving a 20% profit on average.[95] The cost of land as a percentage of the total has risen significantly over the last fifty years.[96]

The high cost of land has also been an issue in Australia where property development has become too expensive in areas such as Sydney since developer profit margin were only 3% compared, for example, to 14% in Perth.[97]

8.11 The allocation of land "development gain"

Once planning permission has been granted for development agricultural land increases many times in value. For example, farmland in Oxfordshire with planning permission for residential housing construction will have a value of £4 million per hectare compared with only £20,000 in its currently agricultural use.[98] The increase in value is retained, in full, by the vendor. If they are a farmer the proceeds can be rolled over and invested in the business and capital gains tax avoided.

Further, under the provisions of the Land Compensation Act 1961, as amended by the Land Compensation Act 1973, the landowner whose land is subject to compulsory purchase also gets the value increase arising as a result of any planning assumptions made about the future use of the land.[99]

There has been considerable concern about who gets this increase in value dating back to at least the mid-19th century.[100] Essentially, the increase in land

93 FTI Consulting, 'Understanding supply constraints in the housing market', (July 2012), 23.

94 Fred Wellings, *British housebuilders: a history and analysis* (Blackwells, Oxford, 2006) quoted in Griffiths, 'We must fix it', 29, supra, note 86.

95 Supra, note 74, (KPMG survey), 31.

96 Supra, note 15, (Aubrey), 4.

97 Wing Hsieh, David Norman and David Orsmond, 'Supply-side issues in the housing sector', (September 2012), *Reserve Bank of Australia Bulletin*, 17.

98 KPMG and Shelter, 'Building the homes we need', (2014), 33. See also Farmers Weekly, "Well-positioned parcels with planning permission have sold for as much as £1 million/acre in the south of England and £600,000/acre further north, while land in north Wales has gone for 50 times its agricultural value" (23 January 2015).

99 Part II, Ss 5 and 6.

100 John Stuart Mill, *Principles of political economy* (published 1848, Oxford University Press, Oxford, 1994), 183–184.

value (known as "planning gain" or "betterment") arises due to the planning decision not because of any action by the owner. In 1947 this increase in value was taxed at a rate of 100% but this tax was abolished in 1953 following a change in government. There have been subsequent attempts by incoming Labour governments in 1964 and 1974 at taxing betterment but these have yielded very little since "the administration was complex, tax avoidance was widespread [and] land was withheld from the market (in part in the hope of a change of government and hence policy)".[101] Each initiative in this area has then been repealed by subsequent Conservative governments.[102]

More successful have been the bilateral negotiations between developers and local authorities using powers under section 106 of the Town and Country Planning Act 1990. Section 106 arrangements are a transfer of economic rents and is a form of "negotiated tax".[103] This has proved a useful source of income for local authorities since the funds accrue locally rather than go to the Exchequer.[104] Much of the cost of the infrastructure for the housing project falls on the local authority (e.g. utilities, transport, schools) and consequently, some of the development gain is repaid to the local authority which is meant to support the provision of these additional services.

There are powers for local authorities to require land for development to be offered first to the local authority. These requirements are being used more frequently with, for example, the percentage of cases doubling from 33% in 2000 to 68% in 2006.[105] However, it is questionable as to its efficiency and effectiveness. It appears that local authorities hold considerable amounts of land suitable for house building but "are constrained from building council homes on the land by their debt caps".[106]

Other jurisdictions have been successful in reducing the cost of constructing new homes by ensuring that the majority of the up-lift in land values arising from the actual granting, or hope, of planning permission does not wholly accrue to the vendor. For example, the housing developments in Amsterdam and in Freiburg in Germany were built on publicly owned land. The increase in the

101 Tony Crook and Sarah Monk, 'Planning gains, providing homes', (2011) *Housing Studies*, Vol. 26, No. 7–8, 997–1018, 1001.

102 A. R. Prest, *The taxation of urban land* (Manchester University Press, Manchester, 1981), 89–96.

103 Supra, note 101, (Crook and Monk), 1012.

104 Edwin Buitelaar, 'Crack in the myth: challenges to land policy in the Netherlands', (2010), *TijdscrhiftvoorEconomische en SocialeGeografie*, Vol. 101, No. 3, 349–356, 352. For example, in 2005 it accounted for 12% of local government income.

105 Sarah Monk and others, 'International review of land supply and planning systems', (March 2013) Joseph Rowntree Foundation, 65.

106 Supra note 98, (KPMG/Shelter), 76. See also Andy Hull, (Institute for Public Policy Research) in written evidence to: Communities and Local Government Committee, Financing of new housing supply: Eleventh Report of Session 2010–12 (The Stationary Office, London, 2012).

land's value was used to finance public services and infrastructure.[107] Nevertheless, while some UK local authorities are keen to build housing, others "are out of the game altogether".[108] This may be because some local authority councils face a dilemma between wanting to build more homes and "being thrown out at the next election" for doing so.[109] There are similar issues in Canada where "opposition from council and community groups also substantially reduces the housing supply".[110]

8.12 Options for increasing the supply of housing

As mentioned earlier, credit provides the fuel to activate latent demand which may increase the price of housing and in turn may motivate existing homeowners to sell and developers to build new homes. As discussed, the increase in the supply of housing may have both a macroprudential effect by increasing financial stability and a positive conduct of business outcome as borrowers would not need to stretch themselves financially as much.

In recent years there has been no lack of high-quality reports of what to do. For example, Sir Michael Lyons published his "Housing Review: Mobilising across the nation to build the homes our children need" ("Lyons") commissioned by the then leader of the Labour party in 2014.[111] More recently, The House of Lords Select Committee on Economic Affairs issued their report, "Building more homes", in July 2016.[112] In addition, the Labour Party Shadow Housing Minister initiated a further review by Peter Redfern which was published on 16th November 2016.[113]

While this is not a work on solving the housing crisis in the UK it is important to consider, albeit briefly, the obstacles and possible solutions to increasing the supply of housing and hence addressing both a macroprudential and conduct of business problem. Kate Barker made the point in her 2004 report that the supply of land for housing does not appear to be responsive to price signals.[114] For example, between 1990 and 2010 the supply of new land for housing fell by 63% in

107 House of Commons, Housing, Communities and Local Government Select Committee Report, 'Land Value Capture', Tenth Report of Session 2017–19, (September 2018), HC 766, 42–43.

108 Supra, note 19, Lord Best's evidence to the House of Lords Select Committee, 55.

109 Supra, note 19, evidence by Kate Barker to the House of Lords Select Committee, 38.

110 Kenneth Green and others, 'The impact of land-use regulation on housing supply in Canada', (July 2016), Fraser Institute, 20.

111 Supra, note 63, (Lyons).

112 Supra, note 19, (House of Lord Report).

113 City AM, 'Taylor Wimpey chief executive Pete Redfern launches a major review into UK home ownership with Labour shadow minister John Healey', (4 February 2016). See Peter Redfern, 'The Redfern Review into the decline of homeownership', (November 2016).

114 Supra, note 2, (Barker), 25.

spite of house prices increasing by more than 300%.[115] Another report described the current housing market as "asymmetric…the price of housing goes up but it is not met by an increase in home building".[116] Moreover, there is a view that UK housing is badly distributed.[117] All of this is having severe, and increasingly bad, socioeconomic effects. If this issue can be addressed and the major market failures corrected then the supply of housing can be significantly increased and the need to increase credit reduced with positive results for macroprudential policy and financial stability.

Other jurisdictions face housing supply shortages, These may be due to geographic issues such as those prominent in Hong Kong (i.e. territorial limits) and in Perth, Australia (i.e. earthquake risk).[118] As already mentioned, there is often strong local objections to new build and local government may be reluctant to designate land for construction.[119] However, others blame the issues on immigrants and the evils of speculative property purchases. For example, Vancouver sees a 'speculative demand [for housing as] a critical barrier to a healthy housing market'.[120]

The more generic issues with current broken housing markets and the lack of housing supply are set out below using examples, largely, drawn from the UK.

8.13 Issues preventing increasing house building

8.13.1 Access to land for development

Lyons refers to an "artificial scarcity of land for housing [which] has created distortion in the land market, limiting the rate at which new homes are built and incentivising the acquisition and trading of land".[121] Currently the eight largest house builders each own around five years supply of land for development and a wider range of options on land for a further five to fifteen years.[122] This means that "large amounts of land suitable for development are tied up in option agreements and therefore not available to other developers".[123] There are many intermediaries in the process of acquiring land and there is little or no transparency as to who own what rights over land and the pricing structures of these

115 Shelter, 'Response to the Lyons review of housing supply', (2014) 3, using Office of National Statistics and Department of Communities and Local government data.

116 Supra, note 93, (FTI Consulting),15.

117 Danny Doring, *All that is solid* (Penguin, London, 2014) 99 and 105–115, who considers that there are sufficient houses but they are inefficiently allocated or simply in need of refurbishment.

118 Trevor Dhu and others, 'Earthquake risk assessment for Perth, Western Australia', 13th World Conference on Earthquake Engineering Vancouver, B.C., Canada, (August 2004), Paper No. 2748, 11–12.

119 Supra, note 97, (Hsieh, Norman and Orsmond), 15–16.

120 Supra, note 5, (City of Vancouver), 5.

121 Supra, note 63, (Lyons), 6.

122 Supra, note 63, (Lyons), 61.

123 Supra, note 63, (Lyons), 62.

rights. For example, it has been calculated that six land agents hold options over some 60,000 hectares suitable for constructing between 300,000 and 400,000 homes.[124] Some of this land many have planning permission for building but remains undeveloped. This issue is considered in more detail later in this section.

8.13.2 Where to build

Only 8.5% of UK land is designated as urban and of this only 1.1% of the total is built on for residential purposes. Some 4% is covered by rivers, lakes, infrastructure, etc., and 87.5% is farm land and other "green space" (within this some 13% is green belt land).[125] There appears to be capacity for large-scale housing development in areas where jobs exist and people want to live (e.g. East Anglia, Hampshire and Bedfordshire, Hertfordshire and much of the Midlands) but these are also areas with the highest land prices outside places such as London, Oxford, etc.[126]

The popular view is that England is in the process of being concreted over to build houses.[127] However, contrary to this perception the UK is not overcrowded and even the most high-density areas in the South East of England have fewer people per square kilometre than many parts of the Netherlands, Belgium, Switzerland and Germany.[128]

8.13.3 Brown and green field site development

Significant capacity to build exists on "brownfield" sites which have no other development use. One recent study estimates that there is space for approximately one million homes on such land.[129] While the National Land Use Database indicates capacity for almost 1.5 million homes on derelict land and of this some one-third would be in London and the South East.[130] However, there

124 Supra, note 63, (Lyons), 62.

125 Quoted in Lyons review, supra, note 63, 35.

126 Glen Bramley and David Watkins, 'Where should we build the extra housing we need in England? Need, demand, opportunity and value', (April 2014) Housing Studies Association conference at Heriot Watt University.

127 Campaign to Protect Rural England, 'Building on Barker: how we can continue to improve housing for everyone without damaging the environment and sprawling over the countryside', (January 2005), 33.

> "Every year 21 square miles of open, undeveloped, green land...is built over in England" and this is mainly for housing.

128 Kristian Niemietz, 'Abundance of land, shortage of housing', (April 2012) Institute of Economic Affairs Discussion Paper No. 38, 6–7.

129 Alex Morton, *Why aren't we building enough attractive homes? Myths, misunderstandings and solutions*, (Policy Exchange, London, 2012), 11.

130 University of the West of England, sponsored by the Campaign for the Protection of Rural England (CPRE), 'From wasted space to living spaces: the availability of brownfield land for housing development in England', (November 2014), CPRE, 8.

is also considerable dispute over the availability of brownfield sites for housing development with the National Housebuilders Federation estimating

> that of the 49,000 hectares of brownfield land in England, 23,500 hectares are suitable for use for housing. Noting this a Parliamentary Committee report said that this would be enough land for approximately one million homes, or four and a half years of housing demand....[131]

The same Parliamentary report commented that "the lower viability and higher costs of developing brownfield sites may be a deterrent for some developers..." and the Committee had "particular concerns about the risk that developers will delay developing brownfield sites because local authorities will be required to release more profitable greenfield sites if insufficient housing is delivered to meet local needs".[132] Developers tend to favour residential developments on greenfield sites since it is generally easier to undertake. Greenfield land is usually subject to a single owner, does not require decontamination and site logistics present fewer problems. In contrast, using previously developed land for housing is more difficult and costly and may take longer.[133]

Consequently, moves to open "Green Belt" sites surrounding some UK cities appears to be a distraction from the main issues.

8.13.4 Planning process

Again contrary to expectations, the planning process itself does not appear to cause undue delays in the process of building. Reports indicate that planning consent can usually be obtained in around sixteen weeks.[134] However, the negotiations on payments under Section 106 of the Town and Country Planning Act 1990 and agreements under the Growth and Infrastructure Act 2013 can take between an additional 22 and 44 weeks.[135] The total lead time to getting planning consent could be a year including certifying compliance with the various planning conditions. Once planning agreement is given developers have approximately three years to start work but "any material operation" is sufficient to satisfy this requirement and there is no time limit on completing the work.[136]

Local planning regulations, such as those common in the US, specifying minimum housing plot sizes and parking, help to maintain existing house prices by

131 Parliamentary Select Committee on Communities and Local Government's Report on the 'Department for Communities and Local Government's consultation on national planning policy', (April 2016) Third Report of Session 2015–16, 13.
132 Ibid., (Select Committee),12.
133 Supra, note 2, (Barker), 58.
134 Supra, note 19, (House of Lords report), 39.
135 Supra, note 19, (House of Lords report), 39.
136 s56(4) Town and Country Planning Act 1990.

restricting the development of more affordable housing.[137] In the US "the bulk of the evidence ...suggests that zoning, and other land use controls, are more responsible for high prices....zoning strictness are highly correlated with high prices".[138] Research in Boston, Massachusetts, found that a restricted supply of new housing resulted in a "remarkable increase in housing prices".[139] This was not due to a lack of available land for development but rather caused by local regulatory barriers; the most important of which were restrictions imposing minimum lot sizes.[140] The tendency has been for local communities to pull the drawbridge up behind them as a means of both increasing current property prices and restricting the number of neighbours viewed as undesirable.

> The zoning regulations most commonly used as exclusionary devices include bans on multifamily housing and a variety of minimum building standards: lot size and width, building size, density Although restrictions such as these do not explicitly exclude specific people or groups of people, they effectively...fosters economic segregation. And given the correlation between race and income, economic segregation has implied racial segregation.[141]

8.13.5 Taxation

The taxation system has an indirect effect on the housing market with a regressive council tax scheme with proportionally more of the tax falling on owners of lower value properties.[142] In addition, there have been proposals to change the taxation system to remove current taxation subsidies for existing home-owners by, for example, the capital gains exemption granted to primary residence sales and deferred inheritance taxation.[143]

8.13.6 Land acquired for development but not developed at all or quickly

The Lyons review found that there were "6,700 sites (containing more than ten homes) with planning permissions that have not yet been completed. These sites have the capacity for 588,000 homes".[144] Some

137 Edward Glaeser and Joseph Gyourko, 'The impact of zoning on housing affordability' (March 2002), Harvard Institute of Economic Research Discussion Paper No. 1948, 21.

138 Ibid., (Glaeser and Gyourko), 21.

139 Edward Glaeser and Bryce Ward, 'The causes and consequences of land use regulation: evidence from Greater Boston', (2009), *Journal of Urban Economics*, Vol. 65, 265–278, 278.

140 Ibid., (Glaeser and Ward), 278.

141 Christopher Berry, 'Land use regulation and residential segregation: does zoning matter?' (Fall 2001), *American Law and Economics Review*, Vol. 3, No. 2, 251–274, 251–252.

142 Supra, note 20, (House of Lords) 6.

143 Supra, note 4, (BHSF, 'The future of housing'), 23–24.

144 Supra, note 63, (Lyons), 65.

> 50,000 of these homes are on sites that are classified as on hold or cancelled, 246,000 are progressing towards construction and 271,000 are on sites that have already started construction. A further 21,000 are on sites that are for sale, have been recently sold or have no information available. In addition to the 50,000 homes that are on identified stalled sites, however, 80,000 unbuilt homes have had planning permission in 2010 or earlier. Of these there are 26,000 homes on sites that have yet to start and 54,000 homes on sites that have started but have not yet completed. In total this means there are 130,000 homes with planning permission, equating to 22% of the total that are either on hold or have been in the system for more than 4 years... [and in addition there] were 270,000 homes on sites that have been in the planning system since 2010 or before which have not yet progressed to planning permission.[145]

There was an interesting review undertaken in 2014 following up an earlier 2012 survey in Greater London.[146] In mid-2012 there were 531 housing schemes which had yet to commence and this cohort of projects was examined again in 2014 to see how they were progressing during a period of rapidly rising property prices and high demand. Although building had started on 262 sites 231 of the remainder were "on-hold" and a further twenty-five sites the planning permission originally granted had lapsed and in thirteen instances planning permission applications were either also on-hold or were being progressed.[147]

8.13.7 Lack of skilled builders

There is a severe skills shortage in the construction industry due to lack of investment in training. In 2016 59% of member firms of the Royal Institute of Chartered Surveyors reported continuing skills shortages which are above the historic average of 43%. This is particularly acute when trying to find both surveyors and bricklayers.[148] The problem is exacerbated by the industry's age profile with many skilled construction workers retiring over the next few years.[149]

Mirroring this, the number of people starting construction, planning and built environment apprenticeships has halved since 2006/2007 with fewer than 10,000 people completing a construction apprenticeship in 2012/2013.[150]

145 Supra, note 63, (Lyons), 65.

146 Mayor of London, 'Barriers to housing delivery – update: private sector housing development on larger sites in London', (July 2014), Greater London Authority, 13. See 2012 report, Mayor of London, 'Barriers to Housing Delivery', (December 2012), Greater London Authority, 9.

147 Ibid., (Mayor of London), 13.

148 Royal Institute of Chartered Surveyors (RICS) 'UK Construction Market Survey', (Q1 2016).

149 ONS, 'Migrant labour force within the construction industry: June 2018', (June 2018), Figure 2: Age distribution of those working in the construction industry by nationality grouping, 2014–2016.

150 Supra, note 98, (KPMG/Shelter report), (construction Funding Agency data on sector specific apprenticeship starts and completions), 44.

In view of these problems, in July 2016 the Parliamentary Select Committee on Communities and Local Government started an enquiry into capacity of the homebuilding industry to meet the demand for new homes.[151] A report is still awaited.

There are similar issues, for example, in the US. In the first quarter 2019 USG Corporation and US Chamber of Commerce Commercial Construction Index continue to indicate labour shortage in the construction industry with firms having difficulties in meeting "deadlines (70%), increase costs for new work (63%), and reject new projects (40%)".[152]

8.13.8 Use of outdated labour-intensive building methods

As mentioned in an earlier chapter, house building methods have not changed significantly for a hundred or more years. Ball notes that "innovation in the ways that houses are constructed is relatively slow".[153] This means that building homes is very labour intensive with a high demand for skilled workers. However, it is reported that these are simply not available in the necessary number thus delaying house building.[154] This may well be because, "for an industry where the key focus may be on land management rather than production, innovation may not have the same priority as other industries".[155] This has produced some problems in the supply chain for construction products such as bricks.[156] However, these appear to be short-term issues.[157]

The lack of innovation presents buyers with a limited choice of designs. In many ways this reflects the wishes of conservative consumers and the need to ensure ease of resale.[158] Nevertheless, it is possible to build relatively cheaply in the UK "using modern technology so that a 1,000 square foot housing unit can be constructed for less than £100,000".[159] However, there is no pressure on builders to produce anything new since due to housing scarcity anything they design and built will be sold. Moreover, developers are more likely to obtain

151 Commons Business Select Committee, 'Capacity of the homebuilding industry inquiry launched', (5 July 2016).

152 The Contractor, '70% of contractors struggling to meet deadlines as labor shortage persists', (14 March 2019).

153 Michael Ball, 'The housebuilding industry: promoting recovery in housing supply', (2010) a report for the Department of Communities and Local Government, 11.

154 Financial Times, 'Shortage of builders hobbles UK housing ambitions', (3 February 2015), *Daily Telegraph*, 'Shortage of builders holding back development, says housebuilder', (17 November 2015).

155 Supra, note 93, (FTI Report), 27.

156 'Britain faces bricks shortage, builders warn', (*Telegraph*, 29 April 2014).

157 Submission by the Modern Masonry Alliance (MMA) an industry trade body to the Lyons review, supra note 63, 116.

158 Michael Ball, 'Chasing a snail: innovation and housebuilding firms strategies', (1999) *Housing Studies*, Vol. 14, 9–21, 12–14.,

159 Legal and General, 'Let's house Britain', (2014) UK Housing Crisis Report, 19. Construction Enquirer 'L&G launches world's biggest modular housing factory', (25 February 2016).

planning permission if they keep to traditional designs.[160] Buildings follow standard formats which are low-cost to design but construction is bespoke with few moves towards off-site modular construction.[161] In addition, the production and assembly of housing components constructed off-site requires housebuilder and sub-contractor investment in staff training and competences. The industry is not structured to do this and has traditionally not invested in these areas.[162]

House building in the UK did go through a period of dynamic growth just as the Second World War ended employing new building methods including pre-fabrication.[163] However the pace was not maintained and house building reverted to its traditional means of construction as the emergency housing programme came to an end.[164] However, a number of European towns and cities have experimented with new methods of housing development and building innovations.[165] For example, Almere in the Netherlands has set aside one hundred hectares of land for some 3,000 self-build homes.[166] There are minimal rules on what can be built with each plot costing about £50,000 and groups can come together to build an apartment building with each flat costing approximately £70,000 although small units can be brought for £25,000 each.[167] The infrastructure is provided by the local authority. There were some moves in this direction to encourage innovation in housebuilding and development prior to 2015 under the UK's coalition government.[168] For example, "Buildoffsite" has been set up to promote off-site building methods and innovation but it is interesting to note that most of the large UK residential home builders are not members.[169]

8.13.9 Machinery of government

Currently housing policy and its implementation is spread over several government departments and agencies (Department for Environment, Food and Rural

160 John Callcutt, 'Review of housebuilding delivery', (2007) Department of Communities and Local Government, 165–166.

161 Ibid., (Cullcutt), 13.

162 Wei Pan, Alistair Gibb and Andrew Dainty, 'Leading UK housebuilders' utilization of offsite construction methods', (2008) *Building Research and Information*, Vol. 36, No. 1, 56–67, 66.

163 James Woudhuysen, *Why is construction so backward?* (James Wiley, London, 2004), xii and 15, describes war-ravaged and disorganised British firms working at the behest of the UK government in a bankrupt country "building 60,000 new pre-fabricated homes, refurbishing 100,000 bombed dwellings and building 34,000 new houses all in fifteen months from April 1945".

164 Brenda Vale, *Prefabs: a history of the UK Temporary Housing Programme* (E&FN Spon, London, 1995), 124–125.

165 Department of Trade and Industry report, 'Modern methods of construction in Germany – playing the off-site rule' (2004). This was part of a programme of Government reviews looking at innovation overseas for lessons for the UK.

166 The Self Build Portal web-site, 'Almere, Holland', www.selfbuildportal.org.uk/homeruskwartier-district-almere, (accessed 25 July 2019).

167 Ibid., ('Almere Holland').

168 Eric Pickles speech at Homes Event on the need for innovation in housing manufacture, 27 November 2014.

169 Buildoffsite web-site, www.buildoffsite.com/about/overview/, (accessed 25 July 2019).

Affairs, Department for Housing, Communities and Local Government, Department for Business, Energy and Industrial Strategy, the Homes and Communities Agency (HCA), and the Department of Work and Pensions and the).[170] This does not enhance "joined-up" government and there is no leading department with sufficient purpose able or willing to lead on promoting a housing policy. Under the coalition government much of the leadership in this area came from HM Treasury but from my own experience the focus was more on programmes to finance demand rather than on increasing supply. Lyons recommended that the HCA be given the task of investing in housing and infrastructure.[171] In the UK, the problem is not helped by the high turnover of government ministers responsible for housing. There have been nine of these since 2010.

As mentioned earlier, a number of reports have suggested proposals to remedy these issues.

8.14 Suggested remedies

8.14.1 Taxation

A number of studies have recommended removing the taxation subsidies on home ownership including the exemptions granted to capital gains exemption and inheritance taxation. Others have gone further and suggested a land valuation tax based on the proposals of the 19th-century economist Henry George.[172] A number of other ideas have also recently surfaced including Professor John Muellbauer's view that the government should acquire land at use value and then arrange for the necessary planning permission.[173] Tim Leunig has argued that land auctions would lead to higher construction rates, whereby "a local community acquires land without planning permission but which is subsequently designated for housing and therefore benefits from the uptick".[174]

8.14.2 Housing development funding

There are several proposals to provide central and local government and housing associations with additional funding to allow a significant increase in house building.[175] In the US, Presidential candidate, Senator Elizabeth Warren has a number of national proposals governing the limiting of local zoning restrictions,

170 In January 2018 the Department of Communities and Local Government had "Housing" added to its title.

171 Supra, note 63, (Lyons), 39–41.

172 Financial Times, 'A British property tax that is fit for purpose', (24 September 2014). See Henry George, *Progress and Poverty* (Robert Schalkenbach Foundation, New York City, 1987).

173 'It is time for the state to jump on the property bandwagon', (*Financial Times*, 2 April 2014).

174 Centre Forum, 'Community land auctions: working towards implementation', (November 2011).

175 Andy Hull, Graeme Cooke and Tony Dolphin, 'Build now or pay later: funding new housing supply', (October 2011), Institute for Public Policy Research Report, 11–14.

re-financing the debt obligations of mortgagees in serious financial trouble and Federal block grants to build affordable housing.[176]

8.14.3 Planning permission and use of compulsory purchase orders

The main thrust of the proposed changes in this area is to encourage building once planning permission has been granted. They include recommendations that permission not used quickly would be forfeit and that there would need to be evidence of substantial work not merely some ditches dug. If construction is progressing slowly, councils could levy an equivalent to council tax on the land as if the proposed homes had been built. In addition, "compulsory purchase order powers should be strengthened…to make it easier for public bodies to acquire land where it is not brought forward and where it is a priority for development".[177]

8.14.4 A return to the roots of building societies and housing associations

Other possible solutions include a return to the original purpose and values of building societies and housing cooperatives to help finance building and ownership of homes by members. However, this would need to be undertaken on a large scale financed by the issue of bonds backed by government guarantees.[178]

8.15 Conclusion

The pent-up demand for housing (and hence credit) unmatched by housing supply has been created over many years and is growing. This major problem has spread to the rental sector with a significant portion of personal income now devoted to housing costs. This is inefficient in economic terms forming a large misallocation of national resources that could be better used in saving and consumption and hence investment.

In parallel, there has been a consolidation of the land development industry and the growth of a complex and opaque network of land option contracts tying up rights over access to large areas of development land for some five to fifteen years hence. This process has been built on high levels of borrowing and may pose a threat to financial stability but one that appears to have been over-looked by the FPC.

176 Elizabeth Warren, 'My housing plan for America', (March 2019), https://medium.com/@teamwarren/my-housing-plan-for-america-20038e19dc26, (accessed 23 July 2019).

177 Supra, note 63, (Lyons), 68.

178 Philip Callan, Phillip Blond and Edward Douglas, 'Going to scale: how a National Housing Fund can unlock Britain's house building capacity', (November 2016) The ResPublica Trust, 6–9.

Looking across a number of jurisdictions there are significant areas with high unmet demand for housing coupled with high housing costs and mortgage debt. This does not always result in financial stability since there appear to be other important factors such as the structure of the banking industry in the jurisdiction and the approach taken by local regulators. Nevertheless, as discussed in earlier chapters, there is significant evidence that a failure to build sufficient housing creates the potential for financial instability due to periodic housing price booms fuelled by the provision of extensive credit. Consequently, the only long-term solution to this risk is a big increase in home building. Even though this is a work on macroprudential and conduct of business policies this issue cannot be ignored since all the regulatory policy measures may provide, at best, only temporary alleviation and not fundamental solutions.

9 Conclusion

This book describes the home ownership aspiration as part of the concept of "hope". Access to finance to help satisfy this desire may be one of the threads that help to hold society together. In recent history there have been surges in home ownership. This was particularly true at the conclusion of the two World Wars and in the 1930s. To a significant extent, this was the result of government policy. In the UK in the early 1980s, the latter was responsible for the collapse of social house building and the increased liberalisation of credit. This process was followed by economic crises centred on residential housing in the early 1990s and again in 2007 and 2008. This is reinforced by evidence from a number of jurisdictions supporting the view that financial crises are commonly linked to over-borrowing to fund the acquisition of residential property.

The macroprudential policymakers are faced with the unenviable task of attempting to suppress the means of financing the homeowning aspiration. In benign economic periods, this may not prove too much of a challenge. Nevertheless, at other times these policymakers may need to implement policies to restrict the growth of credit in the face of political and social pressures. Depending on the circumstances, this may prove both ineffective and a challenge for the macroprudential policymakers and may undermine their legitimacy in the eyes of politicians, the media and citizens.

A systemic financial crisis can result from a number of causes, including those that are episodic such as a war or major operational failure. However, the most common systemic financial crises have at their centre the rapid price inflation of one or more asset classes generated, or at least inflamed, by a surge in the availability of credit. This is true whether it be the schemes of John Law and the Banque Générale Privée in France or John Jacob Astor in New York. By their very nature these threats to financial stability emerge very rapidly and are supported by a range of political, media and public "cheer-leaders". The Economist in 1972 noted that "men of property have been turning stone into gold" in what was described as the "new alchemy".[1]

The macroprudential policymaker needs to identify the issues and to act swiftly, effectively and with resolution. However, there are also pressures to

1 Quoted in Reid, 'The secondary Banking crisis 1973–1975', 63, Chapter 2, n. 108.

chase risk into the next valley resulting in a risk of the policymakers losing focus. They are likely to be acting contrary to the general consensus and those who promote the boom and who talk of "economic paradigm shifts" and "new economic truths". It is also likely that macroprudential policymakers may need to operate contrary to government intentions and actions and, possibly, monetary policy. The consequences may be to undermine the political legitimacy of the macroprudential policymaker. Moreover, these policies, in attempting to restrain credit growth, may result in the risk migrating elsewhere in the economy and financial system. This process may be supported by fiscal and monetary policy.

This does not mean that macroprudential policies should be abandoned. The process of identifying systemic risks and use of macroprudential instruments to provide signals of concern to the market are valuable and not to be underestimated. In addition, macroprudential tools of a microprudential nature, such as increased capital and liquidity, are likely to be effective. It is the quantitative instruments that present the greatest concerns. These measures are designed to have a very direct effect on lending to clearly identifiable individuals. The consequence, if these measures are effective, will be expressions of concern by politicians, the media and general public and may result in challenges to the authority and even the legitimacy of the macroprudential policymakers. Moreover, the evidence suggests that even if these measures are effective for a short period the market will find ways to avoid their effect by, for example, lending being provided by unregulated, or under-regulated, organisations.

This book puts forward the view that these quantitative measures should not be discarded but expectations as to their effectiveness must be lowered. They provide macroprudential signals of concern to the markets, government, and more broadly. It is possible that the government may take steps such as employing fiscal measures to assist in restraining mortgage growth. However, there are other neglected policies and this includes the need for macroprudential policymakers to engage more closely with conduct of business policy.

Conduct of business requirements have the advantages of applying to the function of mortgage lending and not just specific institutions. Moreover, it can be defended since excessive credit and asset price growth is highly likely to threaten individual new borrowers. This form of regulation is always "on" and does not depend on the timeous reaction of regulators. The approach taken, for example, by the VA may be evidence of this policy working both to protect individual borrowers and, to some extent, financial stability.

Nevertheless, there are significant issues with applying conduct of business policy. There is evidence, in the UK, of extensive conduct of business failures in areas outside residential mortgage lending. Further, current UK mortgage conduct of business regulation operations are ponderous requiring detailed information from each prospective borrowers with much of this work carried out by intermediaries who are often less in the regulatory spotlight. The fact that these procedures involve borrowers, lenders and intermediaries, all of whom are keen to undertake the transaction as fast as possible may, in a period of booming house prices and loose credit, undermine the effectiveness of the regulations. It is an area which requires close attention by both the conduct of business regulator and the macroprudential policymakers.

To help counter these risks there may be more innovative methods employed to reinforce both conduct of business and macroprudential policies. First, in the field of "fin-tech" there is likely to be considerable data available on all potential mortgage borrowers from, for example, current account transactions, taxation authorities and employers. With the borrowers' permission, this could be used to assess the affordability of individual loans without them needing to provide any other data. This may reduce the risk of information manipulation and help authenticate the central elements of the affordability calculation thereby making the process more robust.

Second, all regulatory policies involve setting a level of "risk appetite". The US legislation establishing the Consumer Financial Protection Bureau explicitly does this with the "qualified mortgage". This decision has to be made by the legislators since macroprudential policy does not operate in a political vacuum. A public debate about the acceptable level of risk may help strengthen its political legitimacy. However, the concept of assessing and accepting explicit levels of borrowing risk has not been addressed in the UK. It is an aspect which merits consideration.

Finally, the pent-up and unsatisfied demand for housing remains a source of future financial instability. The lack of housing supply at a national, regional and city level results in higher house prices and encourage increased borrowing by purchases. This can only be resolved by a political solution which satisfies this unmet aspiration and helps to ensure financial stability.

The broad conclusion of this book is the need to encourage those from different regulatory cultures and different disciplines to consult and work closely together and to look, in detail, at lessons from other jurisdictions.

Appendix
List of abbreviations

AEI	American Enterprise Institute
AMI	Association of Mortgage Intermediaries
AMTPA	Alternative Mortgage Transaction Parity Act 1982
ARM	Adjustable Rate Mortgage
BBA	British Bankers Association (now part of UK Finance)
BIS	Bank of International Settlements
CFPB	Consumer Financial Protection Bureau
CGFS	Committee on the Global Financial System
CMA	Competition and Markets Authority
CML	Council of Mortgage Lenders (now part of UK Finance)
COBS	Conduct of Business Sourcebook
CRA	Community Reinvestment Act 1977
CSBS	Conference of State Bank Supervisors
DTI	Debt to Income Ratio
EBA	European Banking Authority
ECB	European Central Bank
ECOA	Equal Credit Opportunity Act 1974
ESIS	European Standardised Information Sheet
ESRB	European Systemic Risk Board
FCA	Financial Conduct Authority
FHA	Federal Housing Administration
FPC	Financial Policy Committee
FSA	Financial Services Authority
FSLIC	Federal Savings and Loan Insurance Corporation
FSOC	Financial Stability Oversight Council
GAO	Government Accountability Office
GSE	Government Sponsored Enterprise
HMDA	Home Mortgage Disclosure Act 1975
HOLC	Home Owners' Loan Corporation
IMF	International Monetary Fund
KFI	Key Facts Illustration
LTI	Loan-to-Income Ratio
LTV	Loan-to-Value Ratio

MCOBS	Mortgage Conduct Of Business Sourcebook
MMR	Mortgage Market Review
MPC	Monetary Policy Committee
NBER	National Bureau of Economic Research
NDPB	Non-Departmental Public Body
NIM	Net Interest Margin
OCC	Office of the Comptroller of the Currency
OFT	Office of Fair Trading
ONS	Office of National Statistics
PAC	Public Accounts Committee
PCBS	Parliamentary Commission on Banking Standards
PRA	Prudential Regulatory Authority
PRC	Prudential Regulatory Committee
RDR	Retail Distribution Review
RESPA	Real Estate Settlement Procedures Act 1974
RICS	Royal Institution of Chartered Surveyors
ROCE	Return On Capital Employed
SDLT	Stamp Duty Land Tax
TILA	Truth in Lending Act 1968
TRID	TILA/RESPA Integrated Disclosure rule
TSC	Treasury Select Committee
VA	Veterans Administration

Bibliography

Books, Articles and Reports

Acharya, Viral,

——— 'A theory of systemic risk and design of prudential bank regulation', (2009) *Journal of Financial Stability*, Vol. 5, 224

——— 'Financial stability in the broader mandate for central banks: a political economy perspective', (2015) Hutchins Centre on Fiscal and Monetary policy at Brookings, Working Paper No. 11, www.brookings.edu/~/media/research/files/papers/2015/04/14_financial_stability_central_banks/14_financial_stability_central_banks.pdf (accessed 9 August 2019)

Acolin, Arthur, Xudong An and Susan Wachter, 'Lending competition and non-traditional mortgages', (December 2017).Working Paper, 1–38, http://realestate.wharton.upenn.edu/wp-content/uploads/2018/01/804.pdf (accessed 9 July 2019)

Adelino, Manuel, Antoinette Schoar and Felipe Severino, 'Credit supply and house prices: evidence from mortgage market segmentation', (2012) National Bureau of Economic Research Working Paper 17832, www.nber.org/papers/w17832.pdf (accessed 9 August 2019)

Adrian, Tobias, Daniel Covitz and Nellie Liang, 'Financial stability monitoring', (2014) Federal Reserve Bank of New York Staff Reports No. 601, www.newyorkfed.org/medialibrary/media/research/staff_reports/sr601.pdf (accessed 29 August 2019)

Adrian, Tobias and Hyun Song Shin, 'Financial intermediaries and monetary economics', (2009) Federal Reserve Bank of New York Staff Reports, No. 398, www.newyorkfed.org/medialibrary/media/research/staff_reports/sr398.pdf (accessed 9 August 2019)

Agarwal Sumit and others, 'Do financial counseling mandates improve mortgage choice and performance? Evidence from a legislative experiment', (October 2009) Federal Reserve Bank of Chicago Working Paper 2009–07

Agarwal, Sumit and others, 'Did the Community Reinvestment Act lead to risky lending?', (2012) National Bureau of Economic Research, Working Paper 18609, www.nber.org/papers/w18609 (accessed 9 August 2019)

Aikman, David, Andrew Haldane and Benjamin Nelson, 'Curbing the credit cycle', (November 2010), Columbia University Center on Capitalism and Society Annual Conference, 'Microfoundations for Modern Macroeconomics', New York, www.bankofengland.co.uk/-/media/boe/files/speech/2010/curbing-the-credit-cycle-speech (accessed 9 August 2019)

Aiyar, Shekhar, Charles Calomiris and Tomasz Wieladek, 'Does macropru leak? Evidence from a UK policy experiment', (2012) Bank of England Working Paper No. 445, www.bankofengland.co.uk/working-paper/2012/does-macropru-leak-evidence-from-a-uk-policy-experiment (accessed 9 August 2019)

Ajello, Andrea and others, 'Financial stability and optimal interest-rate policy', (2015) Board of Governors of the Federal Reserve, Working Paper, www.frbsf.org/economic-research/files/1A-Ajello-Laubach-Lopez_Salido-Nakata.pdf (accessed 9 August 2019)

Allen, Franklin and Elena Carletti, 'Systemic risk from real estate and macroprudential regulation', (2013) *International Journal of Banking, Accounting and Finance*, Vol. 5, Nos. 1–2, 28, http://finance.wharton.upenn.edu/~allenf/download/Vita/f681115127329410.pdf (accessed 9 August 2019)

Allen, Franklin, Elena Carletti and Agnese Leonello, 'Deposit insurance and risk taking', (2011) *Oxford Review of Economic Policy*, Vol. 27, No. 3, 464–478

Allen, Franklin and Douglas Gale, 'Financial contagion', (2000) *The Journal of Political Economy*, Vol. 108, No. 1, 1–33, http://finance.wharton.upenn.edu/~allenf/download/Vita/contagion.pdf (accessed 9 August 2019)

Allen, Jason and others, 'The impact of macroprudential housing finance tools in Canada: 2005–10', (August 2016), Bank of Canada Staff Working Paper 2016–41, www.bankofcanada.ca/wp-content/uploads/2016/08/swp2016-41.pdf (accessed 9 August 2019)

Alpanda, Sami, Gino Cateau and Cesaire Meh, 'A model to analyse macroprudential regulation and monetary policy', (2014) BIS Working Paper No. 461, www.bis.org/publ/work461.pdf (accessed 9 August 2019)

Alschuler, Glenn and Stuart Blumin, *The GI Bill: the New Deal for veterans* (Oxford University Press, Oxford, 2009)

Altissimo, Filippo and others, 'Wealth and asset price effects on economic activity', (2005) *European Central Bank Occasional Paper Series*, Vol. 29, 34, www.ecb.europa.eu/pub/pdf/scpops/ecbocp29.pdf?b1c260cfb519aaf7db7b9295eaa2b843 (accessed 9 August 2019)

Alworth, Julian and Giampaolo Arachi, *Taxation and the financial crisis* (Julian Alworth and Giampaolo Arachi (eds), Oxford University Press, Oxford, 2012)

Amiyatosh, Purnanandam, 'Originate-to-distribute model and the subprime mortgage crisis', (2010) University of Michigan, http://papers.ssrn.com/sol3/papers.cfm?abstract_id=1167786 (accessed 9 August 2019)

Amromin, Gene and others, 'Complex mortgages', (November, 2010) Federal Reserve Bank of Chicago WP 2010–17

Amtenbrink, Fabian and Rosa Lastra, 'Securing democratic accountability of financial regulatory agencies – a theoretical framework', in Richard Victor De Mulder (ed), *Mitigating risk in the context of safety and security. How relevant is a rational approach?* (Erasmus School of Law & Research School for Safety and Security, Rotterdam, 2008)

Andenas, Mads and Iris Chiu, *The foundations and future of financial regulation* (Routledge, London, 2013)

Andrew, Dan, Aida Caldera Sánchez and Asa Johansson, 'Housing markets and structural policies in OECD countries', (2011) OECD Working Paper No. 836, 56, www.oecd-ilibrary.org/economics/housing-markets-and-structural-policies-in-oecd-countries_5kgk8t2k9vf3-en (accessed 9 August 2019)

Angeloni, Ignazio, 'European macroprudential policy from gestation to infancy', (April 2014) Banque de France, Financial Stability Review, No. 18, 71–84, www.banque-france.fr/fileadmin/user_upload/banque_de_france/publications/Financial-Stability-Review-18_2014-04_Angeloni.pdf (accessed 9 August 2019)

Arthur, Brian, 'Competing technologies, increasing returns, and lock-in by historical events', (1989) *Economic Journal*, Vol. 97, 642–665

Aubrey, Thomas, 'The challenge of accelerating UK housebuilding', (January 2015) Policy Network Paper, www.housingnet.co.uk/pdf/The_challenge_of_accelerating_UK_housebuilding_By_Thomas_Aubrey.pdf (accessed 9 August 2019)

Austin, John, *The province of jurisprudence determined* (first published 1832, Cambridge University Press, Cambridge, England, 1995)

Australian Bureau of Statistics, 4130.0- Housing Occupancy and Costs, 2017–18, (July 2019) www.abs.gov.au/ausstats/abs@.nsf/0/88BF225497426920CA257F5C000989A8?Opendocument (accessed 17 July 2019)

Avgouleas, Emilios,

——— 'Bank leverage ratios and financial stability: a micro and macroprudential perspective', (October 2015) Levy Economics Institute, Bard College, Working Paper No. 849

——— *Governance of global financial markets* (Cambridge University Press, Cambridge, 2012)

——— 'The global financial crisis, behavioural finance and financial regulation: in search of a new orthodoxy', (April 2009) *Journal of Corporate Law Studies*, Vol. 9(1), 23–59

——— 'Reforming investor protection regulation: the impact of cognitive biases', in Michael Faure and Frank Stephen (eds), *Essays in the law and economics of regulation in honour of Anthony Ogus* (Intersentia, The Hague, 2008), 143–166

Awrey, Daniel, 'Macroprudential financial regulation: panacea or placebo', (2009) *Amsterdam Law Forum* Vol. 1.3, http://ssrn.com/abstract=1410014 (accessed 9 August 2019)

Ayres, Ian, 'Homo economicus, homo myopicus and the law and economics of consumer choice: menus matter', (2006) *University of Chicago Law Review*, Vol. 73, 9

Bagehot, Walter, *The English constitution* (first published between 1865 and 1867, Oxford Classics, Oxford, 2001)

Bailey, Andrew,

——— 'Financial stability – objective and resolution', speech at the Pro Manchester Business and Professional Services Conference, Manchester, 17th March 2011, www.bis.org/review/r110317b.pdf (accessed 9 August 2019)

——— 'Defining the objectives and goals of supervision', speech at the New York Federal Reserve Board conference, 18th March 2016, www.bankofengland.co.uk/speech/2016/new-york-fed-conference-defining-the-objectives-and-goals-of-supervision (accessed 9 August 2019)

Bailey King, C, 'Preemption and the North Carolina predatory lending law', (2004) *University of North Carolina School of Law*, Vol. 8, No. 1, 377–397

Baker, Andrew,

——— 'The new political economy of the macroprudential ideational shift', (2013) *New Political Economy*, Vol. 18, No. 1, 112–139

——— 'The bankers' paradox: the political economy of macroprudential regulation', (April 2015), LSE Systemic Risk Centre Discussion Paper No. 37, 26–27, http://eprints.lse.ac.uk/61998/1/dp-37.pdf (accessed 9 August 2019)

——— 'The gradual transformation? The incremental dynamics of macroprudential regulation', (2013) *Regulation & Governance*, Vol. 7, 417–434

Baker, Andrew and Wesley Widmaier, 'The institutionalist roots of macroprudential ideas: Veblen and Galbraith on regulation, policy success and overconfidence', (2014) *New Political Economy*, Vol. 19, No. 4, 487–506

Baldwin, Robert, Martin Cave and Martin Lodge, *Understanding regulation* (2nd edn, Oxford University Press, Oxford, 2012)

Ball, Jane, 'Using banks: the effect of national attitudes to public intervention in mortgage lending and eviction in French and English law', (2010) *International Journal of Law in the Built Environment*, Vol. 2(2), 118–137

Ball, Michael, 'Chasing a snail: innovation and housebuilding firms strategies', (1999) *Housing Studies*, Vol. 14, 9–21

Ball, Michael, 'The housebuilding industry: promoting recovery in housing supply', (2010) A Report for the Department of Communities and Local Government, http://webarchive.nationalarchives.gov.uk/20120919132719/http:/www.communities.gov.uk/documents/housing/pdf/1526670.pdf (accessed 9 August 2019)

Balls, Ed, James Howat and Anna Stansbury, 'Central bank independence revisited: after the financial crisis, what should a model central bank look like', (2016) Mossavar-Rahman Centre Working Paper Series No. 67, Harvard Kennedy School

Bank of England

2018

——— Bank of England and FCA Mortgage Lenders and Administrators Statistic, (Q3 2018) www.bankofengland.co.uk/statistics/mortgage-lenders-and-administrators/2018/2018-q3 (accessed 30 July 2019)

2017

——— 'Financial stability report', www.bankofengland.co.uk/financial-stability-report/2017/november-2017 (accessed 12 August 2019)

——— FPC minutes of 21 June 2017, www.bankofengland.co.uk/-/media/boe/files/record/2017/financial-policy-committee-meeting-june-2017 (accessed 12 August 2019)

——— Press release, 'FPC's statement from its policy meeting', (22 March 2017), www.bankofengland.co.uk/statement/fpc/2017/financial-policy-committee-statement-march-2017 (accessed 12 August 2019)

2016

——— 'The Financial Policy Committee's powers over housing policy instruments: a draft policy statement', (November 2016), www.bankofengland.co.uk/-/media/boe/files/statement/2016/the-financial-policy-committee-powers-over-housing-policy-instruments (accessed 12 August 2019)

——— 'Financial stability report', (July 2016), www.bankofengland.co.uk/financial-stability-report/2016/july-2016 (accessed 12 August 2019)

2015

——— 'Financial stability report', (July 2015), www.bankofengland.co.uk/financial-stability-report/2015/july-2015 (accessed 12 August 2019)

Bank of England and FCA, 'The failure of HBOS plc (HBOS)', (2015), www.bankofengland.co.uk/-/media/boe/files/prudential-regulation/publication/hbos-complete-report (accessed 12 August 2019)

2014

——— 'Mark Carney's letter to the Parliamentary Environmental Audit Committee', (8 July 2014), www.parliament.uk/documents/commons-committees/environmental-audit/Letter-from-Governor-of-Bank-of-England-on-Carbon-Bubble-risk.pdf (accessed 12 August 2019)

——— 'CP11/14 Implementing the Financial Policy Committee's recommendation on loan to income ratios in mortgage lending', (June 2014), www.bankofengland.co.uk/pra/Documents/publications/cp/2014/cp1114.pdf (accessed 12 August 2019)

——— 'Monetary Policy Committee minutes', (4 and 5 June 2014), www.bankofengland.co.uk/-/media/boe/files/monetary-policy-summary-and-minutes/2015/minutes-june-2015 (accessed 12 August 2019)

2013 and Earlier

——— 'Instruments of macroprudential policy: a discussion paper', (December 2011), www.bankofengland.co.uk/-/media/boe/files/paper/2011/instruments-of-macroprudential-policy (accessed 12 August 2019)

——— 'The role of macroprudential policy: a discussion paper', (November 2009), www.bankofengland.co.uk/-/media/boe/files/paper/2009/the-role-of-macroprudential-policy (accessed 26th July 2019)

——— 'The development of the building societies sector in the 1980s', (1990) *Quarterly Bulletin*, Vol. 503, www.bankofengland.co.uk/archive/Documents/historicpubs/qb/1990/qb90q4503510.pdf (accessed 12 August 2017)

——— 'The supplementary special deposits scheme', (March 1982) *Quarterly Bulletin*, 74–84, www.bankofengland.co.uk/quarterly-bulletin/1982/q1/the-supplementary-special-deposits-scheme (accessed 12 August 2019)

——— 'Competition and credit control', (May 1971) www.bankofengland.co.uk/-/media/boe/files/quarterly-bulletin/1971/competition-and-credit-control-text-of-a-consultatice-document-issued-on-14-may-1971 (accessed 12 August 2019)

Bank for International Settlements (BIS)

——— '84th Annual Report, April 2013-March 2014', (2014), www.bis.org/publ/arpdf/ar2014_ec.pdf (accessed 12 August 2019)

——— Committee on the Global Financial System, 'Operationalising the selection and application of macroprudential instruments', (2012) CGFS Papers No. 48, www.bis.org/publ/cgfs48.pdf (accessed 12 August 2019)

——— 'Central bank governance and financial stability', (May 2011), www.bis.org/publ/othp14.pdf (accessed 12 August 2019)

——— Committee on the Global Financial System, 'Macroprudential instruments and frameworks: a stocktaking of issues and experiences', (May 2010) CGFS Papers No. 38, www.bis.org/publ/cgfs38.pdf (accessed 12 August 2019)

Bank of Israel, 'Financial stability report', (2015), www.boi.org.il/en/NewsAndPublications/RegularPublications/Research%20Department%20Publications/Financial%20Stability%20Report/FSR2015e1.pdf (accessed 12 August 2019)

Bar-Gill, Oren

——— *Seduction by contract* (Oxford University Press, Oxford, 2012),

——— 'The law, economics and psychology of sub-prime mortgage contracts', (2009) *Cornell Law Review*, Vol. 94, 1073–1151

Barker, Kate, 'Delivering stability: securing our future housing needs', (March 2004), *Barker Review Final Report*, http://webarchive.nationalarchives.gov.uk/20130129110402/www.hm-treasury.gov.uk/d/barker_review_report_494.pdf (accessed 12 August 2019)

Barker, Rodney, *Political legitimacy and the state* (Clarendon Press, Oxford, 1990)

Barnett, Michael and Martha Finnemore, *Rules for the World: international organisations in global politics* (Cornell University Press, Ithaca, New York, 2004)

Barr, Michael and others, 'Behaviorally informed financial services regulation', (New American Foundation, October 2008), http://repository.law.umich.edu/cgi/viewcontent.cgi?article=1028&context=other (accessed 12 August 2019)

Barth, James, Joseph Cordes and Anthony Yezer, 'Financial institution regulations, redlining and mortgage markets', (October 1979), The Federal Reserve Bank of Boston Conference Series on 'The regulation of financial Institutions', 101–143

Barthold, Thomas, 'Issues in the design of environmental excise taxes', (1994) *Journal of Economic Perspectives*, Vol. 8, No. 1, 133–151, www.jstor.org/stable/2138155?loginSuccess=true&seq=2#page_scan_tab_contents (accessed 12 August 2019)

Basel Committee for Banking Supervision, 'Core principles for effective banking supervision', (September 2012), www.bis.org/publ/bcbs230.pdf (accessed 12 August 2019)

Bassett, William and others, 'Changes in bank lending standards and the macroeconomy', (2014) *Journal of Monetary Economics*, Vol. 62, 23–40, www.sciencedirect.com/science/article/pii/S0304393213001645 (accessed 12 August 2019)

BBVA Research, 'Macroprudential measures on mortgage lending: country experiences', (2014) *Economic Analysis*, www.bbvaresearch.com/en/publicaciones/financial-systems-and-regulation-watch-macroprudential-measures-on-mortgage-lending-country-experiences/ (accessed 12 August 2019)

Bean, Charles, Matthias Paustian, Adrian Penalver and Tim Taylor, 'Monetary policy after the fall', Federal Reserve Bank of Kansas City Annual Conference Jackson Hole, Wyoming, 16 September 2010, www.kansascityfed.org/publicat/sympos/2010/bean-paper.pdf (accessed 12 August 2019)

Bebchuk, Lucian and Itay Goldstein, 'Self-fulfilling market freezes', (2011) *Review of Financial Studies*, Vol. 24, No. 11, 3519, http://finance.wharton.upenn.edu/~itayg/Files/creditfreeze-published.pdf (accessed 12 August 2019)

Bebchuck, Lucian and Mark Roe,

——— 'A theory of path dependence in corporate ownership and governance', (1999) *Stanford Law Review*, Vol. 52, No. 1, 127

——— 'A theory of path dependence in corporate ownership and governance', in Jeffrey Gordon and Mark Roe (eds), *Convergence and persistence in corporate governance* (Cambridge University Press, Cambridge, 2004), 69–113

Berry, Christopher, 'Land use regulation and residential segregation: does zoning matter?' (Fall 2001) *American Law and Economics Review*, Vol. 3, No. 2, 251–274

Beetham, David, *The legitimation of power* (Macmillan, London, 1991)

Behrens, Carl, 'Legal framework of urban mortgage lending by commercial banks', in Carl Behrens (ed), *Commercial bank activities in urban mortgage financing* (National Bureau of Economic Research, 1952), https://core.ac.uk/download/pdf/6919451.pdf (accessed 12 August 2019)

Belsky, Eric and Susan Wachter, 'The public interest in consumer and mortgage credit markets', (2010) Research Paper No. 10–05 Institute for Law and Economics, University of Pennsylvania Law School, 14

Benes, Jaromir and Michael Kumhof, 'The "Chicago Plan" revisited', (2012) IMF Working Paper, WP/12/202, www.imf.org/external/pubs/ft/wp/2012/wp12202.pdf (accessed 12 August 2019)

Ben-Porath, Sigal, *Tough choices: structured paternalism and the landscape of choice* (Princeton University Press, Princeton, NJ, 2010)

Benston, George and George Kaufman, 'FDICIA after five years', (Summer 1997) *Journal of Economic Perspectives*, Vol. 11, No. 3, 139–158

Berger, Wolfram and Friedrich Kissmer, 'Central bank independence and financial stability: a tale of perfect harmony?', (2013) *European Journal of Political Economy*, Vol. 31, 109

Bergstresser, Daniel and John Beshears, 'Who selected adjustable-rate mortgages? evidence from the 1989–2007 Surveys of Consumer Finances', (2010), Harvard Business School, Working Paper 10–083, https://pdfs.semanticscholar.org/d552/e725215c682443ba478b09258073eae0cb01.pdf (accessed 12 August 2019)

Bernanke, Ben,

——— *Essays on the Great Depression* (Princeton University Press, Princeton, NJ, 2000)

Bernanke, Ben and Alan Blinder, 'The Federal Funds Rate and the channels of monetary transmission', (1992) *The American Economic Review*, Vol. 82, No. 4, 901, http://pages.stern.nyu.edu/~dbackus/Identification/BernankeBlinder_AER_92.pdf (accessed 12 August 2019)

Bernanke, Ben and Mark Gertler,

——— 'Monetary policy and asset price volatility', (2000), National Bureau of Economic Research Working Paper 7559, www.nyu.edu/econ/user/gertlerm/kansasfed.pdf (accessed 12 August 2019)

——— 'Should central banks respond to movements in asset prices?', (2001) *The American Economic Review*, Vol. 91, No. 2, 253

——— 'Inside the black box: the credit channel of monetary policy transmission', (1995) *Journal of Economic Perspectives*, Vol. 9, No. 4, 27, www.nber.org/papers/w5146 (accessed 12 August 2019)

Berndt, Antje, Burton Hollifield and Patrik Sandas, 'The role of mortgage brokers in the subprime crisis', (2010), National Bureau of Economic Research Working Paper 16175

Bernstein, Marver, *Regulating business by independent commission* (Princeton University Press, Princeton, NJ, 1955)

Bezemer, Dirk, 'Schumpeter might be right again: the functional differentiation of credit', (November 2014), *Journal of Evolutionary Economics*, Vol. 24, No. 5, 935–950, www.economicsofcreditanddebt.org/media/research/The_Functional_Differentiation_of_Credit.pdf (accessed 12 August 2019)

Bhutta, Neil and Glenn Canner,

——— 'Mortgage market conditions and borrower outcomes', (2013) *Federal Reserve Bulletin*, Vol. 99, www.federalreserve.gov/pubs/bulletin/2013/pdf/2012_hmda.pdf (accessed 12 August 2019)

——— 'Did the CRA cause the mortgage market meltdown?', (March 2009) *Federal Reserve Bank of Minneapolis*, www.minneapolisfed.org/publications/community-dividend/did-the-cra-cause-the-mortgage-market-meltdown (accessed 12 August 2019)

Bhutoria, Aditi, John Jerrim and Anna Vignoles, 'The financial skills of adults across the world. New estimates from the Programme for the International Assessment of Adult Competencies (PIAAC)', (March 2018), 1, UCL Institute of Education web-site, www.ucl.ac.uk/ioe/news/2018/mar/england-has-one-lowest-levels-financial-literacy-study-says (accessed 17 July 2019)

Bhutta, Neil and Daniel Ringo, 'Assessing the Community Reinvestment Act's role in the financial crisis', (2015) *Board of Governors of the Federal Reserve System, FEDS Notes*, www.federalreserve.gov/econresdata/notes/feds-notes/2015/assessing-the-community-reinvestment-acts-role-in-the-financial-crisis-20150526.html (accessed 12 August 2019)

Black, Julia,

——— 'Constructing and contesting legitimacy and accountability in polycentric regulatory regimes', (2008) *Regulation and Governance*, Vol. 2, No. 2, 137–164

——— 'Critical reflections on regulation', (2002) *Australian Journal of Legal Philosophy*, Vol. 27, 1–36

——— 'Proceduralization of regulation', (2000) *Oxford Journal of Legal Studies*, Vol. 20, 597–614

Blyth, Mark, *Great transformations: economic ideas and institutional change in the Twentieth Century* (Cambridge University Press, Cambridge, 2002)

Bohman, James, 'Complexity, pluralism and the constitutional state: on Habermas's Fraktizität and Geltung', ['Between facts and norms'], (1994) *Law and Society Review*, Vol. 28, 897–930

Bonasta, Christopher, *Knocking on the door: the Federal Government's attempt to desegregate the suburbs* (Princeton University Press, Princeton, NJ, 2006)

Bordo, Michael and Jeanne Olivier, 'Monetary policy and asset prices: does "benign neglect" make sense', (2002) IMF Working Paper, WP/02/225, www.imf.org/external/pubs/ft/wp/2002/wp02225.pdf (accessed 12 August 2019)

Bordo, Michael, Angela Redish and Hugh Rockoff, 'Why didn't Canada have a banking crisis in 2008 (or in 1930, or in 1907 or...)?', (2011), National Bureau of Economic Research Working Paper 17312, www.nber.org/papers/w17312.pdf (accessed 12 August 2019)

Bordo, Michael, 'Central bank independence and financial crises in history', (2010) Oesterreichische 38th Economics Conference 2010, www.oenb.at/en/Publications/Economics/Economics-Conference/2010/Economics-Conference-2010.html (accessed 12 August 2019)

Borio, Claudio

——— 'Macroprudential frameworks: (too) great expectations?', (August 2014) *25th anniversary edition of Central Banking Journal*, www.bis.org/speeches/sp140813.pdf (accessed 12 August 2019)

——— 'The financial cycle and macroeconomics: what have we learnt?', (2012) BIS Working Papers No. 395, www.bis.org/publ/work395.pdf (accessed 12 August 2019)

——— 'Implementing a macroprudential framework: blending boldness and realism', (2010), BIS Paper, www.bis.org/repofficepubl/hkimr201007.12c.pdf (accessed 12 August 2019)

Borio, Claudio and Mathias Drehmann,

——— 'Towards an operational framework for financial stability: "fuzzy" measurement and its consequences', (June 2009) BIS Working Papers No. 284, www.bis.org/publ/work284.pdf (accessed 12 August 2019)

——— 'Financial instability and macroeconomics: bridging the gulf', (2009), paper presented at the Twelfth Annual International Banking Conference, 'The international financial crisis: have the rules of finance changed?', held at the Federal Reserve Bank of Chicago, Chicago, www.dnb.nl/en/binaries/Financial%20instability%20and%20macroeconomics%20bridging%20the_tcm47-224190.pdf (accessed 12 August 2019)

Borio, Claudio and Philip Lowe, 'Asset prices, financial and monetary stability: exploring the nexus', (2002) BIS Working Papers, No 114, www.bis.org/publ/work114.pdf (accessed 12 August 2019)

Borio, Claudio and William White, 'Whither monetary and financial stability? The implications of evolving policy regimes', (2004) BIS Working Papers No. 147, 26, www.bis.org/publ/work147.pdf (accessed 12 August 2019)

Borio, Claudio and Haibin Zhu, 'Capital regulation, risk-taking and monetary policy: a missing link in the transmission mechanism', (2012) *Journal of financial Stability*, Vol. 8, 236–251 www.bis.org/publ/work268.pdf (accessed 12 August 2019)

Boyack, Andrea, 'Lessons in price stability from the US real; estate market collapse', (2010) 10.2139/ssrn.1665124

Boyd, John, Gianni De Nicolò and Abu Jalal, 'Bank risk-taking and competition revisited: new theory and new evidence', (2006) IMF Working Paper WP/06/297, www.imf.org/en/Publications/WP/Issues/2016/12/31/Banking-Crises-and-Crisis-Dating-Theory-and-Evidence-23052 (accessed 12 August 2019)

Braddick, Katherine, 'The changing face of prudential policy', speech at the Future of Financial Services Summit, London, 11 March 2014, www.bankofengland.co.uk/speech/2014/the-changing-face-of-prudential-policy (accessed 12 August 2019)

Bramley, Glen and others, 'Estimating housing need', (November 2010), Department for Communities and Local Government, www.gov.uk/government/uploads/system/uploads/attachment_data/file/6338/1776873.pdf (accessed 12 August 2019)

Bramley, Glen and David Watkins, 'Where should we build the extra housing we need in England? Need, demand, opportunity and value', (April 2014) Housing Studies Association conference at Heriot Watt University

Breger, Marshall, 'Thoughts on accountability and the administrative process', (Summer 1987) *Administrative Law Review*, Vol. 39, No. 3, 399–415

Brener, Alan, 'The golden threads of compliance', (1995) *Journal of Financial Regulation and Compliance*, Vol. 3, No. 4, 344–349

Brunnermeier, Markus, Andrew Crockett, Charles Goodhart, Avinash Persaud and Hyun Song Shin, 'The fundamental principles of financial regulation', Geneva Reports on the World Economy', (International Center for Monetary and Banking Studies and Centre for Economic Policy Research, 2009), www.princeton.edu/~markus/research/papers/Geneva11.pdf (accessed 12 August 2019)

Brunnermeier, Markus and Yuliy Sannikov, 'A macroeconomic model with a financial sector', (2014) *American Economic Review*, Vol. 104, 379

Brunnermeier, Markus and Isabel Schnabel, 'Bubbles and central banks: historical perspectives', (2014), Gutenberg School of Management and Economics & Research Unit Interdisciplinary Public Policy Discussion Paper 1411, http://wiwi.uni-mainz.de/Papers/DP_1411.pdf (accessed 12 August 2019)

Bruno, Valentina and Hyun Song Shin, 'Assessing macroprudential policies: case of South Korea', (2014) *Scandinavian Journal of Economics*, Vol. 116(1), 128–157

Bubb, Ryann and Pasad Krishnamurthy, 'Regulating against bubbles', (2014) *University of Pennsylvania Law Review*, Vol. 163, 1539

Building and Social Housing Foundation (BHSF), *The future of housing* (BSHF Publication, Coalville, 2009)

Buitelaar, Edwin, 'Crack in the myth: challenges to land policy in the Netherlands', (2010) *TijdscrhiftvoorEconomische en SocialeGeografie*, Vol. 101, No. 3, 349–356

Burke, Edmund, *Speeches on America. On conciliation with America*, (first published 1775, Arthur Innes (ed), Cambridge University Press, Cambridge, 1906)

Burk, Kathleen and Alec Cairncross, *Goodbye Great Britain: the 1976 IMF crisis* (Yale University Press, New Haven, 1992)

Busuioc, Madalina, *European agencies: law and practices of accountability* (Oxford University Press, Oxford, 2013)

Caballero, Ricardo, 'A fallacy of composition', (1991), National Bureau of Economic Research Working Paper 3735, www.nber.org/papers/w3735.pdf (accessed 12 August 2019)

Cabinet Office, 'Public bodies 2015', (2015), www.gov.uk/government/uploads/system/uploads/attachment_data/file/506880/Public_Bodies_2015_Web_9_Mar_2016.pdf (accessed 12 August 2019)

Callan, Philip, Phillip Blond and Edward Douglas, 'Going to scale: how a National Housing Fund can unlock Britain's house building capacity', (November 2016) *The*

ResPublica Trust, www.respublica.org.uk/wp-content/uploads/2016/11/Going-to-Scale-1-1.pdf (accessed 12 August 2019)

Callcutt, John, 'Review of housebuilding delivery', (2007) *Department of Communities and Local Government*, http://webarchive.nationalarchives.gov.uk/20070130001032/http:/callcuttreview.co.uk/downloads/callcuttreview_221107.pdf (accessed 12 August 2019)

Calomiris, Charles and Stephen Haber, *Fragile by design* (Princeton University Press, Princeton, NJ, 2014)

Calza, Alessandro, Tommaso Monacelli and Livio Stracca, 'Housing finance and monetary policy', (2009) European Central Bank Working papers Series No. 1069, www.ecb.europa.eu/pub/pdf/scpwps/ecbwp1069.pdf?a4540d3d37de20b3904148303 62131e8 (accessed 12 August 2019)

Campaign to Protect Rural England, 'Building on Barker: how we can continue to improve housing for everyone without damaging the environment and sprawling over the countryside', (January 2005), file:///N:/Downloads/building_on_barker_report.pdf (accessed 12 August 2019)

Campbell, Andrew, 'Designing a framework for protecting bank depositors', in James Devenney (ed), *Consumer credit, debt and investment in Europe* (Cambridge University Press, Cambridge, 2012)

Campbell, Andrew and Rosa Lastra, 'Revisiting the lender of last resort – the role of the Bank of England, in Iain MacNeil and Justin O'Brien (eds), *The future of financial regulation* (Hart, Oxford, 2010), 161–178

Campbell, John, Howell Jackson, Brigitte Madrian and Peter Tufano, 'The regulation of consumer financial products: an introductory essay with four case studies', (September 2010) Harvard Kennedy School Faculty Research Working Paper, 10–040

Campbell, John, Sendhil Mullainathan, Richard Thaler and Susan Woodward, 'Consumer finance policy: implementing two-tier mortgage regulation', (December 2010), *Russell Sage Foundation*, www.russellsage.org/sites/all/files/behavioral_consumer_finance.pdf (accessed 12 August 2019)

Canadian Centre for Economic Analysis, 'Toronto housing market analysis -from insight to action', (January 2019), www.toronto.ca/legdocs/mmis/2019/ph/bgrd/backgroundfile-124480.pdf (accessed 15 July 2019)

Carliner, Michael, 'Development of Federal homeownership "policy"', (January 1998) *Housing Policy Debate*, Vol. 9. No. 2, 299–321

Carney, Mark,

——— 'Three truths for finance', remarks at the Harvard Club UK, Southwark Cathedral dinner, London, 21 September 2015, www.bis.org/review/r150922a.pdf (accessed 12 August 2019)

——— 'Breaking the tragedy of the horizon – climate change and financial stability', speech at Lloyd's of London, 29 September 2015, www.bis.org/review/r151009a.pdf (accessed 12 August 2019)

Carpenter, David, 'The Consumer Financial Protection Bureau (CFPB): a legal analysis', (14 January 2014), *Congressional Research Service*, www.fas.org/sgp/crs/misc/R42572.pdf (accessed 12 August 2019)

Caruana, Jaime and Benjamin Cohen, 'Five questions and six answers about macroprudential policy', (April 2014), *Banque de France, Financial Stability Review*, No. 18, 15–23, https://publications.banque-france.fr/sites/default/files/medias/documents/financial-stability-review-18_2014-04.pdf (accessed 12 August 2019)

Case, Karl, John Quigley and Robert Shiller, 'Comparing wealth effects: the stock market vs. the housing market', (2005) *Advances in Macroeconomics*, Vol. 5, No. 1, Article 1, 26, www.econ.yale.edu/~shiller/pubs/p1181.pdf (accessed 12 August 2019)

Cassidy, Nicolas, 'The Fair Housing Act, disparate Impact and the ability-to-repay: a compliance dilemma for mortgage lenders', (2013) *Review of Banking and Financial Law*, Vol. 32, 431

Castro Coelho, Miguel, Vigyan Ratnoo and Sebastian Dellepiane, 'Housing that works for all: the political economy of housing in England', (October 2014) Institute for Government, 10, www.instituteforgovernment.org.uk/sites/default/files/publications/Political%20Economy%20of%20Housing%20in%20England%20231014F1.pdf (accessed 12 August 2019)

Caverzasi, Eugenio, 'Minsky and the subprime mortgage crisis: the financial instability hypothesis in the era of financialization', (2014) Levy Economics Institute, Bard College, Working Paper No. 796, www.levyinstitute.org/pubs/wp_796.pdf (accessed 12 August 2019)

Centre Forum, 'Community land auctions: working towards implementation', (November 2011), file:///N:/Downloads/Community-land-auctions-working-towards-implementation.pdf (accessed 12 August 2019)

Cerutti, Eugenio, Stijn Claessens and Luc Laeven, 'The use and effectiveness of macroprudential policies: new evidence', (2015) IMF Working Paper WP/15/61, www.imf.org/external/pubs/ft/wp/2015/wp1561.pdf (accessed 12 August 2019)

Cetrino Thomas and Gerald Benjamin, 'Classification of property for taxation in New York State: issues and options', (Fall 2014), Centre for Research, Regional Education and Outreach, State University of New York, Discussion Brief No. 13, www.newpaltz.edu/media/the-benjamin-center/discussion_brief_13.pdf (accessed 21 August 2019)

Chambers, Matthew, Carlos Garriga and Don Schlagenhauf, 'The New Deal, the GI Bill and post-war housing', (2012), Society for Economic Dynamics, Meeting Papers, No. 1050

Chancellor of the Exchequer's Budget speech, 16 March 2016, www.gov.uk/government/speeches/budget-2016-george-osbornes-speech (accessed 12 August 2019)

Chartered Institute of Housing, 'Ticking the box for a welfare system that works', (September 2014), www.cih.org/resources/PDF/Policy%20free%20download%20pdfs/Ticking%20the%20box%20for%20a%20welfare%20system%20that%20works%20Sep%2014.pdf (accessed 12 August 2019)

Chiu, Iris H-Y, *Regulating (from) the inside* (Bloomsbury, Oxford, 2015)

Choplin, Jessica and Debra Stark, 'Doomed to failure: a psychological analysis of mortgage disclosure and policy implications', (2013), 32 No. 10 Banking and Financial Services Policy Report

Christensen, Ian, 'Mortgage debt and procyclicality in the housing market', (Summer 2011) *Bank of Canada Review*, 35–42

Churchill, Randolph, *Twenty-one years* (Weidenfeld & Nicolson, London, 1965)

Cian, Luca, Aradhna Krishna and Ryan Elder, 'A sign of things to come: behavioral change through dynamic iconography', (2015) *Journal of Consumer Research*, Vol. 41, No. 6, 1426

Čihák, Martin and others, 'Financial stability reports: what are they good for?', (2012) IMF Working Paper WP/12/1, www.imf.org/external/pubs/cat/longres.aspx?sk=25470.0 (accessed 12 August 2019)

Claessens, Stijn, 'An overview of macroprudential policy tools', (2014), IMF Working Paper, WP/14/214, www.imf.org/external/pubs/ft/wp/2014/wp14214.pdf (accessed 28 August 2019)

Claessens, Stijn, Swati Ghosh and Roxana Mihet, 'Macroprudential policies to mitigate financial system vulnerabilities', (2014) IMF Working Paper WP/14/55, www.imf.org/external/pubs/ft/wp/2014/wp14155.pdf (accessed 12 August 2019)

Claessens, Stijn, Ayhan Kose and Marco Terrones, 'What happens during recessions, crunches and busts', (2008b) IMF Working Paper, WP/08/274, 34, www.imf.org/external/pubs/ft/wp/2008/wp08274.pdf (accessed 12 August 2019)

Clarke, Stephen, Adam Corlett and Lindsay Judge, 'The housing headwind: the impact of rising housing costs on UK living standards', (June 2016), *Resolution Foundation Report*, www.resolutionfoundation.org/app/uploads/2016/06/The-Housing-Headwind.pdf (accessed 12 August 2019)

Clement, Piet, 'The term "macroprudential": origins and evolution', (March 2010) *BIS Quarterly Review*, www.bis.org/publ/qtrpdf/r_qt1003h.htm (accessed 12 August 2019)

Coase, Ronald, 'The problem of social cost', (1960) *The Journal of Law and Economics*, Vol. 3, No. 2, www.econ.ucsb.edu/~tedb/Courses/UCSBpf/readings/coase.pdf (accessed 12 August 2019)

Cochrane, John, 'Equity-financed banking and a run-free financial system', (2014), comments given at the 'Ending too big to fail symposium', Federal Reserve Bank of Minneapolis, 16 May 2016, https://faculty.chicagobooth.edu/john.cochrane/research/papers/run_free.pdf (accessed 12 August 2019)

Coffee, John, 'Law and the market: the impact of enforcement', (2007), Columbia Law and Economics Working Paper No. 304, www.law.upenn.edu/journals/lawreview/articles/volume156/issue2/Coffee156U.Pa.L.Rev.229(2007).pdf (accessed 12 August 2019)

Consumer Financial Protection Bureau (CFPB)

——— CFPB, 'Ability-to-Repay and Qualified Mortgage Rule Assessment Report', (January 2019), https://files.consumerfinance.gov/f/documents/cfpb_ability-to-repay-qualified-mortgage_assessment-report.pdf (accessed 5 July 2019)

——— CFPB Strategic Plan 2018–22, (February 2018), https://files.consumerfinance.gov/f/documents/cfpb_strategic-plan_fy2018-fy2022.pdf (accessed 26 June 2019)

——— CFPB, 'Supervisory highlights', (Fall 2015), No. 9, http://files.consumerfinance.gov/f/201510_cfpb_supervisory-highlights.pdf (accessed 12 August 2019)

——— CFPB, 'Semi-annual report', (Spring 2015), http://files.consumerfinance.gov/f/201506_cfpb_semi-annual-report-spring-2015.pdf (accessed 12 August 2019)

——— CFPB, 'Consumers' mortgage shopping experience', (January 2015), https://files.consumerfinance.gov/f/201501_cfpb_consumers-mortgage-shopping-experience.pdf (accessed 21 August 2019)

——— CFPB, 'Summary of the ability to repay and qualified mortgage rule and the concurrent proposals', (2013), http://files.consumerfinance.gov/f/201301_cfpb_ability-to-repay-summary.pdf (accessed 12 August 2019)

——— CFPB press release, 'CFPB takes action against Castle & Cooke for steering consumers into costlier mortgages', (7 November 2013), www.consumerfinance.gov/newsroom/cfpb-takes-action-against-castle-cooke-for-steering-consumers-into-costlier-mortgages/ (accessed 12 August 2019)

——— CFPB, 'State supervisory coordination framework', (7 May 2013), http://files.consumerfinance.gov/f/201305_cfpb_state-supervisory-coordination-framework.pdf (accessed 12 August 2019)

——— CFPB, Strategic Plan, 2013–2017, (April 2013), https://files.consumerfinance.gov/f/strategic-plan.pdf (accessed 12 August 2019)

Coogan, Michael, 'Recent developments in the UK housing and mortgage market', (March 1998) Housing Finance International, 3–9, www.housingfinance.org/uploads/Publicationsmanager/9803_UK.pdf (accessed 12 August 2019)

Cooter, Robert and Thomas Ulan, *Law and economics* (6th edn, Pearson, London, 2012)

Copp, David, 'Reasonable acceptability and democratic legitimacy: Estlund's qualified acceptability requirement', (January 2011) *Ethics*, Vol. 121, No. 2, 239–269

Cordero, Guillermo and Pablo Simón, 'Economic crisis and support for democracy in Europe', (2016) *West European Politics*, Vol. 39, No. 2, 305–325

Cordray, Richard, 'Know before you owe', remarks by the Director of the Consumer Financial Protection Bureau at the Consumer Response Field Hearing, Des Moines, Iowa 28 March 2013, www.consumerfinance.gov/about-us/newsroom/prepared-remarks-of-director-richard-cordray-at-the-consumer-response-field-hearing/ (accessed 12 August 2019)

Cotterrell, Roger, *Law's community: legal theory in sociological perspective* (Oxford University Press, Oxford, 1997)

Council of Mortgage Lenders, 'Still aspiring', (10 April 2013) YouGov survey report, www.cml.org.uk/news/news-and-views/508/ (accessed 12 August 2019)

Crafts Nicholas and Peter Fearon, 'The 1930s: understanding the lessons', in Nicholas Crafts and Peter Fearon (eds), *The great depression of the 1930s: lessons for today* (Oxford University Press, Oxford, 2013)

Crockett, Andrew, 'Marrying the micro- and macroprudential dimensions of financial stability', BIS speech, 21 September 2000, www.bis.org/review/rr000921b.pdf (accessed 12 August 2019)

Crook, Tony and Sarah Monk, 'Planning gains, providing homes', (2011) *Housing Studies*, Vol. 26, Nos. 7–8, 997–1018

Crowe, Christopher, Giovanna dell'Ariccia, Deniz Igan and Pau Rabanal, 'Policies for macrofinancial stability: options to deal with real estate booms', (2011a) IMF Staff Discussion Papers, SDN/11/02, www.imf.org/external/pubs/ft/sdn/2011/sdn1102.pdf (accessed 12 August 2019)

Crown Agents Committee of Inquiry, Report by the committee of inquiry into the circumstances which led to the Crown Agents requesting financial assistance from the Government in 1974, (Her Majesty's Stationary Office, London, December, 1977)

Cullen, Jim, *The American Dream: a short history of an idea that shaped a nation* (Oxford University Press, Oxford, 2004)

Cunliffe, Jon,

——— 'Credit: can trees grow to the sky?', speech at the British Property Federation Annual Residential Investment Conference, London, 9 February 2016, www.bankofengland.co.uk/speech/2016/credit-can-trees-grow-to-the-sky (accessed 12 August 2019)

——— Remarks at the Alastair Ross Goobey Memorial Lecture, London, 26 April 2016, www.bankofengland.co.uk/-/media/boe/files/speech/2016/remarks-at-the-alastair-ross-goobey-memorial-lecture (accessed 12 August 2019)

Daintith, Terence, 'Between domestic democracy and an alien rule of law? Some thoughts on the independence of the Bank of England', in Mads Andenas, Laurence Gormley,

Christos Hadjiemmanuil and Ian Harden (eds), *European economic and monetary union: the institutional framework* (Kluwer Law International, London, 1997)

Danisewicz, Piotr, Dennis Reinhardt and Rhiannon Sowerbutts, 'On a tight leash: does bank organisational structure matter for macroprudential spillovers?', (2015) Bank of England Working Paper No. 524, www.bankofengland.co.uk/working-paper/2015/on-a-tight-leash-does-bank-organisational-structure-matter-for-macroprudential-spillovers (accessed 12 August 2019)

Darbar, Salim and Xiaoyong Wu, 'Experiences with macroprudential policy – five case studies', (2015) IMF Working Paper WP/15/123, www.imf.org/en/Publications/WP/Issues/2016/12/31/Experiences-with-Macroprudential-Policy-Five-Case-Studies-43008 (accessed 12 August 2019)

Das, Udaibir and Marc Quintyn, 'Financial crisis prevention and management: the role of regulatory governance', in Robert Litan, Michael Pomerleano and Vasudevan Sundsrarajan (eds), *Financial sector governance: the roles of the public and private sectors* (World Bank/IMF/Brookings Publications, Washington DC, 2002), 163–208

Davis, Philip, *Debt, financial fragility and systemic risk* (Clarendon Press, Oxford, 1992)

De Larosière, Jacques, oral evidence to the House of Lords European Union Committee for its 14th Report of Session 2008–09 on 'The future of EU financial regulation and supervision', 149, https://publications.parliament.uk/pa/ld200809/ldselect/ldeucom/106/10602.htm (accessed 12 August 2019)

Dell'Ariccia, Giovanni and others, 'Policies for macrofinancial stability: how to deal with credit booms', (2012), IMF Staff Discussion Note, No. 12/06, www.imf.org/external/pubs/ft/sdn/2012/sdn1206.pdf (accessed 12 August 2019)

Dell'Ariccia, Giovanni, Deniz Igan and Luc Laevan, 'Credit booms and lending standards: evidence from the subprime mortgage market', (2012) *Journal of Money, Credit and Banking*, Vol. 44, Nos. 2–3, 367

De Mooij, Ruud, Michael Keen and Masanori Orihara, 'Taxation, bank leverage, and financial crises', (2013) IMF Working Paper, www.imf.org/en/Publications/WP/Issues/2016/12/31/Taxation-Bank-Leverage-and-Financial-Crises-40341 (accessed 12 August 2019)

Demyanyk, Yuliya and Elena Loutskina, 'Mortgage companies and regulatory arbitrage', (2015) www.clevelandfed.org/newsroom-and-events/publications/working-papers/2015-working-papers/wp-1220r4-mortgage-companies-and-regulatory-arbitrage.aspx (accessed 12 August 2019)

Demyanyk, Yuliya and Otto Van Hemert, 'Understanding the subprime mortgage crisis', (2008) Federal Reserve Board of St. Louis Supervisory Policy Analysis Working Paper, www.stlouisfed.org/~/media/files/pdfs/banking/spa_2007_05.pdf?la=en (accessed 12 August 2019)

De Nicoló, Gianni, Giovanni Favara and Lev Ratnovski, 'Externalities and macroprudential policy', (2012) IMF Staff Discussion Notes, No. SDN/12/05, www.imf.org/external/pubs/ft/sdn/2012/sdn1205.pdf (accessed 12 August 2019)

Department of Housing, Communities and Local Government, 'House building', Table 244, (updated 4 July 2019), www.gov.uk/government/statistical-data-sets/live-tables-on-house-building (accessed 23 July 2019)

Department for Communities and Local Government White Paper, 'Fixing our broken housing market', (Cmd 9352, February 2017), www.gov.uk/government/uploads/system/uploads/attachment_data/file/590464/Fixing_our_broken_housing_market_-_print_ready_version.pdf (accessed 12 August 2019)

Department of Housing, Communities and Local Government, Budget 2016, UK Housing benefit, Table 1b: expenditure by benefit, www.gov.uk/government/statistics/housing-benefit-caseload-statistics (accessed 28 July 2019)

Department of Communities and Local Government (DCLG), '2014-based household projections: England, 2014–2039', (12 July 2016), 1, www.gov.uk/government/statistics/2014-based-household-projections-in-england-2014-to-2039 (accessed 14 August 2019)

Department of Housing, Communities and Local Government, English Housing Survey Home ownership, 2016–17, Table AT1.1, www.gov.uk/government/statistics/english-housing-survey-2016-to-2017-home-ownership (accessed 25 July 2019)

Department of Financial Institutions, 'FYI financial news – updates from DFI's Consumer Services', (Winter 2014), www.dfi.wa.gov/cs-newsletter/2014/issue1/changing-companies-best-practices.htm (accessed 23 July 2017)

Department of Housing and Urban Development, 'A blueprint for the American Dream: a public/private partnership to increase minority homeownership by 5.5 million by the end of the decade', (2003), https://archives.hud.gov/content/focus/2002-10-18.cfm (accessed 14 August 2019)

Department of Trade and Industry Report, 'Modern methods of construction in Germany – playing the off-site rule', (2004), www3.imperial.ac.uk/pls/portallive/docs/1/40872.PDF (accessed 14 August 2019)

Department of Work and Pensions (DWP), 'Housing benefit expenditure' in 'Benefit expenditure and caseload tables 2019', Table 1b (April 2019), www.gov.uk/government/publications/benefit-expenditure-and-caseload-tables-2019 (accessed 16 July 2019)

Devereux, Michael, John Vella and Niels Johannesen, 'Can taxes tame the banks? Evidence from European bank levies', (2013), Oxford University Centre for Business Taxation, WP 13/25, https://papers.ssrn.com/sol3/papers.cfm?abstract_id=2563634 (accessed 14 August 2019)

Dhu, Trevor and others, 'Earthquake risk assessment for Perth, Western Australia', 13th World Conference on Earthquake Engineering Vancouver, B.C., Canada, (August 2004), Paper No. 2748, www.iitk.ac.in/nicee/wcee/article/13_2748.pdf (accessed 23 July 2019)

Diamond, Douglas and Philip Dybvig, 'Bank runs, deposit insurance, and liquidity', (1983) *The Journal of Political Economy*, Vol. 91, No. 3, 401, www.macroeconomics.tu-berlin.de/fileadmin/fg124/financial_crises/literature/Diamon_Dybvig_Bank_Runs__Deposit_Insurance__and_Liquidity.pdf (accessed 14 August 2019)

Ding, Lei, Roberto Quercia, Carolina Reid and Alan White 'The impact of Federal preemption of state antipredatory lending laws on the foreclosure crisis', (Spring 2012) *Journal of Policy Analysis and Management*, Vol. 31, No. 2, 367–387

Di Lorenzo, Vincent, 'Barriers to market discipline: a comparative study of mortgage market reforms', (2012) *Arizona Journal of International and Comparative Law*, Vol. 29, 517

Di Maggio, Marco and Amir Kermani, 'Credit-induced boom and bust', (2016) Harvard Business School Working Paper 17-010

DiPasquale, Denise and Edward Glaeser, 'Incentives and social capital: are homeowners better citizens?', (1999) *Journal of Urban Economics*, Vol. 45, 354–384

Dolphin, Tony and Matt Griffith, 'Forever blowing bubbles? Housing's role in the UK economy', (May 2011), Institute for Public Policy Research Report, www.ippr.org/files/images/media/files/publication/2011/06/forever_blowing_bubbles_May2011_7576.pdf?noredirect=1 (accessed 14 August 2019)

Doring, Danny, *All that is solid* (Penguin, London, 2014)

Drehmann, Mathias, Claudio Borio and Kostas Tsatsaronis, 'Anchoring countercyclical capital buffers: the role of credit aggregates', (2011) Bank of International Settlement Working Paper 355, www.bis.org/publ/work355.pdf (accessed 14 August 2019)

Dunstan, Ashley, 'The interaction between monetary and macroprudential policy', (June 2014) *Reserve Bank of New Zealand Bulletin*, Vol. 77(2), 15–25

Durkheim, Emile, *The division of labour in society* (first published 1893, Macmillan, London in 1984)

Dworkin, Ronald, *Law's empire* (Hart Publishing, Oxford, 1998)

Dyzenhaus, David, 'Herman Heller', in Arthur Jacobson and Berhard Schlink (eds), *Weimar: a jurisprudence in crisis* (University of California Press, Berkeley, 2000)

Easton, David,

——— *A systems analysis of political life* (John Wiley, New York, 1965)

——— 'An approach to the analysis of political systems', (April 1957) *World Politics*, Vol. 9, No. 3, 383–400

Edey, Malcolm, (Assistant Governor (Financial System) of the Reserve Bank of Australia), 'Macroprudential supervision and the role of central banks', remarks to the Regional Policy Forum on Financial Stability and Macroprudential Supervision, Beijing, 28 September 2012, www.bis.org/review/r121002e.pdf (accessed 14 August 2019)

Edge, Rochelle and Ralf Meisenzahl, 'The unreliability of credit-to-GDP ratio gaps in real time: implications for countercyclical capital buffers', (2011) *International Journal of Central Banking*, Vol. 7, No. 4, 261, www.ijcb.org/journal/ijcb11q4a10.pdf (accessed 14 August 2019)

Eichengreen, Barry and Michael Bordo, 'Crises now and then: what lessons from the last era of financial globalization?', (2002), National Bureau of Economic Research, Working Paper 8716, www.nber.org/papers/w8716.pdf (accessed 14 August 2019)

Elliehausen, Gregory, 'Implications of behavioral research for the use and regulation of consumer credit products', (2010) Finance and Economics Discussion Series, Federal Reserve Board, Washington, DC. www.federalreserve.gov/pubs/feds/2010/201025/201025pap.pdf (accessed 14 August 2019)

Ellis, Luci,

——— 'Macroprudential policy: a suite of tools or a state of mind?', speech at Paul Woolley Centre for the Study of Capital Market Dysfunctionality Annual Conference, Sydney, 11th October 2012, www.rba.gov.au/speeches/2012/sp-so-111012.html (accessed 14 August 2019)

——— 'Macroprudential policy: what have we learned?', Paper presented to the Bank of England's Centre for Central Banking Studies Workshop, London, 6th March 2013, http://studylib.net/doc/10808262/macroprudential-policy--what-have-we-learned%3F-1 (accessed 14 August 2019)

——— 'Prudent mortgage lending standards help ensure financial stability', address to the Australian Mortgage Conference, Sydney, 23rd February 2012, www.rba.gov.au/speeches/2012/pdf/sp-so-230212.pdf (accessed 14 August 2019)

Elliott, Douglas, Greg Feldberg and Andreas Lehnert, 'The history of cyclical macroprudential policy in the United States', (2013) Office of Financial Research Working Paper No. 8, Department of the Treasury, Washington DC, 1–74, www.federalreserve.gov/pubs/feds/2013/201329/201329pap.pdf (accessed 14 August 2019)

Elliott, Douglas, 'Choosing among macroprudential tools', (2011) The Brookings Institution, www.brookings.edu/~/media/research/files/papers/2011/6/07-macroprudential-tools-elliott/0607_macroprudential_tools_elliott.pdf (accessed 14 August 2019)

Elliott, Geoffrey, *The Mystery of Overend and Gurney* (Methuen Publishing, London, 2006)

Engel, Kathleen and Patricia McCoy, 'A tale of three markets: the law and economics of predatory lending', (2002) *Texas Law Review*, Vol. 80, 1255

Ernst, Keith, Debbie Bocian and Wei Li, 'Steering wrong: brokers, borrowers and subprime loans', (8th April 2008), *Centre for Responsible Lending*, www.responsiblelending.org/mortgage-lending/research-analysis/steered-wrong-brokers-borrowers-and-subprime-loans.pdf (accessed 14 August 2019)

Estelami, Hooman, 'An ethnographic study of consumer financial sophistication', (2014) *Journal of Consumer Behaviour*, Vol. 13, 328

European Central Bank (ECB)

——— European Central Bank, 'Housing finance in the Euro area', (March 2009) Occasional Paper Series, No. 101, www.ecb.europa.eu/pub/pdf/scpops/ecbocp101.pdf (accessed 14 August 2019)

——— European Central Bank, 'The concept of systemic risk', (December 2009) *Financial Stability Review*, www.ecb.europa.eu/pub/pdf/fsr/art/ecb.fsrart200912_02.en.pdf?39462a69bb594e9a7f14091c0085c132 (accessed 14 August 2019)

——— European Central Bank, 'Report on the first two years of the macroprudential research network', (2012), www.ecb.europa.eu/pub/pdf/other/macroprudentialresearchnetworkreport201210en.pdf?9128ec92dc0cecb03809405c3dda1cc8 (accessed 14 August 2019)

——— European Central Bank, 'Final report on the macroprudential research network', (2014), www.ecb.europa.eu/pub/pdf/other/macroprudentialresearchnetworkreport201406en.pdf?85baea11d510f7f46f2de53f0c0d1c67 (accessed 14 August 2019)

European Systemic Risk Board (ESRB)

——— ESRB, 'Recommendations on intermediate objectives and instruments of macroprudential policy', (4th April 2013), ESRB/2013/1, 2013/C 170/01), www.esrb.europa.eu/pub/pdf/recommendations/2013/ESRB_2013_1.en.pdf (accessed 14 August 2019)

——— ESRB, 'Vulnerabilities in the EU residential real estate sector', (November 2016) www.esrb.europa.eu/pub/pdf/reports/161128_vulnerabilities_eu_residential_real_estate_sector.en.pdf (accessed 14 August 2019)

——— ESRB, Ferrari, Stijn, Mara Pirovano and Wanda Cornacchia, 'Identifying early warning indicators for real estate-related banking crises', (2015) European Systemic Risk Board Occasional Paper No. 8

EU Commission, 'Green Paper on retail financial services', (December 2015), http://ec.europa.eu/finance/consultations/2015/retail-financial-services/docs/green-paper_en.pdf (accessed 14 August 2019)

EU Parliament, 'Committee on economic and monetary affairs hearing on 15th February 2016', www.ecb.europa.eu/press/key/date/2016/html/sp160215_Transcript_and_QandA.en.pdf?76c3f099ccd202671b1f97e065a74c09 (accessed 14 August 2019)

Evans, Peter, *Embedding autonomy: states and industrial transformation* (Princeton University Press, Princeton, NJ, 1995)

Favara, Giovanni and Jean Imbs, 'Credit supply and the price of housing', (2015) *American Economic Review*, Vol. 105, No. 3, 958–992

Federal Housing Administration, 'Underwriting manual', 'Rating of location: protection from adverse influences, Part II', (1936), https://ontheline.trincoll.edu/images/1936-fha-manual-226.pdf (accessed 15 August 2019)

Federal National Mortgage Association ('Fannie Mae'), 'Securities and Exchange Commission 10-K report for the year to 31st December 2005', www.fanniemae.com/

resources/file/ir/pdf/quarterly-annual-results/2005/form10k_050207.pdf (accessed 15 August 2019)
Federal Register, Vol. 78, No. 183, 20 September 2013, Proposed Rules, 57989, file:///N:/Downloads/2013-21677.pdf (accessed 7 July 2019)
Federal Reserve, 'Quarterly report on balance sheet developments', (November 2016) www.federalreserve.gov/monetarypolicy/files/quarterly_balance_sheet_developments_report_201611.pdf (accessed 15 August 2019)
Federal Trade Commission, 'Improving consumer mortgage disclosures: an empirical assessment of current and prototype disclosure forms', (2007) *Federal Trade Commission, Bureau of Economics Staff Report*, www.ftc.gov/sites/default/files/documents/reports/improving-consumer-mortgage-disclosures-empirical-assessment-current-and-prototype-disclosure-forms/p025505mortgagedisclosurereport.pdf (accessed 15 August 2019)
Ferran, Eilis and others, *The regulatory aftermath of the global financial crisis* (Cambridge University Press, Cambridge, 2013)
Fessler, James, 'The Brownlow Committee fifty years later', (1987) *Public Administrative Review*, Vol. 47, No. 4, 291–296
Field, Alexander, 'The interwar housing cycle in the light of 2001–2012: a comparative historical perspective', in Eugene White, Kenneth Snowden and Price Fishback (eds), *Housing and mortgage markets in historical perspective* (National Bureau of Economic Research, University of Chicago Press, Chicago, 2014), 39–80
The Financial Crisis Inquiry Report, (January 2011), The Financial Crisis Inquiry Commission, www.gpo.gov/fdsys/pkg/GPO-FCIC/pdf/GPO-FCIC.pdf (accessed 15 August 2019)
Financial Conduct Authority
——— FCA, (Consultation Paper P19/17), 'Consultation on mortgage advice and selling standards', (May 2019), www.fca.org.uk/publications/consultation-papers/cp19-17-mortgage-advice-and-selling-standards (accessed 20 August 2019)
——— FCA, 'Our future mission', (October 2016), www.fca.org.uk/publication/corporate/our-future-mission.pdf (accessed 15 August 2019).
——— FCA, 'Call for inputs on competition in the mortgage sector', (October 2015), www.fca.org.uk/your-fca/documents/cfi-mortgage-sector (accessed 15 August 2019)
——— FCA, (Consultation Paper 15/22), 'Strengthening accountability in banking', (July 2015), www.fca.org.uk/static/documents/consultation-papers/cp15-22.pdf (accessed 15 August 2019)
——— FCA, 'Embedding the mortgage market review: advice and distribution: thematic review, TR15/9', (July 2015), www.fca.org.uk/static/documents/thematic-reviews/tr15-09.pdf (accessed 15 August 2019)
——— FCA, 'PS15/9: Implementation of the Mortgage Credit Directive and the new regime for second charge mortgages, feedback to CP14/20 and final rules', (March 2015), www.fca.org.uk/your-fca/documents/policy-statements/ps15-09 (accessed 15 August 2019)
——— FCA, 'Economics for effective regulation', (2014), Occasional Paper 13, www.fca.org.uk/publication/occasional-papers/occassional-paper-13.pdf (accessed 15 August 2019)
——— FCA research by Oxera, 'Review of literature on product disclosure', (October 2014), www.fca.org.uk/publication/research/review-of-literature-on-product-disclosure.pdf (accessed 15 August 2019)

——— FCA, 'Applying behavioural economics at the Financial Conduct Authority', (April 2013), www.fca.org.uk/static/documents/occasional-papers/occasional-paper-1.pdf (accessed 15 August 2019)

Financial Services Authority

——— FSA, 'Policy Statement 12/16 Mortgage Market Review feedback on CP11/31 and final rules', (October 2012), www.fca.org.uk/publication/policy/fsa-ps12-16.pdf (accessed 15 August 2019)

——— FSA, 'Mortgage Market Review, CP 11/31', (December 2011), www.fca.org.uk/publication/consultation/fsa-cp11-31.pdf (accessed 15 August 2019)

——— FSA, 'Fines table: 2011'

——— FSA, 'Consultation Paper 28/10: Mortgage Market Review: distribution & disclosure', (November 2010), www.fca.org.uk/publication/consultation/fsa-cp10-28.pdf (accessed 15 August 2019)

——— FSA, 'Mortgage Market Review, Discussion Paper 09/3', (October 2009), www.fca.org.uk/publication/discussion/fsa-dp09-03.pdf (accessed 15 August 2019)

——— FSA, 'Mortgage effectiveness review: stage 2 report', (March 2008)

——— FSA, 'Treating customers fairly – towards fair outcomes for consumers', (July 2006), www.fca.org.uk/publication/archive/fsa-tcf-towards.pdf (accessed 15 August 2019)

——— FSA, 'Mortgage regulation: draft conduct of business rules and feedback on CP146', (2003), CP 186

——— FSA, 'Approach to regulating mortgage sales', (2002), CP 146

——— FSA, 'Enforcement action against Abbey Life Insurance (part of Lloyds Bank) for mis-selling mortgage endowment policies between 1995 and 1999', (2002), www.fca.org.uk/publication/final-notices/abbey-life_2dec02.pdf (accessed 15 August 2019)

——— FSA, 'Choosing a mortgage, report of a research review and qualitative research on the mortgage buying process', (2001)

——— FSA, 'The draft Mortgage Sourcebook, including policy statement on CP70 (CP98)', (July 2001)

——— FSA, 'Mortgage regulation: the FSA's high level approach', (CP 70), (November 2000)

——— FSA, 'A cost-benefit analysis of statutory regulation of mortgage advice', (October 1999)

Financial Ombudsman Service

——— 'On-line Technical Resource: compensation for being "deprived" of money and for investment loss', www.financial-ombudsman.org.uk/publications/technical_notes/compensation-for-investment-loss.htm (accessed 15 August 2019)

Financial Policy Committee (FPC)

——— FPC meeting minutes, 19 March 2013, www.bankofengland.co.uk/statement/fpc/2013/financial-policy-committee-statement-march-2013 (accessed 15 August 2019)

——— FPC meeting minutes, 20 November 2013, www.bankofengland.co.uk/-/media/boe/files/record/2013/financial-policy-committee-meeting-november-2013 (accessed 15 August 2019)

——— FPC meeting minutes, 24 March 2015, www.bankofengland.co.uk/-/media/boe/files/record/2015/financial-policy-committee-meeting-march-2015 (accessed 15 August 2019)

——— FPC meeting minutes, 25 and 30 November 2015, www.bankofengland.co.uk/-/media/boe/files/record/2015/financial-policy-committee-meeting-december-2015 (accessed 15 August 2019)
——— FPC meeting minutes, 20 September 2016, www.bankofengland.co.uk/statement/fpc/2016/financial-policy-committee-statement-september-2016 (accessed 15 August 2019)
——— FPC meeting minutes 23 and 29 November 2016, www.bankofengland.co.uk/-/media/boe/files/record/2016/financial-policy-committee-meeting-december-2016 (accessed 15 August 2019)
——— FPC, 'Framework for the systemic risk buffer: a consultation paper', (January 2016), www.bankofengland.co.uk/news/2016/january/fpc-framework-for-the-systemic-risk-buffer (accessed 15 August 2019)
——— FPC, 'Statement on housing market powers of direction from its policy meeting, 26th September 2014', www.bankofengland.co.uk/-/media/boe/files/statement/2014/fpc-statement-from-its-policy-meeting-26-september-2014 (accessed 15 August 2019)
Financial Stability Board (FSB)
——— FSB, 'Principles for sound residential mortgage underwriting practices', (April 2012), www.fsb.org/wp-content/uploads/r_120418.pdf?page_moved=1 (accessed 15 August 2019)
——— FSB, IMF and BIS, 'Macroprudential policy tools and frameworks progress report to G20', (October 2011), www.imf.org/external/np/g20/pdf/102711.pdf (accessed 15 August 2019)
——— FSB, 'Thematic review of residential mortgage underwriting and origination practices, peer review report', (17 March 2011) www.financialstabilityboard.org/publications/r_110318a.pdf (accessed 15 August 2019)
——— FSB, 'Peer review of Spain', (January 2011), www.fsb.org/wp-content/uploads/r_110207a.pdf?page_moved=1 (accessed 15 August 2019)
Fiorina, Morris, 'Legislative choice of regulatory forms: legal process or administrative process', (1982) *Public Choice*, Vol. 39, No. 1, 33–66
Fischer, Stanley,
——— 'Macroprudential monetary policy', speech, 59th Economic Conference of the Federal Reserve Bank of Boston, Boston, Massachusetts, 2 October 2015, www.bis.org/review/r151006a.pdf (accessed 15 August 2019)
——— 'Macroprudential policy in action: Israel', in George Akerlof, Olivier Blanchard, David Romer and Joseph Stiglitz (eds), *What have we learned? Macroprudential policy after the crisis* (MIT Press, Cambridge, MA, 2014)
——— Financial sector reform: how are are we?', Martin Feldstein lecture at the National Bureau of Economic Research, Cambridge, Massachusetts, 10th July 2014, www.federalreserve.gov/newsevents/speech/fischer20140710a.htm (accessed 15 August 2019)
Fishback, Price and John Wallis, 'What was new about the New Deal?', in Nicholas Craft and Peter Fearon (eds), *The Great Depression of the 1930s: lessons for today* (Oxford University Press, Oxford, 2013)
Fisher, Paul, 'Microprudential, macroprudential and monetary policy: conflict, compromise or co-ordination?' speech at Richmond University, London, 1 October 2014, www.bankofengland.co.uk/speech/2014/microprudential-macroprudential-and-monetary-policy-conflict-compromise-or-co-ordination (accessed 15 August 2019)
Floros, Ioannis and Joshua White. 'Qualified residential mortgages and default risk', (2016) *Journal of Banking and Finance*, Vol. 70, 86–104

Ford, Gerald, 'Remarks on signing the Housing and Community Development Act of 1974', on 22 August 1974, The American Presidency Project website, www.presidency.ucsb.edu/documents/remarks-signing-the-housing-and-community-development-act-1974 (accessed 25 June 2019)

Foster Lloyd, William, 'Checks to population', (first published 1833 and reprinted 1980) *Population and Development Review*, Vol. 6, No. 3, 473, www.jstor.org/stable/1972412?loginSuccess=true&seq=2#page_scan_tab_contents (accessed 15 August 2019)

Fox, Mark and David Lane, 'Lessons from the US subprime mortgage crisis', (2008) *Journal of International Banking Law and Regulation*, 23(9), 449–457

Francis, William, 'UK deposit-taker responses to the financial crisis: what are the lessons?', (2014) Bank of England, Working Paper No. 501, www.bankofengland.co.uk/-/media/boe/files/working-paper/2014/uk-deposit-taker-responses-to-the-financial-crisis-what-are-the-lessons (accessed 15 August 2019)

Franck, Thomas, 'The emerging right to democratic governance', (1992) *American Journal of International Law*, Vol. 86, 46–91

Fraser, Derek, *The evolution of the British welfare state* (Palgrave Macmillan, Basingstoke, 2009)

Freixas, Xavier, Luc Laevan and José-Luis Peydró, *Systemic risk, crises, and macroprudential regulation* (MIT, Cambridge, MA, 2015)

Frydl, Kathleen, *The GI Bill* (Cambridge University Press, Cambridge, 2009)

FTI Consulting, 'Understanding supply constraints in the housing market', (July 2012), https://england.shelter.org.uk/__data/assets/pdf_file/0006/576906/120716_Understanding_Supply_Constraints_in_the_Housing_Market.pdf (accessed 15 August 2019)

Galati, Gabriele and Richhild Moessner, 'Macroprudential policy – a literature review', (2011), BIS Working Papers No. 337, www.bis.org/publ/work337.pdf (accessed 15 August 2017)

Galbraith, John S. 'The "turbulent frontier" as a factor in British expansion', (1960) *Comparative Studies in Society and History*, Vol. 2, No. 2, 150

Galeoto, Laureen and others, 'The Consumer Financial Protection Bureau: the new sheriff in town', (2012) *Banking Law Journal*, Vol. 129, 702

Garriga, Carlos, William T. Gavin and Don Schlagenhauf, 'Recent trends in homeownership', (September/October 2006) *Federal Reserve Bank of St. Louis Review*, Vol. 88, No. 5, 397–411, https://research.stlouisfed.org/publications/review/06/09/Garriga.pdf (accessed 15 August 2019)

Geithner, Timothy, *Stress test* (Random House Business Books, New York, 2014)

Gelain, Paolo, Kevin Lansing and Gisle Natvik, 'Leaning against the credit cycle', (2015) Norges Bank Research Working Paper, 04/2015, http://static.norges-bank.no/pages/102776/Working_Paper_04_15.pdf?v=12/10/2015104436AM&ft=.pdf (accessed 15 August 2019)

Gerardi, Kristopher, Lorenz Goette and Stephan Meier, 'Financial literacy and subprime mortgage delinquency: evidence from a survey matched to administrative data', (2010) Federal Reserve Bank of Atlanta, Working Paper 2010–10

Gerlach, Stefan, 'Housing markets and financial stability', speech at the National University of Ireland, Galway, 20 April 2012, www.bis.org/review/r120424c.pdf (accessed 15 August 2019)

Giese, Julia and others, 'The credit-to-GDP gap and complementary indicators for macroprudential policy: evidence from the UK', (2014) *International Journal of Finance and Economics*, Vol. 19, No. 1, 25, www.nottingham.ac.uk/cfcm/documents/conferences/2013/julia-giese.pdf (accessed 15 August 2019)

Glaeser, Edward and Bryce Ward, 'The causes and consequences of land use regulation: evidence from Greater Boston', (2009) *Journal of Urban Economics*, Vol. 65, 265–278

Glaeser, Edward, Joshua Gottlieb and Joseph Gyourko, 'Can cheap credit explain the housing boom? (2010), National Bureau of Economic Research, Working Paper, 16230, www.nber.org/papers/w16230.pdf (accessed 15 August 2019)

Glaeser, Edward and Joseph Gyourko, 'The impact of zoning on housing affordability' (March 2002), Harvard Institute of Economic Research Discussion Paper No. 1948

Glinkowska, Beata and Boguslaw Kaczmarek, 'Classical and modern concepts of corporate governance (stewardship theory and agency theory)', (2015) *Management*, Vol. 19, No. 2, 84–92

Goodhart, Charles,

——— 'Lessons for monetary policy from the Euro-area crisis', (2013), 4, Bank of Greece conference on 'The crisis in the Euro-area', Athens, 23–24 May 2013, www.bankofgreece.gr/BogEkdoseis/SCP201317.pdf (accessed 15 August 2019)

——— 'Property finance has been the main common factor', (written evidence to the Parliamentary Commission on Banking Standards, House of Commons, 24 October 2012), www.publications.parliament.uk/pa/jt201314/jtselect/jtpcbs/27/27v_we80.htm (accessed 16 August 2019)

——— 'The macroprudential authority: powers, scope and accountabilities', (2011) *OECD Journal: Financial Market Trends*, No. 2, www.oecd.org/finance/financial-markets/48979021.pdf (accessed 15 August 2019)

——— *The regulatory response to the financial crisis* (Edward Elgar Publishing, Cheltenham, 2009)

Goodhart, Charles and P.J.R. Delargy, 'Financial crises: plus ca change, plus c'est la meme chose', (1999), Special Paper No. 108, London School of Economics Financial Markets Group, 261, http://pages.stern.nyu.edu/~dbackus/BCH/history/Goodhart Delargy_pluscachange_02.pdf (accessed 15 August 2019)

Goodhart, Charles and Rosa Lastra, 'Interaction between monetary policy and bank regulation', (21 September 2015), Report to the European Parliament, 37–54, www.europarl.europa.eu/RegData/etudes/IDAN/2015/563458/IPOL_IDA(2015)563458_EN.pdf (accessed 15 August 2019)

Goodhart, Charles, Dimitrios Tsomocos and Martin Shubik, 'Macro-modeling, default and money', (2013), London School of Economics, Financial Markets Group Special Paper 224, www.lse.ac.uk/fmg/assets/documents/papers/special-papers/SP224.pdf (accessed 15 August 2019)

Goodwin, Matthew, 'The Great Recession and the rise of populist Euroscepticism in the United Kingdom', in Hanspeter Kriesi and Takkis Pappas (eds), *European populism in the shadow of the great recession* (ECPR Press, Colchester, 2015), 273–286

Gorges, Michael, 'The new institutionalism and the study of the European union: the case of the social dialogue', (2001) *West European Politics*, Vol. 24, No. 4, 152–168

Gower, Laurence, 'Review of investor protection: report', Part 1, 6, 1984 H M Stationery Office, London, Cmnd 9125

Gray, Bryce, 'The Secure and Fair Enforcement for Mortgage Licensing Act of 2008', (2011) *Review of Banking and Financial Law*, Vol. 31, 51

Green, Kenneth and others, 'The impact of land-use regulation on housing supply in Canada', (July 2016), Fraser Institute, www.fraserinstitute.org/sites/default/files/impact-of-land-use-regulation-on-housing-supply-in-canada.pdf (accessed 24 July 2019)

Green, Richard, Gary Painter and Michelle White, 'Measuring the benefits of home-owning: effects on children redux', (2012), Research Institute for Housing America: Special Report, http://lusk.usc.edu/sites/default/files/Measuring-the-Benefits-of-Homeowning-11.05.12.pdf (accessed 15 August 2019)

Green, Richard and Susan Wachter, 'The American mortgage in historical and international context', (2005) *Journal of Economic Perspectives*, Vol. 19, No. 4, 93–114

Greenspan, Alan, 'Reflections on central banking', remarks at a symposium sponsored by the Federal Reserve Bank of Kansas City, Jackson Hole, Wyoming, 26 August 2005, www.federalreserve.gov/Boarddocs/speeches/2005/20050826/default.htm (accessed 15 August 2019)

Grice-Hutchinson, Marjorie, *The School of Salamanca, readings in Spanish monetary theory* (Clarendon Press, Oxford, 1952)

Griffith, Matt, 'We must fix it: delivering reform of the building sector to meet the UK's housing and economic challenges', (December 2011), Institute for Public Policy Research, www.ippr.org/files/images/media/files/publication/2012/02/we-must-fix-it_Dec2011_8421.pdf?noredirect=1 (accessed 15 August 2019)

The Group of Thirty, *Enhancing financial stability and resilience: macroprudential policy, tools, and systems for the future* (The Group of Thirty, Washington, DC, 2010), http://group30.org/images/uploads/publications/G30_EnhancingFinancialStability Resilience.pdf (accessed 15 August 2019)

Gurvitch, George, 'Magic and law', (1942) *Social Research*, Vol. 9, No. 1, 104–121

Haakonssen, Knud, 'Hugo Grotius and the history of political thought', in Knud Kaakonssen (ed), *Grotius, Pufendorf and modern natural law* (Dartmouth, Aldershot, 1999), 35–61

Habermas, Jürgen,

——— *Legitimation crisis* (first published in German 1973, translated Polity Press, Cambridge, 1988)

——— *Between facts and norms: contributions to a discourse theory of law and democracy* (Polity Press, Cambridge, 1996)

Haldane, Andrew,

———'Central bank psychology', speech at the 'Leadership: stress and hubris conference', hosted by the Royal Society of Medicine, London, 17 November 2014, www.bis.org/review/r141119a.pdf (accessed 15 August 2019)

———'Macroprudential policy in prospect', in George Akerlof, Olivier Blanchard, David Romer and Joseph Stiglitz (eds), *What have we learned? Macroprudential policy after the crisis* (The MIT Press, Cambridge, MA, 2014)

——— 'Macroprudential policies – when and how to use them', IMF seminar, 'Rethinking macro policy II: first steps and early lessons', Washington, DC, April 2013, www.imf.org/external/np/seminars/eng/2013/macro2/ (accessed 15 August 2019)

——— 'The dog and the frisbee', speech at Federal Reserve Bank of Kansas City's 36th economic policy symposium, 'The changing policy landscape', Jackson Hole, Wyoming, 31 August 2012, www.bis.org/review/r120905a.pdf (accessed 15 August 2019)

——— 'Financial arms races', speech at the Institute for New Economic Thinking, Berlin, 14 April 2012, www.bis.org/review/r120426a.pdf (accessed 15 August 2019)

——— 'Rethinking the financial network', speech at the Financial Student Association, Amsterdam, 28 April 2009, www.bis.org/review/r090505e.pdf (accessed 15 August 2019)

Hallissey, Niamh, Robert Kelly and Terry O'Malley, 'Macroprudential tools and credit risk of property lending in Irish banks', (2014) Central Bank of Ireland, Economic Letter Series, No. 10

Hanson, Samuel, Anil Kashyap and Jeremy Stein, 'A macroprudential approach to financial regulation', (2011) *Journal of Economic Perspectives*, Vol. 25, No. 1, http://scholar.harvard.edu/files/stein/files/a-macropurdenital-final.pdf?m=1360040289 (accessed 15 August 2019)

Harari, Daniel, 'Household debt: statistics and impact on economy', (August 2016) House of Commons Briefing Paper, No. 7584

Harris, Karen, 'Anticipatory regulation for the management of banking crises', (2005) *Columbia Journal of Law and Social Problems*, Vol. 38, 285

Hartmann, Philipp, 'Real estate markets and macroprudential policy in Europe', (May 2015) European Central Bank Working Paper No. 1796

Harvard University, 'State of the nation's housing', (2003), Joint Centre for Housing Studies, www.jchs.harvard.edu/sites/jchs.harvard.edu/files/son2003.pdf (accessed 15 August 2019)

Harvard University, 'State of the Nation's Housing report', (2019), The Joint Center for Housing Studies, www.jchs.harvard.edu/state-nations-housing-2019 (accessed 12 July 2019)

Haughwout, Andrew, Donhoon Lee, Joseph Tracy and Wilbert van der Klaauw, 'Real estate investors, the leverage cycle and the housing market crisis', (September 2011) Federal Reserve Bank of New York Staff Report No. 514, www.newyorkfed.org/medialibrary/media/research/staff_reports/sr514.pdf (accessed 15 August 2019)

Hayek, Friedrich, *New studies in philosophy, politics, economics and the history of ideas* (first published in 1967, Routledge, Oxford, 1978)

He, Dong,

——— 'The effects of macroprudential policies on housing market risks: evidence from Hong Kong', (2014), Banque de France Financial Stability Review, No. 18, www.banque-france.fr/fileadmin/user_upload/banque_de_france/publications/FSR18_DONG-HE.pdf (accessed 15 August 2019)

——— 'Hong Kong's approach to financial stability', (2013) *International Journal of Central Banking*, Vol. 9, No. 1, 299, www.ijcb.org/journal/ijcb13q1a12.htm (accessed 15 August 2019)

Henry George, *Progress and poverty: an inquiry into the cause of industrial depressions and of increase of want with increase of wealth: the remedy* (first published 1879, Robert Schalkenbach Foundation, New York City, 1935), https://mises.org/sites/default/files/Progress%20and%20Poverty_3.pdf (accessed 15 August 2019)

Hensarling, Jeb, 'The Monitor – Hensarling fights for East Texans', speech in Athens, Texas, 14 April 2014, https://hensarling.house.gov/media-center/in-the-news/the-monitor-hensarling-fights-for-east-texans (accessed 14 July 2017) – no longer available since the congressman's retirement in 2018 and the closure of his web-site

Hennessy, Peter, *Whitehall* (Secker and Warburg, London, 1989)

Hills, Robert and other, 'Cross-border regulatory spillovers: how much? How important? What sectors? Lessons from the United Kingdom', (2016) Bank of England Staff Working Paper No. 595, www.bankofengland.co.uk/working-paper/2016/cross-border-regulatory-spillovers-how-much-how-important-what-sectors-lessons-from-the-uk (accessed 15 August 2019)

Hinsley, Francis, *Sovereignty* (Cambridge University Press, Cambridge, 1986)

Hirschi, Caspar, *The origins of nationalism* (Cambridge University Press, Cambridge, 2012)

Hobbes, Thomas, *Leviathan* (first published 1651, Penguin Classics, London, 1985)

Hoggarth, Glenn, John Hooley and Yevgeniya Korniyenko, 'Which way do foreign branches sway? Evidence from the recent UK domestic credit cycle', (2013) Bank of England Financial Stability Paper No. 22, www.bankofengland.co.uk/financial-stability-paper/2013/which-way-do-foreign-branches-sway-evidence-from-the-recent-uk-domestic-credit-cycle (accessed 15 August 2019)

Holmans, Alan, 'New estimates of housing demand & need in England, 2011 to 2031', (2013) Town & Country Planning Tomorrow Series Paper 16, www.cchpr.landecon.cam.ac.uk/Downloads/HousingDemandNeed_TCPA2013.pdf (accessed 15 August 2019)

Home and Communities Agency, 'Get Britain Building, programme prospectus', (December 2011), www.gov.uk/government/uploads/system/uploads/attachment_data/file/345215/get_britain_building_programme_prospectus.pdf (accessed 15 August 2019)

House of Commons, Debates

——— Hunt, Tristram MP, 'The debate on the Housing and Planning Bill', 2 November 2015, Hansard Column 777, www.publications.parliament.uk/pa/cm201516/cmhansrd/cm151102/debtext/151102-0001.htm (accessed 15 August 2019)

——— Hilary Benn MP, debate on housing, 8 January 2014, column 328, https://publications.parliament.uk/pa/cm201314/cmhansrd/cm140108/debtext/140108-0002.htm (accessed 15 August 2019)

——— Debate on investor protection, 16 July 1984, vol. 64, 49–114, http://hansard.millbanksystems.com/commons/1984/jul/16/investor-protection-gower-report (accessed 15 August 2019)

——— Nelson, Anthony MP, speech on the Gower Report debate, Hansard, HC Deb, 16 July 1984, Vol. 64, 49–114, 87, http://hansard.millbanksystems.com/commons/1984/jul/16/investor-protection-gower-report (accessed 15 August 2019)

——— James Kidd MP for Linlithgowshire, debate on Housing Bill, 7 April 1919, Hansard Archive, Vol. 114, 1713–1820, 1754, http:/hansard.millbanksystems.com/commons/1919/apr/07/statement-by-dr-addison#S5CV0114P0_19190407_HOC_348 (accessed 15 August 2019)

House of Commons, Library

——— Library, 'Repossessions and mortgage arrears: statistics', (February 2011), SN/SG/0263

——— Library, 'Endowment mortgages', (8th June 2015), Briefing Paper 570

House of Commons, reports,

——— Housing, Communities and Local Government Select Committee Report, 'Land Value Capture', Tenth Report of Session 2017–19, (September 2018), HC 766, https://publications.parliament.uk/pa/cm201719/cmselect/cmcomloc/766/766.pdf (accessed 22 August 2019)

——— Committee of Public Accounts, 'Departments' oversight of arm's-length bodies', Twenty-first Report of Session 2016–17, 21 October 2016, HC 488, www.publications.parliament.uk/pa/cm201617/cmselect/cmpubacc/488/488.pdf (accessed 15 August 2019)

——— Business Select Committee, 'Capacity of the homebuilding industry inquiry launched', (5 July 2016), www.parliament.uk/business/committees/committees-a-z/commons-select/communities-and-local-government-committee/news-parliament-2015/homebuilding-launch-16-17/ (accessed 15 August 2019)

House of Lords,
——— Select Committee on Economic Affairs, 'Building more homes', (15 July 2016), 1st Report of Session 2016–17, HL Paper 20, www.publications.parliament.uk/pa/ld201617/ldselect/ldeconaf/20/2002.htm (accessed 15 August 2019)
——— European Union Committee, 'The future of EU financial regulation and supervision', (2009), www.publications.parliament.uk/pa/ld200809/ldselect/ldeucom/106/106i.pdf (accessed 15 August 2019)
Hsieh, Wing, David Norman and David Orsmond, 'Supply-side issues in the housing sector', (September 2012), *Reserve Bank of Australia Bulletin*, www.rba.gov.au/publications/bulletin/2012/sep/pdf/bu-0912-2.pdf (accessed 17 July 2019)
Hughes Hallett, A. J., 'Econometrics and the theory of economic policy: the Tinbergen–Theil contributions 40 years on', (1989) *Oxford Economic Papers, New Series*, Vol. 41(1), 189–214, History and Methodology of Econometrics
Hull, Andy, (Institute for Public Policy Research) written evidence to: Communities and Local Government Committee, Financing of new housing supply: Eleventh Report of Session 2010–12 (The Stationary Office, London, 2012)
Hull, Andy, Graeme Cooke and Tony Dolphin, 'Build now or pay later: funding new housing supply', (October 2011), Institute for Public Policy Research Report, www.ippr.org/files/images/media/files/publication/2011/10/build-now-pay-later_Oct2011_8116.pdf?noredirect=1 (accessed 15 August 2019)
Hwang, Soosung, Sanha Noh and Jinho Shin, 'The price impact of deposit in residential lease contracts: the collapse of Chonsei system in Korea', (2015), https://papers.ssrn.com/sol3/papers.cfm?abstract_id=2546549 (accessed 16 August 2019)
Igan, Deniz and Heedon Kang, 'Do loan to value and debt to income limits work? Evidence from Korea', (2011) IMF Working Paper WP 11/297, www.imf.org/external/pubs/ft/wp/2011/wp11297.pdf (accessed 16 August 2019)
Independent Economists Group Report, 'The role of macroprudential policy in the policy framework', (June 2014), www.thecityuk.com/research/ieg-the-role-of-macro-prudential-policy-in-the-policy-framework/ (accessed 16 August 2019)
International Monetary Fund
——— Country Report (January 2014) No. 14/48 on Israel, www.imf.org/external/pubs/ft/scr/2014/cr1448.pdf (accessed 16 August 2019)
——— 'Key aspects of macroprudential policy', (10 June 2013), www.imf.org/external/np/pp/eng/2013/061013b.pdf (accessed 16 August 2019)
——— 'The interaction of monetary and macroprudential policies', (29 January 2013), www.imf.org/external/np/pp/eng/2013/012913.pdf (accessed 16 August 2019)
——— 'When bubbles burst', (2003), IMF world economic and financial survey, Chapter II, 61, www.imf.org/external/pubs/ft/weo/2003/01/ (accessed 16 August 2019)
Isaacs, Julie, Isabel Sawhill and Ron Haskins, 'Getting ahead or losing ground: economic mobility in America', (2008), The Brookings Institute, Washington DC, www.pewtrusts.org/~/media/legacy/uploadedfiles/pcs_assets/2008/pewempgettingaheadfull2pdf.pdf (accessed 16 August 2019)
Jackson, John, 'Sovereignty-modern: a new approach to an outdated concept', (2003) *American Journal of International Law*, Vol. 97, 782–802
Jackson, Kenneth, *Crabgrass frontier: the suburbanization of the United States* (Oxford University Press, Oxford, 1985)
Jácome, Luis and Erlend Nier, 'Macroprudential policy: protecting the whole', (March 2012) IMF Finance and Development, www.imf.org/external/pubs/ft/fandd/basics/macropru.htm (accessed 16 August 2019)

Jácome, Luis and Srobona Mitra, 'LTV and DTI limits – going granular', (2015) IMF Working Paper WP/15/154, www.imf.org/external/pubs/ft/wp/2015/wp15154.pdf (accessed 16 August 2019)

James, David, 'Rousseau on needs, language and pity: the limits of "public reason"', (2011) *European Journal of Political Theory*, Vol. 10, No. 3, 372–393

Jeanne, Olivier and Anton Korinek, 'Managing credit booms and busts: a Pigouvian taxation approach', (2010) National Bureau of Economics Research Working Paper No. 16377, www.nber.org/papers/w16377 (accessed 16 August 2019)

Jebens, Kit, Lautro, a pioneer regulator 1986–1994, (private printing, author's collection, 1997)

Jensen, Siv, Norwegian Finance Minister, 'How to ensure financial stability in a European environment?' speech at the Policy Exchange, 6 April 2018, https://policyexchange.org.uk/pxevents/speech-norwegian-minister-of-finance-siv-jensen/ (accessed 11 July 2019)

Jervis, Robert, 'Unipolarity: a structural perspective', in John Ikenberry, Michael Mastanduno and William Wohlforth (eds), *International relations theory and the consequences of unipolarity* (Cambridge University Press, Cambridge, 2011)

Jiménez, Gabriel and Jesús Saurina, 'Credit cycles, credit risk, and prudential regulation', (2006) *International Journal of Central Banking*, Vol. 2, No. 2, 64–98

Jiménez, Gabriel, Steven Ongena, José-Luis Peydró and Jesús Saurina, 'Macroprudential policy, countercyclical bank capital buffers and credit supply: evidence from the Spanish dynamic provisioning experiments', (December 2017) *Journal of Political Economy*, Vol. 125, No. 6, 2126–2177, www.journals.uchicago.edu/doi/pdfplus/10.1086/694289 (accessed 16 August 2019)

Johnson, Lyndon, 'Special message to the Congress on urban problems: the crisis of the cities.' (22 February 1968), The American Presidency Project website, www.presidency.ucsb.edu/documents/special-message-the-congress-urban-problems-the-crisis-the-cities (accessed 25 June 2019)

Jolls, Christine and others, 'A behavioral approach to law and economics', (1998) *Stanford Law Review*, Vol. 50, 1471

Jones, Greg, 'Mortgage lending: confusing in every language', (2012) *Loyola University of Chicago School of Law, Consumer Law Review*, Vol. 24, 661

Jordà, Òscar, Moritz Schularick and Alan Taylor, 'The great mortgaging: housing finance, crises and business cycle', (2014) Federal Reserve Bank of San Francisco, Working Paper Series 2014–23, www.frbsf.org/economic-research/files/wp2014-23.pdf (accessed 16 August 2019)

Jordà, Òscar, Moritz Schularick and Alan Taylor, 'Betting the house', (December 2014) National Bureau of Economic Research, Working Paper 20771

Judge, Lindsay, 'Housing affordability in the UK', (April 2016) Resolution Foundation charts, www.resolutionfoundation.org/wp-content/uploads/2016/04/slides-for-26-April.pdf (accessed 16 August 2019)

Kahneman, Daniel, 'Maps of bounded rationality: a perspective on intuitive judgement and choice', (8 December 2002) Nobel Prize Lecture, www.nobelprize.org/prizes/economic-sciences/2002/kahneman/lecture/ (accessed 16 August 2019)

Kapodistrias, Ioannis, Letter to A. M. le Chevalier Eynard, February 1830, 'Correspondence de Comte Capodistrias', (1839), 3, Geneva, 472–473, Bibliothèque Université De Genève

Kashyap, Anil and Jeremy Stein, 'The optimal conduct of monetary policy with interest on reserves', (2012) *American Economic Journal: Macroeconomics*, Vol. 4, No. 1, 266, http://scholar.harvard.edu/files/stein/files/optimalconduct.pdf?m=1363374269 (accessed 16 August 2019)

Kaufman, Henry, 'Debt: the threat to economic and financial stability', (1986) *Economic Review, Federal Reserve Bank of Kansas*, Vol. 71, No. 10, 3, www.kansascityfed.org/PUBLICAT/EconRev/EconRevArchive/1986/4q86-D.pdf (accessed 16 August 2019)

Kennedy, Leonard, Patricia McCoy and Ethan Bernstein, 'The Consumer Financial Protection Bureau: financial regulation for the twenty-first century', (2012) *Cornell Law Review*, Vol. 97, 1141

Kim, Choongsoo, 'Macroprudential policies in Korea: key measures and experiences', (2014) Banque de France Financial Stability Review, No. 18, www.banque-france.fr/fileadmin/user_upload/banque_de_france/publications/FSR18_Kim.pdf (accessed 16 August 2019)

Kindleberger, Charles, *Manias, panics and crashes* (Macmillan, London, 1978),

Kiyotaki, Nobuhiro and John Moore, 'Credit cycles', (1997) *Journal of Political Economy*, Vol. 105, No. 2, 211, www-users.york.ac.uk/~psm509/ULB2012/KiyotakiMooreJPE1997.pdf (accessed 16 August 2010)

Koenig, Evan, 'Like a good neighbor: monetary policy, financial stability, and the distribution of risk', (2013) *International Journal of Central Banking*, Vol. 9, 57, www.ijcb.org/journal/ijcb13q2a3.pdf (accessed 16 August 2019)

Kohn, Donald, 'Comparing UK and US macroprudential systems: lessons for China', speech at the Global Financial Forum, Tsinghua University, Beijing, 11 May 2014, www.bankofengland.co.uk/-/media/boe/files/speech/2014/comparing-uk-and-us-macroprudential-systems-lessons-for-china (accessed 16 August 2019)

Kolpfer, Eric, 'A mortgage insurer's look at Basel II and residential mortgage credit risk', (September 2002), *Housing Finance International*, Vol. 17, No. 1, 22–32

KPMG, 'Homebuilding market study: Annex E – study investigating financing for homebuilders' in the OFT's 2008 survey', (September 2008), www.hbf.co.uk/fileadmin/documents/Policy/OFT/OFT_Market_Study__Main_Report__Final._25_September_2008.pdf (accessed 16 August 2019)

KPMG and Shelter, 'Building the homes we need', (2014), www.shelter.org.uk/__data/assets/pdf_file/0019/802270/Building_the_homes_we_need_-_a_programme_for_the_2015_government.pdf (accessed 16 August 2019)

Krznar, Ivo and James Morsink, 'With great power comes great responsibility: macroprudential tools at work in Canada', (2014) IMF Working Paper 14/83, www.imf.org/en/Publications/WP/Issues/2016/12/31/With-Great-Power-Comes-Great-Responsibility-Macroprudential-Tools-at-Work-in-Canada-41551 (accessed 16 August 2019)

Kuncl, Martin, 'Assessment of the effects of macroprudential tightening in Canada', (August 2016), Bank of Canada Staff Analytical Note 2016–2012, www.bankofcanada.ca/wp-content/uploads/2016/08/san2016-12.pdf (accessed 16 August 2019)

Kuttner, Kenneth and Ilhyock Shim, 'Can non-interest rate policies stabilise housing markets? Evidence from a panel of 57 economies', (2013) BIS Working Papers No 433, www.bis.org/publ/work433.pdf (accessed 16 August 2019)

Lamont, Owen and Jeremy Stein, 'Leverage and house-price dynamics in U.S. cities', (1999) *RAND Journal of Economics*, Vol. 30, No. 3, 498, http://scholar.harvard.edu/files/stein/files/leverage-house-prices-rand-autumn-99.pdf?m=1438037130 (accessed 16 August 2019)

Landau, Jean-Pierre, 'Bubbles and macro prudential supervision', speech at Banque de France and Toulouse School of Economics conference on 'The future of financial regulation', Paris, 28 January 2009, www.bis.org/review/r090327e.pdf (accessed 16 August 2019)

Landier, Augustin, David Sraer and David Thesmar, 'Banks' exposure to interest rate risk and the transmission of monetary policy', (2013) NBER Working Paper 18857

Langevoort, Donald, 'The human nature of corporate boards: law, norms, and the unintended consequences of independence and accountability', (2000) *Georgetown Law Journal*, Vol. 89, 797

Lastra, Rosa and Heba Shams, 'Public accountability in the financial sector', in Eilís Ferran and Charles Goodhart (eds), *Regulating financial services and markets in the twenty-first century* (Hart Publishing, Oxford, 2001)

Lastra, Rosa,

——— 'Systemic risk and macroprudential supervision', in Niamh Moloney, Eilís Ferran and Jennifer Payne (eds), *The Oxford handbook of financial regulation* (Oxford University Press, Oxford, 2015)

——— 'Systemic risk, SIFIs and financial stability', (2011) *Capital Markets Law Journal*, Vol. 6, No. 2, 197–213

——— *Central banking and banking regulation* (London School of Economic, Financial Markets Group, London, 1996)

Laufer, Steven, 'Equity extraction and mortgage default', (2013) Finance and Economics Discussion Series Divisions of Research & Statistics and Monetary Affairs Federal Reserve Board, Washington, DC, 3, www.federalreserve.gov/pubs/feds/2013/201330/201330pap.pdf (accessed 16 August 2019)

Lea, Michael and Anthony Sanders, 'Government policy and the fixed-rate mortgage', (2011) *Annual Review of Financial Economics*, 3, 223–234

Legal and General, 'Let's house Britain', (2014) UK Housing Crisis Report, www.legalandgeneralcapital.com/media-centre/publications/lg-capital---media-centre---publications---lets-house-britain.html (accessed 16 August 2019)

Levin, Andrew, 'The design and communication of systematic monetary policy strategies', (2014), Hoover Institution conference on 'Frameworks for central banking in the next century', Stanford University, 29 and 30 May 2014, http://media.hoover.org/sites/default/files/documents/2014LevinThe%20DesignandCommunicationofSystematicMonetaryPolicyStrategies.pdf (accessed 16 August 2019)

Levitin, Adam, Andrey Pavlov and Susan Wachter, 'Securitization: cause or remedy of the financial crisis', (2009), Georgetown Law and Economics Research Paper No. 146285

Levitin, Adam, 'The Consumer Financial Protection Bureau: an introduction', (2013) *Boston University Review of Banking and Financial Law*, Vol. 32, 321, https://papers.ssrn.com/sol3/papers.cfm?abstract_id=2199678 (accessed 16 August 2019)

Li, Wei and Keith Ernst 'Do state predatory lending laws work? A panel analysis of market reforms', (2007) *Housing Policy Debate*, Vol. 18, No. 2, 347–391

Lipset, Seymour, *Political man* (Mercury Books, London, 1959)

Littler, Kevin and Robert Hudson, 'The impact of regulatory change on retail financial product distribution in the UK', (2003) *Journal of Financial Regulation and Compliance*, Vol. 11(1), 71–80

Locke, John, *Second treatise of government* (first published 1689, Cambridge University Press, Cambridge, 1960)

Lombardi, Domenico and Manuela Moschella, 'The symbolic politics of delegation: macroprudential policy and independent regulatory authorities', (2017) *New Political Economy*, Vol. 22(1), 92–108

Luhmann, Niklas,

——— *A sociological theory of law* (first published in German in 1972, 2nd ed in English, Routledge, London, 2014)

——— 'Operational closure and structural coupling: the differentiation of the legal system', (1992) *Cardozo Law Review*, Vol. 13, 1419–1441

Lukes, Steven and Andrew Scull, *Durkheim and the law* (Martin Robertson, Oxford, 1983)

Lund, Brian, *Understanding housing policy* (2nd ed, Policy Press, University of Bristol, Bristol, 2011)

Lyons Housing Review, 'Mobilising across the nation to build the homes our children need', (October 2014), www.policyforum.labour.org.uk/uploads/editor/files/The_Lyons_Housing_Review_2.pdf (accessed 16 August 2019)

McCarthy, Callum, Chairman of the FSA, 'FSA mortgage regulation – one year on', speech to the Council of Mortgage Lenders Annual Conference, 6 December 2005, www.webarchive.org.uk/wayback/archive/20051213120000/www.fsa.gov.uk/pages/Library/Communication/Speeches/2005/1206_cm.html (accessed 16 August 2019)

McCarthy, Yvonne and Kieran McQuinn, 'Credit conditions in a boom and bust property market', (October 2013), Central Bank of Ireland Research Technical Paper 8/RT/13

McCarthy, Jonathan and Richard Peach, 'Are home prices the next "bubble"?', (2004) *Economic Policy Review, New York Federal Reserve Board*, Vol. 10, No. 3, www.newyorkfed.org/research/epr/04v10n3/0412mcca.html (accessed 16 August 2019)

McCarty, Nolan, Keith Poole and Howard Rosenthal, *Political bubbles: financial crises and the failure of American democracy* (Princeton University Press, Princeton, NJ, 2013)

McCoy, Patricia, 'Inside job: the assault on the structure of the Consumer Financial Protection Bureau', (2019) *Minnesota Law Review*, Vol.103(6), 2543–2615.

McDonald, Neil and Christine Whitehead, 'New estimates of housing requirements in England, 2012 to 2037', (November 2015), Town & Country Planning Tomorrow Series Paper 17

McDonald, Oonagh, *Fannie Mae and Freddie Mac*, (Bloomsbury, London, 2012)

McHenry, Patrick, web-site, 'Five years later, Dodd-Frank has failed', 21 July 2015, https://mchenry.house.gov/newsroom/documentsingle.aspx?DocumentID=397906 (accessed 26 June 2019)

McKeen, Elizabeth and others, 'Mortgage underwriting: the qualified mortgage and the ability to repay', (2012) *Banking Law Journal*, Vol. 129, 829

McVea, Harry, 'Financial services regulation under the Financial Services Authority: a reassertion of the market failure thesis?', (2005) *Cambridge Law Journal*, Vol. 64, No. 2, 413–448

Machiavelli, Niccolò, *The Prince* (first published 1532, Penguin, London, 2011)

Madison, James, Alexander Hamilton and John Jay, *The Federalist Papers* (first published 1788, Penguin, London, 1987)

Majone, Giandomenico, 'Regulatory legitimacy', in Giandomenico Majone (ed), *Regulating Europe* (Routledge, London, 1996)

Malloy, Timothy, 'Regulation, compliance and the firm', (2003) *Temple Law Review*, Vol. 76, 451

Malpass, Peter, *Housing & the welfare state: the development of housing policy in Britain* (Palgrave Macmillan, Basingstoke, 2005)

May, Robert, 'Will a large complex system be stable?', (1972) *Nature*, Vol. 238 (5364), 413

Mayor of London

——— 'Barriers to housing delivery – update: private sector housing development on larger sites in London', (July 2014), Greater London Authority, www.london.gov.uk/sites/default/files/gla_migrate_files_destination/Barriers%20to%20Housing%20Delivery%20Update%20Report%20-%20July%202014_0.pdf (accessed 16 August 2019)

——— 'Barriers to housing delivery', (December 2012) Greater London Authority, www.london.gov.uk/sites/default/files/gla_migrate_files_destination/Barriers%20to%20Housing%20Delivery%202012.pdf (accessed 16 August 2019)

Mendicino, Caterina, 'Collateral requirements: macroeconomic fluctuations and macro-prudential policy', (2012) Banco de Portugal Working Papers 11/2012, www.bportugal.pt/sites/default/files/anexos/papers/wp201211.pdf (accessed 16 August 2019)

Merrouche, Ouarda and Erlend Nier, 'What caused the global financial crisis? Evidence on the drivers of financial imbalances 1999–2007', (2010) IMF Working Paper, WP/10/265, 29, www.imf.org/external/pubs/ft/wp/2010/wp10265.pdf (accessed 2nd July 2017)

Mester, Loretta, 'The nexus of macroprudential supervision, monetary policy and financial stability', speech at the Federal Reserve Bank of Cleveland and the Office of Financial Research 2014 Financial Stability Conference, 5 December 2014

Mian, Atif, Kamalesh Rao and Amir Sufi, 'Household balance sheets, consumption and the economic slump', (2013) *Quarterly Journal of Economics*, Vol. 128, No. 4, 1687–1726

Mian, Atif, Amir Sufi and Francisco Trebbi, 'The political economy of the US mortgage default crisis', (November 2008) National Bureau of Economic Research Working Paper No. 14468, www.nber.org/papers/w14468.pdf (accessed 16 August 2019)

Mian, Atif, Amir Sufi and Emil Verner, 'Household debt and business cycles worldwide', (2016) National Bureau of Economic Research Working Paper No. 21581, 22, www.nber.org/papers/w21581 (accessed 16 August 2019)

Mian, Atif and Amir Sufi,

——— *House of debt* (University of Chicago Press, Chicago, IL, 2015)

'The consequences of mortgage credit expansion: evidence from the U.S. mortgage default crisis', (November 2009) *Quarterly Journal of Economics*, Vol. 122, No. 4, 1449–1496

Michailakis, Dimitris, 'Law as an Autopoietic System', (1995) *Acta Sociologica*, Vol. 38, No. 4, 323–337

Mierzewski, Michael and Jeremy Hochberg, 'CFPB proposes new mortgage disclosure rules', (2012) *Banking Law Journal*, Vol. 129, 809

Miller, Geoffrey, 'Independent agencies', (1986) *The Supreme Court Review*, Vol. 1986, 41–97

Miller, Joshua, 'The ghostly body politic: the Federalist papers and popular sovereignty', (February 1988) *Political Theory*, Vol. 16, No. 1, 99–119

Miles, David, 'The UK mortgage market: taking a longer-term view: final report and recommendations', (HM Treasury, London, 2004), http://news.bbc.co.uk/nol/shared/bsp/hi/pdfs/12_03_04_miles.pdf (accessed 16 August 2019)

Mill, John Stuart, *Principles of political economy* (printed 1848, Oxford University Press, Oxford, 1994)

Min, David, 'Faulty conclusions based on shoddy foundations', (2011), Paper for the Centre for American Progress, www.americanprogress.org/wp-content/uploads/issues/2011/02/pdf/pinto.pdf (accessed 16 August 2019)

Minsky, Hyman,

——— *Can 'it' happen again? Essays on instability and finance* (Routledge, London, 1982)

——— 'The financial instability hypothesis: an interpretation of Keynes and an alternative to "standard theory"', (1977), Hyman P. Minsky Archive, Paper 38, 4–6, http://digitalcommons.bard.edu/hm_archive/38 (accessed 16 August 2019)

Mishkin, Fredrick, 'Prudential supervision, why is it important and what are the issues?', in Frederic Mishkin (ed), *Prudential supervision* (University of Chicago Press, Chicago, 2000)

Moench, Emanuel, James Vickery and Diego Aragon, 'Why is the market share of adjustable-rate mortgages so low?', (2010) *Current Issues in Economics and Finance*, Vol. 16, No. 8, www.newyorkfed.org/medialibrary/media/research/current_issues/ci16-8.pdf (accessed 16 August 2019)

Monk, Sarah, Christine Whitehead, Gemma Burgess and Connie Tang, 'International review of land supply and planning systems', (March 2013) Joseph Rowntree Foundation, www.jrf.org.uk/report/international-review-land-supply-and-planning-systems (accessed 16 August 2019)

Montesquieu, Baron de and Charles-Louis de Secondat, *The spirit of the law* (first published 1748, Cambridge University Press, Cambridge, 1989)

Mortgage Nationwide Licensing System, 'Mortgage industry report', (2015) Q2 Update, http://mortgage.nationwidelicensingsystem.org/about/Reports/2015Q2-Mortgage-Report.pdf (accessed 16 August 2019)

Morton, Alex,

———'Why aren't we building enough attractive homes? Myths, misunderstandings and solutions', (2012) *Policy Exchange*, https://policyexchange.org.uk/publication/why-arent-we-building-enough-attractive-homes-myths-misunderstandings-and-solutions/ (accessed 16 August 2019)

——— 'Cities for growth: solutions to our planning problems', (2011) *Policy Exchange*, Vol. 69, https://policyexchange.org.uk/wp-content/uploads/2016/09/cities-for-growth-nov-11.pdf (accessed 16 August 2019)

Mullineux, Andrew, 'Taxing banks fairly', (2012) *International Review of Financial Analysis*, Vol. 25, 154, www.birmingham.ac.uk/Documents/college-social-sciences/social-policy/CHASM/2015/Taxing-banks-fairly2012International-Review-of-Financial-Analysis.pdf (accessed 16 August 2019)

Mullins, David and Alan Murie, *Housing policy in the UK* (Palgrave Macmillan, Basingstoke, 2006)

Mulvaney, Michael, e-mail to CFPB staff, 23 January 2018, 'To everyone from the Acting director', www.documentcloud.org/documents/4357880-Mulvaney-Memo.html (accessed 3 July 2019)

Munnell, Alice and others, 'Mortgage lending in Boston', (1992) Working Paper No. 92–7, Federal Reserve Bank of Boston

Murray, James, *Bruge: cradle of capitalism* (Cambridge University Press, Cambridge, 2005)

Nader, Ralph, *Unsafe at any speed* (Grossman Publishers, New York, 1965)

National Housing Federation Research Paper, 'Intergenerational perspectives on housing wealth', (September 2016), http://s3-eu-west-1.amazonaws.com/pub.housing.org.uk/Intergenerational_perspectives_on_housing_wealth_briefing.pdf (accessed 16 August 2019)

Netelenbos, Benno, *Political legitimacy beyond Weber: an analytical framework* (Palgrave Macmillan, London, 2016)

Netherlands Central Bank (DNB), Financial Stability Committee meeting, (12 May 2012) Policy Conclusions, www.financieelstabiliteitscomite.nl/media/45/80/323341/31/conclusions_of_the_meeting_of_the_financial_stability_committee_of_12_may_2015.pdf (accessed 12 August 2019)

Nicholl, Sheila, (Director of Conduct Policy at FSA/FCA), speech, 'Developing regulatory policy on mortgages at the national, European and international level', 3 November 2011

Niemietz, Kristian, 'Abundance of land, shortage of housing', (April 2012) Institute of Economic Affairs, Discussion Paper No. 38, www.iea.org.uk/wp-content/uploads/2016/07/Abundance-of-Land-Shortage-of-Housing.pdf (accessed 16 August 2019)

Northern Rock, 'Annual report and accounts 2006', www.n-ram.co.uk/~/media/Files/N/NRAM-PLC/documents/corporate-reports/res2006pr-annualreportandaccounts.pdf (accessed 16 August 2019)

Noyer, Christian,

——— 'Macroprudential policy: from theory to implementation', (April 2014) Banque de France, Financial Stability Review, No. 18, 7–11, www.banque-france.fr/sites/default/files/medias/documents/financial-stability-review-18_2014-04.pdf (accessed 16 August 2019)

——— 'Monetary policy and macroprudential policy', speech at a conference on 'The future of monetary policy', Banca d'Italia, Rome, 30 September 2010, www.bis.org/review/r101130a.pdf (accessed 16 August 2019)

Nunn, Alex and others, 'Factors influencing social mobility', (2007) Department for Work and Pensions Research Report No 450, https://core.ac.uk/download/pdf/29018987.pdf (accessed 16 August 2019)

Office of the Comptroller of the Currency National Credit Committee, 'Survey of credit underwriting practices', (June 2005), www.occ.treas.gov/publications/publications-by-type/other-publications-reports/survey-credit-underwriting-practices-report/pub-survey-cred-under-2005.pdf (accessed 16 August 2019)

Office of Fair Trading,

——— 'Annual report of the Director of Fair Trading', (1995), www.gov.uk/government/uploads/system/uploads/attachment_data/file/235603/0475.pdf (accessed 16 August 2019)

——— 'Homebuilding in the UK: a market study', (September 2008), http://webarchive.nationalarchives.gov.uk/20140402142426/http:/www.oft.gov.uk/shared_oft/reports/comp_policy/oft1020.pdf (accessed 16 August 2019)

Office of National Statistics,

'UK Perspectives 2016: Housing and home ownership in the UK', (25 May 2016), http://visual.ons.gov.uk/uk-perspectives-2016-housing-and-home-ownership-in-the-uk/, English Housing Survey (EHS), Table FC21010 DCLG; EHS 2001/02, Table S106, DCLG (accessed 25 July 2019)

——— 'Migrant labour force within the construction industry: June 2018', (June 2018), Figure 2: Age distribution of those working in the construction industry by nationality grouping, 2014 to 2016, www.ons.gov.uk/peoplepopulationandcommunity/populationandmigration/internationalmigration/articles/migrantlabourforcewithintheconstructionindustry/2018-06-19 (accessed 25 July 2019)

Ogus, Anthony, *Regulation: legal form and economic theory* (Clarendon Press, Oxford, 1994)

Olsen, Øystein, Governor of Norges Bank, 'Integrating financial stability and monetary policy analysis', speech given at the London School of Economics and Political Science, 27 April 2015, www.bis.org/review/r150429a.pdf (accessed 16 August 2019)

Ornstein, Stephen and others, 'CFPB ability to replay rule and qualified mortgage definition', (2012) *Consumer Finance Law Quarterly Report*, Vol. 66, 424

Osiński, Jacek, Katharine Seal and Lex Hoogduin, 'Macroprudential and microprudential policies: toward cohabitation', (2013) IMF Staff Discussion Note 13/05, www.imf.org/external/pubs/ft/sdn/2013/sdn1305.pdf (accessed 16 August 2019)

Padoa-Schioppa, Tommaso,

——— *Regulating finance: balancing freedom and risk* (Oxford University Press, Oxford, 2004)

——— 'Central banks and financial stability', speech in Jakarta, 7 July 2003, www.ecb.europa.eu/press/key/date/2003/html/sp030707.en.html (accessed 16 August 2019)

——— 'Central banks and financial stability: exploring the land in between', in V. Gaspar, P. Hartmann and O. Sleijpen (eds), *The transmission of the European financial system* (European Central Bank, Frankfurt, 2003)

Pan, Wei, Alistair Gibb and Andrew Dainty, 'Leading UK housebuilders' utilization of offsite construction methods', (2008) *Building Research and Information*, Vol. 36, No. 1, 56–67

Parliamentary Commission for Banking Standards, 'Written evidence submitted by Professor Michael Devereux and Dr. John Vella to the Parliamentary Commission for Banking Standards', (24 June 2013), www.publications.parliament.uk/pa/jt201314/jtselect/jtpcbs/27/27ix_we_h14.htm (accessed 16 August 2019)

Parliamentary Select Committees,

——— Communities and Local Government's Report on the 'Department for Communities and Local Government's consultation on national planning policy', (April 2016) Third Report of Session 2015–16, www.publications.parliament.uk/pa/cm201516/cmselect/cmcomloc/703/703.pdf (accessed 16 August 2019)

——— Treasury Select Committee, Oral evidence: Bank of England Financial Stability Report (December 2015) HC 780, 26 January 2016, (http://data.parliament.uk/writtenevidence/committeeevidence.svc/evidencedocument/treasury-committee/bank-of-england-financial-stability-report-hearings-session-201516/oral/27787.html) (accessed 16 August 2019)

——— Treasury Select Committee, King, Mervyn, answer to Question 2354, 26 February 2009, 'Banking crisis', Vol. I, Oral evidence, (HC 144–I [Incorporating HC 1167 i–iv, Session 2007–08]), 281, www.publications.parliament.uk/pa/cm200809/cmselect/cmtreasy/144/144i.pdf (accessed 18 August 2019)

——— Treasury Select Committee, Turner, Adair, answer to Question 2168, 25 February 2009, 'Banking crisis', Vol. I, Oral evidence, (HC 144–I [Incorporating HC 1167 i–iv, Session 2007–08]), 281, www.publications.parliament.uk/pa/cm200809/cmselect/cmtreasy/144/144i.pdf (accessed 16 August 2019)

——— Treasury Select Committee report, 'Run on the Rock: oral and written evidence', (House of Commons, Fifth Report of Session 2007–08, Vol. II), www.publications.parliament.uk/pa/cm200708/cmselect/cmtreasy/56/56ii.pdf (accessed 16 August 2019)

——— Treasury Select Committee, questions to Sir John Gieve, (Deputy Governor Responsible for Financial Stability) regarding the Bank of England's role in failing to prevent the collapse of Northern Rock, oral evidence, 20 September 2007, Question

6–8, www.publications.parliament.uk/pa/cm200607/cmselect/cmtreasy/uc999-i/uc99902.htm (accessed 16 August 2019)

——— Treasury Select Committee, 'The run on the Rock', Fifth Report of Session 2007–08, HC 56–I [Incorporating HC 999 i–iv, Session 2006–07], 26 January 2008, www.publications.parliament.uk/pa/cm200708/cmselect/cmtreasy/56/56i.pdf (accessed 16 August 2019)

Paxton, Will and John Brynner, *The asset effect* (The Institute for Public Policy Research, London, 2001)

Peden, G. C., 'New revisionists and the Keynesian era in British economic policy: a comment', (2003) *Economic History Review*, Vol. LVI, No. 1, 118

Peltzman, Sam, 'The effects of automobile safety regulation', (1975) *Journal of Political Economy*, Vol. 83, No. 4, 677–726

Perl, Libby, 'VA housing', (4 February 2013), Congressional Research Service, https://fas.org/sgp/crs/misc/R42504.pdf (accessed 16 August 2019)

Petty, Sir William, 'Collected works of William Petty', in Charles Henry Hull (ed), Collected economic writings of Sir William Petty, (1899 edition, Routledge, London, 1997), Vol. II

Philippopoulos-Mihalopoulos, Andreas and Niklas Luhmann, *Law, justice, society* (Routledge, Abingdon, 2010)

Pickles, Eric, 'Housebuilding: advanced housing manufacture', speech at Homes Event on the need for innovation in housing manufacturing, 27 November 2014, www.gov.uk/government/speeches/housebuilding-advanced-housing-manufacture (accessed 16 August 2019)

Pigou, Arthur, *The economics of welfare* (first published 1920, McMillan, London, 1932), http://files.libertyfund.org/files/1410/Pigou_0316.pdf (accessed 16 August 2019)

Pinto, Edward,

——— 'Fifty years of housing policy failure: how housing policies make homes unaffordable', (October 2015) American Enterprise Institution's International Centre on Housing Risk, 12, www.aei.org/publication/fifty-years-of-housing-policy-failure/ (accessed 16 August 2019)

——— 'Triggers of the financial crisis', (2010) a memorandum to staff of the Financial Crisis Inquiry Commission, www.aei.org/wp-content/uploads/2011/10/Pinto FCICTriggers.pdf (accessed 16 August 2019)

Posner, Richard, *Economic analysis of law*, (8th edn, Aspen Publishers, Wolters Kluwer, New York, NY, 2010)

Pottow, John, 'Ability to pay', (2011), Empirical Legal Studies Centre, Working Paper 237, University of Michigan Law School, 21 http://scholarship.law.berkeley.edu/cgi/viewcontent.cgi?article=1085&context=bblj (accessed 16 August 2019)

Prudential Regulation Authority's approach to banking supervision, (June 2014), www.bankofengland.co.uk/-/media/boe/files/prudential-regulation/approach/banking-approach-2014 (accessed 16 August 2019)

Presidential Archives, 'National Homeownership Month, Presidential Proclamation' (4 June 2002), White House Archive George W. Bush, press releases, http://georgewbush-whitehouse.archives.gov/news/releases/2002/06/20020604-23.html (accessed 16 August 2019)

Prest, A. R. *The taxation of urban land* (Manchester University Press, Manchester, 1981)

Prosser, Tony, 'Introduction: two visions of regulation and four regulatory models', in *The regulatory enterprise: government, regulation and legitimacy* (Oxford University Press, Oxford, 2010)

Purnananandam, Amiyotash, 'Originate-to-distribute model and the subprime mortgage crisis', (June 2011) *The Review of Financial Studies*, Vol. 24, No. 6, 1881–1915
Putterman, Ethan, *Rousseau, law and the sovereignty of the people* (Cambridge University Press, Cambridge, 2011)
Quentyn, Marc and Michael Taylor, 'Regulatory and supervisory independence and financial stability', (2002) IMF Working Paper WP/02/46, www.imf.org/external/pubs/ft/wp/2002/wp0246.pdf (accessed 16 August 2019)
Quercia, Roberto, Michael Stegman and Walter Davis, 'Assessing the impact of North Carolina's anti-predatory law', (2004) *Housing Debate*, Vol. 15, No. 3, 573–601
Rajan, Raghuram,
Fault lines (Princeton University Press, Princeton, NJ, 2011)
——— 'Let them eat credit', (27 August 2010), New Republic, https://newrepublic.com/article/77242/inequality-recession-credit-crunch-let-them-eat-credit (accessed 16 August 2019)
——— 'Why bank credit policies fluctuate: a theory and some evidence', (1994) *The Quarterly Journal of Economics*, Vol. 109, No. 2, 399–441, http://faculty.chicago booth.edu/raghuram.rajan/research/papers/fluct.pdf (accessed 16 August 2019)
Rawls, John, *Theory of justice* (Oxford University Press, Oxford, 1999)
The Redfern Review into the decline of homeownership, (November 2016), https://britainthinks.com/pdfs/TW082_RR_online_PDF.pdf (accessed 16 August 2019)
Reid, Margaret, *The secondary banking crisis, 1973–1975* (Macmillan Press, London, 1982)
Reinhart, Carmen and Kenneth Rogoff, *This time is different* (Princeton University Press, Princeton, NJ, 2009)
Reiss, David, 'Message in a mortgage: what Dodd-Frank's "Qualified Mortgage" tells us about ourselves', (2012), Brooklyn Law School Legal Studies Research Paper 264
Renuart, Elizabeth and Diane Thompson, 'The truth, the whole truth, and nothing but the truth: fulfilling the promise of truth in lending', (2008) *Yale Journal of Regulation*, Vol. 25, 196
Reserve Bank of Australia, 'Submission to the Inquiry into Home Ownership House of Representatives Standing Committee on Economics', (June 2015), www.rba.gov.au/publications/submissions/housing-and-housing-finance/inquiry-into-home-ownership/pdf/inquiry-into-home-ownership.pdf (accessed 23 July 2019)
Rising, George, 'An EPIC endeavor: Upton Sinclair's 1934 California gubernatorial campaign', (1997) *Southern California Quarterly*, Vol. 79, No. 1, 101–124
Rogers, Lamoma, 'A new approach to macroprudential policy for New Zealand', (September 2013) *Reserve Bank of New Zealand Bulletin*, Vol. 76, No. 3, 12–22, www.rbnz.govt.nz/-/media/ReserveBank/Files/Publications/Bulletins/2013/2013sep76-3rogers.pdf?la=en (accessed 16 August 2019)
Rogers, Lamorna, 'An A to Z of LTV ratio restrictions', (2014) *Reserve Bank of New Zealand: Bulletin*, Vol. 77, No. 1, www.rbnz.govt.nz/-/media/ReserveBank/Files/Publications/Bulletins/2014/2014mar77-1rogers.pdf (accessed 16 August 2019)
Rohe, William and Harry Watson, *Chasing the American dream* (Cornell University Press, Ithaca, NY, 2007)
Rohe, William, Shannon Van Zandt and George McCarthy, 'The social benefits and costs of homeownership: a critical assessment of the research', (October 2001) Low-Income Homeownship Working Paper Series 01.12, Harvard University Joint Centre for Housing Studies, www.jchs.harvard.edu/sites/jchs.harvard.edu/files/liho01-12.pdf (accessed 16 August 2019)

Rousseau, Jean-Jacques,

——— *Discourse on political economy* (first published 1755, Hackett, Indianapolis, 2011)

——— *Social contract* (first published 1762, Hafner Press, New York, 1947)

Royal Bank of Canada, Economic Research, February 2019, www.rbc.com/economics/economic-reports/pdf/canadian-housing/Home_Ownership_Feb2019.pdf (accessed 17 July 2019)

Royal Institute of Chartered Surveyors (RICS), 'UK construction market survey', (Q1 2016), www.rics.org/globalassets/rics-website/media/knowledge/research/market-surveys/uk-construction-and-infrastructure-survey-q4-2016-rics.pdf (accessed 16 August 2019)

Rubinstein, William, *Capitalism culture and decline in Britain* (Routledge, London, 1993)

Salazar, Germán, 'Mortgage lending', (2015) 51 March, Arizona Attorney, 18

Samra, Mark, 'New regulation under the CFPB', (2012) 31 Review of Banking and Financial Law, 545

Sants, Hector, Chief Executive, FSA, 'Delivering intensive supervision and credible deterrence', speech at The Reuters Newsmakers event, 12 March 2009, https://webarchive.nationalarchives.gov.uk/20090320233408/www.fsa.gov.uk/pages/Library/Communication/Speeches/2009/0312_hs.shtml (accessed 16 August 2019)

Sargentich, Thomas, 'Contemporary debate about legislative-executive separation of powers', (1987) *Cornell Law Review*, Vol. 72, 430–487

Saunders, Trent and Peter Tulip, 'A model of the Australian housing market', (March 2019) Reserve Bank of Australia, Research Discussion Paper RDP 2019-01, www.rba.gov.au/publications/rdp/2019/pdf/rdp2019-01.pdf (accessed 17 July 2019)

Scales, Len, *The shaping of German identity: authority and crisis, 1245–1414* (Cambridge University Press, Cambridge, England, 2012)

Scanlon, Kathleen and Marja Elsinga, 'Policy changes affecting housing and mortgage markets: how governments in the UK and the Netherlands responded to the GFC', (2014) *Journal of Housing and the Built Environment*, Vol. 29, No. 2, 335–360

Scharf, Fritz, *Governing in Europe: effective and democratic?* (Oxford University Press, Oxford, 1999)

Schembri, Lawrence, 'Housing finance in Canada: looking back to move forward', (November 2014) *National Institute Economic Review*, Vol. 230(1), R45–R57

Schloemer, Ellen and others, 'Losing ground: foreclosures in the subprime market and their cost to homeowners', (December 2006), *Center for Responsible Lending*, www.responsiblelending.org/mortgage-lending/research-analysis/foreclosure-paper-report-2-17.pdf (accessed 16 August 2019)

Schmidt, Reinhard and Gerald Spindler, 'Path dependence and complementarity in corporate governance', in Jeffrey Gordon and Mark Roe (eds), *Convergence and persistence in corporate governance* (Cambridge University Press, Cambridge, 2004)

Schmidt, Vivien, 'Democracy and legitimacy in the European Union revisited: input, output and "throughput"', (2013) *Political Studies*, Vol. 61, 2–22

Schreft, Stacey, 'Credit controls: 1980', (November/December 1990) *Economic Review*, 26–27, www.richmondfed.org/~/media/richmondfedorg/publications/research/economic_review/1990/pdf/er760603.pdf (accessed 16 August 2019)

Schularick, Moritz and Alan Taylor, 'Credit booms gone bust: monetary policy, leverage cycles and financial crises, 1870–2008', (2012) *American Economic Review*, Vol. 102, No. 2, 1029–1061

Schwartz, Alex, *Housing policy in the United States* (Routledge, New York, 2006)

Schwartz, Herman and Leonard Seabrooke, 'Varieties of residential capitalism in international political economy: old welfare states and the new politics of housing', (2008) *Comparative European Politics*, Vol. 6, 237–261

Schwarcz, Steven, 'Systemic risk', (2008) *Georgetown Law Journal*, Vol. 97, 193–249

Scott, Colin, 'Regulation in the age of governance: the rise of the post-regulatory state', in Jacint Jordana and David Levi-Faur (eds), *The politics of regulation* (Edward Elgar, Cheltenham, 2004), 145–174

Scott Wheeler, James, *The making of a world power* (Sutton Publishing, Stroud, 1999)

Seabrooke, Leonard,

——— 'Legitimacy gaps in the World economy: explaining the sources of the IMF legitimacy crisis', (2007) *International Politics*, Vol. 44, No. 2, 250–268

——— *The social sources of financial power: domestic legitimacy and international financial orders* (Cornell University Press, Ithaca, New York, 2006)

Seattle Human Services Department, '2018–2022 Consolidated Plan for Housing and Community Development City of Seattle', (July 2018), www.seattle.gov/humanservices/funding-and-reports/resources/seattles-2018-2022-consolidated-plan-for-housing-and-community-development- (accessed 22 August 2019)

Seitz, Neil and others, 'Bank integrity: the case of subprime lending', (2009) *Company Lawyer*, Vol. 30, No. 9, 277

Sengupta, Rajdeep, 'Alt-A: the forgotten segment of the mortgage market', (January/February 2010) *Federal Reserve Bank of St. Louis Review*, Vol. 92, No. 1, 55–71, https://research.stlouisfed.org/publications/review/10/01/Sengupta.pdf (accessed 19 August 2019)

Shelter,

——— 'Achieving the ambition: building one million homes this Parliament', (August 2016), https://england.shelter.org.uk/__data/assets/pdf_file/0009/1277325/2016_08_23_Achieving_the_Ambition_v.7.pdf (accessed 19 August 2019)

——— 'What salary will a typical first-time buyer need in 2020', (April 2016), https://england.shelter.org.uk/professional_resources/policy_and_research/policy_library/policy_library_folder/research_what_salary_will_a_typical_first-time_buyer_need_in_2020 (accessed 19 August 2019)

——— 'A home of their own', (January 2015), https://england.shelter.org.uk/professional_resources/policy_and_research/policy_library/policy_library_folder/report_a_home_of_their_own (accessed 19 August 2019)

——— 'Response to the Lyons review of housing supply', (2014), https://england.shelter.org.uk/__data/assets/pdf_file/0007/770893/2014_Shelter_Lyons_Review_final.pdf (accessed 19 August 2019)

Shlay, Anne, 'Low-income homeownership: American dream or delusion?' (March 2006) *Urban Studies*, Vol. 43, No. 3, 511–531

Shiller, Robert, *Irrational exuberance* (2nd edn, Princeton University Press, Princeton, NJ, 2005)

Shin, Hyun Song, 'Macroprudential policies beyond Basel III', (2010), Princeton University Policy Memo, http://joaorendeiro.com/wordpress/wp-content/uploads/macroprudentialmemo.pdf (accessed 19 August 2019)

Shinwell, Manny, *Leading with the left* (Cassell, London, 1981)

Simon, Herbert, 'Rational decision making in business organizations', Nobel Memorial Lecture, 8 December 1978, www.nobelprize.org/uploads/2018/06/simon-lecture.pdf (accessed 19 August 2019)

Stein, Jeremy,

——— 'Incorporating financial stability considerations into a monetary policy framework', speech at the International Research Forum on Monetary Policy, Washington, DC, 21 March 2014, www.federalreserve.gov/newsevents/speech/stein20140321a.htm (accessed 19 August 2019)

——— 'Overheating in the credit market: origins, measurement and policy response', (2013), Paper presented to a research symposium sponsored by the Federal Reserve Board of St Louis, www.federalreserve.gov/newsevents/speech/stein20130207a.htm (accessed 19 August 2019)

——— 'Monetary policy as financial stability regulation', (2012) *The Quarterly Journal of Economics*, Vol. 127, 57, http://scholar.harvard.edu/files/stein/files/qje-2012.pdf?m=1401745178 (accessed 19 August 2019)

——— 'Prices and trading volume in the housing market: a model with down-payment effects', (May 1995), *The Quarterly Journal of Economics*, Vol. 110, No. 2, 379, www.jstor.org/stable/2118444?seq=3# (accessed 19 August 2019)

Stephens, Mark and Peter Williams, 'Tackling housing market volatility in the UK: a progress report', (2012), Joseph Rowntree Foundation Report, www.jrf.org.uk/report/tackling-housing-market-volatility-uk-progress-report (accessed 19 August 2019)

Stiglitz, Joseph and Andrew Weiss, 'Credit rationing in markets with imperfect information', (June 1981) *The American Economic Review*, Vol. 71, 393–410

Suchman, Mark, 'Managing legitimacy: strategic and institutional approaches', (1995) *The Academy of Management Review*, Vol. 20, No. 3, 571–610

Sunstein, Cass, *After the rights revolution* (Harvard University Press, Cambridge, MA, 1990)

Sunstein, Cass and Richard Thaler, 'Libertarian paternalism is not an oxymoron', (2003) *University of Chicago Law Review*, Vol. 70, 1159

Swenarton, Mark, *Homes fir for heroes: the politics and architecture of early state housing in Britain* (Heinemann Educational, London, 1981)

Sveriges Riksbank,

——— 'Further measures are needed to manage household indebtedness', (Press release, 25 November 2015), www.riksbank.se/Documents/Pressmeddelanden/2015/prm_151125_eng.pdf (accessed 19 August 2019)

——— 'Financial stability report', (2015:1), www.riksbank.se/Documents/Rapporter/FSR/2015/FSR_1/rap_fsr1_150603_eng.pdf (accessed 19 August 2019)

——— 'Financial stability report', (2015:2) www.riksbank.se/Documents/Rapporter/FSR/2015/FSR_2/rap_fsr2_151125_eng.pdf (accessed 19 August 2019)

Svensson, Lars,

——— 'Cost benefit analysis of leaning against the wind: are costs larger also with less effective macroprudential policy?', (2016) IMF Working Paper, WP/16/3, www.imf.org/external/pubs/ft/wp/2016/wp1603.pdf (accessed 19 August 2019)

——— 'Monetary policy and financial stability', speech at 'Financial liberalization, innovation, and stability: international experience and relevance for China', the Third Joint Conference, People's Bank of China and International Monetary Fund, Beijing, 16th March 2015, http://larseosvensson.se/files/papers/svensson-beijing-monetary-policy-and-financial-stability-text.pdf (accessed 19 August 2019)

Swedish Council for Cooperation on Macroprudential Policy, 'Minutes of the Council meeting', 1 October 2013, www.riksbank.se/Documents/Protokoll/Samverkansradet/2013/pro_samverkansradet_131016_eng.pdf (accessed 19 August 2019)

Swedish Finansinspektionen, 'Amortisation requirement for new mortgages', (20 April 2016), www.fi.se/en/published/press-releases/2016/amortisation-requirement-for-new-mortgages/ (accessed 19 August 2019)

Tacitus, The annals of Imperial Rome, Book II.36, (Michael Grant (trs), Penguin Classics, London, 1956)

Tallman, Ellis and Jon Moen, 'Lessons from the panic of 1907', (May/June 1990) Economic Review, Federal Reserve Bank of Atlanta

Tarashev, Nikola, Claudio Borio and Kostas Tsatsaronis, 'Attributing systemic risk to individual institutions', (2010) BIS Working Papers No 308, www.bis.org/publ/work308.pdf (accessed 19 August 2019)

Tarullo, Daniel, 'Monetary policy and financial stability', speech at the 30th Annual National Association for Business Economics Economic Policy Conference, Arlington, Virginia, 25 February 2014, www.federalreserve.gov/newsevents/speech/tarullo20140225a.htm (accessed 19 August 2019)

Taylor, John, 'Simple rules for financial stability', Keynote address at the Financial Markets Conference 'Maintaining financial stability: holding a tiger by the tail', Federal Reserve Bank of Atlanta, 9 April 2013, https://web.stanford.edu/~johntayl/Taylor%20Keynote%20-%20Atlanta%20Fed%204-9-13.pdf (accessed 19 August 2019)

Teubner, Gunther, *Law as an autopoitic system* (Blackwell Publishers, Oxford, 1993)

Thomas, Matthew and Alicia Hall, 'Housing affordability in Australia', Parliament of Australia Briefing, (2015), www.aph.gov.au/About_Parliament/Parliamentary_Departments/Parliamentary_Library/pubs/BriefingBook45p/HousingAffordability (accessed 16 July 2019)

H M Treasury (HMT)

——— HMT and FCA, 'Financial advice market review: final report', (March 2016), www.fca.org.uk/publication/corporate/famr-final-report.pdf (accessed 19 August 2019)

——— HMT, 'Detail of outcome from FPC's housing market tools consultation', (January 2015) www.gov.uk/government/uploads/system/uploads/attachment_data/file/400448/PU1748_Consultation_Housing_Response.pdf (accessed 19 August 2019)

——— HMT, 'The Financial Policy Committee's housing market tools', (October 2014), www.gov.uk/government/uploads/system/uploads/attachment_data/file/368614/FPC_Housing_Consultation.pdf (accessed 19 August 2019)

——— HMT, 'Response to the consultation paper: regulating mortgages, October 2000', (February 2001), (in author's collection: no longer publicly available)

——— HMT, 'Regulating mortgages', (October 2000), http://webarchive.nationalarchives.gov.uk/20070604000648/www.hm-treasury.gov.uk/media/1AB/8F/77.pdf (accessed 19 August 2019)

——— HMT, 'Regulation of mortgages, a discussion document', (July 1999), (in author's collection: no longer publicly available)

——— HMT, 'Financial Services and Markets Bill: a consultation document, overview of financial regulatory reform', (July 1998), (in author's collection: no longer publicly available)

Trichet, Jean-Claude, 'Systemic risk', The Clare Distinguished Lecture in Economics and Public Policy, Cambridge, 10 December 2009, www.bis.org/review/r091217b.pdf (accessed 19 August 2019)

Tucker, Paul, Simon Hall and Aashish Pattani, 'Macroprudential policy at the Bank of England', (2013) *Quarterly Bulletin*, Q3, 192

Tucker, Paul,
——— 'The design and governance of financial stability regimes: a common-resource problem that challenges technical know-how, democratic accountability and international coordination', (September 2016) *Centre for International Governance Innovation*, Vol. 3, www.cigionline.org/sites/default/files/financial_essay_vol.3_web.pdf (accessed 19 August 2019)
——— remarks at Clare Distinguished Lecture in Economics and Public Policy, Cambridge, discussing Lord Turner's Lecture, 'Reforming finance: are we being radical enough?', 18 February 2011, www.bankofengland.co.uk/-/media/boe/files/speech/2011/discussion-of-lord-turners-lecture-remarks-by-paul-tucker (accessed 19 August 2019)
Turner, Adair,
——— *Between debt and the devil: money, credit, and fixing global finance* (Princeton University Press, Princeton, NJ, 2015)
The Turner review (Financial Services Authority, London, 2009), http://news.bbc.co.uk/1/shared/bsp/hi/pdfs/18_03_09_turner_review.pdf (accessed 19 August 2019)
Turner, Gregg, *The Florida land boom of the 1920s* (McFarland, Jefferson, NC, 2015)
Tyler, Colin, 'The liberal Hegelianism of Edward Caird', (2010) *International Journal of Social Economics*, Vol. 37, No. 11, 852–866
Ullmann, Owen, 'Crony capitalism: American style', (July/August 1999) *The International Economy*, Vol. 7, www.international-economy.com/TIE_JA99_Ullmann.pdf (accessed 19 August 2019)
University of the West of England, sponsored by the Campaign for the Protection of Rural England (CPRE), 'From Wasted space to living spaces: the availability of brownfield land for housing development in England', (November 2014), CPRE, www.cpre.org.uk/resources/housing-and-planning/housing/item/3785-from-wasted-space-to-living-spaces (accessed 19 August 2019)
US House of Representatives Committee on Oversight and Government Reform, chaired by Darrell Issa, 'The role of Government affordable housing policy in creating the global financial crisis of 2008', (released July 2009 and updated May 2010), https://republicans-oversight.house.gov/wp-content/uploads/2012/02/20100512affordablehousingpolicyandthefinancialcrisis.pdf (accessed 19 August 2019)
US Congress,
——— 'Evidence of Thomas Pamperin', (Associate Deputy Under Secretary for Policy and Program Management, Veterans Benefits Administration, US Department of Veterans Affairs) on 20 May 2010 to the House Committee on Veteran Affairs, Sub-committee on Economic Opportunity, www.va.gov/OCA/testimony/hvac/seo/100520TJP.asp (accessed 19 August 2019)
——— 'Testimony of Tim Embree', (Iraq and Afghanistan Veterans of America, Legislative Associate) on 20 May 2010, to the House Committee on Veteran Affairs, Sub-committee on Economic Opportunity, www.govinfo.gov/content/pkg/CHRG-111hhrg57024/html/CHRG-111hhrg57024.htm (accessed 19 August 2019)
——— 'Recognizing national homeownership month and the importance of homeownership in the United States', House of Representatives, Motion 477, 110th Congress (11 June 2007), www.congress.gov/bill/110th-congress/house-resolution/477?q=%7B%22search%22%3A%5B%22recognizing+national+homeownership+month+2007%22%5D%7D&resultIndex=4 (accessed 19 August 2019)
US Military, 'A look at the VA loan appraisal process', www.military.com/money/home-ownership/buying-a-house/a-look-at-the-va-loan-appraisal-process.html (accessed 19 August 2019)

Vale, Brenda, 'Prefabs: the history of the UK temporary housing programme', (E&FN Spon, London, 1995)
Vancouver, City of, 'Housing Vancouver Strategy', (November 2018), https://council.vancouver.ca/20171128/documents/rr1appendixa.pdf (accessed 11 July 2019)
Veblen, Thorstein, *The engineers and the price system* (first published 1921, Viking Press, New York, 1954)
Verhoeven, Amaryllis, *The EU in search of a democratic and constitutional theory* (Kluwer Law International, The Hague, 2002)
Veterans Administration,
——— 'Loan Guarantee Guide', www.benefits.va.gov/BENEFITS/factsheets/homeloans/VA_Guaranteed_Home_Loans.pdf (accessed 19 August 2019)
——— 'Lenders Handbook – VA Pamphlet 26–7', http://benefits.va.gov/warms/pam26_7.asp (accessed 19 August 2019)
Vickers, Raymond, Panic in paradise: Florida's banking crash of 1926, (The University of Alabama, Tuscaloosa, 1994)
Viñals, José, 'Making macroprudential policy work', remarks at the Brookings Institution, Washington, DC, 16 September 2013, www.imf.org/external/np/speeches/2013/091613.htm (accessed 19 August 2019)
Waldron, Matt and Fabrizio Zampolli, 'Household debt, house prices and consumption in the United Kingdom: a quantitative theoretical analysis', (2010) Bank of England Working Paper No. 379, www.bankofengland.co.uk/working-paper/2010/household-debt-house-prices-and-consumption-in-the-uk (accessed 19 August 2019)
Wallison, Peter,
——— 'Dissent from the Majority Report of the Financial Crisis Inquiry Commission', (AEI Press, Washington DC, 2011), www.aei.org/wp-content/uploads/2014/07/-dissent-from-the-majority-report_154941211677.pdf (accessed 19 August 2019)
——— 'Government housing policy and the financial crisis', (Spring/Summer 2010), *Cato Journal*, Vol. 30, No. 2, 397–406, https://pdfs.semanticscholar.org/4b41/94a50373eba21e9f6d0bcda4df3449713605.pdf (accessed 19 August 2019)
Ward, David, 'The public schools and industry in Britain after 1870', (1967) *Journal of Contemporary History*, Vol. 2(3), 37–52
Warren, Elizabeth, 'Unsafe at any rate', (Summer 2007), Democracy, No. 5,
Watson, Matthew, 'Constituting monetary conservatives via the 'savings habit': New Labour and the British housing market bubble', (2008) Comparative European Politics, 6, 285–304
Mawhorter, Sarah, 'Housing Policies in Californian cities', (March 2019), Terner Center for Housing Innovation at UC Berkeley, https://ternercenter.berkeley.edu/blog/local-solutions-statewide-shortfall (accessed 21 August 2019)
Weaver, Kent, 'The politics of blame avoidance', (1986) *Journal of Public Policy*, Vol. 6, No. 4, 371–398
Weber, Max, *The theory of social and economic organization* (first published in 1925, The Free Press, New York, 1947)
Weder di Mauro, Beatrice and Ulrich Klüh, 'Reshaping systemic risk regulation in Europe', in Stijn Claessens, Michael Keen and Ceyla Pazarbasioglu (eds), *Financial sector taxation: the IMF's report to the G-20*, (IMF, 2010), www.imf.org/external/np/seminars/eng/2010/paris/pdf/090110.pdf (accessed 19 August 2019)
Weingast, Barry, 'The economic role of political institutions: market-preserving federalism and economic development', (1995) *Journal of Law, Economics and Organization*, Vol. 11(1), 1–31

Wellings, Fred, *British housebuilders: a history and analysis* (Blackwells, Oxford, 2006)

Wheatley, Martin, Chief Executive, the FCA, 'Human face of regulation', speech at the London School of Economics, London, 10 April 2013, www.fca.org.uk/news/speeches/human-face-regulation (accessed 19 August 2019)

Wheeler, Graeme, 'The introduction of macro-prudential policy', speech at Otago University, Dunedin, 20 August 2013, www.bis.org/review/r130822d.pdf (accessed 19 August 2019)

Whitehead, Christine, Sarah Monk, Anna Clarke, Alan Holmans and Sanna Markkanen, 'Measuring housing affordability: a review of data sources', (April 2009), Cambridge University Centre for Housing and Planning Research, http://webarchive.nationalarchives.gov.uk/20120919132719/www.communities.gov.uk/documents/507390/pdf/1098230.pdf (accessed 19 August 2019)

Whittaker, Andrew, (FSA's General Counsel), 'The role of competition in financial services regulation', speech to the Regulatory Policy Institute, 27 April 2001)

Wiener, Martin, English culture and the decline of the industrial spirit, 1850–1980, (first published 1981, 2nd edn, Cambridge University Press, Cambridge, England, 2004)

Williams, John,

——— 'Macroprudential policy in a microprudential world', (June 2015) Federal Reserve Board of San Francisco Economic Letter, 2015–18, www.frbsf.org/economic-research/publications/economic-letter/2015/june/macroprudential-policy-in-a-microprudential-world/ (accessed 19 August 2019)

——— 'Financial stability and monetary policy: happy marriage or untenable union?', (June 2014), Federal Reserve Board of San Francisco Economic Letter, 2014–17, www.frbsf.org/economic-research/publications/economic-letter/2014/june/financial-stability-monetary-policy/ (accessed 19 August 2019)

Willis, Lauren, 'Decision making and the limits of disclosure: the problem of predatory lending', (2006) 65 Maryland Law Review 707

Wilson, Wendy, 'Housing supply and demand: key issues for the 2010 Parliament', (May 2010) House of Commons Library Research: Key issues for the new Parliament, www.parliament.uk/documents/commons/lib/research/key_issues/Key-Issues-Housing-supply-and-demand.pdf (accessed 19 August 2019)

Wolff, Robert, *In defense of Anarchism* (University of California Press, Berkeley, 1998)

Wolf, Martin, *The shifts and the shocks* (Penguin Books, London, 2014)

Wonder, Nicholas, Wendy Wonder and David Fewings, 'The financial rationality of consumer loan choices: revealed preferences concerning interest rates, down payments, contract length and rebates', (2008) *The Journal of Consumer Affairs*, Vol. 42, No. 2, 243

Wong, Eric, Tom Fong, Ka-fai Li and Henry Choi, 'Loan-to-value ratio as a macroprudential tool Hong Kongs experience and cross-country evidence', (2011), Hong Kong Monetary Authority Working Paper No. 01/2011, www.hkma.gov.hk/media/eng/publication-and-research/research/working-papers/HKMAWP11_01_full.pdf (accessed 19 August 2019)

Woodall, Linda, (Director of Mortgages and Consumer Lending at the FCA) 'Building a Common language in the mortgage market', speech at the Council of Mortgage Lenders' conference, 6 November 2013, www.fca.org.uk/news/building-a-common-language-in-the-mortgage-market (accessed 19 August 2019)

Wood, Geoffrey and Ali Kabiri, 'Firm stability and system stability: the regulatory delusion', in John Raymond LaBrosse, Rodrigo Olivares-Caminal and Dalvinder Singh (eds), *Managing risk in the financial system* (Edward Elgar, Cheltenham, 2011)

Woodward, Susan, 'The long intervention: continuity in the Balkan theatre', (December 2013) Review of International Studies, Vol. 39, No. 5, 1169

Woodward, Susan and Robert Hall, 'Diagnosing consumer confusion and sub-optimal shopping effort: theory and mortgage-market evidence', (December 2012) The American Economic Review, 4, www.stanford.edu/~rehall/DiagnosingConsumerConfusion June2012 (accessed 19 August 2019)

Woolard, Christopher (FCA), 'Smarter consumer communications, DP15/5', speech, 25 June 2015, www.fca.org.uk/static/channel-page/dp-smarter-comms/dp-smarter-comms.html (accessed 19 August 2019)

Woll, Peter, American bureaucracy, (2nd edn, W.W. Norton, New York, 1977)

Woudhuysen, James, Why is construction so backward? (James Wiley, London, 2004)

Wright, Joshua, 'Behavioral law and economics, paternalism, and consumer contracts: an empirical perspective', (2007) *New York University Journal of Law & Liberty*, Vol. 2, 476

Yellen, Janet, 'Monetary policy and financial stability', Michel Camdessus Central Banking Lecture, IMF, Washington, DC, 2 July 2014, www.federalreserve.gov/newsevents/speech/yellen20140702a.htm (accessed 19 August 2019)

Zhang, Longmei and Edda Zoli, 'Leaning against the wind: macroprudential policy in Asia', (2014) IMF Working Paper WP/14/22, www.imf.org/external/pubs/ft/wp/2014/wp1422.pdf (accessed 19 August 2019)

Zilioli, Chiara, 'Accountability and independence: irreconcilable values or complementary instruments for democracy? The specific case of the European Central Bank', in Georges Vandersanden and others (eds), *Mélanges en hommage à Jean-Victor Louis* (University of Louvain, Brussels, 2003), 395–422

Zimmermann, Claus, *A contemporary concept of monetary sovereignty* (Oxford University Press, Oxford, 2014)

Zywicki, Todd, 'The behavioral law and economics of fixed-rate mortgages (and other just-so stories)', (January 2014), *Supreme Court Economic Review*, Vol. 21, No. 1, 157–214

Legislation and Regulations

UK Legislation

Bank of England and Financial Services Act 2016

The Bank of England Act 1998 (Macroprudential Measures) Order 2015

Bank of England Act 1946

Financial Services Act 2012, amending the Bank of England Act 1998

Land Compensation Act 1961 (as amended by the Land Compensation Act 1973)

Town and Country Planning Act 1990

Financial Conduct Authority

Client Assets Sourcebook Rules (CASS), www.handbook.fca.org.uk/handbook/CASS/1/?view=chapter (accessed 19 August 2019)

Conduct of Business Sourcebook Rules (CoBs), www.handbook.fca.org.uk/handbook/COBS/1/?view=chapter (accessed 19 August 2019)

Mortgage Conduct of Business Sourcebook (MCoB), www.handbook.fca.org.uk/handbook/MCOB/11/5.html (accessed 19 August 2019)

Mortgage Credit Directive Order 2015, www.legislation.gov.uk/ukdsi/2015/9780111127742 (accessed 19 August 2019)

The Principles for Businesses, www.fca.org.uk/about/principles-good-regulation (accessed 19 August 2019)

EU Directives and Regulations

Directive 2015/2366 dated 25 November 2015 on payment services in the internal market

Commission Delegated Regulation (EU) 2015/61 of 10 October 2014 to supplement Regulation (EU) No 575/2013 of the European Parliament and the Council with regard to liquidity coverage requirement for Credit Institutions, 10 October 2014

Directive 2013/36/EU of the European Parliament and of the Council of 26 June 2013 on access to the activity of credit institutions and the prudential supervision of credit institutions and investment firm

Regulation (EU) No 575/2013 of the European Parliament and of the Council of 26 June 2013 on prudential requirements for credit institutions and investment firms and amending Regulation (EU) No 648/2012

EU Regulation No. 1092/2010 of 24 November 2010 on European Union macroprudential oversight of the financial system and establishing a European Systemic Risk Board

Insurance Mediation Directive, 2002/92/EC of the European Parliament and of the Council of 9 December 2002 on, Official Journal L 009, 15/01/2003 P. 0003-0010

US Federal Legislation

The Alternative Mortgage Transaction Parity Act of 1982 contained within Title VIII of the Garn–St Germain Depository Institutions Act of 1982 (H.R. 6267 Public Law 97-320)

Bureau of Consumer Financial Protection, 12 CFR Part 1026 CFPB-2011-0008; CFPB-2012-0022] RIN 3170-AA17 Ability-to-Repay and Qualified Mortgage Standards under the Truth in Lending Act (Regulation Z)

Bureau of Consumer Financial Protection, 12 CFR Parts 1024 and 1026 [Docket No. CFPB-2012-0028] RIN 3170-AA19

The Community Reinvestment Act (Public Law 95-128, 91 Statute 1147, contained within Title VIII of the Housing and Community Development Act of 1977 (12 U.S.C. § 2901)

Consumer Financial Protection Bureau: Final rule on simplified and improved mortgage disclosures (November 2013) s1032f of Dodd-Frank codified as 12 USC 5532(f)

Consumer Financial Protection Bureau, 12 CFR Parts 1024 and 1026, RIN 3170-AA19, 12-13)

The Depository Institutions Deregulation and Monetary Control Act of 1980 (H.R. 4986 Public Law 96-221)

Dodd-Frank Wall Street Reform and Consumer Protection Act (124 STAT. 1376 Public Law 111–203—July 21, 2010, H.R. 4173

Equal Credit Opportunity Act (ECOA) 1974, (15 U.S.C. § 1691)

The Federal Housing Enterprises Financial Safety and Soundness Act of 1992,(Public Law 102-550) contained within Title XIII of the Housing and Community Development Act of 1992, (H.R. 533 106, Statute 3941, 12 U.S.C § 4501)

Federal Reserve Act 1913, Sec 24, Public Law 63-43 63d Congress H.R. 7837
Home Mortgage Disclosure Act ('HMDA') 1975, (89 STAT. 1124 Public Law 94-200)
The Housing Act of 1949 (42 U.S.C. 1472)
Housing and Community Development Act 1974, 12 U.S.C. 1706e, Public L. No. 93-383, 88 Stat. 633
The National Housing Act 1934, Public Law 84-345, 48 Stat. 847
Real Estate Procedure Settlement Act 1974 (REPSA) (12 U.S.C. §§ 2601-2617)
The Secure and Fair Enforcement for Mortgage Licensing Act of 2008 (122 Stat. 2810 Public Law 110-289)
The Servicemen's Readjustment Act of 1944 ('G.I. Bill') (Public Law 78-346, 58 Stat. 284m)
TILA-RESPA Integrated Disclosure Rule: Guide to the Loan Estimate and Closing Disclosure forms (January 2015).
Truth in Lending Act 1968 (TILA) (82 STAT. 146, Public Law 90-32)

US State Legislation

N.C. GEN. STAT. § 24-10 (2002); N.C. GEN. STAT. § 24-1.1E (2002)

Other Jurisdictions

Regulations setting up the German Financial Stability Committee (Ausschuss für Finanzstabilität) (January 2013)
German Financial Stability Committee 'Recommendation on new instruments for regulating loans for the construction or purchase of residential real estate', issued on 30th June 2015, AFS/2015/1, basis on section 3 (2) of the Act on Monitoring Financial Stability of 28 November 2012 (Federal Law Gazette I, page 2369)
Irish Central Bank (Supervision and Enforcement) Act 2013
Irish Central Bank (Supervision and Enforcement) Act 2013 (Housing loan requirements) Regulations 2015

Web-sites

Bloomberg, 'The real estate lobby Is ready to rumble', (3 February 2011), www.bloomberg.com/news/articles/2011-02-03/the-real-estate-lobby-is-ready-to-rumble (accessed 14 August 2019)
Buildoffsite web-site, www.buildoffsite.com/about/overview/ (accessed 14 August 2019)
Canada Housing and Mortgage Corporation web-site, www03.cmhc-schl.gc.ca/hmip-pimh/#Profile/2270/3/Toronto (accessed 15 July 2019)
Centre For Public Integrity, www.publicintegrity.org (accessed 14 August 2019)
Consumer Financial Protection Bureau, 'CFPB orders GE Capital to pay $225 million in consumer relief for deceptive and discriminatory credit card practices', (19 June 2014), www.consumerfinance.gov/about-us/newsroom/cfpb-orders-ge-capital-to-pay-225-million-in-consumer-relief-for-deceptive-and-discriminatory-credit-card-practices/ (accessed 14 August 2019)
Council of Mortgage Lenders, 'Data shows housing tenure trends continuing', (5 March 2015), Chart 2, www.cml.org.uk/news/news-and-views/710/ (accessed 14 August 2019)
Cruz, Ted, US Senator for Texas web-site, 'Sen. Cruz, Rep. Ratcliffe introduce legislation to abolish the CFPB', (14 February 2017) www.cruz.senate.gov/?p=press_release&id=3004 (accessed 14 August 2019)

Department of Communities and Local Government, 'House building tables' (updated July 2019), www.gov.uk/government/statistical-data-sets/live-tables-on-house-building (accessed 14 August 2019)

Eurostat: Housing statistics, Eurostat, http://ec.europa.eu/eurostat/statistics-explained/index.php/Housing_statistics#Tenure status (accessed 14 August 2019)

Experian, 'Assess the affordability of each customer', www.experian.co.uk/assets/consumer-information/brochures/affordability-brochure-9.pdf (accessed 14 August 2019)

FCA, 'Financial Conduct Authority provides update on regulatory sandbox', www.fca.org.uk/news/press-releases/financial-conduct-authority-provides-update-regulatory-sandbox (accessed 14 August 2019)

Federal Financial Institutions Examination Council Guidance, www.ffiec.gov/default.htm (accessed 14 August 2019)

GOV.UK, 'Organisation types: a user guide', (updated June 2014), https://insidegovuk.blog.gov.uk/2014/01/13/gov-uk-organisation-types-a-user-guide/ (accessed 14 August 2019)

Home and Communities Agency, 'Kickstart' web-site, http://webarchive.nationalarchives.gov.uk/20140805133148/http:/www.homesandcommunities.co.uk/ourwork/kickstart (accessed 15 August 2019)

id Community web-site, https://profile.id.com.au/australia/dwellings?WebID=250 (accessed 16 July 2019)

Local Government Association web-site, www.localgov.co.uk/The-number-of-unbuilt-homes-reaches-record-high/40098 (accessed 25 July 2019)

National Association of Realtors, 'The Future of Fannie Mae & Freddie Mac and What It Means for You', http://homeownershipmatters.realtor/issues/the-future-of-fannie-mae-freddie-mac-and-what-it-means-for-you/ (accessed 15 August 2019)

National Community Reinvestment Coalition, 'Community Reinvestment Act Q&A', https://ncrc.org/community-reinvestment-act-qa-document-falls-short/ (accessed 15 August 2019)

New South Wales Government Research and demographics web-site, www.planning.nsw.gov.au/Research-and-Demography/Demography/Population-projections (accessed 16 July 2019)

OECD web-site, OECD data, Household debt, https://data.oecd.org/hha/household-debt.htm (accessed 17 July 2019)

OECD web-site, Australia economic snapshot, www.oecd.org/economy/australia-economic-snapshot/ (accessed 17 July 2019)

Ontario, Ministry of Finance, 'Fair Housing Plan: Non-Resident Speculation Tax', www.fin.gov.on.ca/en/bulletins/nrst/nrst.html (accessed 15 August 2019)

Population Australia web-site, Melbourne, www.population.net.au/melbourne-population/ (accessed 12 July 2019)

Self Build Portal, 'Almere, Holland', www.selfbuildportal.org.uk/homeruskwartier-district-almere (accessed 15 August 2019)

Swedish Riksbanks: The Council for Cooperation on Macroprudential Policy/Financial Stability Council (from 2013), www.riksbank.se/en-gb/financial-stability/financial-stability-council/ (accessed 15 August 2019)

This is Money, 'Ombudsman sees record number of mortgage complaints in a year but a third of come from those already falling into arrears', (14 May 2014), www.thisismoney.co.uk/money/mortgageshome/article-2627239/Ombudsman-sees-record-number-mortgage-complaints-year-come-falling-arrears.html (accessed 14 August 2019)

US Census Bureau web-site, California, www.census-charts.com/HF/California.html, https://factfinder.census.gov/faces/tableservices/jsf/pages/productview.xhtml?src=bkmk (accessed 12 July 2019)

US Census Bureau web-site, Seattle City, www.census.gov/quickfacts/fact/table/seattle citywashington, US/PST045218 (accessed 12 July 2019)

US Population web-site, Seattle, https://theuspopulation.com/seattle-population/ (accessed 15 July 2019)

Warren, Elizabeth, US Senator for Massachusetts web-site, 'Sen. Warren praises new CFPB mortgage rules that make families, economy safer', (7 January 2014), www.warren.senate.gov/?p=press_release&id=309 (accessed 15 August 2019)

Warren, Elizabeth, Campaign web-site, 'My housing plan for America', (March 2019), https://medium.com/@teamwarren/my-housing-plan-for-america-20038e19dc26 (accessed 23 July 2019)

Zillow web-site, www.zillow.com/ca/home-values/ (accessed 12 July 2019)

Newspaper Articles

The Architect's Journal, 'Housing minister targets 1 million new homes by 2020', (21 September 2015), www.architectsjournal.co.uk/news/housing-minister-targets-1-million-new-homes-by-2020/8689157.article (accessed 15 August 2019)

Business Reporter, 'Many young female home-buyers "hide family plans from mortgage lenders"', (8 October 2015), http://business-reporter.co.uk/2015/10/08/many-young-female-home-buyers-hide-family-plans-from-mortgage-lenders/ (accessed 15 August 2019)

City AM, 'Taylor Wimpey chief executive Pete Redfern launches a major review into UK home ownership with Labour shadow minister John Healey', (4 February 2016), www.cityam.com/233769/taylor-wimpey-chief-executive-pete-redfern-launches-a-major-review-into-uk-home-ownership-with-labour-shadow-minister-john-healey (accessed 15 August 2019)

Construction Enquirer, 'L&G launches world's biggest modular housing factory', (25 February 2016), www.constructionenquirer.com/2016/02/25/lg-launches-worlds-biggest-modular-housing-factory/ (accessed 14 August 2019)

The Contractor, '70% of Contractors Struggling to Meet Deadlines as Labor Shortage Persists', (14 March 2019), www.contractormag.com/construction-data/70-contractors-struggling-meet-deadlines-labor-shortage-persists (accessed 23 July 2019)

Evening Standard, London, Simon Read, 'Trapped in a mortgage cage', (13 October 2015)

Farmers Weekly, 'Farmland hits £1m/acre for housing', (23 January 2015), www.fwi.co.uk/business/farmland-hits-1m-acre-for-housing.htm (accessed 14 August 2019)

Financial Times

——— 'There are big risks in a hasty rollback of financial regulation', (8 January 2017), www.ft.com/content/042ad561-0294-3d7e-b511-e3e74d318783 (accessed 14 August 2019)

——— 'Shortage of builders hobbles UK housing ambitions', (3 February 2015), www.ft.com/cms/s/2/47ce7222-aab0-11e4-91d2-00144feab7de.html#axzz427eUYR2G (accessed 14 August 2019)

——— 'A British property tax that is fit for purpose', (24 September 2014), www.ft.com/content/94fa6f84-43d0-11e4-8abd-00144feabdc0?mhq5j=e1 (accessed 14 August 2019)

——— 'Bank of England: crashing the party', (24 June 2014), www.ft.com/content/f3a1e166-face-11e3-8959-00144feab7de (accessed 14 August 2019)

——— 'It is time for the state to jump on the property bandwagon', (2 April 2014), www.ft.com/content/4d153a1a-b8e2-11e3-835e-00144feabdc0?mhq5j=e1 (accessed 14 August 2019)

——— 'Bank avoids role in limiting mortgages', (5 April 2012), www.ft.com/content/f608f560-78ea-11e1-9f0f-00144feab49a (accessed 14 August 2019)

——— 'Bankers have been sold short by market distortions', (2 June 2010), www.ft.com/content/9daee5e0-6e70-11df-ad16-00144feabdc0 (accessed 15 August 2019)

——— 'Rate cuts fail to lift house sales, says Bellway', (4 December 2008), www.ft.com/content/2ac562f4-c1e5-11dd-a350-000077b07658 (accessed 15 August 2019)

——— 'Citigroup chief stays bullish on buy-outs', (9th July 2007), www.ft.com/cms/s/0/80e2987a-2e50-11dc-821c-0000779fd2ac.html#axzz4BBODoCe9 (accessed 15 August 2019)

The Guardian

——— 'The Guardian view on the housing white paper: it won't fix a broken market', (7 February 2017), www.theguardian.com/commentisfree/2017/feb/07/the-guardian-view-on-the-housing-white-paper-it-wont-fix-a-broken-market (accessed 14 August 2019)

——— 'Housing benefit is out of control, but there is an alternative', (21 June 2012), www.theguardian.com/commentisfree/2012/jun/21/housing-benefit-out-of-control (accessed 15 August 2019)

——— 'Applying for a mortgage? Prepare for the third degree', (1 June 2012), www.theguardian.com/money/2012/jun/01/applying-for-a-mortgage (accessed 15 August 2019)

——— 'Key repossession ruling opens door to mortgage mis-selling complaints', (22 March 2009), www.theguardian.com/money/2009/mar/22/repossessions-mortgages (accessed 15 August 2019)

Mortgage Solutions

——— 'Mortgage adviser market share held at 69% over H1', (28 August 2015), www.mortgagesolutions.co.uk/news/mortgage-adviser-market-share-maintained-at-69-in-h1/ (accessed 15 August 2019)

——— 'Northern Rock has been voted best overall lender in the 2006 Alexander Hall awards', (29 January 2007), www.mortgagesolutions.co.uk/news/2007/01/29/northern-rock-leadsat-ah-awards/ (accessed 15 August 2019)

Mortgage Strategy

——— 'Northern Rock boasts 18.9% net market share', (25 July 2007), www.mortgagestrategy.co.uk/issues/23-july-2007/northern-rock-boasts-18-9-net-market-share/ (accessed 15 August 2019)

——— 'The Council of Mortgage Lenders (CML) and the Royal Institute of Chartered Surveyors (RICS) in talks over bogus new build buy to let (B2L) valuations', (23 December 2005), www.mortgagestrategy.co.uk/cml-and-rics-in-talks-over-bogus-new-build-b2l-valuations/ (accessed 15 August 2019)

The Scotsman, 'Barlinnie inmates to build Glasgow social housing', (25 July 2015), www.scotsman.com/news/politics/barlinnie-inmates-to-build-glasgow-social-housing-1-3840685 (accessed 14 August 2019)

New Statesman, Tristram Hunt, 'How the English became obsessed with property', (2 February 2004), www.newstatesman.com/node/194947 (accessed 14 August 2019)

The Daily Telegraph

——— 'How borrowers are tricking mortgage lenders', (5 December 2015), www.telegraph.co.uk/finance/personalfinance/borrowing/mortgages/11560371/

How-borrowers-are-tricking-mortgage-lenders-and-why-it-wont-work.html (accessed 15 August 2019)

——— 'Shortage of builders holding back development, says housebuilder', (17 November 2015), www.telegraph.co.uk/finance/property/12000443/Shortage-of-builders-holding-back-development-says-housebuilder.html (accessed 15 August 2019)

——— 'Help-to-Buy 2 shaves six years off first-time buyer age of 37', (5 February 2015), www.telegraph.co.uk/finance/personalfinance/borrowing/mortgages/11378375/Help-to-Buy-2-shaves-six-years-off-first-time-buyer-age-of-37.html (accessed 15 August 2019)

——— 'Is the British dream of home ownership dead?', (3 January 2015), www.telegraph.co.uk/finance/property/11322389/Is-the-British-dream-of-home-ownership-dead.html (accessed 12 September 2019)

——— 'Forty-somethings 'too old to get a mortgage', (11 July 2014), www.telegraph.co.uk/finance/personalfinance/borrowing/mortgages/10959516/Forty-somethings-too-old-to-get-a-mortgage.html (accessed 15 August 2019)

——— 'Mortgage approvals fall amid tough new tests for borrowers', (2 June 2014), www.telegraph.co.uk/finance/personalfinance/borrowing/mortgages/10869463/Mortgage-approvals-fall-amid-tough-new-tests-for-borrowers.html (accessed 14 August 2019)

——— 'Britain faces bricks shortage, builders warn', (29 April 2014), www.telegraph.co.uk/finance/newsbysector/constructionandproperty/10796545/Britain-faces-bricks-shortage-builders-warn.html (accessed 14 August 2019)

——— 'Five dirty tricks in today's rising housing market', (3 October 2013) www.telegraph.co.uk/finance/personalfinance/borrowing/mortgages/10352126/Five-dirty-tricks-in-todays-rising-housing-market.html (accessed 14 August 2019)

——— 'Average first-time buyer is now 35', (11 September 2012), www.telegraph.co.uk/news/uknews/9533491/Average-first-time-buyer-is-now-35-research-finds.html (accessed 14 August 2019)

Wall Street Journal

——— Charles Duxbury, 'Sweden plans tighter mortgage rules to tackle household debt – Swedish financial watchdog seeks to cool borrowing as interest rates remain low', (11 November 2014)

——— Edward Pinto, 'Acorn and the housing bubble', (12 November 2009)

Cases

Corrigan v. Buckley, 271 U.S. 323 (1926), https://supreme.justia.com/cases/federal/us/271/323/case.html, (14 August 2019)

Investors Compensation Scheme v. West Bromwich Building Society, House of Lords, 19 June 1997, Session 1997–98, 1All ER 98 [1998], www.publications.parliament.uk/pa/ld199798/ldjudgmt/jd970619/invest01.htm (accessed 14 August 2019)

Index

Note: *Italic* page numbers refer to figures and page numbers followed by "n" denote endnotes.